Searching
for the
New Liberalism

www.newliberalism.ca

Searching
for the
New **Liberalism**

www.newliberalism.ca

Perspectives
Policies
Prospects

edited by
Howard Aster & Thomas S. Axworthy

mosaic press

National Library of Canada Cataloguing in Publication Data

Searching for the new liberalism: perspectives, policies, prospects
/ edited by Howard Aster, Thomas Axworthy

Includes bibliographic references.
ISBN 0-88962-797-5

1. Liberalism -- Canada. I. Aster, Howard II. Axworthy, Thomas, 1947-

JA84.C3S42 2002   320.51'0971   C 2002-906002-8

Published by Mosaic Press, offices and warehouse at 1252 Speers Road,
Units 1 and 2, Oakville, Ontario, L6L 5N9, Canada and Mosaic Press, PMB
145, 4500 Witmer Industrial Estates, Niagara Falls, NY, 14305-1386, U.S.A.

Mosaic Press acknowledges the assistance of the Canada Council and the
Department of Canadian Heritage, Government of Canada for their support
of our publishing programme.

Mosaic Press in Canada:
1252 Speers Road, Units 1 & 2,
Oakville, Ontario
L6L 5N9
Phone/Fax: 905-825-2130
mosaicpress@on.aibn.com

Mosaic Press in U.S.A.:
4500 Witmer Industrial Estates
PMB 145, Niagara Falls, NY
14305-1386
Phone/Fax: 1-800-387-8992
mosaicpress@on.aibn.com

Le Conseil des Arts | The Canada Council
du Canada | for the Arts

www.mosaic-press.com

Dedicated to the memory of Walter L. Gordon

Acknowledgments

TO ALL THE MANY PEOPLE who have contributed to the success of the first New Liberalism Conference and volume of papers—many, many thanks for your contributions, support, enthusiasm and devotion. We hope that many further gatherings or "new liberalism" will take place across the country in the years to come.

In addition, specific thanks to Tanya Zaritzky for her organizational skills, good humour and absolute commitment to new liberalism; to David Sloly and his innovative team at The Learning Edge for nurturing the *www.newliberalism.ca* website; to Mary Lynn Bratti and the Munk Centre for use of their superb facility; to John Fraser, Master of Massey College and his people for use of their wonderful dining hall; to Barry Appleton, Hugh T. Cameron and Red Wilson for their timely support.

Finally, a special word of gratitude to the Hon. John Roberts who defined the projects for the new liberalism agenda and helped craft the agenda of both the Conference and this volume of papers.

Contributors

DAN ANDREAE is a professor of social policy at the Ontario Institute for Studies in Education and at the University of Waterloo and former policy advisor at the PMO.

HOWARD ASTER is a retired professor of Political Science from McMaster University and has extensive experience as a consultant and policy advisor for numerous Government of Canada departments.

LLOYD AXWORTHY is Director and CEO of the Liu Centre for the Study of Global Issues at the University of British Columbia and former Minister of Foreign Affairs.

THOMAS S. AXWORTHY is Executive Director of The Historica Foundation of Canada and Adjunct Lecturer at the John F. Kennedy School of Government at Harvard University.

PETER L. BIRO is a Partner at the Toronto firm of Goodman and Carr LLP practicing in the areas of civil and commercial litigation.

SANFORD BORINS is Professor of Public Management at the Joseph L. Rotman School of Management at the University of Toronto and Chair of the Division of Management at the University of Toronto at Scarborough.

CANDIS CALLISON is a doctoral candidate in the Program in Science, Technology and Society at the Massachusetts Institute of Technology.

HUGH T. CAMERON is a businessman and entrepreneur, former President and CEO of Cameron Packaing and has developed projects in the forestry, oil and gas and petro-chemical industries.

EDGAR COWAN is the former publisher of Saturday Night Magazine and co-founder of CityTV, and is now a management and marketing consultant in the cultural and mass media sector.

C. DAVID CRENNA is a consultant and writer on Canadian urban, social and environmental policy issues and has taught at Queen's University, Carleton and University of Ottawa.

NATHON GUNN is the co-founder of Bitcasters, a new media company which has launched new media initiatives for Miramax, BMG, CHUM, Fireworks, Universal, Disney and others.

WAYNE HUNT is a professor in the Faculty of Social Science at Mount Allison University.

BROOKE JEFFREY teaches public policy and federalism at Concordia University, where she is Director of the Graduate Program in Public Administration in the Department of Political Science.

CHRIS JONES is the Director of Government Relations at the Railway Association of Canada.

DUNNIELA KAUFMAN is a lawyer at Fraser Milner Casgrain LLP in Toronto where she practices international trade law.

TOM KENT is a Fellow of the School of Policy Studies at Queen's University. He was the Policy Secretary to Prime Minister Pearson.

GRANT KIPPEN is the former Director of Organization for the Liberal Party of Canada and GORDON JENKINS is an electronic business consultant who has worked on e-government assignments in India, Singapore, Hong Kong, Sweden and Australia.

ALISON LOAT is the Director of Development of Canada25 and a candidate for the Masters of Public Policy (MPP) degree from the John F. Kennedy School of Government at Harvard University.

LORNA R. MARSDEN is a former Senator in the Parliament of Canada and is President and Vice-Chancellor of York University.

ANTONIA MAIONI is Director of the McGill Institute for the Study of Canada and is Associate Professor of Political Science at McMaster University and Adjunct Professor in the Department of Health Administration, Université de Montréal.

ELENA MANTAGARIS is a public policy consultant in Ottawa. Currently, she is advising on efforts to modernize the federal government through on-line service delivery.

MICHAEL MARZOLINI is the official pollster for the Liberal Party of Canada and the Chairman and CEO of POLLARA, a public opinion research firm.

DÉSIRÉE MCGRAW is a senior associate with the Ottawa-based consulting firm, Stratos.

MICHAEL E.J. PHELPS is Chairman of the Advisory Board, Duke Energy Gas Transmission—Canada, and currently hold the position of Distinguished University Fellow and Adjunct Professor, Faculty of Commerce, the University of British Columbia.

MARK PODLASLY, a member of the N'laka'pmx First Nation in B.C., has been working with the Harvard JFK School of Government and the Harvard Business School as a Teaching Fellow and Research Associate.

JOHN C. POLANYI, awarded the 1986 Nobel Prize in Chemistry, is a faculty member in the Department of Chemistry at the University of Toronto.

JOHN ROBERTS served as a Cabinet Minister in various portfolios during the Trudeau era and has taught at various universities, including Toronto, Queen's, Trent, Concordia and Royal Military College.

W.T. STANBURY is UPS Foundation Professor of Regulation and Competition Policy, Faculty of Commerce and Business Administration, University of British Columbia.

SHERRI TORJMAN is Vice-President of the Caledon Institute of Social Policy and former Director of The Trillium Foundation.

KIMON VALASKAKIS is the former Canadian ambassador at the OECD, currently president of the Global Governance Group and he has been on the faculty of various universities including University of Montreal, Concordia, Paris, Nice, Alicante

DEBORAH COYNE is a policy analyst who has studied history, economics, law and international relations.

Table of Contents

Section Two : *Policies*

Commentaries

Section Three : *Prospects*

Commentaries

Preface

Thomas S. Axworthy

SIR WILFRED LAURIER, one of Canada's greatest leaders once proclaimed, "I am a liberal. I am one of those who think that everywhere in human beings, there are abuses to be reformed, new horizons to be opened up, and new forces to be developed."

Laurier's spirit of quest and discovery, which he defined so well in 1877, should animate us still. Progressives believe in expanding opportunity and choice, but in every age, problems and situations change and therefore there are new challenges to be overcome, new priorities to be addressed, and new wrongs to right. To that end, as we start a new century a group of concerned Canadians have come together with an overwhelming desire to inject new ideas into a tired political landscape. The "ginger group" of New Liberals met in Toronto, September 27-29, 2002 to discuss Canada's future agenda. Some were well known, such as Tom Kent or John Polanyi, but many were just starting their careers. Some had long associations with a political party; many came from the not-for-profit community. A few were old hands; most were new hands.

The Chinese philosopher Lao-Tze writes, "to hold to the center is to listen to the voice of the inner mind." The "inner mind" of the group that met in Toronto came to a few clear conclusions. In Part I on perspectives, authors like Tom Kent and John Roberts assess the philosophical and political roots of liberalism, while Brooke Jeffery applies this framework to social capital, John Polanyi to science policy and Michael Marzolini to the receptivity of Canadian public opinion to the liberal values.

Part II is devoted to a future policy agenda: Mark Podlasly on urban aboriginals, Désirée McGraw on the environment, Chris Jones on transportation, Michael Phelps on corporate Canada, Lorna Marsden on higher education, Antonio Maioni on health care, Sherri Torjman on social policy and Peter Biro on law reform, have collectively addressed a set of issues that would keep a reformist government busy for years.

But if there was general agreement among the delegates on the continuing validity of liberal principles and on eagerness to apply this framework to a host of concerns, the dominant overwhelming consensus was that the Canadian party and policy process had to be opened up. Papers by Candis Callison, Wayne Hunt, Alison Loat, William Stanbury, Grant Kippen, Deborah Coyne and Sandford Borins each addressed different aspects of Canadian political processes and all were found wanting. There is a clear disconnect between the "inner voice" of the reformers who attended our conference, and the "inner voice" of those who are now in charge of Canada's decision making institutions. This desire for meaningful participation also animates the commentaries of many of those who attended the conference and their contributions, as well as the specific papers on process agree with the sentiments of a young Pierre Trudeau who wrote in exasperation about the closed policy system of 1950, "open up the windows, we are asphyxiating."

Liberalism as a philosophy originates with John Locke in the 17th century; Thomas Jefferson gave its most eloquent expression in the 18th century. The word liberal was a Spanish invention of the 19th century and Lloyd George, Bevenidge Keynes, Roosevelt, Kennedy, Pearson and Trudeau made it the dominant political philosophy of the 20th. Every generation has held to their old truths but adapted them to new realities. Liberalism in Canada is at such a divide today: the philosophy still has resonance but its application to today's problems and opportunities needs a fundamental rethinking. It is to the launching of such a process that this volume of essays is dedicated.

Introduction

Howard Aster

WELCOME TO THE VOLUME of papers entitled Searching for the New Liberalism.

It started some four or five years ago ... for me. I had a conversation with my son who was then a university student. He reminded me of a conversation he and I had with Senator Keith Davey a few years earlier. It was Senator Davey who had turned to me and asked —"what kind of liberal society do you want your son to live in?"

That question had remained unanswered for these many years. But for both my son and me it remained a vital question.

I recall in subsequent years my son turning to me every now and then and asking: "Do you remember that question? Well, don't forget it and make sure that sooner or later you and others try to answer it. It is important for me and my generation."

Well, it took us some many years to get here. But here we are.

The question is still valid and it is my hope that this Searching for The New Liberalism volume will provide, at least, the beginnings of the answer to that vital question.

Flash forward to August 18th, 2002.

It is a warm, Sunday morning. It is near Cracow, Poland. There are over two million people assembled in a field called Blonia. Some 5% of the entire Polish population is assembled on this field. They are there to see Pope John Paul II—probably for the last time.

The Pope chose to address the problems of "...the noisy propaganda of liberalism, of freedom without responsibility..." He calls on his people to fight persistent poverty with "creative charity." That is a most intriguing phrase! He asked his countrymen to help impoverished neighbours, support their families and educate their children.

It is astonishing to me that the Pope would address the problems of liberalism in Poland, to his countrymen, in those circumstances.

A few weeks earlier, it was Prime Minister Tony Blair who invited former President Bill Clinton to England, to a "think tank" to find creative solutions to the apparent plight of "new labour."

Later in August, it was the Socialist Party of France meeting in their annual summer conference asking questions which are not that dissimilar.

Clearly, the fundamental questions and dilemmas which lie at the heart of liberalism are being discussed in many places, by many people, from many political positions.

So, it is now our turn to take up this discussion and debate and to relocate in Canada. In many ways, Canada is the best place to carry forward this discussion on liberalism. One can argue that Canada has had the most successful liberal regime of any country in the world.

Indeed, if one treats the name of political parties seriously, namely that they reflect something about the political ideology from which they spring, then Canadian liberalism is a powerful reminder of how successful the ideology and the party which draws its name from of liberalism has been in this country. No other country in the world can claim such a successful Liberal Party, for so long, directing governments and, by extension, affecting the structure of that society in liberal directions.

But we should also be reminded that liberalism has also been a very, very controversial political ideology and political theory over the past few hundred years. One reading of the history of liberalism would assert that it is due to the failure of liberalism that socialism arose. Indeed, it is the critical interplay between these two competing political ideologies and theories that much of the creative politics of the past 150 years has been played out. One may very well argue that is only the "unfinished" business of liberalism which keeps socialism and democratic socialists alive today.

Also, one must not forget that liberalism has been the focus of an ongoing and at times savage critique from an alternative source, namely the political right. Historically, it began with the critique of liberalism by a decaying aristocratic conservatism. But by the late nineteenth century that critique became merged with the philosophical right of Joseph de Maistre, Papal Encyclicals, Catholic Action, and others, who equate liberalism with modernity, the collapse of value and the excesses of unfettered economic greed. By the mid-twentieth century, this critique becomes extended into more secular terms by political philosophers such as Leo Strauss and Alistair McIntyre. The viability of this critique of liberalism today is sustained, by communitarianism and communitarians such as Charles Taylor—and others.

Debates in political philosophy may appear to be far removed from the struggles which take place in the political arena, where resources must be allocated and re-allocated, where competing interests vie for political ascendancy, where power and influence predominate.

But it is clear today, during the early years of the 21st century, that the search for fundamental political ideas, for vital and viable political discourse is taking many people—from the Pope to Tony Blair—back to the discourse on liberalism.

So, what is it? What is it about Canada which has allowed us to maintain liberal discourse so close to the exercise of political power? Is Canada a liberal society? How have political structures, institutions and policies in Canada over the past century reflected liberal values and liberal discourse? And can these same structures, institutions and policies continue to reflect a viable liberal discourse in this new century?

The papers in this volume are intended to extend the Canadian discourse on liberalism further and to provide a first and incomplete map to further the search for the new liberalism.

It is also my hope that if this is a will of the participants, that we should be able to extend the intellectual discourse on liberalism in Canada on a bi-annual basis through a conference and a volume of pages. I recall my recent experience with international broadcasting where we were able to develop a very successful and very international biannual discourse on the subject, in Canada.

It is my hope that we will be able to re-introduce students of Canadian politics from the high school through the university levels into the discourse on liberalism. As a retired university professor, I find it sorrowful that the "discourse on Canadian liberalism" has had such "bad press," such terrible "academic reviews" and has all but been purged from the curriculum. It is my hope that with some hard work, over a longer period of time, all of this can be repaired. It is, indeed, our duty and obligation to the next generation.

Section One

Perspectives

Liberalism:
The Return of the Perennial Philosophy

John Roberts

FIFTY YEARS AGO liberalism was the prevailing orthodoxy. Democratic liberalism seemed so successful that some political scientists proclaimed "the end of ideology," arguing that there were no longer fundamental cleavages of approach to social problems in the western democracies.

To be a liberal was to be within the generally accepted view of how political issues could be, and should be, practically addressed. Dissenting opinions from the socialists on the left and reactionaries on the right were fringe beliefs to be tolerated, certainly, but not generally to be taken seriously as workable approaches to the domestic economic and social issues of the post war world.

The historical roots of this mid-century liberalism were varied, overlapping and to some extent contradictory—and, though they shared common ground in holding that the individual and his interests were the touchstone for determining the extent of the citizen's rights and the proper limits to the exercise of the powers of the state, they had led to a view of liberalism rather different than that of many liberals in the past.

There were four fundamental strands in the arguments that provided the intellectual foundation for this contemporary liberalism.

One was that there are natural human rights, discovered through reason, religion, tradition, revelation or by whatever other accepted technique of illumination, that are as such inherent to the individual as a human being and which, therefore, ought to be respected since they are the essential attributes to the exercise of the characteristics that define the humaneness of human activity. Necessary for the exercise of a person's reason, or free expression, or free will, or capacity of moral judgement, or free choice of religious belief, or whatever other attribute is held to define this nature, they establish the obligations of (and limitations on) the state to act in the assistance of fulfilling those rights both by promoting and enhancing the conditions for their exercise and by limiting its own activities from restricting their free play.

A second, related, argument for liberalism, appropriate to the growing commercial societies of the 17th century, was founded in the principles of contract. The restraints that should limit the action of the state, as well as define the powers it can legitimately exercise, are to be found in a constitutional contract, either tacit or implicit, made by individual citizens who in their mutual interest agree to abandon their natural unrestrained free action in exchange for establishing a government of limited sovereignty bound by the contract to establish the conditions of external and domestic security without which rights cannot be practically effective. The constitution of government thus binds the state to enforce natural rights on behalf of the citizens and ensure a more effective protection for the conditions of order and safety, but equally binds the state to forego interference in relation to actions beyond the needs of security. The essence of the written or unwritten constitutional contract is to be found in the rule of law, which thus guarantees justice, through government based not on arbitrary force or superior status but on the equal application of written laws formulated within the consensus of the constitutional contract.

When this guarantee of the right to freedom of action was combined—as it was for example in the case of John Locke—with the argument that the individual's exercise of this power of action extended to the creation of things which, thus, became his own (that is, an extension of himself), and that rights therefore extended to his property as much as to himself, contract theory became a powerful doctrine for the protection of established interests.

This attachment of liberalism to property rights became contested, however, by late nineteenth century liberals who sought an expanded role for government. In a society increasingly facing the squalor and instability which accompanied capitalism, industrialization and urban growth, they saw a more active state, properly directed, as a potential means to enhancing the opportunity for individuals to escape or ameliorate these constraining conditions. By acting to correct the abuses in society, even though the traditional property rights of the powerful were infringed, government might enhance the general liberty of the citizens, rather than constitute an inherent restraint upon it. If society is a compact whose conditions establish the opportunity for some to amass wealth because of the laws and structures and stability that public order generates, then the benefits so created collectively should, at least partially, be shared collectively.

This development represented the impact of utilitarianism on liberal thought. It provided not only a justification of redistribution policies to assist the disadvantaged, and supported an active role for the state to enhance the general public good through measures to help realise economic potential, it transformed liberalism into a democratic creed.

Liberalism had traditionally not necessarily been democratic; democracies are not necessarily liberal. Liberalism, particularly when identified with property rights, often provided a protective structure for the defence of established (or "aristocratic") elites against popular (or "mob") demands. Even the framers of the American Constitution, for example, consciously placed structural limitations within it to limit or counterbalance the potential defects of majority rule. And democracies have often been as vigorous as other forms of government in suppressing minority rights that majorities find morally or practically repugnant.

The liberal Utilitarians connected their belief in liberalism with an advocacy of democratic government. They founded their justification of this democratic liberalism on the principle of social utility, and their belief in the individual as a rational calculator of his own self interest. The political structures of society should be arranged so as to achieve the greatest maximization of happiness. Utilitarianism justified democracy not as a set of institutions deriving moral authority from natural rights, nor as an embodiment of a mythic will of the people, but on the basis that democratic institutions were the only way of assuring that the holders of governmental power would act out of consideration for the interests of all (rather than the interests of only themselves) since their failure to do so would lead a universally enfranchised electorate (acting in its own interest) to remove them from office. Utilitarians defended rights not because they are sacrosanct but because they are the best effective means of assuring the diversity, freedom of thought and enquiry, and the freedom of expression, that are the essential conditions for the moral and intellectual progress of society and its individual members and thus a means to the expansion of human happiness.

Utilitarians based rights not on "nature," therefore, but on the equality of the interests of all members of a society, each of whose realization of self should count as much as that of any other. This emphasis on equality comes partially from the English common law tradition but, even more important, it is part of the Christian legacy to liberalism. It is not surprising that the Utilitarians were joined, at least in Victorian England, by staunch Christian advocate—of whom T. H. Green was the outstanding and enormously influential exemplar—who did not consider themselves to be utilitarians but rather philosophical idealists, and who argued that government should intervene to create the conditions of freedom and prosperity in society that would enable individuals equally to freely fulfill themselves. Green endorsed the need of the state to act so as to limit the freedom of some (i.e., the negative freedom of being unrestricted to do what they desire) to enhance the positive freedom of others (i.e., freedom to have the conditions of life that would enable them to fulfil their real desire, the power to live a life of Christian brother hood). Negative freedom should defer to the positive freedom of the deprived to have the conditions necessary to enable their self-realization.

The fourth intellectually significant argument for liberalism was the argument from scepticism. Starting with Wilhelm von Humboldt at the end of the eighteenth century and, especially, with John Stuart Mill, the most influential advocate of liberalism in the nineteenth century, liberalism came to be defended neither on the basis of simple utilitarianism, nor natural rights, nor contract theory. Utilitarianism they believed was flawed by a serious misconception of human character—it saw individuals as rational calculating machines, all essentially similar, rather than understanding the enormous range of their emotions, interests and culture. Nor could one build the structures of society on the guiding principle of the greatest happiness of the greatest number, for no one could pronounce definitively on what others did, or should, find to be true happiness. Nor were natural rights or natural law determining. Humboldt and Mill asked, simply, what are the best conditions, or governmental structures, in which men can live in society? Once those conditions were met it would not matter whether or not they were prescribed by contract or natural law. If contract provisions, or natural law, supported those structures they would be redundant; if not they would be wrong.

In holding that the touch stone for judging the desirability of social and political structures be "the best conditions in which men can live," Humboldt and Mill consciously asserted their own view of human character, empirically observed, the one for which those "best conditions" would be appropriate. That view was that the essential character of men was diverse, unpredictable and, indeed, not definitively knowable. All we can surely know is that pronouncements on what men must be, or should be, to fulfil their nature are uncertain. And this certain uncertainty of human nature Humboldt and Mill (and later thinkers like Talmon, Popper, Hampshire and Berlin) believed was sufficient to justify the structures of a liberal society. For if there is no method in politics or morals for infallibly discovering what men should be, no indisputable technique of reason, science, intuition or religion for discerning the template of proper conduct, and thus no model for forcing individuals to conform as the requisite for realizing their quintessential selves, the alternative was to allow people to choose for themselves in whatever way they wished to lead their lives so long as it was practicable, that is so long as it did not impinge on the ability of others to do the same.

Mill distinguished, that is, between self-regarding actions by an individual (actions that affected only his own interests) and other-regarding actions (those that had an effect on others)—and argued that the category of self-regarding actions was beyond the legitimacy of state action through legal and penal sanction. But the limitation applied only to the activity of the state.

While Mill feared the constricting effects of public opinion, its capacity to stultify original thought, he was not "politically correct" in our contemporary sense. He did not believe that people had a right not to have their feelings hurt, or their self esteem assaulted, or to be free from the derision of others. Rather he thought that progress depended on strong characters with the force of conviction able to withstand such pressures of social conformity and conventional belief, and that it was in society's interest to encourage such characters.

Mill's arguments for liberalism are entirely instrumental. Government, or the state, is a means and not an end in itself. It exists only to serve individual and collective interests, not to constitute an organic manifestation of the moral or cultural nation. In effect he recasts the utilitarian argument by substituting the expansion of opportunity for the maximization of happiness. Happiness, for Mill, was an intangible and elusive concept. Diverse people could hold a wide and conflicting range of views of what happiness is. One cannot make people happy by government fiat, but government can create greater opportunity for people to pursue happiness as they see fit. The expansion of opportunity, even if not exactly quantifiable, was capable of practical application, and in a way that denied (as the traditional Utilitarianism of Jeremy Bentham did not) the right of the state to impose limitations on the individual for his own good. Mill's argument could be used, and indeed would be used, to justify active government—government that engaged itself in actions that would expand the range of choice for citizens in society; but it argued against the government's role as a promoter of moral beings, or emphasized, alternatively, that to be a moral being depended on the expansion of choice. There was no moral truth possessed by governments which defines how people must act, in matters which concern only themselves, and therefore justifies imposing on their freedom to be self-determining through legally imposed standards and sanctions. Individual development, and thus progress, can only be achieved by leaving people to pursue their potential as they themselves interpret it.

This view leads to a liberal advocacy of tolerance and an acceptance of diversity. This was certainly not entirely new. Historically there have been other advocates of tolerance. But many of these accepted it grudgingly as a regrettable necessity to ensure public order. Jean Bodin, in the sixteenth century, for instance, urged it as an expedient for escaping the bloodshed and destruction of the civil and international wars of religion—but only when neither side could prevail through argument or force. Later, in the eighteenth century, tolerance often implied a certain patronizing condescension. To paraphrase the famous quotation erroneously ascribed to Voltaire: "I find your convictions inane, bizarre, and stupid but if you insist on maintaining them I shall accept that inevitability and your right to hold and express them".

The liberal attachment to toleration in the 19th century, however, was neither grudging nor patronizing. Toleration was much more than a practical necessity imposed by the inability of intellectual or military antagonists to prevail. It was, rather, a positive good to be embraced enthusiastically, and championed, both because it reflected the diverse reality of mankind and because it was the essential condition for that diversity constitutes the driving force behind the exercise of the human imagination and intellectual competition that is the source of human advancement.

The sceptics had one other influence on liberalism—they made it pragmatic rather than ideological. If there is no discoverable over-riding, absolute, harmonious, goal for human activity, if (as Isaiah Berlin argued) not all values or rights are at all times mutually absolutely compatible—for instance justice and mercy, freedom from one answer does not respond to all social problems. Political decisions will require perspective and proportion, and a practical consideration of the facts of the moment. Free speech does not extend to libel; tolerance does not extend to the promotion of racial hatred; during a time of terrorism some rights may be temporarily suspended; the pursuit of social justice should not be so dominant that it prevents the market from being an engine of economic growth; rights of property do not extend to activities, like pollution, contrary to a clear public good. One size does not fit all occasions.

Liberals thus eschew procrustean intellectual schemes or universal principles of governmental action. Their concerns are with the law, revenue, expenditure and administration, not the extirpation of personal sin. Pragmatism rather than righteousness should decide the public agenda. For while there may be many people who would be pleased to have their moral viewpoint imposed on others by government, there are very few who wish to have the moral views of others imposed upon themselves. Moral rectitude is not the purpose of government but practical action to enhance the opportunity for individuals to be self-realizing. As President Kennedy remarked, the questions for a governmental leader to ask are "Will it pass?"; "Will it work?"; "Will it help?" (to which we might add, "And then what?").

This does not mean that governmental decisions are necessarily valueless. To ask whether a proposed governmental action will help raises the questions of who is to be helped, and at what cost to others, and to do what. And these ultimately do involve value judgements. They may be immediate practical responses to questions that events have suddenly made important. They may be the incremental response to long-standing issues that require continuing management. They may be undertaken with regard to their practical consequences, not because they fit some preconceived vision of what is intellectually or morally right. But pragmatic decisions are not simply questions of technique or administration. They inevitably reflect the standards and political values of those that make them. For liberal decision-makers their overall effect will likely be the re-enforcement of liberal values.

President Kennedy also famously remarked, in justifying the draft process during the Viet Nam war, that "life is not fair"—and that is true. But liberals historically, from the nineteenth century on, have considered that it is their task to make it fairer. This implies a belief in our ability through experience, knowledge, and intellectual imagination to conceive a future other than that which the unimpeded processes of society, free from action by government, would bring—not through Utopian blueprints, or visionary grand plans, but incrementally by programs that enable individuals to fulfil their purposes by expanding their means to do so through specific interventions.

The practical application of the essential concepts of liberalism was inevitably moulded by the evolution of our increasingly urbanized, industrialized, technologically developed, specialized and thus vulnerable—society. This evolution made more and more apparent the difficulty inherent in Mill's thought—for example his argument that when the individual's free actions do have a discernible effect on the ability of others to act freely they are a legitimate subject for state action. In an increasingly complex world the attempt to distinguish two spheres, those of self-regarding actions and those actions affecting others, with clear boundaries between them, seemed more and more artificial as it became clear that many self-fulfilling actions by some hamper severely the ability of others to fulfil their self-development. Mill's principle, designed to defend individuals against government interference, paradoxically in this new context, became the intellectual justification for an intrusive state.

Liberalism, over time, while retaining the primacy of individual interests as the bedrock of government and the language of rights, diversity and tolerance, has thus shifted from being a doctrine supporting negative freedom, minimal government and the respect of property rights to a doctrine that emphasized the obligation to be active in promoting opportunity, economic reform and social justice—a shift greatly enhanced by the two world wars and their consequences.

This belief in an active role for government in economic policy was enormously strengthened after the 1930's by the emergence of Keynesian economic theory which argued that by government management of economic demand through control of the money supply and the use of fiscal policy, economic cycles of boom and bust could be overcome. Keynesian economics was especially embraced in Canada both because of Canada's historical experience in using active government as a means to generate economic growth through infrastructure and resource development and because of the influential presence in the Canadian civil service of some of Keynes' students. As well, the levers for Keynesian economic management—monetary policy and fiscal policy—were constitutionally within federal hands, and therefore available to the national government, while the instruments for encouraging economic growth through structural policies were largely in provincial hands and not therefore easily used for macro-economic management.

Modern liberalism is as concerned with economic freedom as it is with political freedom. Nineteenth century liberalism tended to be primarily a political doctrine focusing on the franchise, civil rights, and self-determination. Twentieth century liberalism has recognized that a person deprived of economic opportunity can be as cut off from the possibility of fulfilment as one who is deprived of political freedom.

All the subsidiary principles of the liberal philosophy flow from a basic belief in the value of freedom of individual choice, and the conviction that respect for the primacy of the interests of the individual citizens is the foundation of political processes and purposes. Its historical legacy to contemporary liberalism includes, primarily, the following precepts:

- the equality of all members of society, rather than class, religious, ethnic or sexual distinction as the order in principle of government
- the recognition of individual rights, the rule of law and democratic structures as a means to the equal protection of the citizens' interests
- insistence on a secular rather than a spiritual or ideological role for government
- a belief in freedom of thought and expression, and in tolerance and the promotion of diversity, as a means both to individual fulfilment and the generation of progress
- an attachment to property rights and the structure of a free and competitive market economy as the best generator of economic growth and prosperity, and the need for government to provide the legal framework to maintain the free and fair working of that economy
- an obligation on government to ensure that the pursuit of private sector purposes does not generate extraneous adverse social consensus and thus damage the common good
- that government should not only ensure security and stability in society but also play an active role in expanding opportunity for individuals by programs such as infrastructure development, education, research and the provision of essential public services at affordable rather than unregulated costs
- a commitment to ensuring that the benefits of living collectively in a liberal society are used to help achieve the conditions of social justice by narrowing the disparity of opportportunity between those who are disadvantaged and those who are fortunate
- pragmatism in pursuing, and balancing, these goals one with another

These salient characteristics of liberalism are especially appropriate to the social and political conditions of Canada; its size, diversity, federal system, charter of rights, rule of law, democratic institutions, multiculturalizm, historically active role for government in economic development, government provision of essential services, and concern for government as a means to social justice are rooted in its geography, history and cultural traditions.

The defining characteristics of Canadian society have been the search for opportunity and the pluralism that protects and nurtures the independent coexistence of different languages, values, cultural groups, and ideas. Pluralism is at the centre of our society and its political processes. And since liberalism is the political system of pluralism, it has been well suited to the burgeoning development of Canadian society. It emphasized the standard of individual rights to a society comprising individuals seeking opportunity. It stressed the value of diversity in a society made inescapably diverse by its geography and culture. It was democratic, seeking direction from its citizens in a frontier society of individuals proud of their self-reliance. It came increasingly, in the nineteenth century, to promote an active role for the state as the pragmatic means of expanding opportunity for individuals in an economy whose resources could be effectively exploited only through the actions of government in establishing the infrastructure of communications and transportation.

The Liberal party took the framework of theoretical liberalism and applied it in practice to the conditions of Canada. Its cause, historically, has been the driving force of Canada itself—to build a country—on the foundations of the liberalism that is natural to the country itself. Its evolution can be followed through the deliberations at the succession of conferences held by the Liberal party and the political programs based on the conference resolutions.

The first, in 1893, laid the foundation for a national party committed to a federalism that united respect for provincial responsibilities with a growing consciousness of national interests, championed civil and religious freedoms, and advocated Canadian autonomy from imperial control.

The next, held in 1919, was intended to respond to the need to build a solid foundation of national development after the economic disruption that followed the First World War. It was, however, much more than a simple design for economic progress for it recognized that the social effects of industrialization would mean a more active role for government. It strongly endorsed the use of government to create the conditions of economic and social growth through commercial policy, and transportation and communications development. The main resolution, however, was that on "Labour and Industry" which placed the party in the forefront of social reform by outlining twenty specific policy recommendations, including the right to an association for workers, the eight-hour work day, the abolition of child labour, equal pay for men and women and an adequate system of insurance against unemployment, sickness, dependence in old age and other disabilities, (and which would include) old-age pensions, widows' pensions and maternity benefits. These resolutions became the basis for the continuing implementation of the social and welfare reform that is one of Canadian Liberalism's most significant accomplishments.

That commitment was heightened by the experience of the Great Depression. The Liberal party sought to regenerate its programs and policies by holding a summer conference in Port Hope in 1933. The emphasis of the conference and its topics—monetary and financial reform, a national commission for unemployment relief, national agricultural planning—was on practical programs to provide for human need and security. Thinking through the response to the depression strengthened the Liberal party's support for an active role for government in the efficient service of the humanitarian state, a role which was reinforced by Canada's experience in the Second World War.

As the war moved to an end, the Liberal government became preoccupied with the shaping of the post-war years. It would have been unthinkable to return to the conditions of economic collapse that had prevailed during the 1930's. If governments could organize to win a war, surely they could organize to create a society which would secure and protect the conditions of a full life for their citizens. The government published the so-called "Green Book" outlining the path of post-war Liberal policy and emphasizing an explicit commitment to use government to ensure the well-being of society's less fortunate. It proposed increased spending on pensions, health and unemployment insurance, job training and public works. But this was not its sole concern. The foundation for Liberal policies designed by the King government in the 1940's, and built upon by succeeding Liberal governments until the 1980's, had four fundamental elements—the promotion of manufacturing and resource growth in cooperation with the private sector, the support of regional development through subsidy and incentive programs to slow-growth areas, the reconciliation with French speaking Canada by offering francophones an equal partnership in the federal government, and the establishment of large scale security programs.

Post-war Liberal governments focused on much more than the conditions of social welfare. The war had made Canada a leading industrial and manufacturing power. The 1945 White Paper on Employment and Income provided a blueprint for economic growth and national prosperity. C. D. Howe, the government's chief of economic development, believed that if the development of the economy were left to private enterprise alone it would not maintain its industrial growth. He was prepared to use the levers of government to promote the establishment of the solid manufacturing and resource base which was a prerequisite for Canada's post-war economic success.

With the victory of the Conservatives in 1958 the Liberal party turned once again to the party conference as an instrument for policy renewal. The Kingston Conference in 1960 focused on new approaches, which formed the basis for a package of progressive social policies drawn up by the party the following year. When the Pearson government entered office in 1963 it had at hand a waiting program of social legislation—the Canada Pension Plan, Medicare, the Canada Assistance Plan, regional development programs, unemployment insurance, government student loans—a whole array of social security measures which made the Pearson years, over a relatively short period of time, one of the most legislatively productive periods in our legislative history.

Pierre Trudeau maintained this emphasis on social policies (as well as Pearson's activism in international affairs) and succeeded in the constitutional reforms which will undoubtedly be considered his major historical legacy. Indeed Trudeau, both in his thought and his policies, personified almost perfectly those salient characteristics which I earlier described as the precepts that constitute our liberal heritage. That is one of the reasons for his enduring appeal to the Canadian public.

The history of the development of Liberal programs, in short, shows the evolution of policies that are sensitive to the nature of our country and its developing needs. And that is why Liberal governments have held governmental power for most of the past century. It is not the result of some accidental or malign quirk in the electoral process.

Liberals have been elected because the Liberal Party has understood Canada and Canadians better than its political opponents.

But if liberalism has such a convincing intellectual foundation, and if its principles are almost ideally suited to the conditions of Canada, and if its implementation through a succession of Liberal governments has been so successful—how can one account for the disillusion with liberalism (and Liberalism) that has occurred from the mid-1980s until the present day?

The happy, perhaps complacent, celebration of liberal political policies has become contested on all sides. In the world's democracies we have seen the emergence of a multitude of new movements—neo liberals, new conservatives, ecological and environmental parties, libertarians, communitarianism, institutionalised anti-globalization, and a whole range of religious and spiritual cults. Liberalism no longer seems to be the automatic path we should follow to the future. It is attacked on practical grounds—it does not "work"—and on ideological grounds—its values, or professed values, are empty, or a distortion of reality.

What has happened?

It would be tempting—and perhaps to some extent correct—to argue simply that liberalism has become doubted because it has worked. Liberalism seeks to provide opportunity for those who do not have it. To the extent that it succeeds in giving that opportunity —in creating prosperity—it produces a society where more people are better off. It therefore, to some extent, may plant the seeds for its own rejection. As the weight of society shifts to those who are no longer disadvantaged but have advantages they wish to conserve and protect, the impulse for liberal policies of redistribution may be weakened. And a society that prizes novelty, and suffers from the discontent generated by advertising and a media devoted to commercial objectives, may lapse into a frustration of expectations rather than the general mood of optimism and vitality that liberal thinkers had expected.

It is not, however, only the advantaged who have come to suspect liberalism. The disadvantaged see that the North American belief in an egalitarian society conflicts with the real distribution of ownership, wealth and power in our political and economic life. They are frustrated in their aspiration to have more of the community's resources devoted to giving them the opportunities and comforts of those who are well off. It is difficult for them to understand how the promises of technology and progress to provide us with a better life have led to longer working hours for them, wealth for the established, a growing gap between the rich and the poor, and insecurity in their working and family lives. They are discontented with political processes of compromise and brokerage, and electoral financing which seems to ignore their interests, or provides them with too little too late.

The middle classes also have expectations—that they are entitled to enjoy the material rewards of the good life, and that their traditional position in society will be respected. But they bear a heavy tax burden, and they have become more and more suspicious that their tax burden is supporting inefficient and wasteful government programs devoted to others.

So liberalism is not simply a victim of its past successes. Its problems are rooted in the changing nature of our society—in particular the transforming impact upon us of the substance and pace of change.

For two centuries change has been regarded as the ally of liberal reform. Liberals reflected the confident faith that change—properly directed by the wisdom of liberal reformers, of course—could ultimately cure the wretched condition of mankind. Change was seen as a particular remedy for faults in society. It was not viewed as the dominating characteristic of society itself. Now, however, change presents us with pervasive transformation of our social and economic environment. No part of the world is untouched by it; no economic sector is left unaffected.

We live within global networks of production, distribution, exchange and consumption; sometimes these seem to work with dazzling but unfeeling efficiency, at other times they seem not to work well at all. Governments have often seemed powerless to manage these systems and protect individuals from their unintended consequences. In this age of specialization and complication it has become difficult for individuals to identify with the processes of government or the main institutions of society. Government, instead of being seen as a guardian of individual interests, is regarded as an integral part of that incomprehensible system of industrial structures, world markets, military establishments, transportation, communication and information systems, and culture and energy conglomerates that make up the confusing superstructure of our society. Social and political institutions are seen as things which act for citizens, not as things through which citizens act.

And so the conventional wisdom that had supported liberalism and its policies began to change. The characteristic of conventional wisdom is not that it is necessarily wise but that it is convenient. Conventional wisdom is accepted because it comfortably fits the implicit self- interest of those who thus have no incentive to challenge it. By the mid-1980's the precepts of liberalism in action no longer seemed convenient—that is, they no longer seemed to be successful. The old liberal approaches, which had fostered prosperity through the post-war years, seemed not to work in the new world of the 1980's. Keynesian economics failed to manage the problems of stagflation brought about largely by Lyndon Johnson's huge deficits, produced by the waging of the Viet Nam war at the same time he pursued his "Great Society" spending programs, and by the shock of the OPEC energy cost increases. Governments, while happy to apply Keynesian tax reductions to stimulate lagging economies, proved reluctant to apply tax hikes to restrain buoyant demand during good times. Moreover the time lags between the implementation of Keynes's principles and their impact on the economy made them suspect as tools for economic management. Fine tuning the economy through macro-economic management proved a difficult task.

In this context of social frustration and economic confusion, it is hardly surprising that the vacuum was filled by the policies of new conservatism which, with a proud disdain for the public realm, and the attractive notion that the new problems of political and economic management were too complicated for governments to manage, assured us that the simple techniques of market fundamentalism would set all problems to right. One had only to dismantle the role of government to let the "invisible hand" of unfettered markets reward the able and allocate the resources of society in what would ultimately, through social Darwinism, be for the collective good.

The political face of neoconservatism was presented by Margaret Thatcher and Ronald Reagan, but an intellectual establishment gave it respectability. Milton Friedman, preeminently, as an economist justified the rejection of Keynesian economics in favour of monetarist theory. Political theorists like Robert Nozzick argued, on the basis of the primacy of rights, for minimal government and against any role for the state in redistribution, indeed against any role for the state other than the provision of security. Even the most eminent of contemporary liberal thinkers—John Rawls—argued for the acceptability of growing disparities in wealth between the rich and the poor. The precepts of neoconservatism were strongly reinforced by the establishment of right wing think tanks, especially in the United States, in a calculated attempt to provide intellectual and academic respectability for the positions of the priviledged.

Few countries in the western world were immune from these developments. Left wing parties found themselves increasingly challenged, and either shrank or searched for face-saving formulas —such as "new liberalism" of "third way" paths—which enabled them to slide into the acceptance of neo conservative market solutions while maintaining the facade of their traditional social democratic images.

Canada, as much as most countries, was affected by these chang-ing forces. Three dominating assumptions characterized Canada's post-war Liberal governments. One was that economic management could, through economic fine tuning, sustain continuing growth. Another was that government could be good at administration, at running things. The third was that large-scale expenditure programs could meet the needs of social security, diminish poverty, and re-duce the gap in opportunity between rich and poor.

By the 1980's these three beliefs had lost much of their credibility. It was difficult to apply overall macro-economic direction to an economy as open as that of Canada, dependent on foreign markets and hostage to the economic management of other countries, especially the United States. A decade dominated by low prod-uctivity, high inflation, and high unemployment hardly seemed a good argument for the cyclical economic management that Liberals had acclaimed.

Nor with the passage of time did the government appear to be an efficient manager. From the 1930's on, when government depart-ments multiplied and expanded, and a plethora, almost uncount-able, of Crown corporations was established. Government was poor, however, at managing for a variety of reasons—the political processes of government militate against flexibility, decentralization and the delegation of responsibility; personnel management, an essential instrument of management, remains largely outside the hands of political direction; government does not have profit as a bottom-line objective and therefore finds it difficult to apply as a means of bureaucratic control; the objectives of government are as mixed and as varied and as contradictory as the aspiration of the members of society. These amorphous purposes, the lack of precision in purposes, make public management cumbersome rather than streamlined. The public generally assumes that it is simply wasteful.

Thirdly, the public became sceptical of the massive expenditure programs which form the essential network of social security in Canada. Our economy seemed unlikely to expand at a rate that, given the requirements of fiscal stability, would generate automatically the revenues needed to sustain these programs. Hard choices, it seemed, would have to be made.

It is hardly surprising, therefore, that Canada swung towards the Conservatives in the 1980's. But the neo conservative argument is not impressive. It suffers from historical myopia—it neglects our past and forgets how the market place, left unchecked and unbalanced, can undermine human dignity. The painful lessons running through the industrial revolution to the great depression and on to the corporate excess of today—of how markets can ignore human needs when government does not, or cannot, protect the general interest, and how they may give sanction for individuals who pursue only greed and seek prosperity at the expense of their fellows— go unremembered. Nor has neo-conservatism been impressive in action. In both the United States and Canada, in spite of its rhetoric, it saddled governments with extraordinary debt loads; in both countries it led to a growing gap between the rich and the poor; in both countries it has undermined democratic politics by creating a dependence on corporate financing.

The criticisms of liberalism over the past two decades, many of them justified, are not substantially effective criticism of the structure of liberal beliefs and purposes but, rather, criticisms of technique. The underlying principles of action remain sound, the specific applications at times faulty. That is an argument not for the rejection of liberal principles but for a shrewder use of methods to achieve liberalism's goals.

As Benjamin Barber has recently written, the myth of market

fundamentalism is as foolish and wrong-headed as the socialist myth of omnipotent states. It tricks people, he says, "into believing that their own common power represents some bureaucrat's hegemony over them, and that buying power is the same as voting power. But consumers are not citizens, and markets cannot exercise democratic sovereignty. The ascendant market ideology claims to free us, but it actually robs us of the civic freedom by which we control the social consequences of private choices."

But we are now moving,—and recent events both political and economic have reinforced that movement—away from a time when selfish purpose was regarded as the dominant value to one in which social responsibility and concern for others, and how we can work through government to pursue common goals effectively, have returned to the front lines of political thought and discourse.

There is, therefore, once again, an openness to liberal approaches. We do not need a grand new political idea—today's big new idea often becomes tomorrow's bust. We do not need a new overarching intellectual structure for we already have one that has served us well and still corresponds to the values of most Canadians. Nor do we need novelty simply for fashion's sake. That does not mean we do not need new ideas. On the contrary it is vitally important to use our intellectual imagination to come forward with pragmatic approaches to the inevitably difficult problems we will face in this new century. Those new approaches, I believe, will be found within the framework of historical liberalism. It is my hope that this conference will help promote their discovery.

Can the System be Moved?

Tom Kent

OF COURSE IT CAN—sometimes. It has been in the past, and as a society we are not slowing down. So I take the "can" to be shorthand for when and how.

My response has four parts:

First, a generalization about what is needed in order to achieve major change. Second, a lesson from experience in the 1960's. Third a recognition of what is different now. And that will lead, fourth, to a little unsolicited advice to our as-yet Prime Minister. How to give himself a truly locked-in legacy to restore the politics of Canadian liberalism.

However, I expect people like you who are at this meeting will be left with the job. So, what is usually needed for such a job? It is, first, to be boy scouts—be prepared.

There are always barriers to change. But often there is the co-existing wish for that change. This disparity between the barriers for and the wish to change isn't what pollsters may measure, the extent of the two attitudes. Real change is more often inhibited because the defenders of the status quo are more focussed. They know what they are sticking to. The alternative, what may be, is often vague, uncertain; in political terms, it is a promise of a kind and it is usually broken.

That need not be. People who want to change can do better than spin vague proposals without political bite. They can get down to the hard work when it counts most, which is *before* the moment of opportunity for change actually arrives. This means, I repeat, be prepared. It means having the tools for change ready and sharp.

That's hard work in two ways. First, it means choosing priorities: identifying big issues that may soon be made ripe for change. Second, it means preparing, on those issues, firm plans to take out of your back pockets as soon as the time is right.

The reformers who can emerge as victors in the policy battles are those who are poised to seize opportunities.

That's the lesson of experience I draw from the postwar period. For the "under-sixties," I'll summarize. Canada emerged in 1945 with a Liberal federal government willing to build a welfare state. It was frustrated by the provincial governments of Ontario and Quebec. So it turned to managing—well—the postwar economic expansion. But in the process it became the complacent, autocratic establishment party, out of touch with the increasingly confident social values of a new Canada. "Six bucks Harris" said it all.

Electoral defeat was crushing, in numbers, but even more because it showed how heavily the Liberal organization had come to depend on people who were there not for Liberal policies but for the prestige, or advantage, of being with the government party. When the connection ended, these people went into hibernation or whatever. Result: the party became sufficiently a vacuum for a new generation of activists to take it over.

The takeover was maintained, for some years, thanks to the central thing we did right. I come to the thesis. Quite early, *we defined our programs.* There was nothing remarkable about the ideas. Most had been around for years. They were all politically realistic, in the air at the time. What was different from other times was that we wrote out the programs more plainly, more precisely, more firmly. In 1962 and 1963 what a Liberal government would do was made clear to a degree quite different from any time before or since.

The "since" will need defending only if anyone still thinks that the 1993 Liberal Red Book was more than a lavish dressing for what a new government might or might not choose to do. The little pamphlets of 1962 and 1963 were less ambitious, but on key issues they were precise enough to hold the government to a defined course.

Between the writing and the doing there were, of course, fierce battles. The balance of power shifted somewhat when office came into sight. Hibernators emerged. People who had stayed around but accepted positivism perforce, not from conviction, now called for sober second thoughts. The late stages of the Diefenbaker regime apart, the Pearson cabinet was perhaps Canada's most contentious.

The battles were mighty. But the outcome was almost always the same. The guardians of the policy, to borrow a Pearson phrase, were the winners. Their agenda was on the table, their programs publicly declared. It was the revisionists who were usually on the defensive, snared by having gone along in their time of weakness.

I don't mean that the programs as implemented were exactly as proposed. Far from it. But few of the changes were political retreats. They owed more to bureaucratic and other refining. The greatest changes were in the programs that needed baking in the oven of federal-provincial relations. In the case of the retirement package— CPP, QPP, GIS, OAS at 65 and indexed—the outcome was a massive improvement on the original. In the case of medicare, there were improvements but also dilutions; and Sharp, the revisionist, got his consolation of a year's delay.

Essentially, however, the programs held. They would not have held if they had not been ready beforehand, waiting for the time of opportunity. I should note one big retreat. That was on Walter Gordon's investment in nationalism. Significantly, it was the policy segment where definite measures had not been developed and declared in advance.

The book reporting the ideas from this conference will be the right start for wider discussion. But I emphasize that the policy ideas which emerge will deserve better than collection between the covers of some Red Book. You will need to work out priorities and, for the key measures, define the details.

In that area of strategy and tactics, things haven't changed since the sixties. In many other respects they have. They call for substantial institutional changes—in the tax structure, the electoral system, federal-provincial relationships.

I will concentrate, however, on the most immediate need. It arises from one problem that was small for us but is now dominant. *It's the dollar*. I don't mean the exchange rate. I don't mean deficit concerns, government or party. I mean party money from the wrong sources. The Liberal party is now a dependancy of corporate finance.

Of course, it's not alone. And such dependancy is not new. Think of Sir John A. and the CPR. Many people think that money always rules politics. In fact, its role has varied greatly with time and place. It lessened as the confederation matured. The vote for women in 1919 made, I think, a lot of difference. Certainly, for some fifty years thereafter, corporate funding wasn't of much account in Liberal fortunes and policies. The last twenty-five years or so have been greatly different. What is remarkable is the triumph of the spin doctors. They have managed to make the size of the change little noted.

In 1958 the campaign to elect Mike Pearson leader of a national party cost three thousand dollars. This year the leadership of an Ontario party cost three million. True, Pearson was a special case. But not, in this respect, very special. I've no inside knowledge of the 1956 national Conservative leadership campaign, but I was a close observer. I'd be surprised to learn that Diefenbaker's expenses were as much as ten thousand. Today, if there were a serious contest for Liberal leadership, winning would probably cost ten million.

I have Lloyd Axworthy's permission to remind you that the reason Liberals had no opportunity to consider him for the party leadership a decade ago—as I know many would have liked—was that he could not raise the seven figure amount needed to be even in the running. He was not popular with big business.

Politicians and business executives equally claim that political donations are made from the goodness of their heart, not to buy anything. If that's true, they're as illegitimate for the company as million-dollar birthday parties. Businesses are incorporated for specified commercial purposes. They've no right to spend their shareholders' money on being nice to politicians. In fact, of course, the donations do buy influence. Direct favours for particular companies among the many are necessarily restricted to some of them. But cozy interventions in government policy and administration are not. That's why, for years now, the agenda of governments has been so close to the agenda of Tom d'Aquino's chief executive bosses.

Among Liberals the talk may not have changed as much as elsewhere, but the walk certainly has. The contrast between thousand-dollar and million-dollar leaders is palpable. In the 1960's the angriest protests were not in the streets. They came from the boardrooms and executive suites where Medicare and the CPP and all that were denounced as the ruin of the nation.

Orthodoxy now requires all Liberals to claim those measures as the proud embodiments of their values. Does anyone seriously think that such social programs would have been enacted in the 1960's if the politicians of the 1960's had been as beholden to corporate finance as the politicians of today?

Many desirable reforms have been talked about at this gathering. If you want to achieve them, moving the system comes first. Political financing has to be reformed. Federal politics has to catch up with Quebec and Manitoba in the elimination of organizational money. Tough legislation will be needed. Even more than most, it had better be clearly defined before the battle is joined. You could find suggestions in several of my writings.

Let me avoid misrepresentation. The reason to get corporate money out of politics is not that government could then squeeze corporate profits. On the contrary, my view is—has long been—that the corporate income tax should not be reduced but should be abolished entirely, on profits distributed to personal taxpayers. That is, of course, only one item in the package of tax reforms that are required to make Liberalism fit for today.

I'm sorry we haven't spent more time on that. Along with electoral reform, better taxation is one of the main ways to "move the system."

But I return to the first need—to the financing of politics.

I don't know whether this is an area that pollsters have much explored, with questions aimed at what conclusions. But I've no doubt that this is the moment of opportunity. Corporate financing is in disrepute, in even more disrepute than politics. Raising an overwhelming demand to separate the two, to take purchased influence out of politics, would be an easy campaign for any competent group of politicians. It would have been easy even when neo conservatism was dominant. It will be even easier now, especially if you use the new ways to make connections, notably with the lively under-forties, that have been talked about here.

But perhaps, with our present version of democracy, that isn't needed. A for-the-time-being Prime Minister has only to raise his hand. To cleanse political financing, to revive the heart of Liberalism, would be very different from a deathbed conversion to neglected social schemes for which there's little money today and his successor may or may not stick to. By contrast, financial reform of politics would be the least costly, yet firmest and finest of legacies. And he might think that it would discomfort Paul Martin. That would be, of course, incidental, not the motive.

However, I'm not offering to bet that my unsolicited advice will be welcome. The tasks of renewal will remain for you younger reformers.

A Choice not an Echo:
Sharing North America with the Hyperpower

Thomas S. Axworthy

Introduction

> THE HARDEST TASK *for a people forced to change is to acquire new attitudes and unlearn old lessons.*
>
> D.W. Brogan

Pierre Trudeau famously told the National Press Club in Washington, DC, "living next door to you is in some ways like sleeping with an elephant. No matter how friendly or even-tempered the beast, if I may call it that, one is affected by every twitch and grunt." Thirty odd years after Trudeau's quip, the bed has got smaller, the elephant has got larger, and Canadians will have to become quicker and even more supple if we are to stand any chance of maintaining a distinctive way of life while sharing the continent with our superpower neighbour.

Canadian-American relations, like Quebec's role in Confederation and federal-provincial feuding, is a hardy perennial in Canadian history. Canada's first strategy was simply military defence as we resisted the invasions of 1775 and 1812, and fears of a renewed assault after the American Civil War played a role in persuading Britain's North American colonies to unite in 1867. Soon after Confederation, Sir John A. Macdonald launched a second approach: the National Policy of 1879 was an integrated macro-strategy in which tariffs would protect infant Canadian industries, the state would promote massive infrastructure like the railways, while immigration filled the empty West. This was an economic version of the defensive military strategy that had dominated the pre-Confederation years: Canada would build economic walls at the 49th parallel and behind those walls a North America different from the dynamic model to the south would emerge. The National Policy did not go uncontested: in 1854 the Province of Canada had signed a Reciprocity Treaty with the United States, but this experiment in free trade ended when the United States cancelled the agreement in 1865 (lack of access to the U.S. market was another spur to create a larger economic union in British North America). Proponents of free trade, however, looked back fondly at the economic good times associated with Reciprocity, and in 1911, Sir Wilfred Laurier repudiated the tariff component of the National Policy and negotiated a free trade agreement with the United States. Laurier, however, was defeated in the 1911 election and the National Policy continued to be Canada's overall economic framework vis-à-vis the United States until the mid-1980s. By the last Trudeau government, for example, the Auto Pact and the multilateral trade rounds had reduced the efficacy of Macdonald's tariff policy instrument, but it was still hoped that resource endowments and a made in Canada energy policy would give Canada a competitive advantage.

In a momentous break with the past, the Mulroney government in the 1980s fashioned a third strategy which promoted integration, not protection. The National Policy was laid to rest in 1989 by Canada's adoption of the Canada-United States Free Trade Agreement and the successor North American Free Trade Agreement of 1994, which brought Mexico into the free trade fold. NAFTA goes far beyond a mere trade policy: it is a de facto economic constitution for Canada. Once in we will never be out, and NAFTA's terms specifically outlaw the essence of the National Policy which was to use a variety of measures to discriminate in favour of Canadian companies. NAFTA's principle of national treatment means that all companies operating in Canada, foreign or Canadian owned alike will be treated equally. Equally significant, the continental integration initiatives of the Mulroney government coincided with the growing forces of worldwide integration of financial markets or what is commonly called globalization. The die is now cast: to thrive economically, Canada must make the globalization rules of the game work for us rather than kicking against the traces. This does not mean that we cannot engineer what John McCallum calls the Canadian advantage, but it does mean that we have to do so differently than past generations.[1]

Therefore, in the 21st century we must unlearn some of the lessons of the National Policy. We must turn outward, not inward. Our goal must be nothing less than to make Canada the best platform in the world from which to launch a global business. We must be export nationalists, or as Paul Martin put it while running for the leadership of the Liberal Party in 1990, we must have "nationalism without walls."[2]

This calls for a massive change in our historic approach towards the United States. But such transformation can occur. D.W. Brogan, a celebrated British analyst of the United States, for example, wrote in *The American Character* of how the demands of post-war leadership were pressing in on the United States, demanding a different response than the easy isolationism of the past. Brogan's description of how that change should come about is as relevant to Canada's current needs as it was to the United States in 1944:

> It is a world in which all nations have to make
> deep adjustments in their mental habits, have to
> take stock of what is living and what is dead in
> their tradition. But that adjustment must, all the
> same, be made in the terms of the living tradition, according to the spirit.[3]

To chart a sensible course for the future we must take the world as it is: we cannot afford to live in a haze of delusions. But in using our heads to adjust to the modern reality of globalization, we must not lose the habits of the heart and forget the traditions and values which have brought us so far. The instrumentalities of Sir John A. Macdonald's National Policy are no longer relevant, but the values which inspired it—a burning desire to create a distinctive way of life in our part of North America—remains as valid as ever.

The Primacy of Choice

Liberalism is a body of thought dedicated to the proposition that the individual is the unit of supreme value in society. Wilhelm von Humboldt, the founder of the University of Berlin and a philosopher who plainly influenced John Stuart Mill writes that the true end of mankind "is the highest and most harmonious development of his powers to a complete and consistent whole."[4] Freedom, von Humboldt argues, is the first and indispensable condition for developing one's powers, but a second condition is variety and diversity: "even the most free and self-reliant of men is hindered in his development, when set in a monotonous situation."[5] Liberals believe therefore that every individual has a special dimension, a uniqueness that cries out to be realized. As free agents, human beings are capable of defining their own definitions of happiness or versions of the good. Freedom is the ability to make choices and choice is the mechanism by which we achieve ends that we value. As Aristotle emphasized in Book Six of *The Ethics*, "the origin of action…is choice, and the origin of choice is apposite and purposive reasoning."[6] Nineteenth century liberals like Humboldt, Mill, and Constant all promoted the processes that enable Aristotle's primacy of choice.

T.H. Green, Leonard Hobhouse and John Meynard Keynes in the 20th century added to this 19th century liberal framework an emphasis on the actual opportunities that people have to exercise their choices. Amartya Sen, for example, in *Development as Freedom*, is typical of the modern tradition of liberalism in arguing that "unfreedom can arise either through inadequate processes (such as the violation of voting privileges or other political and civil rights) or through inadequate opportunities that some people have for achieving what they minimally would like to achieve."[7]

This philosophical distinction between the right to have choice and the opportunity to exercise it, applies equally well to the collective choices we make as self-governing men and women. Sovereignty is the legal right for all states to make unfettered choices within their national jurisdictions; power is the ability to achieve one's purposes or goals. Traditionally, military or economic resources have been the components of power most useful to get others to do what they otherwise would not do. In recent years, political scientists like Robert Keohane and Joe Nye have examined areas of "soft power" such as cultural reach, the force of example, or the diplomatic skill of some players in converting resources to realized outcomes in the changed behaviour of others.[8] As important as the ability to change the behaviour of others, is the ability *not* to be changed by others, i.e. how much autonomy does a state have on any given issue? No state is fully autonomous, not even the United States, but the critical continuum is the path from autonomy to dependence. Philosophically, liberals do not believe in an absolute good—every individual should be free to decide this for themselves—but we do accord primacy to freedom of choice as the necessary condition to self-empowerment. Collectively, a liberal government should give great weight to expanding as much as possible the power resources that will give future generations the ability to choose. The promotion of choice or enhanced autonomy in an admittedly interdependent world should be a preeminent goal for Canada in the 21st century.

The Unipolar Moment [9]

Promoting Canadian choice and expanding autonomy while living beside the most dynamic and powerful state in the world is no small task. This requirement has always been one of Canada's challenges, but as we enter the 21st century, it has never been so pressing, because the United States has never been so powerful. Hubert Vedrine, the former foreign minister of France, describes the United States not as a superpower, but as a hyperpower with supremacy in "the economy, currency, military areas, lifestyle, language and products of mass culture."[10] Not since the height of Rome has one state so towered over the rest of the world. And we are all very lucky that the United States is a freedom loving democracy—if Napoleon, Hitler or Stalin had enjoyed such a power discrepancy with the rest of the world, it would have meant the conquest of the planet.

Forecasting is always hazardous in politics. It was not too long ago that authors like Paul Kennedy were predicting the decline of the United States because of imperial overstretch and Japan was touted as the coming power.[11] The American economy, of course, could falter, or budget deficits and out of control military spending could become unsustainable, or the United States could even suffer from a terrorist attack with weapons of mass destruction. But the odds of any of Anthony Lake's *Six Nightmares* happening are low, though not impossible, and it is much more likely that the unipolar moment will last, at least for a generation.[12] Since the 1860s, Canada has learned to live with the United States as a major power, then from 1945 on as a superpower, and for the foreseeable future we had better get used to sharing the continent with a hyperpower.

If living in the world of globalization means that Canada must unlearn some of the economic lessons of the past, then dealing with a hyperpower means we must equally unlearn some of the diplomatic verities of the more recent post-war era. The new status of the United States, and changes in the world since the demise of the Soviet Union in 1990, means that two essential assumptions that have governed international relations since 1950— containment as a western balance of power policy vis-à-vis the Soviet Union, and nuclear deterrence, based on a rational state to state interaction model—no longer apply. There is now a large conceptual hole in the theory of international relations. That hole is being filled by a unilateralist school of thought within the United States which includes key members of the Bush administration and which seeks American predominance, not balance, as the central foreign policy goal. The United States now has the power of Rome: crucial to the future of the world will be the internal American debate about whether the United States should also fulfill the imperial mission of Rome.

In its emotional impact, September 11, 2001, has been the day which in the words of many commentators "changed everything." Certainly the awful reality of terrorist threats to innocent civilians, known in the Middle East and Europe for a generation, was finally brought home to North Americans, and with that realization came the even more shocking understanding that however bad September 11 was, it could have been worse. Had the al-Qaeda hijackers flown aircraft into nuclear installations (which had been their original plan), or if they had fashioned chemical or biological weapons (which they were attempting to do in their bases in Afghanistan), the resulting destruction would have been magnified by a horrifying degree. To the nearly 3000 families who lost loved ones in the al-Qaeda attack (including 24 Canadians), September 11 was an awful personal tragedy: for the rest of us it brought home the age old lesson that providing security is the number one responsibility of the state, and that safety can never be assumed, it must be secured.

The debate in the United States about its new position in the world, however, long predates September 11. In fact, the proponents of today's unilateral stance began articulating their position only months after the fall of the Soviet Union. In March of 1992, the *New York Times* broke a story about a secret Defence Planning Guidance study prepared by Paul D. Wolfowitz, the Pentagon's Under Secretary for Policy, and sent to then Defence Secretary Dick Cheney, and National Security Advisor Colin Powell. The classified document rejected the strategy of collective internationalism that had guided the United States since 1945 and argued that America's political and military vision in the post-Cold War world should be to ensure that no rival superpower be allowed to emerge in Western Europe, Asia, or Russia.[14] George Bush senior lost the 1992 election to Bill Clinton and little more was heard of this doctrine of paramountcy as the Clinton administration followed a policy of engaged multilateralism. But the hardliners continued to beaver away in their think-tanks, and the success of George Bush Jr. in winning the 2000 election brought back to power conservatives like Dick Cheney, Donald Rumsfeld, Paul Wolfowitz, Richard Perle and others associated with the 1992 study. What was once a theory has now become an official doctrine.

Almost immediately, the Bush administration showed its unilateralist tendencies by promoting anti-ballistic missile defence, threatening withdrawal from the 1969 ABM treaty, repudiating the Kyoto treaty on global warming, rejecting the International Criminal Court and, for good measure, supporting protectionist duties against European steel and Canadian soft wood lumber. But the September 11 terrorist attack on the United States strengthened the hard line faction even more within the administration, and the President has recently endorsed both the objective of superpower paramountcy and the possibility of preemption if the United States perceives a threat to be imminent, i.e. the United States will strike first. On September 20, 2002, the Bush administration released its "National Security of the United States" report to the Congress. Mr. Bush's document states that "the President has no intention of allowing any foreign power to catch up with the huge lead the United States has opened," and while seeking allies in the battle against terrorism, "we will not hesitate to act alone, if necessary to exercise our right of self-defence by acting preemptively."[15]

If the unilateralist drive of the Bush administration were an aberration, or typical of only a small group of conservatives, it would be worrying but not necessarily critical for the long-term. Uni-lateralism, however, is one of the three predominant schools of American foreign policy and its roots run very deep. The first tradition in America's approach to foreign policy is isolationism, a current that stretches back to Washington and Jefferson's warnings about "entangling alliances." Wishing to avoid Europe's wars and believing that the United States had a special providence from God, Secretary of State John Quincy Adams best articulated the premises of isolationism that made it the lodestar of American foreign policy for more than a century:

> Wherever the standard of freedom and independence has been or shall be unfurled, there will be America's heart, her benedictions, and her prayers. But she goes not abroad in search of monsters to destroy. She is the well wisher to the freedom and independence of all. She is the champion and vindication only of her own.[16]

The second tradition of unilateralism has almost as long a pedigree as isolationism. President Monroe declared in 1823 that the United States would oppose any attempt by the European powers to restore their possessions in Latin America thereby abrogating to itself the role of Latin America's "protector": and as early as 1832 the United States sent a fleet to the Falkland Islands to reduce an Argentine garrison that was interfering with American shipping. In 1844, the United States preemptively went to war with Mexico and increased its area by two thirds, with the annexation of Texas and the conquest of New Mexico and California. Between the Civil War and the Spanish-American War, marines were sent to Cuba, Uruguay, Argentina, Chile, Columbia, and Haiti.[17] The war with Spain in 1898 gave the United States protectorates over Puerto Rico, the Philippines, Guam, and defacto over Cuba. The Jefferson tradition of isolationism and the Monroe doctrine could co-exist because unilateralism and isolationism are ideological twins. "They both spring from the same exceptionalist impulse," writes Michael Hirsh, "a deep well of American mistrust about the rest of the world, especially Europe."[18]

Both isolationism and unilateralism are contested by a third tradition in American foreign policy, liberal internationalism. Forever associated with Woodrow Wilson, its inventor, and practiced to perfection by Franklin Roosevelt, liberal internationalism seeks to build international institutions to create rules of the game, standards of conduct, and international enforcement mechanisms. All of the postwar international architecture—the United Nations, the World Bank and International Monetary Fund, NATO, and the General Agreement on Trade and Tariffs (GATT) and its successor institutions, the World Trade Organization, are American inventions. Today, when an influential body of American public opinion treats the multilateral system it created like Rosemary's baby, we must remember that liberal internationalism has been the dominant influence in American foreign policy since 1945. The unilateralists are winning some innings, but the game is far from over.

What, if anything, can Canada do to tip the balance in the internal U.S. debate toward liberal internationalism? This is the same issue that faced Lester Pearson, Ernest Bevin, and Jean Monnet in 1945-48, although then the debate was between internationalists like Dean Acheson and isolationalists like Robert Taft. The answer is largely the same as in 1945: don't overreact, offer to help, and take your own responsibilities seriously. But in playing a constructive role internationally and in serving as an ally of the liberal internationalist camp within the United States, Canadians must face up to a crucial fact. For years, we have been under investing in foreign policy and military capabilities. We talk the talk but we no longer walk the walk. To be taken seriously as a contributor to one of the great issues of our time—the future role of the United States in the 21st century, and thus the future of the international system itself— we need a radical shift in priorities.

Defence Against Help

Finance Minister John Manley was much criticized lately when he made the statement that Canadians "should grow up" and reflect a more mature attitude towards the United States, but Manley was only speaking some hard truths. To some Canadians anything the United States does is suspect: thus there was opposition to the American led war against al-Qaeda and the Taliban in Afghanistan, even though al-Qaeda was using Afghanistan as a base camp and even though the Taliban had turned that country into one large concentration camp for women. Even when the Americans were right, they were wrong. On the opposite side of the spectrum, there are some who are so fearful about the wrath of the United States that they would have us either support poor ideas—such as the militanization of space—just because the United States is an advocate, or remain silent even when the United States goes off-kilter. Maturity requires that we have the confidence to support the United States when it is right and the courage to oppose them when they are wrong. Meaningful choice implies that we should decide issues on their merits, not by who is the proponent of the idea.

But Canada does *not* have meaningful choices in many areas of international concern, because we have a credibility-capability gap of immense proportions. Walter Lippman, adviser to Woodrow Wilson and the dean of American pundits for four decades wrote that a successful foreign policy "consists in bringing into balance, with a comfortable surplus of power in reserve, the nation's commitments and the nation's power."[19] The real test of a nation's commitment, Lippman wrote, is the capabilities that it devotes to the task. This is a test that Canada is failing. For years we have systematically reduced our investment in foreign policy resources while expanding our rhetorical commitments.

There are three broad avenues of power in foreign policy and, in recent years, Canada has diminished its capacity in every one of them. A starting point is the energy and ability of the men and women who represent our interests or defend our security abroad. The Canadian Foreign Service was once one of the best in the world. Henry Kissinger, for example, writes in his memoirs that "Canadian leaders have a narrow margin of manoeuvre, that they utilized with extraordinary skill."[20] But years of pay-freezes have meant that well-trained Foreign Affairs and military officers face a huge wage disparity compared with the private sector, while spouses find it difficult having a career in a foreign posting. The Department of National Defence is finding it exceedingly difficult to recruit professionals like engineers or doctors. The most worrisome brain drain in Canada is the brain drain away from the military and the Foreign Service.

In our most important foreign posting,—Washington—for example, Canada's human resources pale in comparison with Mexico.

Mexico has consulates in 43 of American cities and the Mexican Ambassador in Washington is almost of Cabinet rank in importance. In contrast, Canada has 10 consulates in major U.S. cities and a very over-worked staff in Washington. There is plenty of American good-will towards Canada, but it takes a tremendous amount of work to penetrate the U.S. bureaucracy, secure a place on the congressional radar screen or get calls placed through the White House switch-board. Indeed, it is not only Senators, Members of the House, or White House staffers who need to be lobbied: the staffs of the myriad of House and Senate Committees and the personal staffs of the politicians are also critical gate keepers. Washington is a constant beehive of activity. In Ottawa, the U.S. ambassador needs to know five or six senior Ministers, a dozen key officials, and some influentials from the Prime Minister's office. In Washington, the Canadian Ambassador needs to influence not a handful of people but literally hundreds of individuals, because the U.S. government is a many splintered thing.

Economic resources are a second component of international power. Canadians certainly have an image of themselves as generous donors committed to the development of the underprivileged. Prime Minister Chrétien rightly placed African development at the center of the recent G-8 meeting in Alberta. But the reality is that we have been punching well below our weight. The Trudeau government made the Canadian International Development Agency (CIDA) a pillar of our foreign policy and increased spending tenfold from $277 million in the late 1960s, to a little over $2 billion in 1984-85. Today, CIDA's budget is still only $2.4 billion which explains why in real terms Canada's percentage of aid to GNP has fallen from .75% in 1975 to .25% today, compared to the Netherlands who spend three times as much at .84% of GNP.

It is military capability, however, that has fallen the furthest. When I first went to work in Ottawa in the mid-1960s, there were over 100,000 men and women in the military, with half in the army. Today, the manpower of all three services is only 60,000 and the army was so stretched by the deployment of 750 troops to Afghanistan that the mission could not be renewed. Today, Canada is 34th in the world contributing to peace-keeping, a far cry from the halcyon days of Mr. Pearson. In 1993, when Prime Minister Chrétien took office, we spent $12 billion on defence. We still do. Our NATO allies on average spend 2% of GNP on defence, we spend less than 1%. This is not failing the Lippman test; these results are so dismal it means that we should not even be writing the exam!

The decline in Canada's capabilities in military and foreign policy resources has a direct impact on Canada's ability to choose sensible policies and to influence the United States to stay on a multi-lateral course. It should surprise no one that security is the number one concern of American policy makers. The United States is a potential target for weapons of mass destruction. Canada can *never, ever* allow itself to be a security threat to the United States. In the days of the Cold War when Canada's airspace was vital to the defence of North America, Canada built and manned three radar networks to provide early warning. In NATO's early days Canada contributed to European defence, squadrons of F-86 fighter jets, then the best fighter aircraft in the world, months ahead of the United States! Terrorism is today a threat to North America similar in magnitude to the Soviet bomber menace in the Cold War, and we must make the same kind of decisions that we did in the era of Louis St. Laurent and C.D. Howe. Either we do the job properly, or the States will rightly insist upon taking its own measures. Both for the protection of our own citizens and to avoid such "defence against help," North America security must return to the priority it commanded in the 1950's.

Under the chairmanship of John Manley, an ad-hoc Cabinet Committee on security has been meeting since September 11. This committee should become permanent and Canada should create a National Security Council to provide integration and consistent advice on security and international issues. Ottawa is organized vertically into silos like immigration or defence. But national security is a horizontal issue that involves a host of departments ranging from Customs, to the Coast Guard, to Immigration, as well as the core departments of National Defence, Foreign Affairs, the Canadian Security Intelligence Service, and the Royal Canadian Mounted Police. The mission of the National Security Council would be "the promotion of a way of life acceptable to Canadian people and compatible with the needs and legitimate aspirations of others. It includes freedom from internal subversion and freedom from the erosion of political, economic, and social values that are essential to the quality of life,"[21] a definition used by the National Defence College of Kingston, Ontario (typically now closed because of the 30% reduction in defence spending).

Over the next decade, Canada must double spending in the envelope of homeland security, foreign aid, diplomacy, and national defence. The 2001 budget had major increases devoted to homeland security needs in cross-border infrastructure and agencies like the RCMP and CSIS. The Senate Committee on National Security and Defence has since usefully pointed out major problems in the security dimension of Canada's ports.[22] Canada never had the "porous" border portrayed by the popular television drama "West Wing," but this belief is now an article in faith in many American circles, and in a country which knows little about its neighbour, this is a serious perception gap. Canada does not have to adopt American procedures and policies on homeland security, and the 30 point plan for a "smart border" for the 21st century jointly announced by Deputy Prime Minister John Manley and Homeland Security Director Tom Ridge in December 2001 is an example of shared, not unilateral, decision-making. But Canada does have to be proactive on homeland security issues, not only because clogged borders hurt the Canadian economy far more than the American, but because we must be acutely sensitive to the overriding security concerns of our neighbour. It should be Canada leading the way in suggesting new procedures and introducing new technology to ease flows at the border while keeping out undesirables. It should be Canada that has an up-to-date emergency measures plan to deal with potential catastrophes. It should be Canada that innovates in protecting the security of our ports and airports. We owe it to our own citizens and to our neighbours.

In the lead up to the G-8 summit in Alberta in June 2002, Prime Minister Chrétien announced an 8% annual increase in Canada's international development budget, leading to a doubling of aid resources by 2010. This commitment should be confirmed by a future Liberal government. If Afghanistan proved anything, it proved that the world cannot "ignore" failed states: here we can offer real leadership, along with Japan, the European Union and the United Nations who understand better than many of the American unilateralist champions that draining the swamp of terrorists requires that you fill in the ditch with productive earth. Trade is the critical piece of the puzzle. Nations in Africa and Asia rightly scorn the West for promoting free trade in theory but protecting agriculture and textiles at home. The Nordic countries lead the world in development assistance: Canada should lead the world in opening our borders to Third World trade. There is real power in being a moral example (not to mention the benefits to Canadian consumers).

Recent budgets have committed resources to homeland security and Prime Minister Chrétien has given a lead by increasing funding for development. But it is in National Defence where the need is greatest and where leadership has been most absent. The Auditor-General, and committees in both the House of Commons and Senate, have made an irrefutable case that just to maintain the military at the existing level of 60,000 troops will require an immediate increase to the defence base budget of at least $1–2 billion dollars. To increase the military to 75,000–80,000 troops will require an annual defence budget of $18–20 billion, instead of today's $12 billion. This is a huge increase, but Canada has been under investing in the military for a generation. So limited has Canada's investment been for so long, that even doubling defence expenditures will only bring us up to the NATO average. The Department of National Defence should receive annual budget increases of $1 billion a year over the next several years until it can sustain a modern well-equipped force of 75,000–80,000 troops.

Canada's credibility gap in international affairs must be closed. We have tried to run an active foreign policy on the cheap but we cannot get away with such smoke and mirrors any longer. It is not national conceit to believe that Canada has something very valuable to offer to the world. In this unipolar moment, the world needs multilateral champions. If we match resources to our values, we can be in the forefront of those states committed to the liberal internationalist ideal. This will require a large shift in national priorities to make our capabilities match our commitments, but in so doing, we will reaffirm the ancient wisdom of Horace that "it is your concern when your neighbour's wall is on fire."

The Canadian Way

Matching resources to Canadian values in international affairs will require one major realignment of priorities; giving Canadians real choices in their economic futures will require a second. A productive economy is both critical in itself—having meaningful and challenging work is one of humankind's most basic desires—and it provides the resources to give us choices in other areas such as social policy. The central issue of our time is how to deliver a superb quality of life through a productive innovative economy that makes the world of deep integration work for us, not against us. If we do not succeed in engineering the Canadian advantage or the "Canadian Way," as the Conference Board puts it in a recent report, then our half of North America will languish, our children will move south, and our corporate assets will be picked clean.[23] We need a strategy that will, in fifteen years, enable us to match the United States in per capita income and to surpass them in a generation. This radical reversal of recent trends will not occur through incremental steps: in a competitive world we need an economic strategy that will break us out of the pack.

The Canadian Way in domestic policy should follow the same precepts that I have advocated in international policy—an investment strategy of major proportions. As in security matters, there are competing camps in Canadian public opinion on how to respond to a world of deep integration. Some still emotionally reject globalization and fight it in all its forms. Others have given up on Canada's ability to chart an independent course and recommend a common currency and even joining a custom union with the United States. The reactions of those worried about globalization are understandable: these are issues of democratic accountability about a world in which private transnational corporations and financial traders have so much power. But I have never understood those who want us to give up such crucial instruments as monetary policy when they have worked so well for us in the recent past. During the negotiation over the Canada-U.S. free trade pact, for example, the great worry of Treasury Secretary James Baker was that Canada would gain U.S. market share by depreciating its currency. That is exactly what has happened. The floating exchange rate, supported by the Bank of Canada, has given Canadian suppliers a decade of competitive advantage vis-à-vis the strong U.S. dollar. This is not a result that can be sustained forever. In time, as current account surpluses pile up, Canada's dollar will increase in value and Canada's suppliers will have to compete on quality, but it is monetary policy that has allowed Canada to adjust so well to continental integration. One only need look to Argentina to see the dangers in tying yourself to someone else's currency.

In creating a distinctive polity in the northern half of North America, the Canadian Way should reject both the institutional integration model of the European Union and the individualistic minimum safety-net approach of the United States. The Euro shows the difficulty of maintaining a one size fits all currency while the cumbersome decision-making procedures of the Union often led to a lower common denominator outcome. The ability of the Canadian Parliament to take decisions quickly is an essential component of the Canadian advantage. Pooling sovereignty between Canada and the United States would also create a problem the Europeans do not have: the overwhelming weight of one of the partners. Institutional integration leads to dependence not enhanced autonomy.

The American model of low taxes, reduced public investment, and weak or non-existent social safety nets would also not be in Canada's interest. Canada has a history of public enterprise and collective investments in key areas like education, health, infrastructure, and poverty reduction will be as important to our future as they have been in our past. Franklin Roosevelt said that taxes are the price we pay for civilization and in order to pay for the investments called for in this paper, Canadians must be prepared to continue to pay a higher percentage of tax than their American neighbours. Rates between tax categories should change—I favour reduced business taxes and increased consumption taxes—but the affluent will continue to pay significantly higher taxes in Canada. It took us a decade to get out of the deficit hole: it will take a decade more of debt reduction and public investment, before Canadian rates on personal income tax can be significantly reduced. A liberal approach to the Canadian Way should explicitly reverse the approach of Ontario and British Columbia of cutting taxes first and making public investments later.

In developing the "Canadian Way," Canada's independent monetary policy shows the value of using what instruments you can to create an advantage. There are many other policies that can be fashioned in a similar way: immigration levels should be increased both to provide skilled workers and to reduce the aging of Canada's labour force; retirement policies should be revised so that Canadians over 65 can still contribute to the work force if that is their choice (skilled labour shortages not unemployment will be our problem in the future): Canada must finally achieve a real internal domestic market—it is ridiculous to have more open borders between Canada and the U.S., than between Ontario and Quebec; and Canada should broaden our trade horizons beyond the United States by seeking out additional trade pacts with Japan, the European Union, and Latin America. But four policy areas should have special political priority: debt reduction, livable cities, tax reform, and investing in children.

In providing choices for future generations, nothing is more important than maintaining budget surpluses and gradually paying down debt. This realization came home to me in a very personal way in my years in working for Pierre Trudeau: in the early 1980's, inflation was high, interest rates were over 20% and with the federal government already running a large deficit, there was little fiscal room to stimulate. Unemployment soared but there were few real immediate options. The policy cupboard was bare. We simply had to let the interest rate policy take its course. No Canadian policy maker should ever be in such a handcuffed position again. After an immense national effort, ably led by Jean Chrétien and Paul Martin, the federal government is now finally in fiscal surplus. Short of war or a national emergency, it must stay in surplus. The investment strategy I am advocating requires surpluses of $8–10 billion a year. If this figure cannot be attained on current projections, then consumption taxes should be raised. Investment instead of consumption is the bedrock for providing future choice. The current policy of making annual reductions in Canada's debt is also wise. Every nickel saved in interest payments is a nickel that can be used in future investment. At present, Canada's debt to GNP ratio is projected to fall to 40% from the sky-high levels of the 1990's: within a decade through higher growth and annual continued reductions, this ratio should be further reduced to 25%. The potential for international economic turbulence is high: Brazil, like Argentina may be the next economic domino to fall and even mighty Japan is having trouble selling its bonds. Prudence should dictate that in an uncertain world you reduce your own vulnerability. Where possible, the provinces should also be encouraged to reduce debt: in Atlantic Canada, for example, there is a real sense of grievance that as their energy resources increase tax yields, the federal government reduces equalization payments. There is little real incentive, except pride, to move from dependency. Instead, the federal government should maintain the equalization formula but direct a portion of the federal transfer to paying off provincial debt. Only when the provinces are out of debt, should equalization payments be reduced.

Jobs are created by productive enterprises. Where companies locate and where they expand are two crucial corporate decisions which Canada's public policy must influence if we are to succeed in giving Canadians real economic choices. The Canadian Way in health care, for example, responds to Canadian values but also gives companies in Canada a real advantage because the state pays for health insurance for workers, rather than corporate coffers. In making a location decision for North American investment, all things being equal, most companies will either settle in the United States because of transportation costs and closeness to markets or in Mexico because of lower wages.[25] One key factor in a firm's decision is the quality of infrastructure which means de facto the quality of Canada's cities. Cities are, of course, more than economic entities: they express our sense of community, our devotion to public space and beauty, and they reflect, too, our diversity and notions of justice. But as Jane Jacobs first educated us, and as a host of analysts have confirmed since the publication of *The Death and Life of North American Cities*, cities are also engines of economic life and incubators of creativity.[24] To have a strong economy in the 21st century, Canada needs thriving, safe, clean, innovative cities where senior executives and employees alike want to live. Continuing investment in urban infrastructure—mass transit, water and sewage, and low-income housing—is both an economic and social priority. In 1945, the forward thinkers of Canada's post-war reconstruction strategy proposed to the provinces a plan in which the federal government would pay 20% of approved capital projects on an ongoing basis. We need such thinking today. Infrastructure should be removed from the stop and go of public works politics to become the mission of a new federal-provincial-municipal foundation charged with joint planning and prioritization of our infrastructure needs. To be effective such a body needs a guaranteed revenue base, so that it can plan for the long-term. Such a body will also give municipalities a place at the decision-making table.

Infrastructure is one location variable subject to public policy.

Taxation is another. Canada has the reputation of being a high tax country, and even with the reductions in corporate tax announced in the 2001 budget, at a 40% rate, Canada is just in the middle of the pack in the cost of doing business. The United States still has significant advantages. Head offices and global champions matter: they create wealth, they invest disproportionately in their home countries, they form hubs of activity in inviting and retaining people, ideas, and capital, and they provide the intangible but very real need for Canadians to be decision-makers, not just decision implementers.[25] If we do not have great Canadian companies at the top of the global game, then Canadians will simply join companies headquartered abroad. Smaller countries like Sweden, the Netherlands or Switzerland have been far more successful in attracting and retaining head offices of major global players than Canada. Part of the problem is branding: as a member of Harvard's executive teaching program, I have visited scores of influential decision-makers in Europe and Asia (as part of an American delegation). In such meetings, one quickly learns who is in the buzz and making an impression on an international audience. For many years, one could not attend such international gatherings on public policy without hearing of Ireland; more recently the example of Finland is often touted. South China attracts enormous interest. Rarely, if ever, is Canada mentioned. We are simply not on the international radar screen.

One way to establish a brand and influence corporate decision-making is to move as boldly on taxation as we did on ending the deficit. Our mantra should be: be daring, be first, and be different. The cost of doing business in Canada must be radically improved. Payroll taxes, which are taxes on jobs, must be reduced, especially the employers contribution to unemployment insurance. Business capital taxes hurt enterprise, because the tax is paid whether or not companies make profits. When Ireland decided in the mid-1980s to cut corporate taxes to less than one-third of Canada's rate and to make tuition free for university students, this combination of reducing the cost of business and investing in brains, created the "Celtic Miracle" and Ireland enjoyed the fastest economic growth in the industrialized world.[26] Canada must do the same. We must not only reduce corporate taxes to U.S. levels, but we should significantly go beyond them. Corporate tax-cutting is one means within our direct span of control to offset the many locational advantages of the United

States. Tax reform—to encourage savings, to promote investment and to reduce the cost of doing business—is the best single way to manufacture a Canadian advantage. Our international brand should be to have the world's most intelligent tax policy.

Lastly, the phrase "lifetime learning for a knowledge economy," has been a slogan not a policy. Canada has a good education record but not an exceptional one. Here, too, investment is needed. At present, Canadians can put money away in registered education plans for students studying full-time at institutions. This should be extended for lifetime learning and professional development. If Canadians save to educate themselves, they should be encouraged. Companies contributing to individual education accounts should therefore get a credit and individuals saving for education should get a deduction similar to the Registered Retirement Savings Plan.

Investing in people should also be concentrated where the need is greatest and where the need is broadest. Aboriginals face the most obstacles in our society. And low-income children, as a group, are the largest number of Canadians who lack real choices. If there is a "silver bullet" in Canadian public policy, it is the work on Early Years education by Margaret McCain and Fraser Mustard.[27] Canada has 1.3 million poor children or 20% of Canada's youth. It is no coincidence that Canada also suffers from a 20% dropout rate. Within the next decade, Canada should eliminate child poverty. Like Medicare, this investment in the social good will also provide immense economic benefits. The National Child Benefit should be increased on a fixed schedule until families are over the low-income line. This schedule should be tied to the $100 billion in tax cuts announced in the 2001 budget. As taxes come down, so too should child poverty. Norway and Sweden have child poverty levels of only 3%: improving the life chances and choices of Canadian children by reaching similar levels within a decade should be Canada's next great social advance. Canadians should never forget the wisdom of Diogenes: "the foundation of every state is the education of its youth."[28]

Conclusion

The language of priorities must be the religion of reform. Taking office in 1993, the Liberal government of Mr. Chrétien rightly made deficit reduction and macro-economic management the overriding national priority. It took two terms but the macro-economic policy framework of Canada is now one of the best in the world, and the results are beginning to show. Canada should lead the OECD in economic growth in 2003. In the decades ahead, we require the same kind of devotion to the investment needs of the micro-economy. To provide enhanced choices for Canadians we must continue to keep the budget in surplus and, where possible, reduce debt. Within this prudent fiscal framework, over the next decade we must attain annual surpluses of $8–10 billion which will give us the resources to invest in urban infrastructure, corporate tax cuts, life-long learning, and ending child poverty. By choosing the Canadian Way of public investment rather than the fixes of adopting the US currency or a customs union, Canada can become the best location in North America to do business without a reduction in autonomy. Canada's margin of manoeuvre will be further enhanced by a steady commitment to debt reduction. While investing domestically, Canada must also forgo our recent habit of starving our military and letting our international development goals shrink. The world needs multilateral champions both to continue to build an international community and to serve as a counterpoint to the unilateralist impulse of some American decision-makers. Preaching won't do the trick but constructive engagement will. To govern is to choose. If we choose well in the next decade, we can ensure that future generations of Canadians will continue to have real choices when they take up the democratic responsibility of defining the good life for themselves.

Notes

[1.] John McCallum, then Chief Economist of the Royal Bank, now Minister of National Defence, told the University of Waterloo in a February 2000 lecture that Canada risks seeing its standard of living slide to only 50% of that in the United States and that without a fundamental policy change Canada would "slide into Americanization and a major challenge to the long term survival of Canada's distinct identity."

[2] Quoted in Richard Gwyn, *Nationalism Without Walls* (Toronto: McClelland & Stewart, 1995), p. 9.

[3] D.W. Brogan, *The American Character* (New York: Time Inc., 1944), p. xlvi.

[4] Wilhelm von Humboldt, *The Limits of State Action*, ed. J.W. Burrow (India napolis: Liberty Fund, 1969 edition), p.10.

5   Ibid, p. 10.

6   Quoted in John Adair, *Great Leaders* (Guilford, Surrey: The Talbot Adair Press, 1989), p. 74.

7   Amartya Sen, *Development as Freedom* (New York: Alfred A. Knopf, 1999), p. 17.

8   Robert O. Keohane and Joseph S. Nye Jr., *Power and Interdependence*. (Boston: Little Brown & Co, 1977), pp. 27-29.

9   Charles Krauthammer, "The Unipolar Moment," *Foreign Affairs* (Winter 1990-91), pp. 23-33.

10 Hubert Vedrine, *France in an Age of Globalization* (Washington, DC: Brookings Press, 2001), p. 2.

11. See Paul Kennedy, *The Rise and Fall of the Great Powers* (New York: Random House, 1987).

12. See, for example, Anthony Lake, *Six Nightmares* (Boston: Little Brown & Co, 2000).

13 See the *New York Times* March 9, 1992, "U.S. Strategy Plan Calls for Insuring No Rivals Develop," by Patrick Tyler, p.1.

14 *New York Times*, September 20, 2003, "Bush to Outline Doctrine of Striking Foes First," by David E. Sanger, p. 1.

15 Quoted in Henry Kissinger, *Does America Need a Foreign Policy?* (New York: Simon and Schuster, 2000), pp. 238-239.

16 For a fascinating review of the history of American foreign policy see Walter Russell Mead, *Special Providence* (New York: Alfred A. Knopf, 2002).

17 Michael Hirsh "Bush and the World," *Foreign Affairs*, (September/October), p. 20.

18 Walter Lippman, quoted in *Walter Lippman and the American Century* by Ronald Steel (New York: Vintage Books, 1981), p. 406.

19 Henry Kissinger, *White House Years* (Boston: Little Brown and Co., 1979), p. 383.

20 Quoted in the Report of the Standing Senate Committee on National Security and Defence, "Canadian Security and Military Preparedness," February 2002, p.51.

21 Ibid, pp. 108-116.

22 See, The Conference Board Report, *Performance and Potential 2001 – 2002*, Ottawa, 2001.

23 For a good discussion of the location decisions of firms see Jack Mintz, *Most Favoured Nation* (Toronto: C.D. Howe Institute, 2001), pp. 5-25.

24 Jane Jacobs, *The Death and Life of Great American Cities* (New York: Vintage Books, 1961).

25 These points are made well in Thomas Paul D'Aquino and David Stewart-Patterson, *Northern Edge* (Toronto: Stoddart, 2001), pp. 217-262.

26 Ibid, p. 248.

27 For a follow-up on what has happened in Ontario to the Early Years study note *The Toronto Star,* September 6, 2002, "Broken Pledges on Early Years," by Vanessa Lu, p. 1.

28 Adair, *Op.cit*, p. 143

Social Cohesion and Nation-Building:
The Role of Liberal Values
in Connecting Canadians

Brooke Jeffrey

IN A COUNTRY where the Queen is asked to drop the puck at an NHL game, where *Hockey Night in Canada* leads the TV ratings and a contract dispute between the show's anchor and CBC management receives front page coverage in the national news, the genius of the Molson brewing dynasty in linking its image with the national pastime seems self-evident. Yet after years of successful "lifestyle" commercials, the company's abrupt shift to an ad with political overtones during the 2000 NHL playoffs led some industry insiders to question whether Molson's marketing team was losing its touch. This scepticism quickly faded. The *"I am Canadian"* campaign—featuring an average 'Joe' ranting about differences between American and Canadian culture—went on to become one of the most popular commercials in the annals of Canadian television. By the end of the season there were groups of fans in living rooms and bars around the country reciting "the rant" along with the ad's star, an unknown actor whose career took flight when he was asked to perform the monologue at non-sports events across Canada long after the season ended.

The ad was not popular with everyone, however. Many political observers viewed it with dismay, arguing it was filling a void in public consciousness caused by an absence of political leadership. Canadians would not be clinging so desperately to a beer commercial to define their identity, they argued, if a meaningful new political vision had been presented. Others maintained the ad was merely a harmless outlet for the expression of Canadian patriotism, into which little else should be read.

Both sides in the debate appeared to ignore the fact that the monologue contained not only distinctions based on popular culture, but references to important differences in political *values*. True, Joe's rant included such trivial matters as the correct pronunciation of letters of the alphabet and the proper term for a sofa. But it also highlighted Canadians' support for peace-keeping, multiculturalism and an activist role for government, and their rejection of American-style law-and-order and cultural assimilation.

There is an important message in this subtext. In his seminal work, *Continental Divide*, political scientist Seymour Martin Lipset has demonstrated how Canadians have long defined their national identity in contradistinction with their American neighbours, primarily on the basis of differing values.[1] Countless polls have reaffirmed Lipset's conclusions. As Gregg and Posner put it, "What made us distinct was that we weren't Americans, and we were proud of it."[2] It should come as no surprise, then, to learn that the values identified by Lipset which allow Canadians to distinguish themselves from Americans are precisely the type of liberal values referred to in the Molson ad. Intentionally or not, the *"I Am Canadian"* ad confirmed the deep-rooted commitment of most Canadians to the underlying values of modern liberalism.

Liberal Values and the Welfare State

Historically the most important of liberal values has been the supremacy of the individual. This concept underpins other well-known liberal values such as tolerance of diversity, equality of opportunity, fairness and equitable treatment. However in many modern liberal democracies, and particularly in Canada, these traditional liberal values have been accompanied by an ingrained appreciation for the collective good. This modern strand of liberalism resulted in the politics of inclusion and a sort of "social solidarity" in which citizens were persuaded that the interests of the individual would be best served by collective action and/or government assistance for the less fortunate or disadvantaged. [3]

Of course this modern liberal vision of an activist role for government was epitomized following the Depression and the Second World War by the emergence of the welfare state. Virtually all of the western liberal democracies created programs to achieve this objective, but there were variations in approach as each government responded to particular circumstances. In the United States, for example, President Roosevelt introduced the New Deal. But, as Lipset and many others have noted, despite this initiative most Americans also continued to cling to the more traditional liberal emphasis on the individual. As a result they had the least attachment to the concept of the collective good, while Europeans embraced this modern liberalism most enthusiastically.

Canadians also embraced the welfare state. Moreover the standard social programs—such as health care and unemployment insurance—were accompanied by policies of equalization and regional development, two important and distinctive aspects of the modern liberal vision in this country. (Indeed, the concept of equalization was considered so integral an element of our political culture that it was entrenched in the constitution amendment package of 1982.)

This difference in approach explains much of Canadians' tendency to distinguish themselves from Americans. Not only did Canadians embrace the welfare state, but they accepted the idea that the state could play a positive role in society and act in the public good, while Americans continued to view the state as a potential threat to individual liberty.

Regardless of the nature of the programs established, however, it is important to note that modern liberalism justified the various initiatives of the welfare state not simply on the basis of altruism but, as American economist and former Secretary of Labour Robert Reich has stressed, by demonstrating that they were in *everyone's* long-term self-interest. Many programs contained provisions to highlight this sense of collective benefit. The concept of universality, for example, reinforced the vested self-interest of the middle class in maintaining these programs, which were largely financed by them. For Canadians, the idea that "we are all in this together" was applied not only to individuals but to regions, strengthening the attachment to the federation. What Reich terms the "liberal idea of common dependence" was even extended to international affairs in the early years of the post war era, with liberals in all western democracies coming together to forge "common security" policies such as the creation of the United Nations and the Bretton Woods agreement on international trade.[4]

Reich's point, of course, is that the emphasis on an individual's long-term self-interest has been increasingly downplayed or even ignored by many liberal politicians in recent years, at the expense of public support for some of their initiatives. The persuasive argument that "we are all in this together" has been lost. A corollary to this observation is that the discourse of modern liberalism is in danger of losing its ability to connect citizens.

Since this presentation is part of a panel on "Culture, Cohesion and Connecting Canadians," where others will be speaking about the role of cultural institutions and technology in achieving this objective, I want to emphasize the continuing importance of liberal *values and ideas* as a means of connecting Canadians. This point can hardly be overstated in a country where political integration is still a work in progress.

Political Integration and Liberal Values

All states need to achieve and maintain a healthy level of political integration. For many of the countries of western Europe the existence of a well-established national identity was taken for granted. This natural cohesion provided a base on which liberal-minded governments could easily build democratic institutions and programs. But new states, and especially ones like Canada—a country which Prime Minister Mackenzie King famously declared had too much geography and too little history—first need to *create* an overarching national identity with which citizens can identify.

Naturally the symbolic trappings of the state—anthems, flags, or legislative buildings, for example—have a role to play in achieving national identity, and one might assume they would be the first order of business for a new state. Certainly they should not be dismissed lightly in terms of their potential role in uniting citizens. However, meaningful integration requires considerably more substance in order to achieve lasting citizen loyalty. In Canada, where many of these symbols took nearly one hundred years to create, their role was even less significant. Nation-building was left almost entirely to substantive state initiatives, from railways to the CBC, and notably to national projects resulting from liberal values.

As public opinion polls have repeatedly demonstrated, the various elements of the welfare state, and particularly the national health care plan, consistently rank among the most important aspects of national identity for Canadians. That this is true across regions is even more striking. A recent Canada West poll, for example, found that the political values of Albertans differ very little from those of other Canadians, especially on social issues. In fact, Albertans' support for a publicly funded medicare system is among the highest in the country.

Of course integration is particularly important in countries with plural societies (like Canada) where minority groups—religious, ethnic or linguistic—need to feel not only protected but positively engaged in the national project. As Michael Ignatieff has argued, the success of many states with plural societies depends on their ability to create a national identity based first and foremost on the concept of "civic nationalism." [5] For these states, the political values expressed through the constitution, political institutions and government policies are the glue that unites all citizens, regardless of their ethnic or linguistic diversity.

Ignatieff's notion of civic nationalism is especially important for Canada. The *Constitution Act, 1867* contained several important measures to achieve this. The rule of law, the protection of civil liberties and the choice of a federal system of government—as well as the numerous guarantees of linguistic and religious freedom—revealed an overarching set of common values with which all Canadians could identify from the beginning, a point made forcefully by Quebec Liberal Leader Jean Charest in his address to the November 1999 Forum of Federations Conference at Mont Tremblant.

Over time additional government initiatives reflecting these liberal values, such as the *Official Languages Act*, multiculturalism policy and, most recently, the *Charter of Rights and Freedoms,* have built on the original constitutional measures to strengthen civic nationalism and, by extension, national identity. Like the welfare state, these liberal initiatives have served to connect Canadians across regions and mainstream political parties to an extent that sometimes is underappreciated by Liberal politicians. Despite the best efforts of the neoconservatives, for example, polls consistently show very high levels of public support for the Charter in all parts of Canada, including Quebec. Perhaps equally surprising is the Ipsos-Reid poll of April 2002 which found support for the Charter stood at nearly 70% in Alberta.

While this may seem reassuring, it is hardly a license for liberals to become complacent. More than a decade of neoconservative discourse may not have affected Canadians' underlying liberal values to a great extent, but it has certainly sown the seeds of concern and confusion about the programs designed to implement those values. Take two of the issues that will be discussed later in this conference. Despite considerable evidence to the contrary, many Canadians now believe the health care system is in crisis. More importantly, they increasingly believe it is unaffordable. The consequences of these misconceptions can be found in other polling data which reveal growing numbers of Canadians are prepared to consider heretofore unacceptable options such as private sector delivery of some medical services or even user fees, apparently believing they have little choice.

Attacks by neoconservatives on the Charter, multiculturalism, bilingualism and aboriginal self-government have all been based on the premise that the state has no role to play in assuring equality of opportunity, but rather must treat all citizens "equally." Likewise government initiatives to promote equality of opportunity or access—such as affirmative action plans or grants for groups representing the disadvantaged—have been routinely described as "unfair" by the New Right. Many Canadians, committed to values of equality and fairness, now increasingly find themselves confused as to the real impact of such programs.

A similar situation exists with respect to the activist role of the state generally. Many Canadians now seem to believe it is inappropriate if not actually undemocratic for the federal government to implement any new programs if doing so might result in a deficit, however temporary. And, while many of these same respondents repeatedly indicate they favour increased spending on health care, postsecondary education and training programs and national home care or drug plans, they also reject any increase in taxation, instead supporting further reductions in personal taxation levels. Clearly the liberal concept of government spending as an investment, to improve the quality of life of citizens, has been lost, as has the link between taxation and the provision of programs and services for citizens. These linkages have been severed by neoconservative rhetoric that remains largely unchallenged, rhetoric such as Alberta Premier Ralph Klein's outrageous but widely-publicized remark at the founding meeting of the United Alternative in February 1999 that Alberta's tax dollars go east and disappear into the "black hole" of the federal government. Perhaps even more significant has been the increasing prevalence of neoconservative discourse in national debate. With Canadians now accustomed to being referred to as "taxpayers" and "consumers," but rarely as "citizens," the notion that "we are all in this together" is fading rapidly.

In light of such claims it is not surprising that the degree of regional alienation, particularly in western Canada, also appears to be on the increase. Despite decades of being on the receiving end of equalization payments, and despite the irrefutable "per capita" fairness of funding formulae for national social programs, many Canadians in the west believe their region is not treated fairly by the national government. One of the major reasons for this perception, of course, has been the inflammatory discourse of the Reform/Alliance leadership. But it has also been exacerbated by the neoconservative discourse of Premiers such as Ralph Klein and Mike Harris, both of whom have utilized a "we versus they" framework to challenge basic liberal tenets such as equalization.

As a result I would argue the two major challenges faced by liberalism over the past twenty years have been the emergence of a neoconservative public discourse and the phenomenon of globalization, which provided the opportunity for this discourse to emerge. In my view liberals have not yet responded appropriately to these challenges, although progress has certainly been made since 1993. After briefly reviewing some of the consequences of the lack of comprehensive liberal response to this neoconservative attack, I would like to propose a course of action which should help to repair the psychological damage and restore public confidence in liberalism.

The Challenges of Neoconservatism and Globalization

Few would disagree that the phenomenon of globalization, and the technological revolution on which it was founded, have produced a major societal upheaval. Many would argue the disruption to institutions and individuals has been equivalent to that caused by the industrial revolution. Certainly it has led to widespread questioning of some of the basic premises of both modern capitalism and liberalism. Just as Keynesian economics has been challenged by Milton Friedman and his disciples, so liberal concepts of the role of the welfare state have been challenged by the public choice theories and social Darwinism of so-called neoconservatives.

One of the most insidious effects of globalization has been to foster what Linda Weiss refers to as "the myth of the powerless state."[6] With international corporations acquiring more wealth than many states, and new technologies that make it increasingly difficult if not impossible for national governments to legislate or regulate the activities of these corporations, two important political changes have taken place. First, public attention has shifted from national governments to international organizations, where it is believed the real power now lies. Many of these organizations are perceived—rightly or not—as undemocratic and unaccountable. A corollary to this development is that citizen participation in domestic politics, and especially in political parties, has declined significantly, an issue addressed in detail by another panel later in this conference.

The second important change flows directly from the first. As citizens in most western liberal democracies increasingly began to question the ability of national governments to protect them from the worst consequences of globalization, they also questioned the role of the state generally. Many began to return to the older liberal view of the supremacy of the individual, believing they needed to take their own measures to protect themselves and their families, and accepting the neoconservative argument that the less the state intervened the better.

As I have argued elsewhere, this change occurred in large measure because of the non-response of liberals to these developments.[7] Or, as Robert Reich has put it, the neoconservative "parable" to explain these developments was persuasive largely because liberals failed to construct an acceptable alternative parable. In Canada as elsewhere this appears to have been partly the result of an unwillingness on the part of political elites to recognize that there was a problem or that each generation must be reintroduced to the underlying concepts of liberalism. John Kenneth Galbraith makes this point in painful detail in his scathing analysis of the Reagan years, demonstrating how successive generations of middle-class Americans came to believe they were responsible for their own success and failed to recognize the many benefits they received from the state to help them achieve this success.[8] In a speech delivered at the University of Toronto in early 1998, Michael Ignatieff decried the neoconservative attack on liberal values and the failure of liberals to respond, stating that "nothing has done the electoral and moral credibility of liberalism more harm than the failure to take this attack seriously."

One of the most serious consequences of this development has been what Christopher Lasch called the "revolt of the elites."[9] For those of the middle class who were losers in the globalization sweepstakes, the state not surprisingly became less meaningful because of the cutbacks introduced to the social safety net imposed by a neoconservative agenda. But Lasch points out the state also became less relevant for those winners in the middle class, who succeeded despite the turbulent economic times. Many now believe they can continue to survive without the benefits of the welfare state, which in any event have been severely diminished. At the same time, as Reich has argued, the techno-elites produced by globalization have in many cases not only ceased to identify with the values of the welfare state but also with the idea of the nation state itself. Until very recently these upper middle-class professionals have been able to cross borders at will and sell their technical services to the highest bidder. The "secession" of these elites from national politics has created a global class of political dropouts whose only allegiance is to capitalism.[10]

In the United States the term "liberal" itself was almost totally marginalized during the Reagan/Bush years. Robert Reich's humiliating account of the Dukakis campaign is highly instructive. He recalls how the Democratic presidential candidate aggressively denied he was a liberal until the last days of the campaign, when he was trailing his Republican opponent so badly that an admission of liberal tendencies no longer mattered.[11] Similarly Kevin Phillips, a former respected Republican adviser who became a fierce critic, nevertheless argued the only way to defeat the GOP was to avoid the "l" word and resort to an earlier Democratic tactic of proposing a new "economic nationalism."[12] As Michael Marzolini's paper shows the liberal stigma lingers on. Recent polling reveals that barely 8% of American respondents identify themselves as liberals.

Marzolini's figure for the United States compares with the nearly 50% of Canadians who indicated in his poll that they would actively describe themselves as liberals. Other polls by Compass, Gallup and Ekos have found similar or even higher levels of support. Moreover, when Canadian respondents are asked to indicate their views of various liberal programs, rather than liberalism itself, this support increases. Proof that the majority of Canadians remain overwhelmingly liberal in their outlook can also be found in the analysis of the 2000 election campaign carried out by Blais, Gidengil and Nadeau. They found among other things that this was unquestionably a "values" election in which the campaigns of the major opponents—the Liberals and the Alliance—were focussed on defining quite different visions for the country, notably through the famous debate on health care.[13]

Yet since then Alliance Opposition and premiers Klein and Harris have managed to raise significant public doubts about the affordability of the health care plan as we now know it. These attacks have led increasing numbers of Canadians to consider dismantling the state program and/or to assume they cannot "afford" to invest in pharmacare or home care programs, environmental protection or infrastructure repair.

In my view this cause-and-effect relationship has been ignored by liberals for far too long. The result is a schizophrenic situation in which Canadians overwhelmingly support liberal values but believe they are not entitled to liberal programs reflecting these values to enhance their quality of life. Left unchallenged, neoconservative discourse will continue to eat away at the base of support for any future liberal programs and initiatives. Yet Canadians will respond positively if these programs are correctly framed. This means, first and foremost, that liberal *values* need to be defended, not altered. At the same time, and keeping in mind Reich's argument about the seemingly outdated nature of the traditional liberal "parable," these values must be presented within the context of a coherent overarching framework, one that responds directly to the new realities of the postindustrial era and the arguments of the neoconservatives. Only by meeting these objectives will a liberal parable succeed in recapturing public imagination. One possible source of inspiration for this framework may be found in Europe, home of both liberalism and the welfare state.

Liberalism and Social Cohesion

Faced with many of the same economic and social problems as Canada, and deeply engaged in constructing a European identity for their own political integration project, Europe's leaders have adopted the discourse of "social cohesion" to heighten the legitimacy of their liberal initiatives. The specific impetus for this new approach was the growing social inequality apparent even as the economic integration of the Union was meeting with considerable success. In announcing the various provisions of the Treaty of Amsterdam and the Stability and Growth Pact, many of which were designed to combat this inequality, French President François Mitterand famously declared at the closing meeting of Heads of State that "Europe will have failed if the benefits of economic integration are not shared by all."

The disconnect between the European Union's economic and *political* integration projects also increased exponentially during the 1990's, leading to the calls for a European constitution and Charter of Rights and eventually to the decision to establish a Convention on the Future of Europe. In this context, another proposal being seriously examined by the Convention is the entrenchment of a Social Charter. This proposal clearly recognizes that the promotion of social cohesion can also produce beneficial results for political integration.

Not only the European Union but also the OECD and the Council of Europe have adopted the discourse of social cohesion. At the Council of Europe's Summit in October 1997 an intergovernmental body called the European Committee for Social Cohesion was created to develop and implement a Council-wide strategy for social cohesion. The press release announcing the Committee's creation was particularly blunt in making the linkages between economic and political integration. It stated that "social cohesion is an essential element for democratic security" and "divided societies are not only unjust but cannot guarantee stability in the long term." The Final Declaration of the Heads of State made the same point. It identified social cohesion as "one of the foremost needs of the wider Europe and an essential component to the promotion of human rights and dignity."

The emphasis which European politicians have placed on social cohesion as a *public good* is also noteworthy. Indeed, the use of the term "public interest" is an important element of the social cohesion discourse. Liberal programs are explained and/or justified in terms of their ability to promote social cohesion, which in turn is seen as providing long-term benefits to all citizens. Perhaps most important, social programs are not justified simply as being cost-effective or good for economic growth. Actually the reverse is true. In Europe, economic growth is promoted as a means of achieving an improved quality of life, which is considered the ultimate objective of the state. This is clearly an approach which would resonate with Canadians.

New Approaches to Liberal Discourse

What conclusions can we draw from the preceding analysis? First, there is no need to throw the baby out with the bathwater. The "new" liberalism does not need to reinvent liberal values, but it *does* need to construct a new discourse. Presenting a mix of programs without an overarching rationale or national purpose with which citizens can identify has not proven sufficient to counter neo conservative rhetoric, despite the excellent start made on the next "round" of liberal initiatives by the Chrétien government through such measures as the National Child Benefit, the Millennium scholarships and the Canada Infrastructure Program. Similarly, whatever proposals come out of this conference concerning new social programs or a plan to ensure sustainable development and meet our Kyoto commitments will not receive widespread public support if they are not presented within the context of a liberal vision.

Second, I would argue that now is the ideal time to tackle this challenge. While the Chrétien government was obliged to spend much of its mandate eliminating the deficit, the past few years of surplus have led Canadians to think once again of the possibilities of government. Moreover the shock of September 11 has forced many of Reich's techno-elites to reconsider their allegiance to capitalism and the borderless society. This return to legitimacy for the state has been further heightened, of course, by the dot-com meltdown and the crisis of corporate governance. Not for more than a decade has the possibility of linking taxation positively to government programs been so obvious.

Tom Axworthy's paper calls for major increases in government spending on existing and new programs over the next decade in order to bring Canadians into the 21st century. This spending would need to be financed in part by ensuring that there are no further reductions in taxation. While there may be differences of opinion among liberals on the relative merits of his specific proposals, few would disagree with his conclusion that there are many urgent areas requiring government investment to enhance our quality of life or even to prevent a deterioration in current standards. The question, as he later posed himself, is how to convince Canadians that this "decade of investment" is necessary?

Prime Minister Chétien has demonstrated that part of the answer lies in convincing Canadians we are taking a "balanced" approach. Michael Marzolini's polling data bear this out. Liberals must find a way to counter the neoconservative critique that we "tax and spend," the clear implication of which is that there is no underlying purpose. Contrary to neoconservative critiques, Liberals are also prepared to encourage economic growth. Their underlying purpose, however, is not growth for growth's sake, but to enhance citizens' quality of life—in part by reducing disparities and promoting social cohesion.

In my view the concept of "investment for the future" is key to this turnaround in the liberal image, as are the concepts of collective or public good and what Galbraith has termed the "humane agenda." Perhaps the best current example of this balanced approach—which has been the hallmark of Canadian liberalism—can be found in the proposed broadband initiative, a project which has the potential not only to encourage economic competitiveness but also to ensure equality of opportunity and access for rural, northern and disadvantaged Canadians across the country. With apologies to Marshall McLuhan, I am essentially arguing that it is the message and not the medium that is important.

Michael Marzolini's paper notes that former prime minister Pierre Trudeau achieved the highest level of public support for liberal values, or liberal "branding," because of his ability to articulate these values in ways which resonated with Can-adians, whether through initiatives such as the Charter or through concepts such as the "Just Society." I would add that it was also Trudeau, in his critical response to the "distinct society" provision of the Meech Lake Accord, who remarked that "*Canada* is the distinct society." For many Canadians this statement was self-evident It is up to new liberal politicians to provide the leadership that will ensure Canadians continue to believe this is true.

Notes:

[1]   S.M. Lipset. *Continental Divide: The Values and Institutions of Canada and the United States*. (New York: Routledge, 1990)

[2]   A. Gregg and M. Posner. *The Big Picture*. (Toronto: McFarlane, Walter and Ross, 1990).

[3]   See for example Louis Hartz.(ed.) *The Liberal Tradition in America*. (New York: Harcourt Brace, 1953) and Ken McRae,"Louis Hartz's Concept of the Fragment Society and its Application to Canada", *Etudes Canadiennes*, vol.5, 1978. pp.17-30.

[4]   Robert Reich. *The Resurgent Liberal*. (New York: Random House, 1989) pp. 279-80.

[5]   Michael Ignatieff. *Blood and Belonging*. (Toronto: Penguin Books, 1993) pp. 6-7

[6]   L. Weiss. *The Myth of the Powerless State*. (New York: Cornell University Press, 1998)

[7]   B. Jeffrey. *Hard Right Turn: The Rise of Neoconservatism in Canada*. (Toronto: Harper Collins, 2000) pp. 442-9.

[8]   J.K. Galbraith. *The Culture of Contentment*. (Boston: Houghton- Mifflin, 1992)

[9]   C. Lasch. *The Revolt of the Elites and The Betrayal of Democracy*. (New York: W.W. Norton and Co. 1995)

[10]   Robert Reich. *op. cit.* pp. 274-5

[11]   Robert Reich. loc. cit.

[12]   K. Phillips. *The Politics of Rich and Poor: Wealth and the American Electorate in the Reagan Aftermath*. (New York: Harper Collins. 1991)

[13]   A. Blais, E. Gidengil and R. Nadeau. *Making Sense of the Vote: The 2000 Canadian Election*. (Toronto: Broadview Press, 2002)

Choices and Consequences
in a Liberal Foreign Policy

Lloyd Axworthy

IT'S A TIME FOR Canadian liberals to make choices and consider consequences on how to conduct our foreign policy in the post-September environment.

Let's begin by looking at two statements:

On September 20th, 2002, in a report to Congress, President Bush said the following:

> Our forces will be strong enough to dissuade potential adversaries from pursuing a military buildup in hopes of surpassing or equaling the power of the United States. To forestall or prevent such hostile acts by our adversaries, the United States will, if necessary act pre-emptively.

This pretty much sums up the new prescription for a global Pax Americana solely determined by the military might of our superpower neighbour. We are told by many in this country that we have no choice but to join the parade.

Consider the alternative:

> These terrorist attacks are a further, horrifying indication of the pervasiveness of threats to

people's safety, rights and lives. As the international community faces the implications of these
tragic events, we must recognize that innovative
international approaches are needed to address
growing sources of global insecurity, remedy it's
symptoms and prevent the recurrence of threats
that affect the daily lives of millions of people.

This, unlike many of the outpourings of feelings and official
statements in the dark days that followed September 11, was not a
rousing call to arms seeking retaliation or revenge. It did not up-
hold the right of an aggrieved country to protect its sovereign national interest. It did not assert the need to strengthen borders or
amass overwhelming military power.

Instead, it recognized the widespread nature of the problem and
called for innovative, international answers. Most important, it put
the threat to people—the risk to individuals—as the central issue.

This was the statement of the Human-Security Network, an association of 13 countries founded in 1999 out of an initiative by Norway and Canada. Its purpose was to collaborate and cooperate on
concrete human-security matters on the international agenda at
the time, such as a small-arms treaty, the international criminal court
and the protection of children.

This group of like-minded nations worked from the premise that
the basic right of people to live in freedom from fear was challenged
equally by two overwhelming threats—the uncontrolled forces of
state-inspired violence, and the newer, murkier dangers arising from
a global underworld of human traffickers, arms traders, criminals
and terrorists. As we all know, such advice was not heeded. The
war on terrorism has become the dominant and over-arching
objective of the United States and its allies. It has given license to a
variety of interventions, a massive increase of expenditure on arms,
a justification for severe limits on human rights and a cover for all
kind of nasty suppressions of various groups and interests around
the world.

As practised by its chief proponent, counter-terrorism is the new
crusade. It is the litmus test of loyalty to the faith: you're either for
us or against us. Its primarily a military response, noncollaborative
in approach and defiantly opposed to most forms of international

efforts at alternative solutions, as witness the recent attempt to undermine the International Criminal Court.

Giving renewed vigour to the apostles of *realpolitik*—bringing out of the shadows all those who find notions of humanitarian co-operation, international justice and the rule of law to be anathema— it has given birth to a doctrine of pre-emption, which arrogates to the United States the right to be judge, jury and prosecutor against any country, or anyone it considers a threat. Of course, this runs contrary to half a century of international law and the Charter of the United Nations.

This assertion of pre-emption sets in precedent the right of any strong state to move against a weaker neighbour solely on the basis of its own calculation otherwise known as the law of the jungle. As such it is leading inexorably into further crisis and will continue to expand the orbit of danger and accelerate the cycles of violence, such as the impending attack on Iraq.

I want to make the case that this approach is a mistake. If we want to successfully combat the terrorists—and all others who threaten the security of innocent people, whether they be commuters on a plane to Los Angeles, children in Northern Uganda, bomb victims in the Middle East or kidnapped civilians in Columbia—then we need to apply the common sense and pragmatism of a human-security approach.

If we don't, any attempt to deter global criminal activity is doomed to failure. And unless and until we can strike a better balance and forge a different pathway based on human-security principles, we also face a serious regression in the level of international co-operation on a myriad of crucial global issues and the receding of hope of a more peaceable, secure world.

Attempting to beat terrorists into submission through military action cannot be effective. There may be a momentary restriction on the activities of terrorist organizations—it may send them further underground and may eliminate some of their human resources. But the global reach and religious fanaticism that defines terrorist organizations such as al-Qaeda make a successful, persistent military deterrent unlikely. More importantly, there are too many pre-existing tensions which military attacks exacerbate rather than quell. Military responses feed the anger, poverty, rhetoric—the climate of grievance—which create and sustain terrorist intentions.

Terrorism will never be eliminated, but its attraction can be significantly diminished by addressing causes: poverty, despair, disenfranchisement, religious fanaticism, absence of effective and meaningful democracy, etc. Some of these efforts have already been undertaken. They are complex, resource-intensive and require innovative international co-operation.

Furthermore, building an effective global network of law enforcement and justice that applies the same capacity for collaborative action that terrorists themselves often employ can substantially deter terrorism. Efforts to dismantle or ignore collaborative action only strengthen the terrorist ability to undermine an effective international response.

I don't come to these conclusions from any lofty philosophical heights. I write as a former practitioner, a survivor of twenty-seven years in elected politics and twelve years as a minister of the Crown— not occupations that usually lead to the kindly contemplation of the incongruities of life. As Canada's Foreign Minister for close to five years, I had to deal with the hard realities of living in a world of war, genocide, ethnic cleansing and premeditated violence. I was party to decisions on whether to engage in enforcement actions—I am no stranger to that dilemma.

As a neighbour and appreciative ally to the biggest kid on the block, I've also worked on numerous ways to co-exist and co-operate with the United States. I'm fully aware of the power of our partner on the North American continent to be a force for good. But I also come with a sense of apprehension about the present mood and dominant politics of that country.

It is because of that experience that I see the need to depart from conventional wisdoms and seek out new navigational guides to aid in the search for security. Not to replace the template of basic protection of national security, but to layer onto it new responses to global threats and risks which don't lend themselves to flexing biceps and going it alone.

This is especially critical in scoping out answers to the dark side of globalization. The same information networks that allow capital to move around the world in seconds or bring scenes of suffering into global living-rooms give international predators the capacity to establish integrated, world-wide connections that overwhelm the resources and capability of individual nation-states to protect their citizens. To give one example, drug-trafficking is a multibillion-dollar business that confronts police forces around the world with the most sophisticated tools of communication, transportation and organization.

Halting steps are being made at the UN, the G-8, OECD and other international forums to build a sense of teamwork to tackle such threats. But there is an opposite pull. The strong hold of beliefs in national sovereignty and the increasing pressure of localism generate substantial resistance from many governments to participate in multilateral co-operative ventures. The philosophy of "go it alone" is alive and well in the world, even in the face of a shared reality of common risk. Human-security is the lens through which this changing international scene should be viewed. The security risk to individuals must be the focal-point of a strategy that sees like-minded countries, partnering with non-governmental organizations, working towards new standards of international behaviour based on protection of civilians.

What makes this idea of human-security work is that it fits well with where we are as Canadians at the turnover from the 20th to the 21st centuries. Canadian efforts to forge a new diplomacy inclusive of civil groups point the way to a new era of democratic decision-making at the international level. Our push for treaties and institutions based on humanitarian values could be the foundation of an international rule of law that respects and protects the rights of the individual. Our experiments with the use of "soft power techniques," such as the Internet, open up ways of enhancing the delivery of public goods and public policy. Our effort to mobilize a coalition of states dedicated to co-operative international efforts creates a force for reform in the global system.

One such effort is the International Criminal Court—the cornerstone of a global judicial system incorporating co-operation on investigation, forensic evidence-gathering, police and enforcement action, and prosecution, and all done according to the precepts of respect for rights acting as a balance against the capricious use of force in the hands of leaders.

But the ICC is not a stand-alone example—there are other initiatives under way. One of the most important is the report of the Canadian-inspired, global Commission on Intervention and Sovereignty, an attempt to rethink and redefine the meaning of sover-

eignty in light of the experiences of the last decade with acts of genocide and ethnic cleansing around the world.

Last December, the Commission proposed that sovereignty be
redefined as the responsibility to protect, thus shifting the perspective from what it endows to the state to what it obliges the state to
do. To quote from the report: "Such a responsibility implies an evaluation of the issue from the perspective of the victim, not the
intervener; if a state cannot provide the protection or is the author
of the crime, then it forfeits its sovereign right and the international
community steps in, not just to protect, but to prevent and rebuild."

This fundamental shift of perspective to the view of the victim,
not the intervener—from the right of sovereign interest to the responsibility to protect—has particular relevance as we contemplate
the preparations for an attack on Iraq. This adventure is part of the
emerging U.S. anti-terrorist policy which asserts the right of
pre-emptive intervention at a time, place and target of its own choosing. It is not enough simply to oppose, wring hands and wail. There
must be an alternative, based on the perspective of the victim—in
this case, the Iraqi people, who face double-jeopardy from their own
government and now from the United States.

It's time to start fresh by asserting a strong interest by the
international community in human protection. That can be done
by requiring Iraqi compliance and disarmament based on resolution 1284 weapon inspections, backed up by robust enforcement,
detailed intelligence gathering and severe limitations on procure-
ment from other countries, along with a lifting of sanctions, once
full disclosure and disarmament are properly certified, by respect-
able international observation and evaluation. These are a series of
tasks to which Canada could well make an effective contribution.

This is a human-security approach, not the scorched-earth strategy proposed by the U.S. administration. And it must be clearly
stated soon, in the councils of government and the UN. It is a real
chance to present an alternative, rather than exacerbating the cause
of terrorism and creating further resentments in the Islamic world.

One year after the tragic events of September 11, there is an opportunity to go the human-security route and find solutions based
on the rule of law and the practice of justice. We must think about
these issues one year after the sad anniversary of a terrible atrocity
against the rights of innocent people.

The Commission leads to a much broader strategy on how to insure the prevention and protection of the rights of individuals. Canada, supported by a coalition of NGO's and other like minded governments is working towards having it appear as a General Assembly resolution in the next year—giving the Assembly the power to exercise a mandate of directing the Security Council, similar to what it did in defining he rules governing self-determination and colonial trusteeship. To have such a strategy succeed there will have to be the release of creative energy, in the civil gatherings, the chancelleries and the academies and the 52nd floor. It does offer an opening for a new process of renewal, giving needed energy and credibility to the UN for efforts at renewal and reform. It is not just an idea, but a catalyst for real action.

What's more it takes the concept of responsibility to protect beyond the realm of war and conflict, and into a basic re-thinking of the ways in which responsibility must be applied in the risks to economic and environmental security, which are those root causes of inequity and humiliation that are part of the terrorist breeding ground.

In both cases the global architecture is non-existent, archaic or discriminatory. Let me draw your attention to my recent trip to Mongolia where I learned that the IMF was demanding a rescinding of wage increases for civil servants, and a reduction in care for children. The IMF was citing the mantra of today's new economic priesthood of macro stability!

The Gobi dessert, which is a product of both economic imperative and climate change, eats away the pasture land which in turn causes dust storms that sweeps across East Asia and reaches the shores of North America. Who is responsible, who has the right to impose sanctions, exercise protection?

Other examples abound—the hollowing out of Argentina, the smoke from Indonesia, the trade discrimination, the spread of AIDS, all are now managed in an ineffectual and desultory way.

There is a recognition that the present system of economic and environmental governance isn't working. There are attempts to reform and change—Doha, Monterey, G-8 and Africa, Johannesburg. The problem is that there are the advocates of old fashioned power politics who want to enhance and keep their dominance and engage in a form of treaty-cide to abort and cleanse the global system of acts and institutions of cooperation. There are the apostles of the multi-lateral status quo, the diplomats and politicians who constantly ask if they dare to eat a peach. Do I dare disturb the universe? And convene meeting after meeting to repeat the same old nostrums with nary a thought to any new thinking. And, the wizards of the IMF's who swoon about in their hermetically sealed cocoons of fiscal orthodoxy.

There is one way to break down this resistance—inertia through the power of the people, the full rein of global democracy and its application to our forms of global governance. There is presently a disconnect between where people are and the decision makers. A poll we conducted in eleven countries found most people concerned with personal safety, the threat of natural disaster and climate change, not Osama bin Laden and his terrorist groups. Yet, in western countries this is the preoccupation. The same disillusionment is setting in with international institutions and their relevance to real problems whose expression we see vividly portrayed in the streets at every international meeting. Unless there is serious reform of our political structures, nationally and internationally, the credibility of our way of taking decisions will begin to crumble and then the terrorists will have really won the day.

It is, I believe, a unique liberal task to help write the primer on global citizenship. The place to start is what we believe about our own social contract and how we approach fundamentals such as cooperation and tolerance in our own society. We must establish a culture of rights, of social commitment, of negotiation and compromise in a domestic political system and translate that into the same values internationally.

We have been leaders in using our federal system and our Charter of Rights to define sovereignty in other than traditional nation-state term. Authority can be shared by different levels of government, loyalties and attachments diffused to different centres of commitment. This in turn has given our citizens a sense of belonging to a broader community. Our civil groups, in particular, see themselves as belonging to a world-wide network of activists and advocates. Now the pressure of changes in our own demographics. Create a situation where our ability to make a living and preserve our well-being will depend increasingly on our participation in global constellations of cities, propelling us into taking that concept of global citizenship onto an ever-widening and inclusive plain.

This plain stretches far beyond the shores of our own territory and continent. If there is one truth that will dominate the lives of the millennium generation it is the way their lives will be affected by people, events and actions from around the globe, bound ever more tightly by links of commerce, information, travel and trade. Wherever one resides, a sense of calamity will prevail unless there is a radical change in the way we do business globally. Just before the opening of the Sustainable Development Summit in Johannesburg, the World Bank released a study which forecast a world twenty years from now of 9 billion people and a global GDP of 140 trillion—staggering numbers, and ones leading to environmental disaster and social breakdown, unless policies are dramatically changed.

It is not a doomsday scenario. It can be fixed by the appropriate levels of international collaboration, sharing of wealth and change in consumption by industry and consumers in the industrial world. That will be the acid test of global citizenship—are we ready to limit or change our present consumerism and levels of economic growth for the sake of cleaner air and water, security against violent climate change and a more equitable distribution of wealth, as prescribed by international agreement and supranational regulation and decision-making? The contrast in positions was seen soon after Prime Minister Chrétien made a commitment to ratify the Kyoto agreement during the Johannesburg meeting, followed by the denunciation by certain provincial premiers and business-based lobby organizations. Exercising global citizenship is not necessarily a universal commitment in Canada, especially with some provincial politicians and industry leaders!

The task we face is not only in changing the nature of citizenship to a multiple set of references and responsibilities, but to insure that as the role of global citizenship grows over the next fifty years it is a democratic one.

For that reason it is a priority that we seriously reform the way decisions are made at the national level in order to get things right in what we can accomplish globally.

First, let's deal with what is now called the democratic deficit, a buzz-word that properly expresses a feeling of frustration that the opportunity for full representation of views and public participation are limited.

One major problem is our electoral system—the first past the post, single constituency arrangement. This type of system can lead to gross representation—a small plurality of votes results in a huge majority of seats. What should be looked at is a hybrid system that combines the constituency-based model with a modified proportional representation that reflects popular vote. That would be one means of further democratizing, thereby energizing, our politics.

It would also be a way of improving the access and opportunity for more women to get elected and exercise their rightful role as full participants in the governing of the country, I believe that this inequity affects what we do or more accurately don't do globally. It has been my experience that women are more supportive of human-security agendas, especially so when it came to issues such as the protection of civilians and promotion of peace-building matters. A revised election system is one place to start in insuring that women will have a greater say in what Canada does in the world.

Another way to improve our democracy in this new century is to reform the Senate. It is anachronistic to have an appointed body making decisions in this day and age. I grant there are a number of highly competent people serving in the Senate, bringing special talents to the job. The same people would have even greater influence if they were elected and accountable.

An elected Senate could come to have a special role and responsibility in the carrying out of debate and overview of Canada's global role. There is a potential in our parliamentary system that has only barely begun to be tapped. One limitation of our present system is the severe restrictions on time, resources and range imposed on individual MPs by dint of their various constituency, caucus, and assembly duties. There needs to be some degree of specialization, where international matters would receive a more than passing glance. If the Senate were elected it could bring real credibility to that task.

One very important set of tasks would be to choose the representatives we send to represent us in global forums. Perhaps we should think of more direct election of key posts—ambassador to the UN, directors on the World Bank and IMF, our Environment ambassador could be designated as part of a slate election to the Senate, allowing each party leader to choose very distinguished Canadians to be their nominees for certain posts, and then have them explain and defend their views and qualifications during the election. Think what it might do in engendering a serious look at international global issues if each party had to nominate specific people with clear views on a global role for Canada and have issues discussed in a fully transparent electoral campaign and have those choices ratified by parliament!

Pending such fundamental changes to the Senate, such as making it an elected body, Parliament, as a whole, should have a much clearer, more direct advice and consent role for approving candidate's international postings, combined with a clear schedule of periodic reports to the appropriate committee. Parliament is a crucial cog in connecting people to the increasingly complex world of decision-making on global matters. It can continue to play an ever more valuable role, but until it is made substantially more democratic by changing the system of election and reforming the Senate, its possibilities will be limited and not sufficient to the task.

A third area of democratic reform is to further restrict the distorting influence of money in our national political system—both in the electoral process and in the party selection of candidates and leaders. Make no mistake, big money resources are used to sway crucial decisions affecting Canada's international role. In the past this power was used with telling effect during the free trade election of 1988. Today, money is being channeled through a number of business-oriented think tanks to promote Canadian support of the right-wing policies of the Bush Administration, and opposition to Kyoto and further military integration.

There is an antidote. The Doer government in Manitoba passed legislation limiting donations to individuals, excluding corporations and unions. Alberta has done he same. Such initiatives are a good beginning in reducing the need for the bagman and limiting the power of organizations with big financial resources. The Manitoba limitations on political funding need to be replicated in other jurisdictions if we are to have a reasonably level policy playing field.

Another sure way to curb the misuse of power and concentrated wealth is by increasing the influence and involvement of the public through a broad sharing of information. The water scandal in Walkerton, the revelations on corporate malfeasance washing over North America, the admission of neglect by intelligence agencies in the wake of September 11th are stark reminders of how disclosure and transparency are powerful and necessary tools in a modern democracy. The advent of the Internet creates a further breakthrough by shattering the control of the expert or the insider. The ability of ordinary people to exert influence on decisions through the glare of information is a substantial, perhaps quantum, change in the nature of democratic practice—what Mary Graham of the Institute of Governance calls techno-populism.

Techno-populism may have its greatest impact in the international arena. This can be affirmed by recent experience in developing a human-security agenda. World wide populist campaigns for the Land Mine Treaty and the International Court were made possible to a significant degree through the power of information technology. The future scope of developing the use of information is limitless and should be one of the most serious undertakings of Canada in the years ahead. Perhaps its most potent use is in the development of a global civic culture that binds people into a global community. But, already we see efforts to curtail its use, limit the flow of information through intellectual property rights and limit access to sources of public private behaviour. The cause of openness internationally is one that Canada should espouse.

Reform of our political institutions is one priority, but without a substantial investment in their global education structural reforms will not produce the level of involvement that is desired and needed. This is especially important for the education of today's young people. For these charter members of the Internet generation the idea of borders and boundaries have little meaning. Their cyber universe encompasses the world, communicating in an instant with counterparts to play games, extract information, chat about music and, alas, peek at pornographic portals.

The Internet generation has access to any number of sophisticated, technically awesome means of entertainment—games, costing hundreds of millions for development and promotion, available from Mongolia to Sweden to Vancouver Island, Hollywood films extolling action, adventure, war and violence, a mass media controlled by gargantuan conglomerates that extol reality television, sports extravaganzas, and talk show diatribes. We should, by comparison, be inventing to develope comparable tools for education using the best graphics and interactive techniques. And, we must be mindful of John Kenneth Galbraith's comment of private affluence and public poverty. In a time when we decry the great divides between cultures of the East and West, hear the plaintive wail of commentators in the United States about why Americans are not liked, watch the propagation of historic grievance, fanaticisms and hatreds, the bypassing of potential tools to engage in an open educational exercise is irresponsible and foolhardy. We need to see a globally based system of educational programs using information technology as a fundamental public good.

This has special meaning when we use the language of the Digital Divide, a gap that separates rich from poor, urban from rural and North from South. Everyone, from the Secretary General of the UN to the communication giants, expresses their concern. Lost among all the talk of e-commerce, and e-government is the possibility of e-community—the potential for web based education for connecting researchers around the world to look at our common problems of disease, literacy, and security, of training and educating in the vital fields of conflict or crisis management or environmental security, forging a global public network of information and interactivity that can spur the advance of democratic development.

Here is an exciting role for Canada to play with our information know-how, the skill of our software companies and the "mentality for seeing a borderless world of our Internet generation." We have a reservoir of good will, good people and good public institutions to span the cyber atmosphere and jump over traditional stages of development, putting a public face on the Internet. We can fulfill the McLuhan prophecy of being the foremost inhabitants of the global village.

Redefining our democratic institutions is crucial to enable Canadians to participate fully in the debates and discussion that shape our international role. Recall the warning by Robert Dahl in his book *Controlling Nuclear Weapons* that we are in danger of forfeiting democracy by not finding ways to insure that there is a competence by citizens to be involved in making decisions on complicated contemporary matters affecting humankind, such as the use of nuclear weapons. He still believes, however, "that the ancient vision, now twenty-five centuries old, of a people governing itself through the democratic process, and possessing all the resources and institutions necessary in order to govern itself wisely can be adapted yet once again, as it has been in the past, to a world drastically different from the world in which that vision was first put into practice."

Democratic governance also must be effective governance. It has to be smart, efficient, coherent and adaptable. It needs to provide the openness and participation of citizens in decisions and implementation. It needs to set the proper funding to achieve its public goals. One of the recognized accomplishments of the Chrétien government was to get the fiscal situation of the federal government in order and seek an incremental reform of the federal system.

Now the federal government needs to reorganize around a team concept for managing its global policies and activities. The purpose would be to insure compatibility of policies and avoid duplication and inter-departmental rivalry—in other words to see Canada's global obligations and opportunities in all its dimensions, not in singular and uni-departmental terms. The strategy group should be assigned a global budget envelope that is worked out between respective departments to reflect agreement on overall priorities, insuring against uneven and uncoordinated expenditures.

It is not, however, only a matter of reorganization or strategy. The federal government has to spend more money on the tools it needs to play an effective global role. One place to start is the refurbishing of our diplomatic and trade services. There should be an expansion of the Canadian infrastructure into areas that are vital to us, such as the United States and other posts in the western hemisphere. To maintain a global presence we have to open posts in areas where our representation is virtually non-existent, such as Central Asia, and strengthen our represenation in Central Asia. This needn't be expensive. The advent of sophisticated information systems opens all kinds of opportunities to extend the Canadian presence.

Development assistance is another funding priority. Our contributions presently hover around 0.4% of GNP, a far cry from the 0.7% promised by Lester Pearson. Prime Minister Chrétien is taking steps to increase foreign aid—committing to a doubling of funding by 2010. The recent focus on Africa and his support for the NEPAD exercise is a good demonstration of targeting resources and encouraging regional responsibility. The reduction of trade barriers adds further value. What's missing from this Africa initiative is a complimentary effort to increase our diplomatic presence, a plan to provide military assistance to deal with breakdowns in security, help in policing the rules against small arm trading, provision of skilled people in administration, and a major effort to work with the African states to overcome AIDS. There must be a much more comprehensive, integrated approach to development than simply handing out dollars to fund a series of discrete projects.

Then there is defence. Since September 11th the clamour of the pressure groups, the arms industry, certain editorialists, the senior military brass and the US ambassador have been in full throat, demanding increases in defence expenditure. And, I agree—it should be a priority, although I daresay for different reasons and for different purposes than the defence lobby would wish.

In my time in government I always supported adding to the defence budget when it was designed to improve our capacity for peace-making, coastal surveillance, disaster missions, improved living standards for personnel and special roles such as de-mining, military training for emerging democracies and service in international missions. What I objected to was the way in which hundreds of millions were spent in development and research on weapons systems reflecting US determined military objectives, such as space-based technology.

What I strenuously object to now is the slippery slope of integration which we are embarked on, all in the name of battling terrorism, which step by step leads to a loss of choice. The immense amount spent by the US on military matters—thirty times what the next thirty countries expend—naturally leads to a overwhelming predominance of military anchored solutions to global issues, avoiding all the other tools in the kit. It also leads to the US drawing other military forces into their orbit and making them dependent— witness the northern command proposals and the latest move at NATO to set up a US dominated rapid reaction group to go beyond NATO borders to fight terrorists. The implications for Canada are serious and far reaching in terms of severely limiting what we may want to design as an alternative approach to security.

Where I would like to see increased expenditure for our defence forces is in the supply of equipment, personnel and logistics to actively support a human-security policy. In particular, this means transport capable of carrying troops and supplies on rapid reaction missions on behalf of conflict resolution efforts, or in aid of internationally approved humanitarian assignments, modern naval capacity for sea-based peace-keeping and coastal surveillance, especially in arctic regions, enhanced intelligence gathering using Canadian technology of satellite sensoring which we would be prepared to share with UN peacekeeping operations, efficient health and disaster relief units and the building up of a mobile well-trained reserve that can be used as a fully competent supplement to regular forces.

What this would provide is the means to adapt to the changing nature of global conflict and security issues, to make decisions to act in concert with other nations in cooperative missions and untie some of the strings that presently bind us to US military systems and strategy. We should begin discussions with the European Union on how to work out joint plans for a rapid reaction force as part of our trans-Atlantic partnership. This would require more added investment on building such a capacity. In particular we must resist plans being put forward by the Bush administration for a US-controlled rapid reaction force. Talk about becoming even further entwined in the web of military strategies set by an administration that shows no interest in peacekeeping or peace-making.

Another area where we need to substantially upgrade our military capacity is in providing surveillance, monitoring and patrol of our northern regions. Arctic ice is melting. Trade routes are opening. There is increased exploration and resource development. The dangers of pollution and disruption grow. The Arctic Council, a unique Canadian international innovation, sets the stage for a model form of cooperation involving states and people in collaborative decision-making, leading to agreements on how to manage the region for the welfare of its habitants and its habitation. This will be frustrated by unilateral actions and assertions, particularly from the Russians and the Americans, unless we have a capacity to affirm an independent position on behalf of cooperative circumpolar development. We need the appropriate military presence to insure that our preferred policy direction is respected.

Our military can also make a major contribution in the pursuit of new international agreements and collective action in dealing with the growing threats in the arena of biological weapons and cyber warfare. These will become increasing threats, especially in the possession of terrorists or criminals. There needs to be continuing research into methods of detection, verification and control, and removal. All necessary requisites for any future agreements. The same requirements are necessary to pursue international agreement to control the use of weapons in space. In these ways, provided that freedom of action is maintained, our military can make a positive contribution to advancing the human-security agenda in the age of terrorism.

This, then, is the case for a made in Canada approach to security, designed to serve, what I believe to be, the interest of Canadians in seeing a world built on foundations rooted in our own respect for law, rights and the protection of people. It is not an easy road. It will face the hostility of the present US administration and those in this country who want us to be their deputy sheriff. But it is a role that would give support in the United States to those who decry the present war mentality and want to see a restoration of US leadership around principles of international cooperation. It would also find friends and favour in many other parts of the world by many who see the disruption and danger of the Bush doctrine. Most importantly, it would at least set out a direction for future generations to follow as they look to present leadership to strike a proper course.

Ferdinand Armesto, the Oxford historian, has concluded in his massive study of the past millennium "that some small group of people have the ability to decisively influence the rest of mankind through the power of their ideas, to adapt technology and their willingness to explore." This is a role that I passionately believe Canadians can fulfill, even when faced with the implacable opposition of the world's powerful, and the indifference of so many who prefer their comfort to the joy of discovery. That I believe is what must draw people together in the healing circle of discussion and dialogue in this post-September 11th atmosphere, the kind of exercise that we are involved in today where as true liberals our view should be unrestricted, and like the explorers of old we look to see great distances in every direction. And once we set our sights, it is important that we start our voyage. To quote the Spanish poet Antonio Machado:

" Traveler there is no path, paths are made by walking."

A Liberal View of Science

John C. Polanyi

IT IS MY HOPE that The New Liberalism will turn its piercing gaze briefly in the direction of Science Policy as it applies to the universities, where most of the nation's science is done. This is a little-known byway of national policy. Conservatives and Liberals have let it become over-grown with illiberal practice. Not only is this obstructing the traffic in science, it is in danger of invading the wider thoroughfares of policy.

Canadian scientists have too little collective consciousness, and even less of a tradition for political action. Instead the community mutters to itself, in casual two's and three's, rather than constituting a countervailing force to bureaucracy.

What is the problem the science administrator must address? It is to maximize the returns on a considerable investment in university science. The university scientist has the responsibility to deliver on that investment.

He or she must contend with the complexity of nature. It is the highest art to separate the problem one wishes to solve from the hundred other unknowns with which it is entangled. This skill is one which the practitioner cannot sufficiently describe, and the unskilled observer cannot sufficiently conceive. For it is a skill which is learnt not from books but from other practitioners through apprenticeship. Its external attributes can be listed, but they do not provide a basis for judging performance.

The external attributes of scientific discovery include such characteristics as interdisciplinary research, the formation of teams, and the activity of networking. However, it is not helpful, though we do it, to *demand* these attributes. Nor is it sensible to assess the quality of a scientific research proposal according to the extent to which it embodies these attributes.

But why, apart from the desire of governments to govern, should one want to apply these dubious criteria? It is because they are regarded as being objective. They constitute a form of accountability that can be quantified and appreciated by anyone. That is appealing. The drawback is that it is unreliable.

We would do better to explain that to the public. We must trust them to understand that performance in the arts, of which science is one, can only be judged by those skilled in the art. The process is not new; it is called "peer review." Peer review has, in fact, never been used more widely in science than it is today. But what is not acknowledged is that it is being subverted. We will soon be left with the appearance rather than the reality of peer review.

Let me explain with an example. It is an important example. Noting the existence of skill in the performance of science, governments both federally and provincially have set up Centres of Excellence. The title is promising. "Excellence" is needed because insights come mainly to the minds of a small group of visionaries. "Centres," because sharpness comes from steel rubbing against steel.

But the description, "Centres of Excellence" is misleading. The so-called "Centres" are often virtual, extending over large regions. Still more damaging, the excellence can also be virtual, since the quality of the science counts for less in judging the centres than the "style" (the elements of interdisciplinarity, networking and management structure, to which I alluded).

To make things worse, the criterion of style is coupled with an assessment of potential for "wealth generation." This depends on an impossible calculation involving the nature of the as yet unmade discovery and the way it will interact with other discoveries to make possible a device. That device must be of such a nature as to bring wealth to the jurisdiction (federal or provincial) of the funding agency. And all this is, optimistically, to be validated through peer review.

This is how it comes about that a puzzled colleague in Bad-Wurtenburg is faced by a form in which he must give a rating to the likely economic benefits to the province of Saskatchewan of some proposed research in non-linear optics.

A further exercise, among many, is the provision of milestones for the research. These cover a several-year period. They can be categorized as to the particular "thrust," and "task" within that thrust. They are written a year before the project begins. At a suitable later date progress must be reported directly beneath each of the original millstones (as they are sometimes mistyped).

Woe betide the researcher who hares off in pursuit of the unexpected. Fortunately some do because this country has excellent science, in spite of over-management.

But our scientists are asking themselves why they should be required to make discoveries by subterfuge. A few, who are the most mobile, go in search of jurisdictions where it is less necessary to do so.

I leave to you the wider question. Has this new accountability, which in principle we welcome, in practice involved us in damaging exercises? Are senior officials in many areas spending time and money in chicanery, to the detriment of their work?

Of course they are. But I leave the question open, Canadian style.

However, I would like to add one thing. You may think me guilty of hyperbole. What I am really guilty of is stating the problem too narrowly. It is not a problem primarily of bamboozling bureaucrats, but of losing opportunities. To vary the simile, the general in the field observing a gap in the enemy ranks may decline to order a charge. Why? Because winning the war has become subsidiary to following the plan. This has invariably been the undoing of the centralized state.

Let me summarize. It is the mark of creative activity, in whatever sphere, that it surprises. If it doesn't surprise it is re-creative, a hobby. But in order to surprise it must be given the freedom to do so. In scientific research we should insist on the freedom to succeed. Of course we expect to be held accountable. We are not asking for the freedom to fail, but to be judged on what we do. To judge us in any other way is to ensure that we do less than we might.

I am aware that I have painted on too small a canvas for this ambitious meeting. Science policy is not only *thought* to be peripheral; it is peripheral. It looms larger when one considers that the entire spectrum of creativity is similarly vulnerable. For if liberalism means anything, it means an openness to the changes that the exercise of imagination can bring.

In this important sense, to be a scientist is, automatically, to be a liberal. Science embraces whatever change carries the hallmark of truth. So, when a stateless patent clerk in Berne, Switzerland, challenges the greatest living scientists, attention is paid. In short order, Einstein was plucked from obscurity. The Establishment of science rejoiced in the revolution he had wrought.

This ruling body has in fact been knocked flat a dozen times in the past century, with the advent of new notions of matter, energy, time, life and the universe. The community it rules has emerged each time strengthened by change.

Sadly, but not surprisingly, the liberal imagination of the scientist extends only a little way beyond the laboratory door. But that little matters, as practitioners of politics know. My fondest hope for science is that its habit of renewing itself through change, and hence its tolerance of dissent, will spread beyond its professional boundaries.

The task of the liberal today is what it has always been; shaping a world without war or want. What is new, and science has something to do with it, is that we live in a time of runaway change in which we are being forced to implement that dream. The political scene is mined with explosive information and expectation. And also with explosives.

In a Statement first circulated in July 2001 a group of Nobel prize winners spoke of this:

> The most profound danger to world peace in the coming years will stem… from the legitimate demands of the world's dispossessed. If, then, we permit the devastating power of modern weaponry to spread through this combustible human landscape, we invite a conflagration that can engulf both rich and poor.

> The only hope for the future lies in co-operative international action, legitimized by democracy. It

is time to turn our backs on the unilateral search for security, in which we seek to shelter behind walls.

… To survive in the world we have transformed we must learn to think in a new way. As never before, the future of each depends on the good of all.

By the time, two months later, that September 11th woke up the world, some 35 prize winners had signed. Shortly thereafter the number increased to 110—the great majority of this international community.

The Nobel Statement was, I would say, liberal to its core. On September 11, 2001 you might not have thought that there were 110 liberals around, particularly since (being Nobel prize winners) they were mostly American. But, in fact, liberals abound, and global realities are in the process of creating more. The president of the United States is one when he excoriates the United Nations for being a paper tiger. The challenge that we face, and I am confident we shall be up to it, is to be more liberal than the president of the United States.

Polling Alone:
Canadian Values and Liberalism

Michael Marzolini

IN ADDRESSING THE progressiveness of Canadian Liberalism with respect to the Liberal government's social policy, it is very important to consider that Liberalism itself is not static. It moves and progresses, along lines defined by changing public opinion, cultural values and need. Today's Liberalism has much in common with yesterday's Conservatism, give or take a margin-of-error of about 50 years. It evolves slowly, though in the past 10 years the velocity of movement has increased dramatically, and public attitudes toward the role of government, both socially and economically, have changed from what they were just a decade ago.

Public opinion and Liberalism evolve together in quite remarkable fashion. Liberal values mirror the values of the public. Six in ten Canadians, when forced to make a choice, identify themselves as "small-L" liberal. This is twice the number that labels themselves as "small-C" conservative and six times as many who consider themselves socialist. This greatly facilitates the ability of Liberalism to evolve and adjust to changes in public opinion.

In most cases, Liberalism, manifested in the actions of Liberal governments, have trailed, but followed reasonably closely on the heels of public opinion. That is, in my view, the way it *should* be. Changes in public opinion need time to be realized, and adjusted to, by the public itself. Only when governments or activists forge too far ahead of public opinion do they risk losing the public's confidence. We saw this very recently with the release of a "trial balloon" suggesting a 10% GST—thankfully killed within hours, but not without cost.

But taking strong and immediate action *ahead* of public opinion is often necessary for government to do its job responsibly. The 1995 Budget is an example; the public only became convinced of the necessity to kill the deficit mid-way through the campaign. It would have taken too long to get them on-side first.

But while one can lead public opinion on specific *policy*, there are great risks to being too far ahead of public opinion in the broader context of *Liberalism*. The former is an opinion, subject to rapid change. The latter is a value, which only changes slowly over time.

Liberalism is not a brand; it is a product category. This category consists of brands, which have been defined at various times in history by strong brand managers—ranging from C.D. Howe, Paul Martin, Walter Gordon, to all the Liberal Prime Ministers to varying degrees.

Pierre Trudeau provided the strongest brand identity, one whose values endure as well today as they did during his term in office. But public expectations of government today are far different than they were in the "golden era" of political entrepreneurship.

Liberalism has been the most successful political ideology in Canada for the single reason that it has never failed to evolve. It has rarely been left in the dust of public opinion. It is centrist, with no inhibitions about making forays into the left and the right of the political spectrum.

Indeed, political "spectrum spanning" has had limited opposition opportunities for growth and maximized Liberal Party support for many years. And it is these forays, both to the left and to the right, which have served to fine-tune Liberalism against the ever-changing map of public opinion.

This isn't easy, considering that the political center is always moving, like a pendulum, from right to left and then back again. It is further complicated by the subdivisions within this pendulum, very different public agendas with respect to social and economic policy. During the last decade both agendas have moved quite independently from each other, to varying degrees—socially to the left, while

at the same time economically to the right. This makes it very difficult for any political party except the Liberals to position themselves
closely with the public.

In looking at the question, "Can the System be Moved?" there is
certainly in Canada a willingness to embrace a revitalized and progressive social policy. There is a concurrent desire to enjoy a higher
standard of living. These have manifested themselves in two very
different government approaches: one is the innovation agenda, while
the other is the social cohesion agenda. Both in concert, provide a
balanced approach to spectrum positioning.

Social cohesion of course, has been in the spotlight as a result of
Robert Putnam's book, *Bowling Alone*, which was a best-seller in Ottawa but not widely read in Toronto. He points to the decline in
organized activities, such as bowling leagues, to illustrate a fragment-
ing social cohesion among the public.

But Putnam's study was very much a Made-in-America product,
and one that parallels but doesn't reflect completely the state of affairs in Canada. Earlier this year, POLLARA sponsored a national
survey for Kroeger College of Public Affairs, exploring many of the
Canadian values surrounding social cohesion, with an attempt to
assess the opportunities and limitations in the agenda. These data
provide many perspectives on this Canadian value-map, and on social cohesion's potential place in the broad context of Liberalism,
especially with respect to the innovation agenda.

Preferred Role of Government

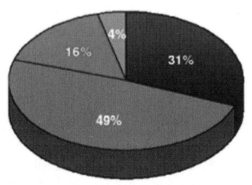

■ Solve problems & protect people from adversity
■ Help people equip, solve their problems
■ Stay out of people's lives and not interfere
▨ No opinion

The goal of the latter is to provide a higher standard of living to Canadians. Social cohesion's goal is to develop shared values, challenges and opportunities in Canada, based on increased hope, trust and reciprocity among Canadians. These goals are not contradictory; together they actually produce a wide straddling of the political center. But many of the government interventions by which each can be achieved, *do* conflict, not only in policy, but also in public opinion.

Governments around the world have embraced social cohesion agendas primarily as means to counter the increasing public disconnection and isolation from their democratic institutions. They now have to determine what roles they can play that are both appropriate and effective. And more importantly, how the social cohesion agenda can be bought into by a public that will never endorse a solution without fully understanding the problem.

In the thirteen years POLLARA has been tracking the preferred role for government, we've seen a lot of change. Thirteen years ago, a slim majority of Canadians wanted highly active government— a government that would solve their problems and protect them cradle to grave. They were introspective, protectionist, and dependent. The boundaries of their world ended at the US-Canadian border, and since they strongly *opposed* the FTA, even the strength of this border was regarded with trepidation.

Concepts like a guaranteed annual income, which make most Canadians shudder today, were popular back then. The national deficit and debt were not even in our vocabulary, and unemployment was something to be solved with mega-projects and direct government employment. The demands on government were far greater than before this time, and had a much different orientation from what they are today.

Since that time we've seen a steady and marked shift, to the point where the largest number of Canadians now desires a government that is active in making people more independent, and more able to solve their own problems. When unemployment is high, they no longer expect government to provide direct employment as was common back in the 70's and 80's. They now look to government for training and direction, and to create the economic environment that stimulates private sector hiring.

A majority now welcomes NAFTA, and thinks that globalization

Competition

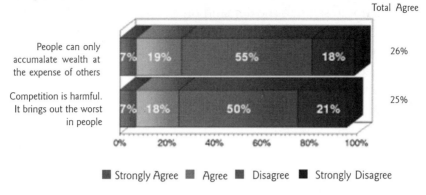

Total Agree

People can only accumalate wealth at the expense of others	7% 19% 55% 18%	26%
Competition is harmful. It brings out the worst in people	7% 18% 50% 21%	25%

0% 20% 40% 60% 80% 100%

■ Strongly Agree ■ Agree ■ Disagree ■ Strongly Disagree

Social Justice

Total Agree

People in this country are in need because there is injustice in our society	15% 52% 26% 5%	67%
Incomes should be made more equal	29% 35% 26% 6%	64%

0% 20% 40% 60% 80% 100%

■ Strongly Agree ■ Agree ■ Disagree ■ Strongly Disagree

Individual Initiative

Total Agree

Indivduals should take more responsibility for providing for themselves	36% 50% 11% 2%	86%
In the long run, hard work usually brings a better life.	34% 49% 13% 2%	83%
People in this country are in need because of laziness and lack of will power	13% 42% 33% 10%	55%

0% 20% 40% 60% 80% 100%

■ Strongly Agree ■ Agree ■ Disagree ■ Strongly Disagree

will provide benefits not only to them, but also far more to their children. They are now budget conscious and more sensitive to public spending. They were asked to tighten their belt to get the deficit under control, and they don't want to give up the gains they helped work for. They may worry about their pension, but they've increased their savings ratio and given more thought to retirement planning.

This is not to say that the demand on government is reduced. The 16% of Canadians telling us that the proper role of government is to stay out of people's lives and *not interfere has not changed significantly* in ten years. Rather, the only shift has been from "cradle to grave" orientation to wanting government to "help us help ourselves." And this is the overlay through which they see each of the factors that make up social cohesion.

This shift toward self-reliance was not forced upon Canadians; they came to this conclusion as a result of five key factors: NAFTA, the move to fuller employment, globalization, the war on the deficit, and the Internet. These have all helped Canadians become more independent and outward looking, more entrepreneurial and dedicated to individual initiative, and in many ways more economically sophisticated.

Canadians believe in individual initiative and hard work. They also believe that competition is not a bad thing in itself and that people *can* accumulate wealth without hurting others. These serve as rigid confines on the level of economic intervention and approach that government could make with respect to promoting social cohesion. The OECD concept of social cohesion tends to recognize this. The Council of Europe approach is less applicable to Canadian attitudes and values.

At the same time, there is a belief and a desire across Canada for social justice. There is some recognition and concern that Canada, especially with the growth of globalization and technology, may now be approaching a trend of *two-tier* economic development.

New technologies, many people feel, may widen income and opportunity disparities instead of closing them.

The federal government's broadband strategy, albeit under-funded due to lack of resources, is clearly a key component of both the innovation and social cohesion agendas. That program was not designed to equalize incomes, only to provide more equalization for opportunity and access for a high standard of living. Despite a desire for more equal distribution of wealth across Canada, straight and simple income redistribution is *not* a desired course of action on the part of most Canadians.

Cross-analyzing the results of those proposing more equal incomes reveals that these same people also believe strongly in competition, hard work, and individual initiative and responsibility. Most of them consider themselves to be Liberals. To them, lack of opportunity is a social injustice and its resolution would be beneficial both individually and collectively.

Canadian's Attitudes on Taxation and Government Spending

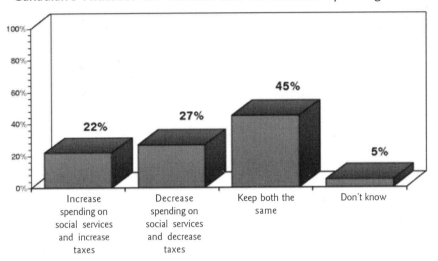

Government Involvment in Commercial Operations
Should Be Decreased

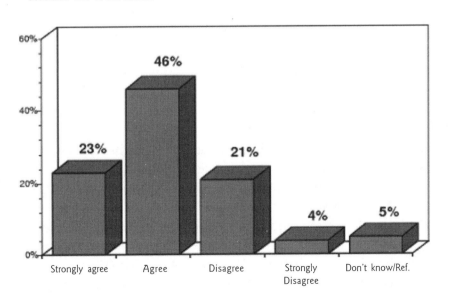

Further evidence of the confines of the government's abilities to promote social cohesion is provided by the lack of Canadians willing to make the trade-off between increased spending on social services and higher taxes. Despite their concern over social injustices, there is not the public will, which impacts political will, for more money to be thrown at the problem. Politically, the status quo is the government's easiest position.

Political positioning however is often based on simple majorities of public opinion. It often overlooks the significant minorities, in this case one-in-five Canadians, who would be prepared to pay higher taxes for more social spending. This is why segmenting and analyzing these population clusters will be very important to understanding this issue, and to make the case against the tyranny of the majority.

A similar quarter of all Canadians, most of them the same people endorsing high taxes and social spending, also oppose the move to privatization of government commercial operations.

Having polled on the CN, PetroCan and Air Canada privatizations, as well as those of many provincial utilities, we can state that this number doesn't change significantly across sectors. It is a hard-core collectivist group of well-educated New Democrat and left leaning Liberal supporters who oppose any move toward private ownership. Similarly, supporters of privatization are to be found in the Alliance, PC and centrist-Liberal support groups.

And it is this latter group that has the most impact on political decisions involving all issues related to both innovation and social cohesion. No political party wishes to isolate its own supporters, and Liberal voters are firmly in the center. But where this sometimes limits the efficacy of government in promoting some aspects of social cohesion, it also encourages the social cohesion agenda in many other ways.

Politically, the social cohesion agenda complements the innovation agenda. Government, especially one straddling the political center, cannot afford to stake out an unbalanced position on the right or the left. It must stay anchored in the center, and while some aspects of social cohesion tend to run counter to individualistic views (which are more aligned with the innovation agenda). They enhance social cohesion, nevertheless, the appeal of the whole package to both collectivists and individualists.

It is a political risk for government to promote either the innovation agenda, or the social cohesion agenda, alone. A package of the two minimizes this risk while promoting the maximum good.

This is not to say that those who support parts of a social cohesion agenda are smaller or less significant than would support parts of an innovation agenda.

Support for Governmental Involvement in Social Services, Health and the Environment

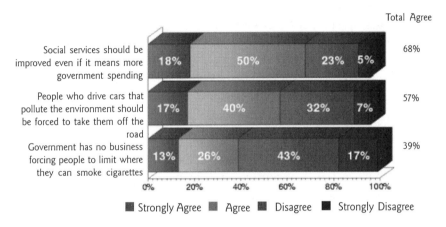

Indeed, despite their lack of willingness to pay higher taxes, there is majority support in Canada for improved social services even if it means more government spending. The state is also seen to have the right to intervene in many social issues, notably environmental and health-related.

Canadians very much take a menu approach to all the individual facets of collectivism and individualism. What they tend to choose could be termed contradictory, but we tend to view it as more balanced.

We may want less government intervention generally, and that mainly confined to giving us the tools to do the job ourselves, but there is recognition that many aspects of our life should not be run by private enterprise, and that there are areas in which the government must intervene.

This balanced approach is politically encouraging for both agendas, giving government more efficacy, while removing unwanted obligations from the private sector.

While it is important that the encouragement of social cohesion by government be along lines currently acceptable to Canadians, it should be remembered that this level of acceptability will move back and forth like a pendulum. Politically, opinion polls have always been tracking the movement of the political center from right to left and back again, in durations lasting about five years.

Currently, the economic political center is to the right, though socially it is still marginally on the center-left. Both will eventually return or move further to the left, and it is likely that government and institutions will increase in importance, trust will increase and community spirit will be enhanced.

We have seen some of this post-September 11th, but whether this is a brief check in public attitude or a more lasting effect it is too early to tell. We are looking forward to tracking some of these questions later this year.

Social participation may have been declining these past few decades, but Canadians are not writing off its importance. The importance of social interaction and involvement are at least recognized by Canadians as being important. In this we compare very favourably with American attitudes. Again, these levels of importance will be fascinating to track next year, after Canadian memories of September 11th move further into the past.

Former US Speaker Tip O'Neil once said that "all politics is local" and it is predictable that Canadians feel closer to their towns

Canadian Attitudes on Community Spirit in Canada

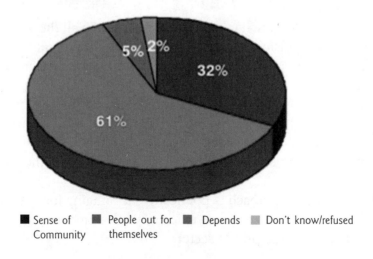

5% 2%

32%

61%

■ Sense of Community   ■ People out for themselves   ■ Depends   ■ Don't know/refused

Importance of Various Factors in Creating Community

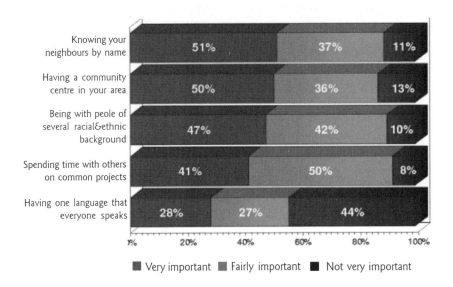

Knowing your neighbours by name — 51% Very important, 37% Fairly important, 11% Not very important

Having a community centre in your area — 50%, 36%, 13%

Being with peole of several racial&ethnic background — 47%, 42%, 10%

Spending time with others on common projects — 41%, 50%, 8%

Having one language that everyone speaks — 28%, 27%, 44%

■ Very important ■ Fairly important ■ Not very important

Degree of Closeness to Various Geographic Areas

Total Agree

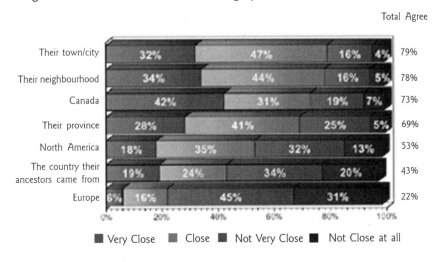

Their town/city — 32%, 47%, 16%, 4% — 79%

Their neighbourhood — 34%, 44%, 16%, 5% — 78%

Canada — 42%, 31%, 19%, 7% — 73%

Their province — 28%, 41%, 25%, 5% — 69%

North America — 18%, 35%, 32%, 13% — 53%

The country their ancestors came from — 19%, 24%, 34%, 20% — 43%

Europe — 6%, 16%, 45%, 31% — 22%

■ Very Close ■ Close ■ Not Very Close ■ Not Close at all

and neighbourhoods than to their country. But the *intensity* of closeness is greatest with respect to the idea of the nation. This surprised me, as I've seen a lot of data suggesting that we are actually identify more closely to our provinces than our country.

But while this may seem encouraging, it is again the minority opinion that must be taken into account. A fifth of Canadians seem to feel little connection to their town or neighbourhood even though they've lived there for an average 14 years; and even worse, more than a quarter feel no connection to Canada itself.

This is a very high number and far greater than the percentage of separatists in the country. However, this is a problem that *can* be directly approached by government, through communications messaging and the fostering of a stronger and more unique brand identity sensitive to our values and culture.

Levels of community spirit are even more alarming and problematic in Canada. Only one-third of the population really believes that people in general feel a sense of community with others—most believe they are only out for themselves.

It will take further analysis and correlating with the other questions on the survey to explore fully the reasons behind this situation. It could be a mixture of crime, the growth of individuality and competition, and a growing lack of public trust for individuals and institutions.

We know from our regular quarterly tracking report, *Perspectives Canada*, that confidence and trust in all individuals and institutions has been falling throughout the last eight years—both in the private and the public sectors.

A couple of waves of our yearly "Public Trust index" can be found on the www.Pollara.ca web-site, ranking trust in about 50 institutions and occupations. This year however, post-September 11th, we've seen a small recovery in trust and confidence, for every type of institution.

Public utilities, banks, insurance companies, oil and gas, and telecom companies, have joined governments at all levels in moving ahead in both impression and trustworthiness.

Whether this is short-term or will have a more lasting impact we can't determine at this time , but we will track this, and hope for at least a significant residue of improvement. Currently, the most socially cohesive attitude we've measured is that everybody seems to hate Air Canada.

But when it comes to Canadians' trust in their government, this is the area in which the most improvement is needed, and indeed which may be driving many other unproductive attitudes.

Canadians have always been cynical toward government, and this

Canadians' Attitudes About Democratic Systems

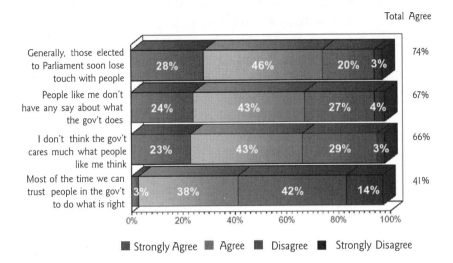

Total Agree

Generally, those elected to Parliament soon lose touch with people — 28% / 46% / 20% / 3% — 74%

People like me don't have any say about what the gov't does — 24% / 43% / 27% / 4% — 67%

I don't think the gov't cares much what people like me think — 23% / 43% / 29% / 3% — 66%

Most of the time we can trust people in the gov't to do what is right — 3% / 38% / 42% / 14% — 41%

■ Strongly Agree ■ Agree ■ Disagree ■ Strongly Disagree

Satisfaction with Level of Democracy in Canada

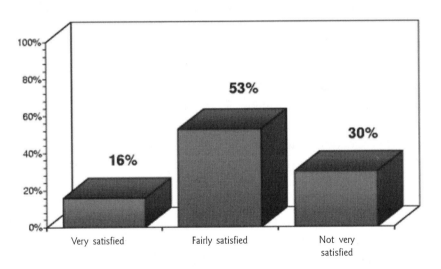

16% Very satisfied 53% Fairly satisfied 30% Not very satisfied

should be expected to some degree. However, the sense of disconnection that we currently have with our governments is quite significant and rather ugly. It paints a picture of a people who have been isolated by governments that are perceived as out of touch, not caring what the public thinks, inaccessible, and not always out for the public's best interests.

This is not a recent occurrence. Indeed the results were actually worse more than a decade ago, during the Mulroney administration, when on a scale of one to ten, where one is not at all impressed and ten is very impressed, each of the federal government, the civil service and the Party in office all rated lower than a "3" average. All are now over "5", but still have far to go.

If it is not happy with the institutions, and if it feels disconnected from government, the public is equally subdued when it comes to its satisfaction with the level of democracy. Again, the emphasis must be on the 3 in 10 Canadians who are not very satisfied, and further exploration of the issue is needed.

In terms of the social cohesion issue a lot has been made about the problem of declining voter turnout. Participation levels in society are not where we would like them to be but we strongly believe that too much has been made of this issue where it applies to voting. In 1988, there was a very high turnout as a result of a divisive issue, Free Trade, which many Canadians felt would threaten their livelihood. In 1993, there was a lower turnout, though closer to the historical average as the issue was jobs; there were many people out of work, and the incumbent government was highly unpopular.

Since then there have been two more federal elections, each one progressively more boring, progressively less threatening to anybody's way of life, and resulting in progressively lower turnouts.

But in 1995, during the Quebec Referendum, in the *ultimate* of threatening situations, more than 90% of eligible voters cast their ballots.

In every election, and at every level of government, the turnout has always been proportional to the threat posed by the issues being debated. When the issue is important, Canadians *can* be counted on to vote.

Many in the Liberal Party could easily design a party election platform so radical that 90% of the public would be motivated to vote, but of course they'd be voting against us.

There is no evidence of the need for mandatory voting, or for moving to a system based on proportional representation—both of which have been suggested by academics and the media.

But though voter participation has clearly declined through the last three elections, in a way that appears to have little to do with social cohesion, Canadians do see the importance of voting and the importance of civic duty.

Political Participation

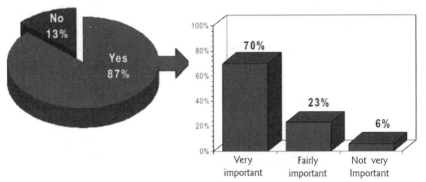

Voted in 2000 Federal Election

Importance of Civic Duty in Decision to Cast Vote

Subsample: Voted in 2000 federal election

Involvment in Other Political Action in Past Year

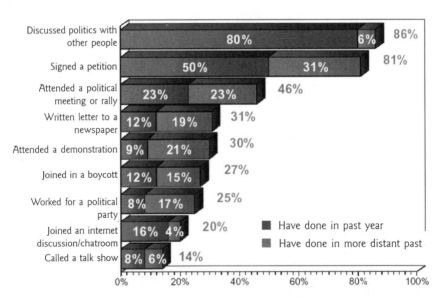

Witness that some 26% of the public would lie to the pollsters on a survey such as this, saying they had voted when the actual turnout was 61%. They at least recognize a social stigma resulting from not bothering to vote.

While Canadian's political involvement compares favourably with that of Americans, there is no dispute that it *could* be higher and that this would be beneficial down the line.

Over the past decade there have been some small victories for the public, which created a feeling of greater empowerment. The negative option cable television issue, when the industry caved into public pressure; the reversal of the NHL taxpayer bailout, when the people spoke and the government listened; and Air Canada's decision to back off their Aeroplan point reduction changes, are a few such victories from the past year.

Participation in Groups or Associations

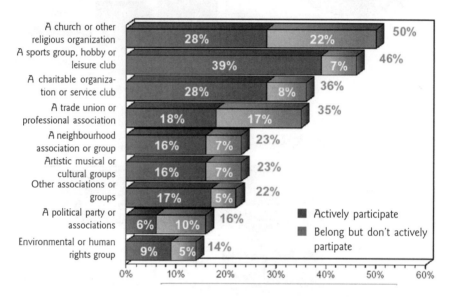

Voluntary Work

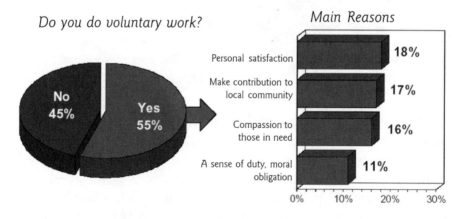

Subsample: Those who do voluntary work

But this hasn't been enough, and a majority of Canadians still don't actively participate in public affairs. This is not surprising, given the majority who feel that they can't have any effect, and that the government doesn't care what people like them think.

Though POLLARA did not ask specifically about bowling leagues or choral singing, as Putnam did in his study, we do find that group participation in Canada is limited to a minority, the same core people involved in multiple organizations.

There is much that governments can do to stimulate the development of a community of shared values and inclusiveness. However, most of the standard methods result in only short-term improvements. Longer-term improvements need to be based on a greater spirit of trust and goodwill with respect to these institutions, and these levels are low to begin with.

There are more questions than answers to be found in the issue of social cohesion. The one that many people spend the most time thinking about is "What level of social cohesion is desirable?" Having too much would likely be as damaging as having too little. The perfect example of extreme social cohesion is the Hells Angels biker gang.

However, we have a long way to go before we worry about this question. Currently only significant minorities of the public are participating and getting involved in public issues. The rest are isolated and disconnected and this affects both their outlook and their usefulness to society.

Only in the area of voluntary work do we find anything approaching a majority level of participation, and then we still have that significant minority that is not participating.

Conclusion

For government, it is easy to approach some of the components of social cohesion. Securing the means to achieve equal opportunity is an *industry* within the government. Government has always strived in this direction and will likely always do so. The broadband strategy is just one in a long line of these initiatives, but one that deals with the threat of two-tier economic development.

Participation and sense of community can be artificially, though only partially stimulated, through the encouragement and founding of organizations such as Katimavik, CUSO and similar programs of national youth service, both for the domestic market and for export.

Branding the Canadian identity as unique and valuable could stimulate patriotism and connection, as could positioning Canadian history as more relevant to our heritage.

Communications can play a key role in fostering participation, identity and connection. However, in the current economic climate, the government has neither the funds nor the political will for such communication.

The public has always viewed the government as being self-serving and wasteful, especially in the past six months. Perhaps we need to look at all government communications within the framework of promoting social cohesion, and give it enhanced priority under this new agenda.

To do this would also mean putting the issue of social cohesion on the table for public discussion and input. The public won't endorse a solution until they understand the problem, and I doubt that one person in twenty has ever even heard of the term social cohesion, much less what it means.

Advertising is not the only confinement that government must face in dealing with social cohesion. The Canadian public holds both individualistic and collective values, and there is much to the agenda that they would embrace and refuse, sometimes at the same time. Income redistribution, changes to tax structure, government ownership of commercial operations, or any regulatory change that impacts too bluntly on Canadians' strong feelings of individual initiative, are too *risky* to approach today. This could change with time.

But the major political asset to the agenda, that will ensure its place at the table, is that social cohesion is political insurance when proceeding with the innovation agenda. Its inclusion puts the government, and indeed Liberalism, in *balance*, with *anchors* on both the political right and left, and enhances the appeal of both as a package.

Such a package minimizes the political risk to the government, while at the same time promoting the maximum good.

Section Two

Policies

Canada's New Millennium:
The Role of the Corporate Sector

Michael E.J. Phelps

WHETHER CANADA'S search for a brighter future is to proceed along the lines of a new liberalism or not, one condition must be satisfied and that is, Canada must have the ability to make its own choices.

The ability to make these choices is at the heart of the concept of national sovereignty and for these purposes I refer to sovereignty in the fullest sense of the word, that is economic, political and cultural. This is a challenge and indeed, in Canada's case, this particular challenge may be more pronounced than similar challenges facing any of the world's leading industrialized nations. Our geographic proximity to the United States, as well as our cultural similarity, and taking into account our much smaller population, makes our aspirations for full sovereignty somewhat more problematic than is the case for western European countries or even Australia. I am reminded of being in Melbourne just a few years ago and picking up the morning paper to read that Melbourne would be graced that evening by the arrival of two well known American entertainers, Bryan Adams and k.d. lang. It is very easy to confuse Canadians for Americans.

In this quest for a brighter future, Canada's Corporate Sector will have a key role to play. Corporations will serve as the primary funding engines for our quality of life aspirations. The ability to create, on a sustained basis, a healthy economy is one of the foundations of Canada's ability to stay separate. This does not mean that the economies of the two countries will not continue to be closely linked. This does not mean that there will be significant acquisitions or mergers of Canadian companies by U.S. entities or indeed of U.S. companies by Canadian ones. Still, our ability to stay separate requires, for the most part, that the Corporate Sector itself retain sufficient independence to play a role in the promotion of sovereignty.

One further point needs to be emphasized and that is that our separateness, in every sense of the word, is a part of our overall quality of life. The world's economies and capital markets are integrating every day but this does not mean complete integration. Canada's quality of life will be enhanced by resisting complete economic or cultural integration.

All of this being said, what can we look to from the Corporate Sector in Canada to promote our aspirations? As we sit here in the second half of the year 2002, current events make it difficult to feel much confidence. The news, on a worldwide basis, at least insofar as the economy is concerned, has been unremittingly negative. It is hard to pick up a newspaper and find anything positive on the economic or corporate fronts. The world has witnessed, amongst other things, the following events:

- The implosion of valuations in the technology sector over the course of the last two years.
- An outright recession as defined by negative economic growth over at least two successive quarters.
- The terrorist events of September 11th in New York City and Washington, DC.
- A significant escalation in the risk of unleashing weapons of mass destruction, whether in Iraq or Kashmir.
- The bankruptcy of major companies such as Enron, WorldCom and Global Crossing.
- A high incidence of scandal, corporate theft and fraud in such cases as Enron, Tyco and Adelphia Communications.
- Questions regarding the quality and integrity of reported financial statements. Doubts were even expressed about such high quality and reputable names as IBM and General Electric.

- Auditors themselves being subjected to skeptical review, especially after Arthur Andersen was convicted of Obstruction of Justice by shredding Enron files.
- Instances of excessive executive compensation in companies such as Tyco, Hydro One in Canada, and even General Electric. These abuses are particularly unpalatable in the face of a recession and three years of falling stock prices.
- A daily litany of stories relating to conflicts of interest in the world of investment banking, including suggestions that equity research analysts distorted stock purchase recommendations in an effort to gain investment banking business. As well, press stories revealed that potential investment banking clients were given allocations of scarce initial public offerings of technology stocks in an effort to garner business. These stocks were sometimes resold within hours or days of being allocated.
- The Canada / U.S. trade relationship has been marred by a series of measures emanating from private quarters in the United States, designed to hinder trade between the two countries in such sectors as agriculture, steel and softwood lumber.

Taking all these factors together has resulted in the most precipitous drop in stock market values since the 1930's.

All of this is important, for without a recovery in the tone and confidence of the capital markets, there will be no recovery because there will be nothing available to fund it.

That being said, efforts are under way to bring about changes. Reforms are being implemented on both sides of the Canada—U.S. border which will promote auditor independence and provide greater confidence in the quality of accounting. Equity research is in the process of being separated from investment banking. Executive compensation will necessarily be modified to reflect public concern and cynicism.

These changes will serve to improve public and corporate confidence in capital markets.Much of this will be accomplished by a change of attitudes.Boards of directors will have to play a more diligent role in exercising an oversight function.

Government legislation and regulation will need to increase confidence and trust in the working of the economy generally, and in capital markets specifically. That being said, an overly stringent and detailed set of rules will not do the job. What is needed is a balance between careful oversight and regulation and leaving enough room to allow the creative qualities of businesses to flourish.

Assuming that this recovery is to be accomplished over the course of the next couple of years or so, Canada must acknowledge that we still face challenges in being fully sovereign in the corporate and economic sphere. These challenges arise in ways that may appear to be excessively technical, but they have a profound effect on the day-to-day workings of Canada's economy.

All of this starts with the need to maintain a vibrant and separate financial services industry in Canada. This is easier said than done because the enormous size and liquidity of the U.S. capital markets serves as a significant magnet for Canadian companies seeking access to capital. Larger and more liquid markets are more efficient and yield better pricing for the issuers of stocks and bonds. The fact of integration in Canadian and U.S. capital markets, and considering relative sizes, means that there is a disproportionate influence of U.S. tax and accounting rules. It is hard for Canada to maintain separate and different rules for disclosure and accounting, in the case of those companies that seek access to both markets. This is a problem unique to Canada. Insofar as I know, American companies do not spend a lot of time worrying about other countries' accounting rules. They are fully occupied contending with their own. In the case of Canadian corporations, we have to worry about both. Similarly, in the case of tax, (and I do not mean levels of tax but rather rules of tax), the United States offers certain advantages for consolidating tax returns with subsidiaries, thereby making them more competitive internationally than Canadian corporations. Again, there are undoubtedly good reasons for separate Canadian tax rules, but it can be problematic when they are different than American ones.

As I stated earlier, these issues may appear to be technical and narrow, but they are important in the day-to-day workings of Canada's Corporate Sector. They are part of our struggle for sovereignty.

The upshot of all of this is that Canada must work hard to pursue a multilateral approach to tax and accounting issues. Post-September 11th, the United States does not seem much given to pursuing multilateral approaches in any sphere. Historically, U.S. financial regulation has served to provide exemptions for European and Canadian companies that follow their own domestic rules. Acceptance of these exemptions seems to be on the wane. Much of the U.S. regulatory thrust these days is to compel issuers seeking access to American markets to fully comply with American rules. Again, this means that Canadian companies will have to comply with two sets of rules with the inevitable but perhaps slow push to standardize them in order to reduce complexity and compliance costs. In respect of all of this, we have much common ground to share with Western Europe. Western Europe may represent our best hope for a multilateral approach to these issues.

Finally, governments at all levels in Canada and the public generally will have to recognize that the benefits of our separateness come with a certain cost. Our society will need to arrive at a stronger consensus in an effort to pursue the advantages of this separateness. If it is simply a matter of the highest gain or highest value, our sovereignty will not have much long-term prospect of success. We have every reason to aspire to create world class competitive corporations but in the search for shareholder value, if that is the only goal, we will lose out to the much larger force to the South of us. Canada must arrive at a consensus where returns from companies and stock markets are exceedingly important but not the only consideration in determining economic decision-making.

Over the course of the last decade, as Canada's population has sought higher returns from equities in the face of extremely low interest rates and low returns from deposits or bonds, the pressures to pursue shareholder value have been growing enormously. This is not as a result of the forces of Bay Street or Wall Street or the banks of Zurich. This is about Canadians doing it to Canadians. We have demanded low-risk, high dividends and high returns, much in the same way that we want cheap airfares but extraordinarily well maintained aircraft with first-class meal service. Something has to give in all of this. In our case, we must understand that some cost, perhaps slight, to maintain our separateness is well worth the price. Leadership in this respect should come from public sector fiduciary institutions, such as teachers and government civil service pension funds. They are the owners of much of the economy through their shareholdings and they should seek to make sure that non-financial goals are not completely eliminated. No one should think that placing financial goals on a secondary basis will lead to much success in the economy. That being said, non-financial goals such as sovereignty ought not to be excluded from consideration either.

By way of summary, therefore, two points should be made:

- The current economic and capital markets climate is as negative as anything seen in the last 70 years. Time will be requred for a recovery in the Corporate Sector. Regulation and attitudes will need to be modified.

- Canada's proximity to, and cultural similarity with, the United States makes sovereignty a greater challenge for Canada than for other industrialized nations. For the Corporate Sector, this includes the difficulty in maintaining different tax and accounting rules than those facing U.S. companies. This does not mean falling in lockstep with U.S. rules. It does mean, however, that we need to be conscious of the cost of these differences and the advisability of pursuing multilateral approaches.

Some Thoughts About a Liberal Legal Culture:

Considering Canada's Anti-Terrorism Act, the Constitution and the HR Revolution

Peter L. Biro

> THE REAL PURPOSE *of laws, then, is to educate the citizen in the common good, and persuade him to behave in the public interest, rather than than to command and restrain.*
>
> P.E.T.[1]

One of the great paradoxes of the liberal state is that, while citizen participation in the political life of the state is optional on an individual basis and is never coerced, there can be no liberal state without an intellectually vibrant and politically engaged citizenry. Unlike any other political tradition, liberalism depends, for its sustainability, on the notion that the individual members of society will remain continually engaged in the never-ending process of balancing personal aspirations with community objectives and, wherever possible, actualizing one in the pursuit of the other.

The laws have a persuasive and salutary role to play in this process. Participatory democracy in the liberal state requires a constant critical, if not also grudging, compliance with the laws. This compliance respects and affirms the laws, but only provisionally, and only insofar as it results from a genuine belief that such laws continue to educate society's members in the common good and that the individual's own identity and potentialities have the greatest chance of being most fully realized under such circumstances.

The relation of the citizen to its government is nowhere more complex and sophisticated than in the liberal state. This is because there is no social contract more dynamic and more fluid than the contract between and among the citizens of a liberal state. Liberalism is not, unlike other traditions, concerned first and foremost either with hierarchies or with their abolition. It is less ideological and doctrinaire than any other political tradition. It is less preoccupied with any preconceived notion of the "correct" social order and more interested in ensuring that the societal arrangements of the day best protect and promote the interests of all members of society.

But to know best about one's own interests, each citizen has to be encouraged, I dare say, almost "incentivized," into learning, listening, speaking out and taking action. A failure to participate in the political life of one's country leads not only, as Trudeau once suggested while paraphrasing Plato, to being governed by those less fit than oneself to do the job, but worse, it may lead to the imperceptible end of the liberal society *per se*.

There is no snobbery or pretension in this observation. One of the essential purposes of the laws and of the legal system is precisely to foster a political environment in which the individual is driven to remain engaged in the debates of the day. This can only be achieved in a truly pluralist society; one in which the individual citizen associates or identifies his or her fullest development and self-expression with a particular set of societal arrangements. It can only be achieved, moreover, when the laws and the legal environment do not discourage self-expression; for when they do, that is, when people view social and political expression as manifestly unwelcome, they become anti-social, disengaged, disinterested and apathetic.

The laws really do have a direct impact on the nature and quality of political discourse in our country.

One can speak about law reform, about an agenda for liberalism, for the Liberal Party of Canada, for the country. I am suggesting that such an agenda should be driven by a reminder and a restatement of fundamental liberal principles: pluralism as a cardinal political value, law as a means to protect and empower, but never as a system that silences voices and stifles expression. We must reaffirm our preference for a legal system and legal culture which encourages us to express who we are, lest we end up with laws which dictate only who we must not become.

The "law reform" agenda in Canada will be a full one for national and provincial governments in the coming years. It will include reforms concerning, *inter alia*, the civil status of the person—e.g., same-sex marriages; radical reform in our laws and policies concerning our aboriginal citizens and peoples; the decriminalization and possible legalization of certain controlled substances, whether for therapeutic or other purposes; revisiting the law governing "compassionate killing," euthanasia and assisted suicide; the overhauling of the entire penal system and the rethinking of traditional approaches to sentencing and punishment in the criminal justice system; expanding the role of alternative forms of dispute resolution in the civil justice system; "internationalizing" Canada's approach to the prosecution of war crimes and crimes against humanity; aggressively addressing the scourge of "corporate" or "white-collar" crime; revamping and modernizing privacy and intellectual property laws to more effectively address the internet and other technological developments; and, perhaps of greatest and most vital importance for any liberal democracy: the "access-to-justice" and legal aid brief.[2] These and so many other important aspects of the law and of our legal system are crying out for attention and reform.

I wish, however, to use these pages to focus on three matters that ought to be of concern to liberals and Liberals alike in Canada. I seize upon these matters precisely because of my liberal preoccupation with the law's ability to liberate and empower the individual and, equally, to intimidate and repress her.

In addressing a colloquium whose guiding mission is the search for the "new liberalism," I cannot help but note in passing that a "new liberalism" must, nevertheless, be a "true" liberalism. In addressing new challenges and in seeking a road map for the future, we ought to consider whether Canadians have always been true, in recent years, to the most timeless principles of liberalism. Have we, in our laws, in our constitution, in our culture, measured up to liberalism's imperatives? I submit that we have not.

In a sense, each of the three matters that I discuss below calls for a reconsideration of the way liberals understand their relation to each other and to government; each offers liberals an opportunity to highlight the uniqueness, indeed, the moral unassailability, of their way of thinking about government and politics—a golden opportunity to differentiate themselves from the "competition"— whether on the battlefield of ideas or in the legislatures on all ends of the ideological and party spectrum. We ought to go back to the well of first principles for some of the most promising "new ideas" that might really take hold in the public imagination. As nothing more than a starting point in the critical self-examination that I propose, here are three projects, among so many other important reforms to be considered, that Canadians can and should be discussing and undertaking:

- Enhancing the legitimacy of our national security protection measures by respecting civil liberties and property rights: Giving the *Anti-terrorism Act* a true "sunset clause."
- Acknowledging our political maturity: Repealing Section 33 of The *Charter*.
- Reconsidering the HR revolution: Giving people the freedom to speak again!

In entertaining these projects, we can begin to correct our recent deviation from the liberal path. The search for the new liberalism entails, at least in part, an acknowledgment of our betrayals of the true liberal tradition.

1. Enhancing the legitimacy of our national security protection measures by respecting civil liberties and property rights: Giving the Anti-terrorism Act a true "sunset clause."

In October 1970, faced with what it said was an "apprehended insurrection" in Quebec, the Trudeau government invoked the *War Measures Act* and effectively instituted a state of martial law. The *FLQ* was the terrorist face of Quebec separatism and Trudeau would not miss the opportunity to use the might of the state to smash this particularly hated enemy from within. Ultimately, this internal security threat—which Trudeau did not, after all, fabricate, whether or not one accepts the view that his government misled Parliament and the Canadian public as to the actual existence of an "apprehended insurrection"[3]—gave the Prime Minister an opportunity to dispel any notion that the ugly nationalism against which he had railed throughout the 1950's and 60's would make any inroads through violent means. That nationalism, manifesting itself principally in the movement for Quebec secession and sovereignty, would have to make its case through the peaceful, though sometimes duplicitous, process of constitutional reform and through democratic political discourse and the use of democratic institutions.[4]

What is clear is that the government of the day characterized the situation as one of national emergency and it reacted accordingly, invoking the use of emergency powers and conducting government business in a fashion that signalled that the extraordinary—even if over-reaching[5]—use of the *War Measures Act* was, as the law required, both provisional and temporary.

On September 11, 2001, the twin towers of the World Trade Center in Manhattan succumbed to the evil of international terrorists who had as their professed target the very foundations of Western liberal democracy.

On October 15, 2001, the *Anti-terrorism Act* [6] had its first reading in the House of Commons. On November 28, it was passed by the House of Commons and on December 18, it received Royal Assent, with most of its provisions coming into force on assent.

I do not propose to debate the wisdom of or the need for a powerful, decisive and extraordinary government response to the threat of terrorism, international or otherwise. It is not a question. Nor do I doubt the good intentions of Western countries who are reacting, even if they are over-reacting, to President Bush's demands that they all fall into line, lest the downing of the towers become a foreshadowing of the collapse of civilization as we know it.

But among my deep concerns about Canada's legislative answer to the insecurities of a post-9/11 world is that there is really nothing provisional or temporary about it. Notwithstanding the celebrated "safeguards"—including a mandatory three year Parliamentary review—contained in the statute, to which subject I shall return, the *Anti-terrorism Act* is, unlike the proclamation of the *War Measures Act* and the *Public Order Regulations* which were revoked on December 3, 1970, unquestionably intended to be a permanent feature of our legal landscape.

It is difficult to think of any piece of legislation of the magnitude and with the sweeping impact of the *Anti-terrorism Act* that was introduced and brought into force and effect with the lightning speed with which Bill C-36 became law. In a matter of weeks, the House of Commons was presented with legislation that amended some seventeen statutes with consequential amendments to an additional five statutes. It would be inaccurate to charge the government of the day with ushering the draft legislation through Parliament without entertaining debate and criticism. A number of well-considered submissions were made to the House of Commons Standing Committee on Justice and Human Rights,[7] and scholars, human rights experts and advocates as well as parliamentarians spoke out on the need for important amendments to the bill.[8] Unfortunately, many of the most important recommendations from a variety of well-respected authorities failed to find their way into the final version of the bill.[9]

I wish to address, from a broader perspective, the nature of this legislation. We must appreciate that the *Anti-terrorism Act* is no ordinary bill. It does not merely aim, in modest and unobtrusive fashion, to repair minor social, political or economic ills facing the nation. It does not and cannot purport even to resolve the problem at which it takes aim. That would be too smug and presumptuous a claim. It does, however, make one of the more ambitious commitments contained in any piece of drafting to come off the government printer in recent times:

> Whereas the Parliament of Canada, recognizing that terrorism is a matter of national concern that affects the security of the nation, is committed to taking comprehensive measures to protect Canadians against terrorist activity while continuing to respect and promote the values reflected in, and the rights and freedoms guaranteed by, the *Canadian Charter of Rights and Freedoms* . . .[10]

There can be no question that, in order to deliver on such a commitment to both security and freedom jointly, acknowledging that this commitment is based upon the recognition that people everywhere "are entitled to live their lives in peace, freedom and security,"[11] there will have to be some accommodating, compromising and balancing between security and freedom. It may be worth noting the subtlety of the language in the recital. It does not undertake to guarantee absolutely the rights and freedoms in the *Charter*. It undertakes to "respect and promote the values reflected in, and the rights and freedoms guaranteed by" the *Charter*. This is important because it demonstrates Parliament's recognition that *Charter* rights will be abridged by the legislation, but only in accordance with the principles of fundamental justice, and only in accordance with the principle, which I discuss in the next part of this essay, that rights can be legitimately limited only once their primacy and inalienability have been expressly acknowledged. The Department of Justice states that the government,

> . . . has taken steps to combat terrorism and terrorist activities at home and abroad. . . .The new package of legislation creates measures to deter, disable, identify, prosecute, convict and punish terrorist groups. . . . It provides new investigative tools to law enforcement and national security agencies; . . . it ensures that . . . the root causes of hatred are addressed through stronger laws against hate crimes and propaganda.[12]

A few inconveniences might have to be suffered, a few sacrifices made, in order to deliver on the promises contained in this "package of legislation." The legislation is replete with abridgments of both procedural and substantive *Charter* and other rights and freedoms. In an effort to ensure that no stone would be left unturned in the fight against terrorism, Parliament has, calmly—and without too much fuss—laid the groundwork for permanent war-time government in a time of peace. In other words, the legislation, in my submission, has reconfigured some of the basic operating principles of our legal framework. If we are to accept this reconfiguration, we had better first understand what it means.

But this essay assumes this startling proposition to be true, rather than demonstrating that it is the case. I can only point in a general way to some of the features of the legislation that produce this worrisome result, while also directing the readers' attention to the submissions and essays referred to in footnotes 7 and 9 herein.

The *Anti-terrorism Act* casts a very wide and, in my submission, indeterminate net in its definition "terrorist" activity.[13] The non-discrimination principle in the provision designed to protect minorities is inadequate and opens the door for such methods as racial profiling as a standard means for fighting terrorism.[14] The provisions dealing with preventive arrest and detention are intricate and create potential uncertainty as to the duration of the period of detention. The power of the Solicitor General to list "terrorist" groups and organizations is far too arbitrary, sweeping and lacks a sufficient system of accountability and due process.[16] The powers to freeze, seize and forfeit property[17] are absolutely awesome and, particularly as they affect innocent third parties with otherwise valid interests in the property of alleged terrorists or even of unwitting facilitators of terrorist plots, they cut deeply into liberal conceptions of property rights. Moreover, particular note must be made of the provision which obliges all Canadians, indeed, all persons, to report their own possession, custody or control of any terrorist property.[18] This will require such persons/ all persons to make a determination as to the scope and content of "terrorist activity" and to conduct their own due diligence for the purpose of complying with the law. Moreover the disclosure requirements in the statute may well undermine solicitor-client privilege and confidentiality.[19]

I will say that the reconfiguration of operating principles to which I refer above is as much about how we view ourselves in relation to the state as it is about the minutiae of the legislation itself. In the climate of fear which ensued following the devastating events in New York City and the subsequent war conducted from caves far far away from Urban Anywhere, we have acknowledged that we are prepared to compromise a great deal of the liberties on which a truly liberal state is founded. That is to say, we are prepared to postpone our enjoyment of those liberties in the interest of ensuring that we will be able to reclaim them in the future, not as abstract symbols of our potential as free moral persons, but as the mundane load-bearing girders in the infrastructure of the towers that we inhabit daily.

We have to know that we will get all of our rights back; that is, that the rights and freedoms which might currently be classified as conditional or as being in animated suspension, but which, nevertheless, remain "ours," must be reclaimed. And to those who say that the tenuous and conditional suspension of those rights is now a permanent fact because the conditions of national and international security, or rather, of *insecurity*, are permanent features of our universe, we must respond by saying, "be that as it may, give us back our freedoms so that we can, if reasonably necessary, again agree to forebear from exercising them for a period of time."

The legislation provides for a qualified "sunset clause" only in respect of the powers concerning investigative hearings and preventive arrest.[20] But even then it is not a true "sunset" clause, for it gives Parliament the ability to extend the application of such powers by resolution.

There is no "sunset clause" whatsoever in respect of the remainder of the legislation. There is only a requirement that a Parliamentary committee review the *Anti-terrorism Act* as a whole in three years and that such committee submit a report on the review to Parliament within a year after that review is undertaken.[21] There is also a requirement that the provincial and federal Attorneys General and Solicitors General report annually to Parliament on the use of the preventive arrest and investigative hearing provisions in Bill C-36.[22]

We must, as so many have demanded from the outset, have a true "sunset clause," that is, a clause which brings this extraordinary legislation to a close so that we can, if so advised, debate the merits of it all over again. There are certain matters that need to be revisited, restated, repeated and ultimately, reversed. Any law that tampers with the enjoyment of the rights and freedoms that underpin our way of life, however well-advised it may be, must be required to make the case for itself over and over and over again, if necessary and appropriate.

In one of its press releases calling for a tighter definition of "terrorism" and a "true sunset clause," the Canadian Bar Association issued the following statement:

> The CBA acknowledges that there is pressure to pass the legislation quickly. "We believe that quick passage must be accompanied by a sunset clause," says the CBA. "Given the far-reaching nature of the Bill, we need more than a review. If Canadians can be assured that the provisions in the legislation are temporary, they will accept them in this period of immediate response to an extraor-

dinary threat."[23]

In a liberal society we must adopt an attitude of active impatience with measures that we willingly accept as restrictions on our rights and freedoms. We must be eager always to revisit the grounds on which we provisionally sacrificed the recourse to and exercise of our liberties, particularly when that entails relinquishing power over our liberties to agents of the state.

Moreover, as discussed more fully in the last part of this essay, we are conditioned by the laws we enact and live under. Our ability to think and speak critically about our own best interests depends upon the encouragement that we receive and the freedom we enjoy to do so. This is the sense in which I refer to law as being either engine of citizen self-actualization or instrument of stagnation and repression.

We must insist on a true "sunset clause" in the *Anti-terrorism Act*.[24] Liberalism, whether "new" or tradional, demands nothing less.

2) Acknowledging our political maturity: Repealing Section 33 of The Charter.

It has been twenty years since the *Canadian Charter of Rights and Freedoms* was entrenched in our Constitution. Over these last twenty years our courts and tribunals have had ample opportunity to exercise their supervisory responsibility in respect of legislative compliance with and conformity to the principles enshrined in the *Charter*. During this period, our nation's highest court has produced a rich and voluminous jurisprudence both defining the substantive content of the rights and freedoms enumerated in the *Charter* and developing the test for determining whether government measures or actions which limit or restrict those rights and freedoms do so in a manner that can be said to be "reasonable" and "demonstrably justified in a free and democratic society."

The balancing of individual rights and freedoms with the state's interest in measures which result in the compromising of those rights and freedoms is no mundane judicial exercise. Prior to the introduction of the *Charter* to our legal system, judges were generally unfamiliar with this kind of balancing act. Prior to 1982 the principal constitutional doctrine to which the courts resorted in order to strike down or limit the effect of legislation which jeopardized basic civil liberties was the doctrine of "legal federalism," which entailed rendering nugatory laws which were inconsistent with the distribution of legislative powers between Parliament and the provincial Legislatures as enumerated in the *B.N.A. Act*. With the possible exception of the "Implied Bill of Rights Doctrine,"[25] civil liberties had little or no express constitutional standing and the defence of civil liberties generally had to be undertaken on the jurisdictional battlefield.

But for twenty years now, our justices have been refining and applying the test that must be met by the party seeking to justify the right-limiting measure—i.e., the state—in order to save it from being judicially disembowelled. For twenty years our courts have been striking down laws that infringe the rights and freedoms enumerated in the *Charter* but they have also been sparing those laws that could be demonstrated to have met the elaborate test developed under section 1 of the *Charter*. The essential feature of the test is that it requires the limitations on the rights and freedoms at risk to stand or fall based upon the state's ability to establish that the substantive limiting measure is necessary in order, ultimately, to advance the aims of a free and democratic society. In other words, the test is not whether some other legislative objective is more important or valuable than the rights which will be restricted, but whether the restriction of the rights in the particular instance of the measure under review is justifiable on the basis that this will contribute to the growth and preservation of a society which is ultimately founded upon a respect for individual rights and freedoms and for the equal moral personality of each member of that society.

A good deal of judicial ink has been spilled fashioning and applying the "Section 1 Test." The principle of proportionality between the importance and the salutary effect of the right-limiting measure, on the one hand, and the nature and seriousness of the deleterious effect of that measure on the rights and freedoms at issue, on the other hand, has become as central a feature of our constitutional landscape as is the text of the *Charter* itself into which this principle has breathed life.[26]

Section 1 is a magnificent text, both as a work of elegant and noble prose, but also as a masterpiece of nation-building. Section 1 both guarantees the rights and freedoms set out in it and stipulates the sacred formula for regulating all government measures which limit those rights and freedoms.[27] Section 1 is where democracy finds its highest expression in our Constitution; not in the provisions granting suffrage; not even in the democratic rights provision of section 3 of the *Charter* itself. For it is in section 1 that we acknowledge our governments' power over the scope of our liberties, but only in circumstances in which that power ultimately respects and preserves those liberties.

It is lamentable that, some thirty-two sections further into the document, we find the lowest form of "democracy" expressed in our Constitution. Section 33, the infamous *notwithstanding clause*, sits there as a reminder that there were those among us, when this *Charter* was crafted, who believed that democracy was not linked to inalienable rights and freedoms. There were those who believed that, in certain circumstances, if the will of the people clashed with the rights of the people, then will should prevail over rights.

Section 33 confers on Parliament and the Provinces the power to declare that legislation which abridges the fundamental freedoms, legal rights and equality rights of Canadians—indeed of all persons situate in Canada—shall operate notwithstanding the provisions which entrench those rights and freedoms in the *Charter*.[28]

The conceptual bifurcation and divorce of individual rights from legislative supremacy was one of the great fallacies in the so-called democracy argument and, but for the historical fact that section 33 was the ransom that had to be paid to the *Charter's* kidnappers lest the captive foetus be stillborn, it is not an article of the Constitution that we should reluctantly embrace and diligently interpret over time. Instead, Section 33 is a blight on our Constitution and we should get rid of it.

There have been many accounts of the events and political machinations behind the deal that gave Canada a *Charter* with a notwithstanding clause[29]—and I need not revisit those events since a number of the participants in this weekend's proceedings were actually there—but one thing about the birth of this override clause should be clearly stated. Both for its opponents and for its proponents it was understood as being antithetical to section 1 and to the idea that rights and freedoms must never be limited except in the service of a liberal state founded on the primacy of those very same rights and freedoms. The notwithstanding clause made a mockery of the whole notion that rights could not be restricted unless the restrictions were justified and defended, explained and accounted for, and not just in political terms.

But our courts have now spent almost twenty years holding governments to account and administering the test that must be passed by governments seeking to limit the rights and freedoms of Canadians. Our Supreme Court has required governments to show that there is a matter of sufficient importance that warrants overriding protected rights and freedoms. It has required Parliament and the Provinces to demonstrate that there is a rational connection between the legislative objective and the limiting measure, that the limiting measure under review impairs the right or freedom at issue as little as possible, and that there is proportionality between the importance and salutary effects of the limiting measure, on the one hand, and the deleterious effect of that limiting measure on the right or freedom at issue, on the other hand.[30]

Having for so long subjected the exercise of state authority to such rigorous standards of review when rights and freedoms were at risk, it is simply unconscionable, at this stage of our political maturity, that we should tolerate, in the name of democracy or regional distinctiveness, the possibility of a constitutionally approved resort to a device which enables our legislatures to unilaterally insulate their laws from scrutiny under Section 1.

The use of the notwithstanding clause in 2002 is the political equivalent of an athlete on performance enhancing steroids in a sport that has not yet banned the use of such drugs. It is simply no longer morally acceptable or even politically defensible to maintain this provision anywhere in the Constitution. We don't need it. It doesn't safeguard democracy or the supremacy of legislatures; it diminishes the integrity and undermines the legitimacy of the institutions that would invoke Section 33 for any purpose.

We already have constitutional doctrines that enable Parliament to act dramatically and decisively in circumstances of national emergency or where the nation's security is in peril.[31] And in developing the Section 1 test, our Supreme Court has demonstrated that the Constitution permits restrictions on rights and freedoms in circumstances in which the state is able to make the case that, while such restrictions provisionally deprive individuals of the full exercise and enjoyment of those rights and freedoms, they are imposed with complete and utter respect for the moral personality of each individual who is required to bear the burden of the limiting measure. This is because Section 1 requires the justification of the limiting measure to be made only once it is determined that a constitutionally protected right has been infringed. The acknowledgement of that infringement, however grudging it may be on the part of the lawyers for the state, is one of the cardinal distinctions between the operation of Section 1 and the invocation of Section 33. For the resort to Section 33, even with its five-year sunset clause, amounts to a denial, however provisional it may be, of the very existence of the rights and freedoms that are expressly overridden.

Many will insist, nonetheless, that it is naïve, if not just politically foolhardy, to speak seriously about constitutional reform at this time in our nation's history. After all, Quebec separatism is on the wane and talk of removing Section 33 will only raise the nationalist ire of the only province to have regularly invoked it in the name of cultural preservation, if not also political sovereignty. The Constitution does not even figure on the radar screen of public opinion at this time. Talk about the Constitution is divisive, detrimental to national unity, they will say, and, frankly, it is one of those issues that is just too abstract to sell on page one of the next Liberal Party Red Book.

Yet there are few issues of principle that should never be permitted to drop off the page of any truly liberal policy agenda— even if it is just to say: "This is what we stand for. If the country isn't "ready" for reform today, we will come back to this soon, once we have made the case more adequately, once we have earned the trust and gained the support of our compatriots in the West and in Quebec." And to those who say that this position is condescending to or dismissive of the "regions," I say that we are nation-building and Section 33 does not enhance the uniqueness of the regions, it divides and fragments the nation. A strong nation in which no government can establish "freedomless" jurisdictions, even provisionally, need not be one that is hostile to the regions or to the project of preserving and promoting diversity "distinctness."

Once Canadians understand that we are demonstrating the profoundest and highest respect for their individuality and their equal moral personality, once we show them that this enhances the quality of their citizenship and boosts the esteem in which their political institutions and leaders hold them, we will have little difficulty talking over the heads of the demagogues in democrats' clothes who are most inconvenienced by freedom's supremacy and who purport to speak for "ordinary Canadians."[32]

As the philosopher John Rawls argued in his seminal treatise on justice, certain matters are simply not within the government's competence as defined by a "just constitution."[33] In light of the true majesty of the text of Section 1 of the *Charter* and of the heroic work that our Supreme Court has done to give full effect to the intention of that text, we must surely be convinced that democracy in Canada has reached a level of maturity that makes the continued existence on our books of Section 33 seem silly and unnecessary at best and absolutely patronizing, insulting and disrespectful of our equality as moral persons at worst.

Therefore, let us work towards a consensus among "extraordinary Canadians" on the imperative of repealing Section 33 of the *Constitution Act, 1982*. We are surely now mature enough to acknowledge what we knew at the time of the Patriation of the Constitution, that the complete abrogation of rights and freedoms that is contemplated in Section 33 is simply not within the competence of our governments as defined by a just and truly liberal constitution.

3) Reconsidering the HR Revolution – Giving People the Freedom to Speak Again!

We have done an admirable job - though not a perfect one by any means—of reversing the tide of sexism, racism and discrimination in the workplace and in our society. Let me not be taken to mean that these scourges are not still with us. But we can be proud of the fact that we have made a concerted effort to educate each other about the pernicious nature and effects of these ills. In so doing, we have sought to make our workplaces environments in which, for the most part, people of all races, religions, ethnic backgrounds, genders, and sexual orientations and people with various disabilities and special needs and challenges can come to work knowing that their differences and particularities must not make them especially vulnerable to abuse and must not disadvantage them in matters concerning their security of tenure, their opportunities for advancement and the quality of their work environment. People understand that there are laws which protect them against abuse, and discrimination and they understand that there are recourses available to victims of such mistreatment and adverse consequences for those who commit the impugned acts.

Walk through the warehouse, the mailroom, the offices, the coffee stations and the washrooms of most workplaces and there is a good chance that you will see, posted on the wall right next to the fire safety and emergency procedures and the workers' compensation accident reporting procedures, a copy of the sexual harassment policy or the employee code of conduct. Increasingly, employers are producing employee handbooks and policy manuals containing elaborate policies and directives with respect to behaviour in the workplace. These policies tend to go far beyond a restatement of the basic principles of non-discrimination set out in our human rights legislation. They tend to be proactive in the extreme, sometimes even anticipating every imaginable scenario in which some employee might be made to feel uncomfortable, offended, insulted, embarrassed or otherwise inconvenienced. Some workplaces even have policies purporting to govern and restrict the sorts of relationships fellow employees are permitted to engage in with one another—even on their own time.

The HR Revolution to which I refer is not the "Human Rights" revolution, though that is the *sine qua non* of the revolution in question. It is what I refer to as the "Human Resources" revolution that followed and that was itself spawned by the human rights revolution. This is the HR Revolution that should be great cause for concern and that, in my submission, offers one of the most instructive examples of the power of the laws to both "educate the citizen in the common good, and persuade him to behave in the public interest" and also to discourage genuine discourse. It offers an example of that power of the laws gone awry. The HR Revolution took its cue from our human rights laws. But then, in an atmosphere of fear and paranoia—nudged on by U.S. court decisions awarding millions of dollars in damages to complainants whose bosses had taken quite inappropriate liberties with them—anticipating litigation and human rights complaints at every turn, HR departments began to legislate behaviour in the workplace on a scale and to an extent not expressly required or even contemplated in any of the actual human rights statutes. Dress codes were introduced to proscribe potentially offensive attire; protocols of behaviour and procedures for every conceivable situation in the workplace were developed.

Now the workplace is, indeed, a relatively safe place to be. The glass ceiling, while not yet completely eradicated, is a great deal higher than it had previously been. The demographics of the average workplace scream "diversity" in every way. And individuals are far less frequently singled out for unfair or discriminatory treatment by virtue only of their distinguishing particularities.

But this HR Revolution has claimed its own victims: Individual self-expression and political discourse. The culture of compliance and docility in the workplace, where most Canadians spend the better part of their waking hours, has now trickled out into our homes, our streets and our legislatures. The "right to be heard," that sacred legal principle of procedural fairness, while still very much alive in our courts and tribunals, has not been reinforced elsewhere because its political counterpart, the "freedom to speak" together with the liberal psychological ideal, namely, the craving urge to criticize, have been neutered in the workplace, mainly by provincial human rights laws. These laws, whether by design or by effect, have virtually legislated the bounds of acceptable speech. "Mainstream" public political discourse has been reduced absolutely and unquestionably to two basic social and political imperatives:

"Always say the right thing. But whatever you do, never say the wrong thing."

Without going to the texts of the statutes, one need only peruse sections 3(1) of the *Alberta Human Rights, Citizenship and Multiculturalism Act* and 14(1) of the *Saskatchewan Human Rights Code* for representative examples of laws that prohibit speech which might offend or which are "likely to expose persons to hatred or contempt" or which "tend[s] to expose to hatred, ridicules, belittles or otherwise affronts the dignity of any person" based on an enumerated ground of discrimination.[34]

While we must not confuse the human rights revolution with its misguided offspring, the HR Revolution, neither should we confuse it with its natural parent, the civil liberties revolution—which got started sometime between Locke and Trudeau, depending on who you ask. While this may not be the place to offer explanations for the evolution and mutation of laws designed to recognize and protect the moral personality of free citizens everywhere, one thing needs to be made absolutely clear because it is at the heart of the argument here today: The HR Revolution, as well-intentioned as it may once have been, was terribly misguided and became the enemy of civil liberties everywhere, and, therefore, of a liberal society.

What is the relation of the legislated political correctness in our workplaces to the rules that govern political debate elsewhere? It is simply that we have been educated by the laws to be docile, to be quiet, inoffensive, without opinion or conviction on matters of *gravitas*. The expression, in the workplace, of strongly held views on issues of public concern are not merely a matter of "bad form," they verge on being downright unlawful—or so one might be forgiven for believing. We have surely all witnessed—and participated in—the heated and passionate debates amongst our colleagues over whether the Leafs ought to have pulled their goalie in the dying minutes of the game, or whether Britney shouldn't have slept with Jake on Survivor before first giving Lance back the engagement ring he almost died acquiring while doing a guest appearance on Fear Factor. These sorts of angst-filled discussions are perfectly acceptable in the office or on the shop floor. Why? It is because they are of no social or political consequence. It is because they just don't matter.

But watch icicles form in nano-seconds when someone attempts to talk about something that really does matter. The response to a serious statement about "the human condition," the "state of the nation" or world affairs, which I submit is absolutely a conditioned one—i.e., conditioned by our legal culture—typically ranges from bewilderment and bemusement to plain outrage. Politics is just off-limits altogether in the workplace. People have been chastised and disciplined for talking politics in the shop.

And the consequences of talking politics outside the shop are often even graver.

"9/11" certainly hasn't helped matters one bit either. After 9/11 it has, in some circles, effectively become illegal to express certain thoughts and views, even in the most reticent and equivocal manner. Readers are directed back to the text of the *Anti-terrorism Act*.

When our Prime Minister is lambasted in Parliament for having made a fairly tame and not particularly earth-shattering public pronouncement on the possible connections between terrorism and unconscionable disparities between wealthy and desperately impoverished nations, we can see, first hand, why true liberalism is in need of rescuing. I submit that the distance between the legislated intellectual docility of the workplace and the extreme intolerance for free expression of new and diverse ideas and opinions in our "public squares" and legislative assemblies is a short one.

The first thing we can do about this is to acknowledge the phenomenon. Next, we can agree that this is a real problem for a political tradition whose principal virtue is that it, more than any other tradition, views the state as the product of the "general will" in a way in which the "individual will" finds its fullest expression— yet another paradox of liberalism. And when we bring this home to the Canadian polity, we can see that the political parties that don't identify with the "liberal" brand don't have the same problems that Liberals have. They don't have liberalism's problems because they don't have the Liberal Party's opportunities. It is a real struggle to remain relevant; and one achieves this not by ramming a pre-packaged and out-dated ideology down the collective throat of an already disengaged and weary public. One does it by waking everybody up and inviting them to think for themselves and to talk— out loud—about what they believe. One invites them to ask questions and to suggest answers, explanations and solutions without fear of ridicule or reprisal.

The NDP hovers on the precipice of irrelevancy in this country— although it is now embarking on its own process of renewal and revitalization—because it has remained the voice of a now almost outmoded political correctness, and the voice of a very limited constituency, while failing to offer fresh solutions to the problems of that constituency. The hackneyed call for increased entitlements and more radical distribution of wealth, while perfectly legitimate as part of a more complex approach to the problems of inequality and disadvantage in our society, has not alone empowered enough people—instead it has only romanticized their perpetual victimization—and has not been heard as a siren call for citizens to become more engaged in the public life of their community.

The parties on the "right" have been self-destructing for some time, but that silliness will not last much longer. And once the "right unites," the challenge will become more obvious: What do liberals have to offer that conservatives don't? Liberalism. Given the current state of political discourse in the suites and in the streets, in the offices and in our House of Commons, liberals and Liberals alike must nod their heads in disappointment, take a look around and then recognize that they can have the entire field to themselves, if only they understand that they must earn it by giving Canadians the freedom—indeed, the will—to speak again...everywhere.

The human rights revolution has been a good thing and we would not choose to forsake it regardless of its unhappy by-products, principally the HR Revolution. But we must now acknowledge and deal with the HR Revolution and reverse its life-sapping effect on the body politic. For just as the laws have had the effect, even if unintended, of stifling public discourse, they can equally serve to revitalize discussion and debate.

A commitment to living in an authentically liberal state requires of us that we adopt the liberal attitude to our laws and to our legal culture. The reforms that I have proposed herein and that I suggest should be part of an agenda for Canada in the coming months and years are liberal measures. Canadians must strive to work together to identify and fashion the most suitable means to these fundamentally liberal ends.

If, as a celebrated Canadian Prime Minister once said, to be a citizen of Canada is to be a citizen of the world, then, in an era of global engagement when internationalism and multilateralism are being challenged by the unilateralism of the "hyperpower"[35] immediately to the south, what is really at stake here is the quality of world citizenship.

Notes:

1   *Approaches to Politics* (Toronto: Oxford University Press, 1970), p. 50; from the essay, "A State Made to Measure" which appeared in French in 1958 in a collection of Trudeau's essays published by Jacques Hébert in the journal *Vrai* under the title *Les Cheminements de la politique.*

2   The subject of legal aid is deserving of its own conference and volume devoted exclusively to the issues surrounding access to justice. Especially in a liberal democracy, legal aid needs to be explained and understood not merely as a socialized legal defence fund, in criminal cases, or socialized family assistance, in civil family cases, but as a means to convert alienated cynics into citizens. In a pluralist society in which the law and legal institutions purport to recognize the equal moral personality of each individual, the ability to advance one's interests before the courts and other public and

private tribunals must be a fully realizable right. In a report of the Canadian Bar Association entitled, *Making the Case: The Right to Publicly-Funded Legal Representation in Canada*, (Ottawa: CBA, February, 2002), the argument for a constitutional right to legal aid is explored in some depth. The CBA has itself made the legal aid brief one of its major priorities. The CBA argues that legal aid is an essential feature of Canadian democracy, that it is required, though not expressly, by the *Charter*, that it is promised in Canada's international commitments, that it is intrinsic to the rule of law. It has called on the federal government to take four main steps to ensure national equity in legal aid: increase its financial contribution to criminal and civil legal aid, lead in negotiations of national standards for legal aid, enact federal legislation on essential legal services, create a national civil legal aid tariff. (www.cba.org/CBA/Advocacy/legalAidAdvocacyResourcekit) We need to support all of these measures. But it is also vital to make the case for legal aid in terms of law, *qua* engine of citizen self-actualization. In her presentation at this conference, Sherri Torjman spoke of "citizen engagement." This must be the ideal, the goal of social justice reform. It is essential that legal aid be understood not merely as a social program for those needing the assistance of the state to protect their own vital interests, but also as a proud institution which has the mandate of demonstrating to otherwise disadvantaged and disengaged members of society that the machinery of the state can actually work for them. It affords individuals the opportunity to actively participate in the workings of the state not merely as subjects of a gigantic and anonymous *Leviathan*. As people are afforded the ability to interact with their fellow citizens and with the state through the medium of an accessible and responsive justice system, they inevitably feel more empowered, less alienated from government— from "the system"—and feel less excluded from participation in the political process. That is, at the very least, one of the working assumptions of theorists of participatory democracy.

We must, in any event, acknowledge that the entire legal aid system is in crisis. Witness the rash of recent "Fisher Applications" which have sought orders compelling the Attorney General to fund legal aid retainers at rates substantially above the current limits set by legal aid. Even when legal aid certificates have been granted, they are frequently refused by lawyers who simply cannot reasonably be expected to provide proper representation at the fixed rates. See both David Gambrill's article, "The floodgate's open," 13 *Law Times*, (Sept. 16, 2002) 1 and Cristin Schmitz's "Trial judges order Crown to pay premiums above current Ontario legal aid rates," 22 *The Lawyers Weekly*, (Sept. 20, 2002) 1. Note the most recent uproar over the Ontario Government's decision to resort to duty counsel and the much criticized public defender system in lieu of a properly funded legal aid system in which individuals would have the right to be represented by counsel of their own choosing. This crisis will not go away. It must be understood as a "social justice" issue—akin to health care —which will require a substantial commitment of funds on the part of both provincial and federal governments.

3   See Reg Whitaker, "Apprehended Insurrection? RCMP intelligence and the October Crisis," *Queen's Quarterly* 100:2 (Summer 1993) pp. 383-406.

4   The subsequent use by a succession of Quebec governments of the *notwithstanding clause* (s.33 of the *Constitution Act, 1982*) in the service of that nationalism certainly calls into question the legitimacy of those institutions and the quality of their democracy. This is the subject of the next section of the paper.

5   The Trudeau government's proclamation into force of the *War Measures Act* in October 1970 has largely been seen to be nothing short of a "remarkable suspension of civil

liberties," which would not have been justified on the basis only of the true nature and extent of the threat posed by the "ill-organized FLQ, which could not actually have mounted an insurrection". See Peter Hogg, *Constitutional Law of Canada*, (Toronto: Carswell, 1977) p. 253. The same passage appears in the subsequent editions of Hogg's opus.

6   *Bill C-36 - An Act to amend the Criminal Code, the Official Secrets Act, the Canada Evidence Act, the Proceeds of Crime (Money Laundering) Act and other Acts, and to enact measures respecting the registration of charities, in order to combat terrorism.* (S.C. 2001, c.41)

7   Among the most compelling submissions were those of The British Columbia Civil Liberties Association (November 7, 2001), the Canadian Bar Association (October 2001), and the Canadian Jewish Congress (November 6, 2001).

8   Professor Irwin Cotler, M.P. in particular, has managed to be all of these things.

9   Irwin Cotler, "Thinking Outside the Box: Foundational Principles for a Counter-Terrorism Law and Policy" in R.J. Daniels, P. Macklem and K. Roach eds., *The Security of Freedom: Essays on Canada's Anti-Terrorism Bill,* (Toronto: University of Toronto Press, 2001) at 111; Cotler, "Constitutional Democracy: Balancing Security and Civil Liberties, CIAJ Conference, *Terrorism, Law and Democracy: How Is Canada Changing Following September 11th,* (Montreal: March 25-26, 2002); Don Stuart, "The Anti-Terrorism Bill C-36: An Unnecessary Law and Order Quick Fix that Permanently Stains the Canadian Criminal Justice System," CIAJ Conference, *Ibid.*; Errol Mendes, "Between Crime and War: Terrorism, Democracy and the Constitution," CIAJ Conference, *Ibid.*; Sujit Choudhry, "Protecting Equality in the Face of Terror: Ethnic and Racial Profiling and s.25 of the Charter," in *The Security of Freedom supra*; Bnai' Brith Canada's report on Bill C-36 (November 6, 2001).

10 From the preamble to the statute. It is perhaps worth noting that the drafters have sought refuge, rightly, in the jurisdictional haven of the "national concern" branch of the Peace, Order and Good Government (P.O.G.G.) power in s. 91 of the Constitution Act, 1867.

11 The first recital in the preamble is, in a way, even more powerful, for it acknowledges the right of all people to "live their lives in peace, freedom and security."

12 This "Backgrounder," which I have paraphrased in places, appeared on DOJ's web-site following the coming into force of the legislation – www.canada.justice.gc.ca/en/ news/nr/2001/doc_28217.html.

13 S. 83.01.

14 See Cotler, "Constitutional Democracy: Balancing Security and Civil Liberties" *supra.*

15 S. 83.3. See Gary Trotter, "The Anti-Terrorism Bill and Preventative Restraints on Liberty," in *The Security of Freedom, supra* at p. 240.

18 Ss. 83.1 and 83.11.

19 Ss. 83.1 and 83.28.

20 Ss. 83.28, 83.29 and 83.32.

21 S.145.

22 S. 83.31.

23 "CBA Calls for Tighter Definition of Terrorism, True Sunset Clause in Bill C-36," (October 31, 2001)

24 The CBA has recommended that the "sunset clause" apply not only to the power of preventive arrest, but also to the listing of entities provisions, the wiretap authorization provisions, the provisions pertaining to the *Access to Information* and the *Privacy Act,* and the provisions pertaining to the non-disclosure of evidence against a person or entity. CBA Release (December 6, 2001). I would also

insist on extending it to the provisions dealing with freezing, seizing and forfeiture of property.

25   It was perhaps only for one brief shining moment that this doctrine was given its due, and even then, its champions, Abbott and Rand JJ. gave expression to the doctrine only in *obiter*. The case was *Switzman v. Elbling*, [1957] S.C.R. 285.

26   The seminal case is *R. v. Oakes*, [1986] 1 S.C.R. 103, with an important refinement to the proportionality test coming later in *Dagenais v. CBC*, [1994] 3 S.C.R. 835.

27   Section 1: "The *Canadian Charter of Rights and Freedoms* guarantees the rights and freedoms set out in it subject only to such reasonable limits prescribed by laws as can be demonstrably justified in a free and democratic society."

28   The fundamental freedoms are set out in s. 2 and include freedom of conscience and religion, of thought, opinion and expression, of assembly and of association. The legal rights set out in ss. 7-14 include the right to life, liberty and security of the person as well as all of the most sacrosanct procedural protections that underpin all civilized notions of the rule of law and all liberal criminal justice and law enforcement systems. The equality rights set out in s.15 have been the subject of numerous critically important judicial decisions; they have been at the core of a substantial number of social reforms and have, perhaps more than any other aspect of the *Charter*, influenced not only law-making in this country, but also—for better or for worse—the conceptual framework in which we think and speak about rights.

29   Stephen Clarkson and Christina McCall compellingly describe these events leading up to the Faustian bargain in *Trudeau And Our Times - Vol. 1: The Magnificent Obsession* (Toronto: McClelland and Stewart, 1990), pp. 357-386.

30   This is but a crude synopsis of the marvellously crafted test that has been painstakingly worked out in *Oakes* and later refined in *Dagenais* and other cases.

31   For example, section 91 of the *Constitution Act, 1867* gives Parliament the power "to make Laws for the Peace, Order, and Good Government of Canada," and the courts have developed a "national concern" and an "emergency" branch of the POGG power.

32   If we would only stop talking about and making a virtue of "ordinary Canadians" and start convincing each and every Canadian just how EXTRAORDINARY he or she truly is or can become, maybe we might be able to elevate the level and quality of political discourse in this country. Let the NDP keep talking to and about "ordinary Canadians." We need to start treating people with greater respect for their extraordinary

33   I refer to Rawls' first edition of *A Theory Of Justice* (Cambridge, Mass.: Harvard University Press, 1971), in which the original thesis was first published in one comprehensive volume. It would be foolhardy to purport to summarize the argument or to identify the one passage which can be singled out as authority for the proposition asserted above. The text of *A Theory Of Justice* is replete with references to a "just constitution," including on page 212 of the edition cited herein, in which Rawls states that "the government has no authority to render associations legitimate or illegitimate any more than it has authority in regard to art or science. These matters are not within its competence as defined by a just constitution." This follows a chapter in which Rawls discusses the priority of liberty in the context of freedom of conscience, explaining that the reasoning here can be generalized to apply to other freedoms. There can, Rawls posits, be no compromise of one's religious, moral or philosophical interests unless there is no alternative. See Rawls' discussion of this in the context of his "original position" at p. 206. Perhaps no thinker in modern times has more comprehensively and systematically worked out a theory of rights and social justice ("liberal" or otherwise).

34   These provisions were cited a few years ago (with reference to corresponding statutes

then in effect) in a bold newspaper editorial entitled "Give Free Speech A Very Long Leash—The law always protected offensive speech until human-rights codes came along." *The Globe and Mail*, (January 15, 1999).

35   This description of the United States appears in Thomas Axworthy's essay in this volume, "A Choice, Not an Echo: Sharing North America With The Hyperpower."

Health Care
and the Search for New Liberalism in Canada

Antonia Maioni

LIBERALISM IS NOT *so much a party creed or set of fixed platform promises as it is an attitude of mind and heart, a faith in man's (sic) ability through the experiences of his reason and judgment to increase for himself and his fellow men the amount of justice and freedom and brotherhood which all human life deserves...The only basic issue... is whether our government will fall in a conservative rut and die there, or whether we will move ahead in the liberal spirit of daring, of breaking new ground."*[1]

John F. Kennedy, 1960

Liberalism stands for the middle way: the way of progress. It stands for moderation, tolerance, and the rejection of extreme courses, whether they express themselves in demands that the state should do everything for the individual, even if it means weakening and destroying him in the process, or in demands that the state should do nothing except hold the ring so that the fittest survive under the law of the jungle ... In other words, Liberalism accepts social security but rejects socialism; it accepts free enterprise but rejects economic anarchy; it accepts humanitarianism but rejects paternalism.[2]

Lester B. Pearson, 1962

Recent events in the development of Canadian health care are a cautionary tale for those who believe in the public system: however much one believes in the effectiveness and viability of the Canadian public model, health care cannot be considered an immutable "sacred trust" that the Canadian public will continue to support at any cost. Basically, if health care systems do not deliver on promises and address dissatisfaction about the quality of care, and—just as importantly—if political leaders do not succeed in establishing confidence in the public model's ability to meet future needs, then supporters of alternative visions are likely to become much more vocal and powerful in advocating change, however far from existing principles that such change may seem.

This paper looks at health care and the new liberalism through three lenses. First, I raise the issue of a Canadian paradox in Canadian public opinion, between support for the health care system and the perception of crisis and anxiety about its future. Second, I look at the interplay between ideas and institutions in the politics of health care reform in Canada, past and present; and third, I offer some reflections on the new liberalism's challenge in renewing a commitment to the public model in Canadian health care.

The Context of a Canadian Paradox

The pressures on health care in Canada are well-documented : the transformation of health care delivery systems for both routine and chronic conditions; advancements in technology in the treatment of specific conditions; demographic pressures, particularly those associated with aging populations, although the jury is still out about the true costs of an aging population; the pressures related to costs, including the rising use and costs of prescription drugs; and concerns about inequality in and access to quality health care services.

But talk of the "crisis" in health care also refers to the challenges governments face in restricting public sector spending and in the intergovernmental squabbles over fiscal balance and imbalances. There is considerable debate over whether health care costs are really soaring out of control or not in this country, and the extent to which publicly-financed services are more or less efficient in the delivery of health care. Increasingly, there are signs that the fiscal capacity—and the political will—of governments to carry on the responsibility for health care is being sorely tested.

In light of this situation, there has emerged, I would argue, a Canadian paradox: on the one hand, there exists considerable support for the broad principles of public health insurance—generalized support for the modern liberal tenets of equality, redistribution of wealth, solidarity and universalism broadly stated—and the system is often hailed as a constitutive part of the country's identity. Indeed, this summer, an Environics poll revealed that the highest numbers of Canadians—fully 46%—considered the advent of public health insurance as the most important event in the 20th Canadian experience. In addition, in survey after survey, the vast majority of Canadians claim that they are satisfied with the care they or their family actually receive, and only a small minority would readily trade their current system with, for example, a predominantly private-insurance US model.

But on the other side of the story, the growing concerns about the problems in health care delivery and financing have led many Canadians to question the fundamentals of the system. The principles of the Canada Health Act for example, while still solidly entrenched in the public's psyche, may be losing some ground (Table 1).[3] In addition, measures of satisfaction with the way the federal and provincial governments are handling health care show a clear deterioration of approval, starting gradually in the 1980's and accentuating throughout the 1990's. From the mid-1990's onward, a majority expressed dissatisfaction toward both levels of government. Although the approval of federal action is slightly higher, the difference is small and the trend is just as clearly negative. Indeed, given that provincial governments have carried most of the burden of budget cuts and other unpopular measures through the 1990's, a wider gap might have been expected.

More startling is the widespread perception of the health care system in crisis. A recent Environics poll has found that 67% of Canadians agreed with the statement that "the health care system is in a state of crisis." For the sake of comparison, a matching question in the United States found that 63% of Americans perceived the US health care system to be in crisis.[4] The data for Canada holds constant across age, gender, and socio-economic status; the most interesting divergences are found in regional attitudes. Respondents in Quebec and British Columbia were the most negative in their perception of crisis; respondents in Ontario and Alberta were, relatively speaking, less negative.

A statistical fluke? On the contrary. This data confirms resilient trends that have been developing for some time. In the US, this generalized unease has been constant for at least the past decade.Iin Canada, meanwhile, opinion trends reveal a dramatic fall in satisfaction with the health care system in recent years. A most telling example of the decline in public confidence in the Canadian healthcare model can be gleaned from cross-national studies conducted by the Commonwealth Fund. In 1988, 43% of Canadians thought that their system had major or fundamental flaws; last year, this number had swelled to 77%. Only 5% of Canadians then thought the system had to be completely overhauled; today, almost a quarter of Canadians are willing to see the system rebuilt from the ground up.[5]

Are these perceptions justified? That is debatable. The media makes much of health care system shortcomings. Hardly a week passes without media reports of major problems with the health care system in Canada—from emergency rooms that cannot cope with patient demand to reports about overstressed health care workers, not to mention the constant haggling between federal and provincial governments over who should foot the ever-increasing bills for the publicly funded system.

Amidst this general mood of pessimism, optimists rightly point out that Canada' universal medicare system produces enviable outcomes in terms of the overall health of the population, including a slightly higher life expectancy and lower infant mortality rates—all this at a fraction of the cost of the U.S. system (9% of GDP in Canada, compared to 14% in the U.S). While the Canadian health care model has been relatively successful at controlling costs and providing quality care, there have been trade-offs. Waiting lists, particularly for specialized care, have become a major concern among Canadians. A recent Statistics Canada study based on a survey of 14,000 respondents shows that 18% of the 23 million Canadians who used health services in 2001 experienced difficulties with access. As a proportion of the whole population, 11% claimed that some of their needs had remained unfulfilled, mostly because of the length of waiting lists or the unavailability of some services in some places.[6]

Does this perception of crisis, real or exaggerated, matter? Absolutely, and policy-makers ignore it at their peril. To be sure, the observation that two-thirds of Canadians perceive a crisis in health care does not mean that as many would support privatization of health care financing, for example. In fact, it has been well documented, in particular in POLLARA surveys, that opinion on user fees and privatization remains divided.[7] Nonetheless, there is a cognitive dissonance between the values underpinning universal health care in Canada, and the narrow rhetoric on both sides of the public debate over health care, from that of markets and managerialism, and from some political elites to those who see the Canada Health Act as the Ten Commandments that cannot be touched.

The perception of crisis is important for at least two reasons: first, we know that opinions on major policy issues tend to be coherently structured around core beliefs upon which citizens can rely to form a coherent opinion about complex issues, even if they are far from completely informed.[8] Second, we should remember that opinions about core issues such as health care are shaped not only by people's perception of the current situation but, more importantly, by their view of how the system will respond to future needs. While Canadians are not so disillusioned that they are willing to try *anything* to remedy the situation, they may become increasingly open to alternative solutions, even if they seem to contradict the underlying principles of the public model.

Where do these perceptions come from and why have they changed so rapidly over such a relatively short period of time? We know that the relationship between opinion and policy is not linear; the way in which preferences affect policy will depend on a number of factors. In fact, the historical development and institutionalization of existing policies may create their own parameters that can constrain policy-makers responses in terms of the range of feasible choices and the extent of change: for example, the expectations raised and popular support enjoyed by universal, or "middle-class", benefits such as health insurance. As such, politicians may be loath to pay the political price—in opinion polls and at the voting booth—associated with dismantling popular social programs. But this reasoning may underestimate the capacity of the public to perceive crisis situations in existing policy models and to seek alternative solutions: the presence and relative power of viable alternatives are crucial elements in setting the policy-making agenda. In the last decade there has been no shortage of signals from the policy community, interest groups, elite opinion leaders, and the media pointing to a crisis situation in health care.

A review of newspaper editorial coverage of health care issues over the last decade shows two trends.[9] The first is the simple—yet significant—fact that the volume and depth of coverage and analysis of health care issues has increased, as anyone who has been even moderately attentive to the news would easily ascertain. The second—and perhaps more portentous—trend is the way in which the health care system has been subjected to a barrage of criticism by opinion leaders, and how alternatives to the existing system have appeared on the radar screen of public debate. In addition, a keyword count of articles on health care in the past decade shows a heady increase in the use of the word "crisis" to describe the health care system and its woes.[10]

The Significance of Health Care in New Liberalism

Why is the health care story significant in the quest for a new liberalism? Modern liberalism in Canada was born in the post-war reconstruction period and reinforced the idea that governments were responsible for reconstructing a post-war order that would extend beyond physical defence to an essential role in securing freedom and opportunity through social programs. This modern liberal ideal is embedded in Canadian health care policies. Health care is regulated as a "public good" and governments have a role to play in ensuring that this good is available to all citizens.

In many ways, health care defines the relationship between state and society, between governments and citizens, in Canada. The impact of service provision in promoting citizenship regimes and the tensions inherent in sustaining the commitments to such provision are evident in most modern welfare states. In the Canadian experience, health care has been heralded as a singular achievement of what states and citizens can do best together: effecting regulation and pooling resources in an effort to ensure health care provision based on need rather than ability to pay. Because Canada is a federal polity, the "success" of health care policy can also be considered an example of how decentralized governance can coexist with the promotion of a shared sense of national identity. Some would say the design of health care in Canada also reflects a commitment to collective responsibility and to the bonds of community in a diverse society.

Health care represents perhaps the most important example of the way in which service provision by governments can enhance citizenship and state legitimacy. Through its involvement in health care, the modern state takes on a crucial role in social protection in the sense of literally "protecting" its citizens from the effects of ill health. In helping to finance the provision of health care services, governments offset the potentially catastrophic costs associated with illness. In regulating the health care sector, governments shape the rules of the fundamental relationship between providers and patients. In essence, involvement in health care represents a way in which the state can help establish the boundaries of social consensus and mutual rights and responsibilities between citizens.[11]

But health care places an enormous responsibility on the modern state, one that many governments are finding difficult to sustain. Precisely because health care is so important—the most personal in its impact, the most frequently used by individuals and families—it is also the sector in which governments are most vulnerable to the effects of citizen involvement, participation and feedback. Because health care is a service provided by highly specialized professionals in increasingly complex technological and administrative settings, the linkage—and accountability—between state and citizen is often less than transparent. And because health, in effect, has no real "price" in terms of supply and demand patterns associated with typical consumer goods, governments are attempting to regulate an industry for which the inflationary potential is practically limitless, thus putting enormous pressure on state treasuries even in heavily regulated health care systems and opening avenues for lucrative private-sector alternatives.[12] Another reason that the health care story is relevant for the new liberalism is that it offers a telling history of the interplay between ideas and institutions in Canadian political life, and the way in which political change can happen.[13] In terms of ideas, it is important to remember that it did, in effect, take a long time to achieve a consensus around the public model in Canada. and that this consensus is not immutable to change or to challenge. The ideas embedded in the

Canadian model were developed by social forces and political parties infused by progressive platforms of the left and centre-left that no longer have the same resonance and vibrancy in Canadian political debate. Remember Port Hope, circa 1933? Mackenzie King was not convinced of social-democracy, or even US-style New Deal liberalism, but he could not risk alienating the progressive wing of his party or the public. Later, reformist elements in the Liberal party (such as Paul Martin, Sr.) were able to keep the health care agenda alive in part through the recognition of the left-wing presence in federal and provincial politics. Remember Kingston, circa 1960? The Kingston conference was geared to expanding the party base and building a new progressive policy, including support for health insurance. Pearson later recalled that, "My desire was to forget about the old party, to stop looking to the past...We could no longer be successful unless we were a truly liberal party, progressive enough to attract people who might otherwise turn to the New Democratic Party."[14]

It is still the case, as in the past, that policy change is more difficult in the US because of the configuration of political institutions: Bill Clinton learned to his chagrin what Harry Truman had experienced forty years ago—the separation of powers and the plethora of veto points for powerful interests groups makes major policy change difficult.[15] In Canada, governments have been better able in a parliamentary system to legislate change when the political will was available to do so. Even though health care legislation was a long time coming in Canada, and subject to considerable party infighting, it was possible to introduce and implement important initiatives. But that same political will can potentially be used to change the existing system, whether in Ottawa or in the provinces.

Federalism is the other significant institution shaping health policy in Canada. In constitutional terms provinces have primary jurisdiction over health care matters, and provinces have continually served as laboratories of innovation in the past and continue to do so today. Today, however, it is not a relatively less well off province with a social-democratic government, like Saskatchewan, nor a government pushing the state into modernity, as in Quebec, that are at the forefront of change in health care. It is not insignificant to note that the solutions being touted as "innovative" today are emanating from richer provinces under more fiscally conservative governments with health reform agendas that are based on stretching the flexibility of the public model to perhaps a breaking point. Part of this tension stems from the fact that the public health care model that developed in Canada was based on the understanding that provinces would organize and implement, but that the costs of the health care system would be shared between the provinces and the federal government. To ensure consistent standards, the federal government eventually legislated the Canada Health Act in 1984, which sets out certain conditions to which provincial governments must adhere—in their own way—in order to receive federal money: universality, comprehensiveness, equal access, portability, and public administration. But, like most incentives, this arrangement was predicated on what economists like to refer to as the "golden rule." The Canada Health Act is a statute, not a constitutional provision. It can only function if the means are there to do so. Those who see the Canada Health Act as the beacon for stability are reminded that without a sustained deep fiscal and political commitment attached to the principles it is designed to protect, the Canada Health Act is not a powerful rampart.

Health Care and the Search for Direction

Specific prescriptions for health care reform are emanating from provincial commissions of inquiry and the Royal Commission on the Future of Health Care in Canada. What does all this mean in term of the relationship between health care and the new liberalism? There are two main points to remember about health care in this search for the new liberalism; or, alternatively, there are two main points about new liberalism that can infuse the search for health reform in Canada.

The first is the recognition that, even though the contours of the public model of health care remain in place, the playing field of health care politics has changed irrevocably. The problems associated with health care delivery and financing in Canada are not short-lived concerns that have a magic bullet—or magic pill—solution. The scope of the policy debate has widened considerably, more and new voices are being expressed, and the public is being tuned into both the problems of the existing health care model and alternatives for its reform.

In this context, the challenge of the new liberalism is to be attentive to the public voice. This does not mean pandering to the polls

—or to the pollsters. But nor does it mean ignoring the signals that reveal both a commitment to and anxiety about the long-term viability of the public health care model. The public is not, on the whole, irrational or incoherent in their opinions about health care. The new liberalism should understand and respect that the public is uneasy—and at times confused—for specific reasons. Canadians who come into contact with the health care system may be satisfied (in retrospect), but discontent tends to be driven by a perception of overall crisis in the future (prospective concerns). And in fact, it is precisely these measures of anxiety toward the care that an individual expects to receive in the future that most strongly correlate with the perceived need for major change in the system, and this has a clear effect on their assessment of the need for change.

The new liberalism also has to work toward articulating health care as a public rather than consumer good. In many ways, the Canadian health care model reflects much of the liberal tradition in Canada, and is a crucial element in shaping and maintaining beliefs about social justice in Canada. Unlike other social conditions, and despite the environmental and social factors that shape health outcomes, health is the great equalizer with which most everyone can empathize. Chronic problems or life-threatening accidents can strike anyone, anywhere, anytime. The sense of otherness or distance that can affect perceptions of other social issues—such as poverty or homelessness, for example—are much more muted when it comes to health.[16]

If the new liberalism includes a vision of health care as a public good, it will have to work towards defending that vision for the future. It must capture and express the reasons why governments are important in health care and it must renew confidence in the public system. In other words, this means reconciling what people are saying—that they consider health care important, that they consider the public model worthwhile—with what can be achieved to realize these goals. Part of that task involves disengaging in demagoguery and instead opening up broad discussions, evaluating needs and priorities, exploring feasible alternatives, and helping the public engage in an informed debate about feasible choices. There are relatively large bodies of evidence to suggest that public health care systems do better in providing care and controlling costs, that health care systems focused on preventive and integrated care work better in keeping populations healthy. In that sense, the new liberalism should be able to express the idea that governments should not abdicate their role in ensuring equal opportunity in health care, that the real challenge is to adapt rather than abandon the public model.

The second challenge for the new liberalism is to really understand what the middle way, or progressive way as Pearson puts it, really means. The middle way may seem like a safe place but it is ultimately a dangerous one, since it is easy to get run over in the middle of the road. Or, worse still, to become irrelevant or blurred in the muddle of ideological sparring. To that end, the new liberalism has to commit to the real root of its name: "liberare" or to liberate. Liberalism's true function, throughout history and across political systems, has been to push the boundaries of the "liberation" of the human condition toward freedom and equality. In contrast, "conservatism" has been concerned with "conservare" or preserving traditional social and economic hierarchies. What the new liberalism must do is to redefine what "new" ideas really are, to build on the convictions of existing principles that define liberalism's purpose. The radar screen of health reform debate today is littered with "new" ideas that are not at all new and certainly not progressive, yet they capture public imagination in search of fresh—i.e., different—ideas.

The cognitive dissonance in Canadian political discourse, between a generalized support for the modern liberal tenets of equality, redistribution of wealth, solidarity and universalism broadly stated, and the rhetoric of "new" ideas of markets and managerialism emanating from political elites, has had a profound impact on Canadians' perceptions of and confidence in the public health care model. The Canadian model of health care, as it currently subsists, is not a sacred trust that the public will continue to support at any cost. If the system does not deliver on its promises, if dissatisfaction about the quality of care grows, and there continues to be an erosion of confidence in the system's ability to meet future needs, the public is likely to become much more vocal in advocating change. In such a context, radical departures may be perceived by many as a panacea, and those voices that can successfully ride the wave of public discontent are likely to win the day. The new liberalism, to succeed in a social justice agenda, must have not only the courage of ambition, but also the courage of conviction to harness public imagination and support. This involves giving voice to coherent ideas, articulating reasonable arguments, and delivering the real resources needed to ensure sustainable health care that can ensure loyalty to the public model, and give pause to those who exit towards other alternatives. Without this courage of conviction, change in health care may happen without policy decisions and, more damaging still, without coherent policy direction.

Notes:

[1]   Senator John F. Kennedy, at the acceptance of the New York Liberal Party nomination, September 14, 1960.

[2]   L.B. Pearson, Introduction, in J.W. Pickersgill, *The Liberal Party* (Toronto, 1962)

[3]   Stephen Vail, "Canadians' Values and Attitudes on Canada's Health Care System: A A Synthesis of Survey Results," Report 307-00, The Conference Board of Canada, p.6

[4]   Environics Group, Cross-national Comparison of Poll Results, and Campbell Institute of Public Affairs, Maxwell School of Syracuse University, September 2002.

[5]   Blendon, Robert J. et al. (1990) "Satisfaction with Health Systems in Ten Nations" *Health Affairs*, Vol.11, No.1, pp. 2-10; and Blendon, Robert J. et al. (1999) "The Cost of Health System Change: Public Discontent in Five Nations" *Health Affairs*, Vol.18, No.3, pp. 206-216

[6]   Statistics Canada, Access to Health Care in Canada Survey, July 2002.

[7]   Tracked in Vail, Stephen, "Canadians' Values and Attitudes on Canada's Health Care System: A Synthesis of Survey Results,"; on the Pollara survey and its interpretation, see: Hugh Winsor, "The Power Game: Context Is Everything When Polls Make Policy," *Globe and Mail* (January 17, 2000), p.4

[8]   Benjamin I. Page and Robert Y. Shapiro, *The Rational Public: Fifty Years of Trends in Americans' Policy Preferences* (Chicago: University of Chicago Press, 1992)

[9]   Research in progress; the newspapers surveyed include *The Globe and Mail,* and *The Ottawa Citizen* and *Le Devoir.*

[10] Research in progress; the newspapers surveyed include *The Toronto Star* and *La Presse.*

[11] Banting, Keith G., "The Past Speaks to the Future: Lessons from the Postwar Social Union" in Harvey Lazar (ed.), *The State of the Federation 1997: Non-Constitutional Renewal,* Kingston, Institute of Intergovernmental Relations, Queen's University, 1998.

[12] This passage from Antonia Maoini, "The Citizenship-building effects of policies and services in Canada's universal health care regime" (Canadian Policy Research Net works, 2001).

[13] See Carolyn Tuohy, *Accidental Logics: The Dynamics of Change in the Health Care Arena in the United States, Britain, and Canada* (New York: Oxford University Press, 1999); on political institutions and health care in comparative context, see Antonia Maioni, *Parting at the Crossroads: The Emergence of Health Insurance in the United States and Canada,* Princeton: Princeton University Press, 1998.

[14] Lester B. Pearson, Mike: The Memoirs of the Right Honourable Lester B. Pearson, Volume 3: 1957-1968. Toronto: University of Toronto Press, 1975, 54.

[15] On the US case, including the parallel between Clinton and Truman, see Theda Skocpol, Boomerang: *Health Care Reform and the Turn Against Government* (New York: Norton, 1996).

[16] See Grant Reeher, "Reform and Remembrance: The Place of the Private Sector in the Future of Health Care Policy", forthcoming, Journal of Health Politics, Policy and Law, April 2003.

Higher Education:
Moving on in a Positive Climate

Lorna R. Marsden

IN THE WINTER of 2001, the eminent French sociologist, Alain Touraine, stunned a meeting of deans of graduate schools of Canada and their guests by declaring that the USA has a monopoly of important universities. There are, he said, about a dozen major universities in the world—those to which all the very best minds and researchers go, graduate from, or work in—and all are in the USA, with the possible exception of Cambridge.

Coming from a prominent (although safely retired) professor from France, this was a strong claim. And yet in the post-war period Americans have focussed their considerable public and private influence and resources on building outstanding, exciting places of learning that influence governments, private sector organizations and international institutions everywhere. They have also built up an amazing range of institutions of higher education that are less influential but highly successful. Given what is sometimes seen as US isolationist sentiment, US universities draw in a huge proportion of all foreign students. They in turn influence world institutions and leaders throughout the world.

To a Canadian audience dedicated to building our own universities, this was distressing but true. All of us have tried to hire and retain faculty in a variety of fields only to have the brightest exit to Harvard, Stanford or Chicago. We all try to hire graduates from the top ten or twenty universities and are very pleased when our graduates are accepted into those universities for graduate programs or faculty positions. Virtually all of us list sabbaticals, conferences, invited lectures or some association with those outstanding institutions.

Some in Canada believe we should mimic the US system, pouring our resources into a few institutions and build the US style "tiered" system of universities and colleges. Others believe that we can more successfully nation build by supporting access to a good quality of education and research across the country and that, in addition, provinces are likely to try to do this regardless of the hopes of some. It is one of the key debates in this country and public policy is not transparent on this highly controversial topic. I will return to this debate later.

In Canada, we pride ourselves on offering in all our universities the type of good, solid undergraduate education that gives the best students entry to the "best" graduate and professional schools and the richest scholarships. Is this a sufficient goal in the current environment? Can we sustain even this standard?

In a world of mass higher education, of increasing costs associated with teaching and research, in a period of high participation rates and strong demands for highly qualified and motivated workers, there are some key steps we can take to support our ambitions.

The Government of Canada has shown great leadership by its student financial support and its research agenda and now the Innovation Agenda announced in February 2002.[*1] For the past decade, the Government of Canada has been building a series of policies and programs that have responded well to the requirements of our economy, our universities and to students. What they have not done is make any definitive clarifying policy statements about higher education.

So what have they accomplished and what might we do next to meet the challenges of living next to the empire of learning and working in a globalized economy?[2]

I. The Limitations to Public Policy

Creating public policy for higher education in this country, as in other federations, presents some considerable challenges and these have to be considered in looking toward Canada's future in this field.

First, universities are ancient institutions with considerable autonomy in attitude and substance. From one point of view we are a highly regulated sector with provincial and federal reporting and funding requirements that are quite out of control. For example, York University in a recent typical year filed 983 reports to all three levels of government generating quite a few jobs and a lot of expense in this part of the administration. Although regulation is clearly growing in Ontario and probably across the country, nonetheless professors are autonomous scholars and scientists and are so protected by rules of academic freedom and by their very powerful associations and unions.

Even more significant is that this autonomy must be in place if the best work is to be done. It is out of the question that research and scholarship should be confined within a particular nation, region or era. Faculty do now and have always gone to the sources of their data (archives, archaeological sites, laboratories, libraries, communities, oceans/fields and forests, etc) wherever they may be. Research is always compared to the best in the world, not to local standards, and scholars and scientists are highly peripatetic.

This is a condition of good work and wherever it is interfered with (e.g. during the Cold War and most of the hot wars as well) standards of science and research suffer. Scientists and scholars are by definition global—they are deeply and intensively integrated into their fields of expert knowledge and the people in that field wherever they may be.[3] The entire world and beyond is their workplace. This frequently leads to disputes with governments over matters of funding, visas, research leaves, etc.

Second, governments are beholden to their voters and taxpayers and want to demonstrate their delivery skills. It is very difficult to demonstrate the value of much research and scholarship in terms that the ordinary taxpayer understands. The media frequently use the titles of research projects and theses to make jokes or scandals about university research. Some of it may be scandalous but, by and large, it is serious and well, peer-reviewed, research that fits somewhere into the building of knowledge and understanding.

However, taxpayers understand all too well when their son or daughter does or does not get into the university/program of his/her choice and so the concerns of students and their parents get considerably more attention than the building of knowledge. Colleges of the technical variety are better understood than universities but neither commands the rapt attention given to the k-12 schools. And for those whose children go neither to college nor university, and yet do not thrive in the workplace, the options are not understood, are expensive and are limited.[4]

Public policies set by governments are, therefore, a small though vital part of higher education policy and thinking that must be carried out if Canada is to forge ahead in higher education. Much of the policy and public thinking has to be done by the governors of universities, by the administrators and the interested public.[5] Universities are an integral part of civic society. They are very important to the values of civil society and they need protection, promotion and understanding not simply as a means to an economic end, but as the source of and depository for Canadian society and culture.

Third is the inescapable impact of the division of powers in our Constitution which, from the beginning of Confederation, gave provinces exclusive domain over education. This is a problem for all levels of government and increasingly so in higher education, as the competitive standards have risen, and research fuels economic growth. The division of powers certainly curtails the best policy and planning agendas as the rituals of intergovernmental disputes, the blame game and the competition for the tax dollar and voters obscures the necessity for a coherent higher education approach.

Much as some of us dream about a different constitutional division of powers, it is not going to happen and so the barriers have to be overcome—and are often overcome—by the creative thinking of politicians and public servants on each side of the big divide. Where governments decide to cooperate, collude or connive to make important things happen in higher education, they often do provide great benefits for Canadians.

II. An Agenda for the Decade

In the federal domain, research and student support are successful strategies and both are crucial in the near term. But as the struggle over elite focus versus opportunity for general levels of education is joined, there will be pressure on the government to reveal coherent choices now visible only in expenditure decisions. So the following three goals would make a rich agenda for the decade.

- tackling the real issues facing students and their families as they make the decision to go to university, college or elsewhere
- pushing the research agenda as far as possible and diffusing it throughout the culture and economy as far as possible
- working out the goals for higher education: the national purpose, the provincial objectives and the joint strategies.

III. Students: Quality, Choice and Access

While the majority of students one encounters are most preoccupied with getting into the university, the program and the courses they want; while they will discuss the virtues or otherwise of their professors at length; and while their lifestyles are certainly the most fascinating aspect of students for those of us who work with them closely, their official associations appear to be focussed on only one matter: money.*2

Student associations are preoccupied with the cost of tuition, access to funding, and student debt issues. An evening spent with the web sites convinces one that not only are governments at all levels perniciously raising the costs of higher education but that the majority of students are loaded permanently with debt.

There is no question that the costs of higher education—to the student, provincial and federal coffers and to the taxpayer—need serious attention and solution.

From a public policy point of view, however, the question is broader: what sort of internationally competitive and locally useful education are students being offered in our colleges and universities for the dollars spent? For if our Canadian graduates are so well equipped that they can graduate into the best jobs, graduate schools and professional programs in the world, then the question of cost is one thing. If, on the other hand, they are not internationally competitive, then it is another.

How is a student or parent to know? In a country where the only public rankings are those in *Maclean's* magazine which does not give academic quality indicators and does not intend to do so, we have a serious problem. *Maclean's* is about consumer choice and lifestyle at institutions. In every university and college some programs are better than others and furthermore programs change with faculty moves, research funding and departmental choices. Students go to programs more than institutions and employers, graduate and professional schools judge program performance more than institutions (much as institutions would like to believe).

In the USA, graduate programs are assessed and ranked frequently by subject discipline. (And I stress that I am referring to program assessments and rankings and not to accreditation). Those carrying out rankings keep a close eye on which faculty are where, the research and publications emanating from a department,[6] and the graduate students who are associated with the department. Research funding, employers and the informed public are well served by such rankings. In the UK, research rankings were imposed during the Thatcher years and have evolved into a rankings scheme that has its critics and downsides but which has certainly focussed the attention of the universities on their standing. In Europe, rankings of programs are an increasingly important part of the landscape.

In Ontario, all graduate programs are assessed for quality on a regular cycle through the Ontario Council on Graduate Studies. The programs are categorized, though not ranked, but the results are not made public. In Ontario undergraduate university programs will also be reviewed in a similar manner. These reviews are not about student satisfaction (although that is one element) but are peer reviews which examine the faculty, the department, the institutional support, planning, research and publications.

How do such rankings help students? When they are of a public nature, they help students understand where they might apply in order to enter the most competitive program in any major subject. Maclean's can then supplies the life-style data. They help students explain to their parents why it is important to get into a particular program (not a particular university).

If costs vary by programs, then so should scholarship and bursary support. If universities know that some of their programs are highly ranked and others less so, they will put their resources to one or another policy: either pull all programs up to high standards or focus on their strengths. But in such a situation, they will focus their attention on attracting and keeping the very best students and faculty.

For these reasons, the initial step in tackling the student costs question is such data. To collect it on a valid and reliable basis, we need in Canada an independent highly qualified body of individuals who provide an assessment of the academic quality of programs in every one of the 96 universities and university colleges now members of AUCC. Equally we need the same for the technical and polytechnical institutions. The embryos of such assessments exist in the rankings reviews of graduate programs through, for example, OCGS. This project needs the subscription of federal and all provincial governments and all the universities but to be accepted and successful it cannot be a government program but must remain a peer-reviewed one. Establishing and setting to work such assessments would take nearly a decade but would be a basis for maintaining Canadian strength and reputation in an increasingly complex world.

Then we can properly assess and reassess the funding situation for students.

There is no question at all that a university education is expensive for students and their families. It is even more expensive for the taxpayer. The question is always: who pays?

We have moved from a country in which religious denominations began and provided support for colleges and universities in large part, with families bearing the most significant part of the costs, to one where most institutions of higher learning are secular and provincially supported. The costs for students in the form of tuition, foregone earnings and living costs have risen but so have the sources of financial support. Whereas most students leaving high school could not aspire to university in the 1950's and earlier, now most can go to university but they must worry about potential savings plans or debt burdens.

This is why a clear and transparent public policy statement is required from all political parties. In Ontario, where tuition fees have been regulated, the issue was fully engaged when the Harris government came into power. Their policy was to "share the burden." Tuition would rise and students have to pay more while the general taxpayer paid no more. This took the form of tuition rises until about one-third of the cost of a university undergraduate education was paid by the students, and of deregulated fees for graduate and most professional programs.[7]

Both opposition parties opposed these moves. The NDP preferred no tuition costs to students and the Liberals proposed lowered tuition costs and no deregulated costs. Now all three parties are reconsidering their positions. In provinces where tuition has not risen, universities are starving for funds and losing their reputations and their faculty.

In the meantime, the Government of Canada—and some provincial governments—have been focussing on the problem of student debts. The banks have forcefully made the case that something must be done: graduates or drop-outs were not paying off their debts; all too many young people were declaring bankruptcy; and debts were mounting. They considered at length the income contingent loan plans. There are variants but in general ensure that paybacks of loans are contingent upon earnings. They are biased against graduates who go into low-paying sectors of the economy (e.g. the arts, social work, nursing) and, in general, benefit those who focus on early high rates of earnings. The same logic underlies the University of Toronto tuition plan in law which has been so controversial over the past two years.

But at the end of the day, more scholarship and direct support has been the answer through the Millennium Fund and Canada Study Grants—through higher levels of student loans and a variety of tax incentives for endowed scholarship support from the public and corporations; and tax incentive programs for savings for higher education. These are universal programs in that the student then takes those funds and applies them to the program of his/her choice.

Public policy can be improved in this area in several important ways: First, improvements in existing programs of support would see a focus on realistic planning for families, students and governments. While universities and colleges explain to their students how to finance their education, that does not help families make the initial choice of whether to go to higher education or not. Along with the RESP program, much education of families is needed to bring the focus and concern to the levels of US families is needed. While improving the educational side of RESP's, looking at the flexibility of US 529's would also be useful in improving support for higher education in Canada.

Survey data of applicants indicates that the higher education choice is often made in grade 11 or 12 and the correlation between low family income and late choice is very high.[8] Clearly schools are not or cannot provide this education to families. A national program is needed to convey realistic information about how much a college, university or other form of post-school education costs, how much time it takes away from earning and what the long term benefits are.

Second, the Millennium Scholarship fund through the Foundation was a brilliant and welcome idea. It is the application of that idea that contradicts liberal concerns. In order to avoid the constitutional challenges, the Foundation negotiated with each province separately. In some provinces it works well, but where a student must apply for a student loan in order to receive a Millennium Scholarship it does not. The working poor—a focus of Liberal concern for a long time—appear to be more debt averse and less likely to want to take loans or to reveal to governments their family financial situation. A study of how students finance their education shows that of the roughly half of students who graduate debt free (or with no debt outside their families), many are from the working poor. They save, they work full or part-time while they study, and they do not take student loans. They need those scholarships and they are excluded all too often. This can be reformed..

A review of the Millennium Program—as assessment of its first years and of its future—and a tune-up should be a high priority for the government of Canada and provincial governments.

Canada Study Grants are another initiative that provide support for students with special needs. A recent useful study by Statistics Canada has shown that students from lower and moderate income backgrounds are far less likely to go to university or college if they must go beyond commuting distance.[9] Once again, living distant (80Km or more) is a greater deterrent for low income families. In short, living at home is viewed as making higher education possible. Expanding either the Canada Student Loan program or the Study Grants program to be sensitive to this issue could have positive results.

Some of the commuting issue is cultural and some students are needed at home on a daily basis. For example, if the student is the only English/French speaker in the household, then that student is needed to provide services for other family members in daily life. One also suspects that the gender differences remains crucial. In some cultures the young women will not be permitted to live in a campus environment. So providing access across the country is crucial. In BC, the university-college measures have greatly improved access, for example.

Third, new measures are needed to improve the quality of the post-secondary academic experience. In our economy where trade and international issues are the life-blood of our existence, bringing more and more students into the international arena is obligatory. Universities and colleges are highly aware of this.[10]

In Canada, attention is all too often focussed on providing international education experiences for students. In recent years the Canadian embassies and consulates have greatly enhanced their attention to higher education which is most helpful and conducive to institutional responses from colleges and universities. As the Innovation Strategy has already suggested, we also need highly prestigious scholarships to attract the world's best students to study in Canada.

The government of Canada could help provide such prestigious scholarships by providing special tax incentives to those prepared to endow such internationally recognized scholarships at high levels e.g. those prepared to endow a scholarship worth say $100,000 (four years of tuition, living and travel) which would require an endowment of $2m at the normal 5% payout should get extra tax benefits. The Millennium Foundation could provide the proper services and guidance which would result in the donor receiving the appropriate recognition and benefits. The Innovation Strategy has identified the need for a "Rhodes-like" scholarship to bring great students to Canada and it is an excellent priority.

Equally, highly recognized academic scholarships are required. In my view, the Millennium Scholarship missed the point by focussing on financial need rather than great academic qualities, however defined. It is good for universities to have such scholarships to attract students, but it is equally good for the country to have scholarships comparable to the Woodrow Wilson Fellows and the Marshalls.

In summary, there are three key steps for the coming decade in support of students:

1. Provide better guidance to students and their families by focusing on program quality and rankings (not institutional rankings) and by establishing better and broader public know-

ledge and expectations on the costs of higher education and available savings and support programs.

2. Improve the existing scholarship and loan programs to serve the working poor, lower middle income and non-urban students and families

3. Raise the stakes on international education both by supporting students to study and work elsewhere and by creating prestigious scholarships for students to study in Canada.

IV. Research: Keeping up the Pace

The Government of Canada has made some bold and very successful new steps in ensuring Canada's competitiveness through university research in the last few years. It reformed the MRC into the CHRI to promote health studies beyond the medical; it created the Canada Foundation for Innovation to focus research dollars and projects on research and it invented and supported the Canada Research Chairs, a series of faculty appointments to both build capacity for research in all universities and to attract back to Canada some of the talent abroad. Best of all, in the past budget, it paid some of the indirect costs of research to the universities, a measure which will truly ensure a change in the climate toward research and innovation across the country. This agenda has been imaginative, sensitive to needs and highly applauded.

The Innovation Agenda of the past February 2002, in the paper Achieving Excellence, announces a series of further goals, targets and priorities to achieve the objective of supporting our economic future by absorbing innovation into the business of Canada, creating value at home and building talent for the future.

By AUCC calculations, universities and university colleges do one-third of the research in Canada. By Government of Canada standards it is one-quarter. Under any circumstances, it is important and has the potential to fuel the economy.

Research transfer is another and more complicated matter. Universities are not always good transmitters and Canadian businesses are not always good receivers. In provinces like Quebec where the Government of the province has focussed on the space industry and pharmaceuticals there has been a major payoff. It is the concentration of instruments and resources—tax incentives, industrial inducements, labour force availability and research institutions— that have worked well. In Montreal, in Edmonton and Calgary, and in Vancouver/Lower Mainland there are equally good opportunities as well as many smaller centres. But there is the wider scope: in most places, invention/improvement and good ideas have no natural receivers and will not see the light of day unless there is an institution to move those ideas around. The Innovation Agenda commits government to "leverage the commercialization potential of publicly funded academic research," to provide incentives in some fields, to increase venture capital and to recognize innovators.

The CFI has that potential. What it does not now have is a cadre of individuals sophisticated in intellectual property, industry/universities, and investing to spur the system forward. Could it do this job? In collaboration with the NSERC, SSHRC and CHRI a powerful collaboration could be developed and conveyed. Industry/sectors, however, have to listen to the idea and to be willing to work together. Overcoming this hurdle is a major challenge which can be strongly supported by governments both directly and indirectly. But it is a culture change in this country and requires breaking down areas of mistrust and misunderstanding that run very deeply. The current opposition to the "corporate agenda" and the myths about ivory tower thinkers have set up barriers to understanding that will emerge only with some successes, most of which have to be between the university and industry partners. They are not successful when forced but only when encouraged.

Indirect costs were funded by the federal government for the first time last year. This is a very welcome move on the part of Government and has already made a significant change in the capacity and motivation of university researchers everywhere. A continuation of this policy is crucial for the increased productivity and creativity in university and college based research. The Innovation Agenda strategy includes the funding of the indirect research costs at the 40% level. The results of such funding will provide a good background for understanding what happens next, i.e. will there be further collaborative steps to be taken of a trilateral nature?

Universities, through the AUCC, have committed to doubling the amount of research we perform to help make the target of being among the top five countries in R&D by 2010; to increase research collaboration; to triple commercialization performance; to work with their communities in these areas as well as others.

But the question is: will the Innovation Agenda be successful? Will higher education individuals and institutions rally to the cause?

There is enormous goodwill and a lot of work going on. There is great hopefulness but the answer turns to some considerable extent on the clarity of policy on higher education reinforced by allocation of resources and that returns us to the question posed earlier. Is it federal public policy to focus resources on a few institutions to create "best in the world institutions" or is it to focus on the excellence, talent and progress wherever it is found?

V. Clear and Transparent Policy

The Innovation Strategy, in particular, is Liberal in its intent and a brilliant piece of work. This Government of Canada has achieved a lot in support of students and research. The other moves have been bold and focussed as they have spent the dividend of debt repayment and fiscal prudence.

The problems lie in the operationalization of some of those ideas and in the failure to resolve the major debate about the country's future in higher education.

In operationalization, the Millennium Scholarship issues have been identified earlier. Is the objective to encourage talent, to encourage the brainy regardless of background? In that case, the program should require academic performance beyond the usual and supply financial support without a means test. The goals are now confused.

The Canada Research Chairs represent another operationalization issue. They are distributed according to a formula based on an institution's share of the existing granting councils awards. This distorts the CRC's in the direction of universities with medical, dental and engineering schools because those programs apply researchers are applying to the granting councils which are the best funded. It assumes that the bulk of chairs should go to those areas of study chosen by the fewest students because the grant funding goes there. As an example, most undergraduate students study in the social sciences and humanities and researchers in those fields are offered the least grant funded research, so the new faculty are going to those fields that already have the fewest students, the most research funding and the least influence on building the research culture. This is a distortion *unless* you subscribe to the view that a few institutions should receive the bulk of the resources to build the "best institutions in the world".

So what is the public policy coming from Ottawa? Have they concluded that they will build the capacity at a very few universities to try to achieve some level of competition with the top US institutions? Funding for the CRC's and some actions would indicate this approach is what lies behind the allocation of resources. (This, of course, begs the question of whether that is possible even if it is desirable). Or are they concerned to ensure that resources support excellence wherever it is found, that opportunities are created for talented students and researchers and that capacity be built in many parts of the country even if for specific and differentiated objectives? The Millennium Scholarships, indirect costs, and parts of the Innovation Strategy point to this thinking? Or are they just hedging their bets?

A clear statement of intentions and, if possible, a statement coordinated with the provinces would be a major accomplishment and a great step toward a great future for higher education in Canada.

That statement should differentiate policies directed to access and opportunity for students (with variations by province if necessary), the clear research intentions settling the question of whether a few selected institutions will succeed or all may compete, and the role and limitations of government in changing the climate and culture of our country in higher education and research, strengthening internationalization goals abroad and at home, and building institutional strength to achieve targets and objectives.

The Liberal approach would be one of creating access and opportunity rather than elite focus, supporting initiative and excellence in individuals rather than rewarding institutions and eliminating remaining barriers and facilitating accomplishments rather than choosing winners and losers.

Notes:

1 * For the full story on the Innovation Agenda see www.innovationstrategy.gc.ca/cmb/innovation

2* *see, for example,* www.cfs-fcee.ca

1 This debate can be seen for example in the *National Post* article of 17.08.2002 by Heather Sokoloff "Law Students may be asked to share future pay" in which Mc-Gill and Queen's representatives are paraphrased as "Many Canadian schools can do just fine without large contributions from students. But what if you want to be the best in Canada What if you want to compete with the best in the world?"

2 For many of us, the leader of the country/party is judged on three main issues of almost equal importance:

- the leader's concept of how to balance the relationship with the USA with our longstanding commitment to international economic development and peacekeeping: how would she/he maintain those complex relationships?

- the leader's proven ability to ensure that the economy is strong now and in the long term while at the same time narrowing the gap between the well-off and the struggling groups in Canada: is there a plan?

- the leader's commitment to the strengthening and reforming of our major institutions which include confederation, parliament, and civil and cultural institutions: will Quebec and Alberta stay in Canada as willing participants; will Parliament keep up with contemporary democratic practices; will education, health, cities/communities, and our key national parks, museums, libraries, universities and other centres of culture thrive?

Successive governments have made advances on these issues by inventing new institutions (e.g. peacekeeping), reforming institutions (e.g. the Constitution), fighting inflation and reducing deficits, and addressing US relations. But the challenges are renewed with each change in leadership.

3 This use of the word "global" follows the very helpful discussion by Sylvia Ostry in her Walter Gordon Lecture in Public Policy at Massey College, 23 May, 2001 and published with the Sixth, Eighth and Ninth Lectures by Massey College, 2002, pp 75-98.

4 This complex subject is addressed in the HRDC paper "Knowledge Matters" which accompanies the Innovation Strategy and in which the government tries to gain some purchase on this subject. It has received all too little attention, mostly in my view because the institutional structure is not there to provide support for apprenticeships and other forms of education.

5 There are myriad resources for discussions on higher education and the future of universities, colleges and other forms of higher education. The best source is Canada is the AUCC and their website (AUCC.ca); in the USA, the AAHE (AAHE.org) and especially their Futures Project which is the source of much stimulating thought, much of it published in their magazine Change (see futuresproject.org). Many good ideas have emerged in the last few years and I touch on only a very few here and only those that link to public policy.

6   Of a recent article published by the AAHE which shows that program rankings and faculty research productivity are highly correlated in the USA

7   In fact, the proportion paid by student tuition varies from one-third to almost one-half depending upon other sources of revenue for universities and its mix of programs.

8   Such data are collected by, for example, a survey of all applicants to Ontario's universities organized by the OUAC – Ontario Universities Application Centre in Guelph.

9   Statistics Canada, "Too Far To Go On? Distance to School and University Participation," June, 2002

10   see for example the AUCC response to the Innovation Agenda, "A Strong Foundation for Innovation: an AUCC Action Plan," July 2002.

The New Liberalism:
Ideas and Ideals

Sherri Torjman

IN SEARCHING FOR the *new liberalism* (small "l"), the most important factor to remember is the small "l." The new liberalism must be far more than a set of *ideas*. It also must embrace a set of *ideals* that embody a clear direction for the country.

In recent years, these ideals have been missing from public discourse. The social policy field, in particular, has drifted without apparent direction. Aside from the major advance in social policy represented by the National Child Benefit, which had been proposed and designed by my colleague Ken Battle, the country appears to be floundering when it comes to definitive protection for and promotion of human well-being.

This feeling was reflected by three national organizations—the Coalition of National Voluntary Organizations, United Way/Canada and the Canadian Council on Social Development—when they approached the Caledon Institute to write a national social vision. They wanted to find ways to place social well-being and environmental protection on the table as issues equal in importance to economic growth. They also wanted to ensure that the voluntary sector was at the table in helping to define key social issues and formulate possible policy options. The first challenge, though, is to find that decision-making table; its location remains, to this day, somewhat of a mystery.

The need for direction in the country reflects an apparent lack of commitment to social issues. Both the passion and poetry have gone from public life.

In response to their request, I wrote a paper entitled *Reclaiming our Humanity*, which was intended not as a definitive blue-print for social policy, but was meant, rather, to provide a springboard for discussion to enable groups across the country to talk about social issues and find ways to make public their concerns.

Reclaiming Our Humanity looks at both communities and governments. It comes as no surprise that communities have been struggling for years to tackle difficult and complex problems, such as poverty, family violence, high unemployment and racial intolerance. Despite these enormous challenges, there is some exciting and significant work under way. This is not to imply that communities are *new* or that their importance has been rediscovered. The voluntary sector was alive and well long before the fact of public provision. And the answer certainly is not a return to communitarianism.

Emerging Forms of Community Governance

What *is* new is that communities throughout Canada—and indeed throughout the industrialized world—have started to work far more strategically than before. They have adopted an approach referred to in the literature as "comprehensive community initiatives." This approach is beginning to be applied widely in the US and the UK, with its nationally funded neighbourhood regeneration approaches.

It is a method in which communities effectively make an explicit decision to tackle, systematically and comprehensively, a major concern. The initiative generally is identified by a community organization or local government, which assumes the role of convener.

Many different forms of comprehensive community initiatives are now under way. The Lutherwood Community Opportunities Development Association in Waterloo Region, for example, spearheaded Opportunities 2000, a community-wide effort to reduce poverty. The Mayor of Ottawa convened Partners for Jobs, a multisectoral task group concerned with finding solutions to unemployment and underemployment. The Community Foundation of Hamilton undertook a *Strengthening Civility* effort in the aftermath of September 11. The United Way movement in more than 200 Canadian and American cities started *Success by 6*, which promotes collaboration among organizations involved in the early years. The United Way and Chamber of Commerce have joined forces to tackle the high rates of unemployment and poverty in the City of Toronto.

Typically, comprehensive community initiatives will define the overall problem they seek to address. The convener organization will then bring together the players who can help do something about it. These initiatives often seek organizations or sectors that are not the *usual suspects* but try instead to broaden the scope of involvement to harness new ideas, expertise and resources. Because these efforts seek to engage sectors that have not worked together in the past, they are often able to create new and successful solutions. In the City of Ottawa, for example, the welfare department and several key industries collaborated around customized training, a short-term, highly market-relevant form of skills development. Welfare recipients were trained to work in the key clusters of the local economy, including high tech, tourism and photonics.

Comprehensive community initiatives generally adopt a long-term view that is necessary for tackling complex problems. They recognize that difficult issues such as poverty do not start on fiscal year April 1 and end on March 31. Many of these efforts are developmental in that they focus not only upon pressing and obvious concerns but also upon the positive elements in the community. They try, for example, to help families build financial assets or restore the natural or physical assets of a neighbourhood, town or city.

The Caledon Institute currently is engaged in a major national effort called Vibrant Communities. It was developed by the recently created Tamarack Institute for Community Engagement and is receiving multi-year, multimillion-dollar support from the McConnell Family Foundation in Montreal. Human Resources Development Canada is funding the policy component of this work. Selected conveners from 15 cities across the country are involved in a Pan-Canadian Learning Partnership in which they come together on a monthly basis to share ideas, resources and strategies regarding local solutions to poverty reduction. They effectively 'scale up' their individual efforts through this collaborative strategic approach.

In addition, five communities will receive substantial funds to support their poverty reduction work. In order to qualify for these funds, they must convene a multisectoral steering group that takes responsibility for the initiative and helps create a community-wide vision as well as a strategic plan with detailed actions. This steering group *must* include representatives from at least four sectors: business, government, anti-poverty groups and the voluntary sector.

Our role at the Caledon Institute is to support the work of the Pan-Canadian Learning Partnership. We help identify the various models for poverty reduction that have been employed successfully both within and outside the country. Caledon is also responsible for the policy aspects of this national initiative. For example, we wrote a paper on the role of local government with respect to community-based poverty reduction. While the document was prepared for the Waterloo-based Opportunities 2000 project, several local governments have used it as a guide to remove barriers to self-sufficiency that may be embedded in their policies and programs. In response to problems arising from the transition from welfare to work, Caledon also prepared a paper entitled *More Money in the Pocket* to make the case for income tax relief for low-income earners.

At the very least, the new liberalism must be aware of the wide range of innovative approaches that are emerging to help communities undertake strategic actions to improve their well-being. The new liberalism should seek to create links between formal policy-making processes and new mechanisms for local decision-making. The economic and social problems confronting Canada are too big and complicated to be tackled by governments alone. Business, labour, municipal governments, the educational system, interest groups, researchers and communities must play an active role in various forms of working partnership.

Governments can also assist these new forms of governance through support for deliberative learning, which seeks to promote the continual and strategic exchange of ideas and local solutions. Another enabling role for governments is to make available knowledge and research that further the efforts of diverse comprehensive community initiatives. The development of templates for local labour market information, for example, can help cities and regions create profiles of their workforce and both actual and potential employment opportunities. In short, the new liberalism must seek to understand the links between traditional governments, and new and emerging forms of governance.

But while community work is necessary and indeed essential, it is by no means sufficient for tackling complex economic and social issues. Communities can never replace a strong public sector. They are an indispensable complement and supplement to—but not a replacement for—strong government. And here's where the problem lies in recent years.

If Tom Axworthy were to write a book right now about the current state of public affairs, he likely could not call it *The Just Society*. He would have to call it *The Justify Society*. The changed title would reflect the new way of making decisions in the country and the ongoing requirement to justify every component of public investment, especially in social policy. And it is not merely an ethical or humanitarian case that is called for—which would be a reasonable expectation. Instead, there needs to be a *business case* for social investment—to prove that every dollar of social investment will yield at least one dollar in associated benefits.

All this justification is part of the move towards evidence-based policy-making, which has become the new buzzword in Ottawa. On the one hand, the approach makes sense in a knowledge-based world in which information and research are seen as essential ingredients for making intelligent decisions. It also reflects, from a political perspective, the need for return-on-investment arguments. The public is increasingly demanding proof that its tax dollars are being well spent.

But there is already substantive and compelling information in many areas of social policy. We simply fail to act on it. Perhaps Tom Axworthy needs to write yet another book. He can call it *The Just Do It Society*.

The Evidence for Social Investment

We know that strong and sustainable social programs can enhance Canada's economic competitiveness by supplying the vital social infrastructure—health care, education, a skilled and knowledgeable workforce—that bestows comparative advantage on the global economic stage. Persistent and growing inequality of both opportunity and outcome is a costly economic deadweight in terms of lost productivity, lost revenue, reduced consumer spending and higher costs for income assistance, social services and health care.

An intelligently designed tax and income transfer system can do much to mitigate the inequality gap.

We know the importance of early childhood development. Opportunities are created—or denied—in children's critical early years, when their development is forged along multiple dimensions—physical, emotional, social, linguistic and intellectual—that significantly shape their destiny as adults. Early childhood development has been shown to improve children's subsequent performance in school, lessen the learning risks linked to low income, and enhance parents' childrearing and coping skills. And early childhood development is not just for families whose parents are in the workforce. Such services also can help families that care for their children at home.

The social and economic benefits of high-quality child care, in particular, are well documented. A recent report by University of Toronto economists Gordon Cleveland and Michael Krashinsky calculates the costs and benefits of high-quality, publicly funded, early childhood care and education for children between the ages of 2 and 5. For every dollar invested in high-quality child care, they found a $2 return. The report analyzes several studies that measure the effects of early childhood education on school performance—a major factor enhanced by high-quality care. Regardless of socioeconomic background or mothers' employment status, children who participate in early childhood education were found to perform significantly better in school than those who do not participate.

Public investments in high-quality early childhood programs benefit not only parents and children. Society gains significant benefits from the long-term impact of enhanced childhood development, economic productivity and lower costs of supports, like welfare and social services. The public benefit also comes from the increased workforce participation of parents. The investment in early childhood produces lower social spending on families, higher tax revenues to government and greater future economic security for mothers.

There is also substantial evidence on the health, social and economic benefits of decent affordable housing. Dozens of studies corroborate the profound and far-reaching connections between housing and well-being. We know from a wide range of research the effects of unsafe and unhealthy housing. Poorly maintained housing is responsible for many childhood injuries. Damp, moldy interiors are linked to higher risk of respiratory disease and asthma. Unstable living arrangements, made worse by parents' inability to pay the rent, have a deeply negative impact upon the emotional, behavioural and cognitive development of children.

A US National Task Force has named decent housing as the foundation of family life, without which all other activities are severely challenged. A decent home is the platform for dignity and self-respect; a base for hope and improvement. It allows people to take advantage of opportunities in education, health and employment—the means to self-reliance.

At Caledon, we base our proposals on this wide body of compelling evidence. Our proposals are also founded on a clear set of values—value that seek the reduction of poverty and improvement of economic and social well-being for all Canadians. We have woven together our proposals into a framework (or architecture, to use the European term) that sets out the fundamental building blocks for public investment in social programs.

Key Pillars in the Social Architecture

A paper which my colleague Ken Battle and I recently wrote, entitled *Social Policy That Works: An Agenda,* puts forward a set of proposals for reconstructing Canadian social policy over the next decade or more. Only the highlights, rather than the details, of the extensive body of recommendations are presented here.

Sustaining Canada's *health care system* is clearly central to the agenda of smart social policy, and medicare is one of the best examples of how social programs can contribute to an economy's competitive advantage on the world stage. Core reforms should include: an increase and stabilization of federal funding for medicare, raised through earmarked taxes; expanded coverage of national health insurance to incorporate pharmaceuticals and home care; and major reform of primary health care to provide access to round-the-clock services through multidisciplinary group practices.

Health care (including prescription drugs) not covered under medicare, as well as dental care, are financed through employer-provided insurance as a benefit to employees or by individually purchased insurance. Typically, provincial and territorial welfare systems provide some form of supplementary health care, though these are uneven in availability and scope across the country. Under the National Child Benefit, some provinces are using their savings from welfare expenditures on children (which are being replaced by enrichments to the federal Canada Child Tax Benefit) to extend supplementary health care to the working poor.

However, many Canadians—generally those with below-average earnings and those who work for employers that do not provide supplementary health insurance—either have to pay out-of-pocket for health benefits that are not covered by medicare and for dental care, or go without. *Supplementary health benefits* (e.g., prescription drugs, dental care, eyeglasses and supplementary health services) not covered under medicare should be made available to low and modest-income Canadians not insured under employer-provided health plans. The federal government could share the cost of this program with the provinces/territories.

Income payments on behalf of children—better known as *child benefits*—are another major building block in the social architecture and a key weapon against child poverty. Child benefits help fill the gap between wages and needs, especially for families with low or modest earnings for whom the labour market cannot provide a living wage. Child benefits also help acknowledge the heavier financial burden faced by all families with children compared to equal-earning families and individuals without children to support. Children are not a purely individual consumer choice: Society has a strong stake in ensuring the well-being of children as future workers, consumers and citizens.

The Canada Child Tax Benefit currently pays a maximum $2,422 for the first child and $2,218 for the second child and is scheduled to rise to at least $2,520 for the first and $2,308 for the second child by July 2004. The federal government should accelerate the pace of investment in the Canada Child Tax Benefit by announcing a $2,600 maximum benefit for the July 2002-June 2003 payment year (the rise would be retroactive to July), which basically would reach the crucial goal of an *integrated* child benefit system that replaces welfare-delivered child benefits.

Ottawa should then launch a second stage of reform that gradually expands the Canada Child Tax Benefit to achieve the ultimate target of a $4,400 per child maximum amount by 2010 for low-income families. Because the first stage will have removed child benefits from welfare, further increases in the second stage will benefit welfare families as well as the working poor. The second stage should also improve child benefits for non-poor families.

Income benefits are not the only important measure for children and their families. A strong system of *early childhood development* services for families—child care and early childhood learning, pregnancy and early parenting services, and parenting and community supports—makes both economic and social sense. Unfortunately, Canada's early childhood development services are deficient in supply, affordability and quality control. Services are uneven between and, in most cases, within provinces and territories. There is nothing approaching a national system. Most families rely on unregulated child care bought or traded on the market (typically from neighbourhood providers) or provided by relatives.

Ottawa has already committed a cumulative total of $2.2 billion over five years to help provinces invest, over and above what they already spend, in four areas: promoting healthy pregnancy, birth and infancy; improving parenting and family supports; strengthening early childhood development, learning and care; and strengthening community supports for families with children. While better than nothing, the new federal money is too little to carry much weight. Provinces and territories can spend the money with no strings attached except that it must go to some form of early childhood development services. Thus the money will do little, if anything, to help build a comprehensive system of early childhood development services across Canada.

The federal government should increase substantially its financial contribution to early childhood development. In return for its larger financial investment, Ottawa should negotiate bilateral agreements with the provinces and territories so that strategic investments can be made towards constructing a comprehensive child care and early childhood development system, in accordance with guiding medicare-like national principles (comprehensiveness, universality, accessibility, quality and accountability), objectives and good practices as jointly developed by the two levels of government. Immediate priority should be placed on increasing the supply of licensed child care spaces.

The federal and provincial/territorial governments should launch a joint reform of *income security, employment supports and lifelong learning* for all Canadians in the workforce—both unemployed and employed. Major areas for reform should include strengthening Employment Insurance to provide income support for employees who are temporarily and infrequently unemployed and for employed Canadians who want to upgrade their skills and education. The outmoded and stigmatizing welfare system would be replaced by a Basic Support system, composed of three main elements.

A *Basic Wage* would assist employable unemployed Canadians who do not qualify for or who have exhausted Employment Insurance. The Basic Wage would represent real remuneration for real work (not dead-end make-work, but goods and services with value), but with procedural safeguards to protect workers from abuse. The Basic Wage would also provide employment-related benefits, such as federally financed EI and C/QPP coverage and supplementary health and dental benefits. *Training Allowances* would assist individuals undertaking skills and learning development that enhances their employability. The third component would be *Basic Assistance* to fulfill welfare's originally intended roles as an emergency safety net until people in need get into mainstream programs and/or paid employment, and as a source of adequate support for Canadians who cannot work and do not qualify for other programs.

This *Employment Skills and Learning Strategy* would include a set of measures, including customized training and job supports, to facilitate the retention of paid employment—e.g., regular on-site visits, short-term counselling, advocacy, referral, problem-solving and mediation. The Strategy would include a policy framework to support *community economic development*, one of the most promising areas of economic and social development. A systemic approach is required to facilitate the labour market entry of *skilled immigrants* in their field of expertise.

Many Canadians with disabilities are unable to find employment because they do not have access to the disability supports they need to go to or stay at work. The federal government should collaborate with the provinces and territories to establish a *Disability Supports Fund* that would consolidate existing programs and promote the development of a comprehensive network of supportive goods and services throughout the country.

The reality for many Canadians—including persons with disabilities—is that they are not employed full-time. Current federal programs including the Canada Pension Plan disability benefit need to be reviewed from the perspective of both access and adequacy. Existing tax benefits for persons with disabilities have an institutional bias towards care (e.g., the medical expense credit and child care expense deduction). They also tend to be exclusionary in their provision. The disability tax credit is based on a restrictive definition of disability. The medical expense tax credit allows a designated, but relatively narrow, list of eligible items. The infirm dependant tax credit and the caregiver tax credit employ limited definitions of age. Aside from the small supplement for working poor households permitted by the medical expense tax credit, other relevant measures provide no assistance to poor Canadians who pay little or no income tax. Yet they still incur disability-related expenses.

Weaknesses in the current programs need to be resolved through the reform of existing provisions. In the long run, Ottawa should consider the development of a new *National Disability Benefit* in order to redress the myriad problems that have the effect of disqualifying applicants and some beneficiaries rather than providing the assistance they need to live independently.

Decent affordable housing is another major pillar in the social architecture. At last count (1995), one in seven households lived in "core housing need." This means that their housing was lacking in the number of bedrooms per family size, the safety of the dwelling was inadequate and/or they paid more than 30% of household income on accommodation.

The federal and provincial governments must play a far more active role in the housing area. They have several options. They can reduce the cost of accommodation by investing in the supply of affordable housing. They can also bolster Canadians' ability to pay for housing through rent supplements or income assistance. In November 2001, Ottawa put $680 million on a federal-provincial table for a modest reinvestment in affordable accommodation. The new dollars have attracted five provinces and two territories to match the federal contribution—but the total funding and potential output remain woefully low. The federal government, in conjunction with provinces and territories, should build on this initial injection in order to make a real dent in the housing crisis. Such investment could comprise part of a federal agenda for cities.

The Ideals Behind the Ideas

We recognize that it is not possible to move on all fronts at maximum speed—or even on all fronts. Public expenditure clearly must be made within the context of a solid fiscal framework. At the same time, it is essential to have an overall roadmap that sets out the major directions that ideally, as a nation, we seek to achieve. It is important to know the ultimate or desired destination within which the individual routes can be charted.

Ottawa must reassert its crucial role in helping provinces and territories to reform and finance social and health programs that fall within their jurisdiction. The federal government's superior fiscal capacity and its historic responsibility for national social policy—though now as an equal partner with the provinces and territories instead of its former role of first among equals—demand that it become again an active, intelligent and confident player, in a game where virtually all problems are complex and do not respect neat jurisdictional borders or government organization charts.

The federal government should also provide visionary leadership. It should see itself as more than a vehicle simply to fund a disparate set of social programs. Rather, it is the key institution for promoting social well-being in Canada.

Here's where the new liberalism can play a crucial role. It should start talking openly and explicitly about the importance of smart social investment. It should articulate clearly the concept of the public good. It should weave together various *ideas* into a tapestry of strong *ideals*. And it should do this with confidence, passion and commitment.

Transportation in Canada:
Solutions to the Gridlock

Chris Jones

> LIKE ALL PUBLIC *monopolies, highways give you the impression of a free good. They are not. I ask that we bear in mind one simple adage: just as there is no such thing as a free lunch, there is no such thing as a "free way." The only real questions are: who pays, who benefits and how much.*

Former U.S. Senator Daniel P. Moynihan

My objective in this paper is to shed some light on the root causes of the problem in the surface transportation sector in Canada and to propose some solutions that policy makers may wish to consider in addressing these causes. In the first part of the paper, I situate my argument for a different kind of transportation policy in the context of a longstanding theoretical debate about liberalism.

The conference took as its theme the search for a new liberalism. The implicit assumption is that the old liberalism has been found to be wanting. In the area of transportation, I would suggest that the recent historical evidence of outcomes in this sector lends support to this view. Canadian liberalism, understood as a prescriptive philosophy of government designed to improve the general welfare, has been applied in too restrictive a manner in the transportation field. In the surface transportation sector, the core belief of the past fifty years, one clearly reflected in policy, has been that freedom of individual choice trumps concerns about societal good.

Negative Liberty and Transportation

To substantiate this assertion, I propose to examine the empirical evidence in the sector using the theoretical constructs of "negative" and "positive" liberty made famous in Isaiah Berlin's inaugural lecture as the Chichele Professor of Social and Political Theory in the University of Oxford. Applying Berlin's insights from the 1950's to practical policy problems of today holds, as David Greenberg argues, "untapped promise for reconceiving the premises of our most basic political debates."[1] In the lecture, entitled "Two Concepts of Liberty," Berlin makes a distinction between negative liberty, which he understands to mean the casting off of chains or the freedom from restriction, and positive liberty, which he suggests is consistent with limiting some freedoms to achieve a higher good. Negative liberty essentially means leaving individuals alone to pursue their own ends, a condition which Berlin ultimately endorses given his stated concerns about the risks of misguided paternalism.

It is my contention that negative liberty has been enshrined as the guiding principle in the policy arrangements that underpin transportation. The mix of incentives that exist in this sector are heavily skewed towards enhancing a private conception of individual mobility (automobile use) irrespective of the costs that this imposes on society or the environment. Individual choice is the preeminent value while very little is done by governments to make transparent the consequences for society of our transportation decisions. In urban areas particularly, the emphasis on negative liberty or permitting individuals to exercise their transport choices unencumbered by concerns for society's overall well-being, is becoming problematic.

Below I discuss how Berlin's concept of negative liberty may be seen as informing the guiding principles and practices of surface transportation policy.

There is no dedicated charge for road use in Canada; we do not have a system of user pay. Roads are paid for out of consolidated revenue funds or general tax revenues. Those of us who drive pay, to different levels of government, a combination of provincial special motor fuel taxes, federal excise taxes on road fuels, vehicle registration and driver licence fees. Tolls account for only a small portion of total government revenue. The fact is that governments tend to adopt a very narrow definition of the costs associated with road-building and maintenance. At present they include the costs of construction, maintenance and a part of the expenditure on enforcement, safety and policy activity. They adopt a straight cash flow accounting model, lumping capital spending in with operational spending.

Governments don't factor in the total economic costs of road spending; they neglect to include the opportunity costs of the capital invested in the highway network. For example, paying an amount equivalent to the cost of constructing a new road to pay down the national debt may have generated a significant saving in debt-servicing costs. Capital deployed elsewhere may contribute more to the maximization of overall public welfare. Nor do they account for the depreciation costs of the road network that affects the useful life of the asset in question. It was estimated by Transport Canada in 1993 that the failure to include economic costs of roads meant that, in reality, there was annual shortfall of $5.5 billion in road revenues compared to road costs.[2] There are also questions about how much of the fuel tax collected should be considered road revenues. Railways, after all, do not use the roads, but they still pay fuel taxes.

Other factors such as social costs and externalities are also left out of the economic calculation of the cost of roads. The costs of congestion—for example the extra fuel consumption of idling engines or delays in deliveries due to stalled traffic—have been estimated to be around $2 billion annually in Toronto and $1.5 billion in Vancouver. Environmental costs—the costs of toxic pollutants, greenhouse gases, noise, damage to adjacent farmland or greenspace etc.—are substantial. The Organization for Economic Cooperation and Development has noted:

> Transport's environmental impacts occur mainly
> during the operation of motorized transport, but
> are also caused during the production and main-
> tenance of vehicles, the construction of infrastruc-
> ture, the provision of energy and fuels, and the

disposal and decommissioning of vehicles and infrastructure. All impacts during the entire life cycle
have to be taken into account.[3]

Social costs may include treating asthmatics whose admissions to
hospital increase during smog alerts, or rehabilitating road accident
victims. This year Ontario has recorded the greatest number of smog
alerts in its history (27), compared to the previous record of 23, set
last year (2001). Both of these numbers represent significant increases
over the 14 smog days registered in Ontario in 1995, the previous
highwater mark. Ground-level ozone, the main consituent of photo-
chemical (summer smog), formed from the action of sunlight on
NOx (nitrogen oxide) and VOCs (volatile organic compounds), is
believed to be responsible for between 10 and 20% of hospital admissions for respiratory ailments during the summer months in
North America.[4] According to the Ontario Medical Association,
1,900 people died prematurely in the province in the year 2000
from the effects of air pollution. In respect of accidents, Transport
Canada estimated the annual cost of traffic crashes to be $25 billion
in 1999. As recently as 1998, the Ontario Association of Chiefs of
Police (OACP) was lamenting the huge allocation of police resources
to dealing with motor vehicle accidents. In 1998, the police devoted 800,000 hours of time to dealing with 215,000 traffic accidents in which 1,000 people lost their lives and 90,000 were in-
jured. As the Chief of the OACP remarked at the time:

> ...if we had a similar number of murders there
> would be an extraordinary outcry. Traffic colli-
> sions deserve the same kind of outrage when you
> look at both the cost in human life and the social
> costs.[5]

Using conservative assumptions, the costs of environmental
remediation, health care costs, emergency scene attendance, lost
productivity to the economy, and other factors amount to billions of
dollars which the Canadian taxpayer must absorb. In Europe, the
OECD estimates that transport's unaccounted costs amount to some
8% of the GDP of OECD European countries.[6]

The point of furnishing these statistics is to illustrate how much
of the actual cost of roads remain unaccounted for. Given the sig-

nificant tacit subsidy to road use, it is hardly surprising that Canadians drive a great deal. In fact, the recent report of the Canada Transportation Act Review (CTAR) Panel has predicted that on the basis of past patterns, total car use will be 50 to 60% higher in 2015 than in 2000.[7] That a significant monetary subsidy operates to the benefit of private vehicle users is not in doubt. The CTAR Panel is worth quoting at length on this point:

> ...road users do not have to cover the whole cost of road use, because of the way governments fund road infrastructure, and because most users do not have to deal personally with some of the unwelcome social effects. If they had to do so – if road users were charged directly on each trip for the cost of maintaining the road network, as well as for the costs of congestion, environmental damage and accident risks that their road use imposes on others – it seems likely that their choices would change and more of the alternatives would be used.[8]

This brings us to Berlin's notion of negative liberty. Policies that might constrain or shape an individual's transportation choices (road tolling, green taxes) and that would work to the benefit of society or the environment, have been largely shunned. Of Canada's total network of 900,000 kilometres of roads, the portion which is tolled amounts to a total of 344 kilometres or .04% of the total. France has more than 6,300 kilometres of toll roads while the United States has 7,589 kilometres of toll roads.[9] Roads and highways continue to be viewed as free public goods, which governments, for political reasons, feel obligated to provide. No effort is made to link vehicle use to incremental pavement costs, environmental degradation or increased congestion. Surface transportation policy has been developed so as to directly encourage the individual to exercise his mobility options by means of the car. Not surprisingly, individuals act on these signals and incentives, and privatize the benefits (of mobility) while socializing the costs (the externalities). The upshot is we have SOVs commuters in SUVs —single occupant vehicle commuters in sport utility vehicles—and our major urban areas, such as the Greater Toronto Area or the Greater Vancouver Region, are increasingly experiencing traffic tie-ups of the kind we used to believe were restricted to Southern California. Coupled with the modest sums spent on transit and commuter rail and the lack of intermodality in our system, the logical and often the only rational choice is to drive. Canadian governments, especially provincial ones, have embraced a vision of mobility that is unimodal (road-centric) and based on the view that the maximum amount of individual liberty should obtain with respect to discretionary car use. It is a paradigm firmly rooted in the post-War road-building boom when, for electoral reasons, governments were eager to satisfy their voters' desire for enhancements to their newfound sense of mobility. As Myers and Kent put it: "subsidies tend to go where the votes are, and the votes are in the driver's seat."[10] Finally, it would be naive to neglect to mention the addiction that federal and provincial treasuries have to the revenue they collect from fuel excise taxes, from licence fees, from the sales of new vehicles, and other transport related activities.

While growing private car use is a problem, especially in our major urban centres, a more egregious example of the dysfunctional character of surface transportation policy lies in the commercial freight sector.

Modal Distortion in Commercial Freight Haulage

The conditions that encourage rampant car use are also critical factors that distort modal market share in the freight sector: namely, subsidized infrastructure, a largely laissez-faire approach to emissions and pollution, and an indifference to urban blight and the destruction of greenspace resulting from sprawl and heavy traffic volumes. The unfettered licence that road users enjoy, which I contend represents an exaggerated version of negative liberty, has an equally potent impact on the commercial freight transportation market.

In the freight transport sector, the swollen market share obtained by commercial trucking reflects both the infrastructure subsidy described above, uneven tax treatment of the different surface modes, and the lack of good data on the relative pavement damage done by different categories of vehicles. It is here that the lack of vigilant oversight of the burgeoning truck sector has produced its most dysfunctional policy and market outcomes. Partly this can be explained by the fact that, since 1954, trucks have been regulated provincially—the rail, air and marine modes continue to be regulated federally—and data collection on proliferating extra-provincial truck movements has been patchy. It is easy to see why. There are more than 10,000 provincially regulated, for-hire motor carriers in Canada operating over 250,000 heavy commercial trucks. Trucks have no proprietary interest in the roadway. This is in contrast to the 60 railways in the country, all of which are vertically integrated operations; that is they are responsible for the infrastructure they run on. The trucking industry has been a highly successful opponent within provincial capitals of any move towards a user-pay policy. They have a vested interest in maintaining the status quo, as most informed estimates suggest that they enjoy a 50% subsidy on the cost of the Canadian roadways that they run on.[11]

Governments have continued to regard road provision as a public good and to under-price it, a position which enjoys widespread support among motorists, notwithstanding the distortions this causes in the freight market where other modes are at a serious disadvantage. However, more recent research has begun to illuminate the extent of the cross-subsidy that private motorists are providing to commercial truck users of the roadways. A U.S. study shows that while commercial trucks account for 30% of the vehicles on the road (passenger cars, light trucks, and buses account for 70%), they account for 99% of the pavement impact.[12] In fact, cost recovery for the heaviest commercial trucks averages only about 40%. The Railway Association of Canada is driven to conclude that:

> The current fee structure (fuel taxes, annual fees)
> does not properly reflect the costs of vehicles with
> different mass and operating characteristics.[13]

This conclusion is supported by a growing body of empirical evidence from within North America and abroad. However, rather than developing a methodology to improve data capture on pavement damage by vehicle type, a precursor to the politically thorny question of road user (weight-distance) charges, provincial governments continue to allow heavy goods vehicles hugely discounted access to public roads.

What explains this reluctance? The trucking industry is large, well-organized and vocal. But this is only part of the answer. It is undeniable that trucks carry, by value, a significant share (60%) of the goods exported to the US. Hence, they have evolved into a key part of the economic distribution system. However, the proliferation of the trucking industry has causes that are more systemic. Trucking has grown in response to the interplay of a variety of economic development, industrial planning, land use, transportation and environmental decisions. Among the contributing factors are: the growth of new edge and satellite cities on the periphery of existing urban areas; new models of outsourcing and inventory management; and the desire of local municipalities to secure development fees from "big box" warehouse, distribution and logistics facilities located in non-traditional locations served only by roads. Sprawl is not simply applicable to residential housing; it also applies to manufacturing and warehousing operations and ultimately, according to this model's perverse logic, the only way to service these nodes is by truck. Additionally, Transport ministries everywhere espouse the basic belief that mobility can only be enhanced by adding road capacity and hence they tend to act as de facto lobbyists for the laying of new asphalt. New infrastructure spending on roads clearly benefits trucks. One of the biggest factors, though, has been the unwillingness of policy makers to impute the full cost of environmental impacts generated to the individual modes responsible. Trucking is a highly fuel intensive mode of transport and the pollution that is a by-product of its activities is absorbed by society in general.[14]

Intermodalism

If the 1950s was an era imbued with optimism about the unlimited possibilities that road travel promised, fifty years later that optimism has diminished as we have become distinctly aware of the drawbacks to rampant private vehicle and commercial truck use. Although advances in engine technology have mitigated emissions somewhat, the sheer, inexorable increase in vehicles on the road has rendered many urban areas close to high volume roads virtually unfit for human habitation. As a recent enquiry by the Toronto Public Health Department into the presence of cancer-causing chemicals in Toronto's air put it:

Two of the ten carcinogens—benzene and polycyclic aromatic hydrocarbons (PAHs)—are present in outdoor air at levels that are ten times higher than the levels considered tolerable and should be given high priority by the City for actions that will reduce emissions. *The transportation sector is likely the most significant source of emissions for both these contaminants within the City.*[15]

The key is to decouple transport growth from economic growth and to develop an alternative to the present unimodal focus on roads. To do this we need a new vision for transportation that places the accent on transparency, sustainability and intermodality, characteristics that are more or less absent from the current surface transportation system. Intermodalism means linking two different modes together seamlessly to take advantage of the intrinsic benefits of each. In its recent Transport Policy White Paper, the European Union has expressed an official commitment to intermodality, stating:

Intermodality is of fundamental importance for developing competitive alternatives to road transport. Action must therefore be taken to ensure fuller integration of the modes offering considerable potential transport capacity as links in an efficiently managed transport chain joining up all the individual services.[16]

A good example of an air-rail intermodal link is the leading-edge high-speed rail terminal situated in the heart of Terminal 2 at the Roissy-Charles de Gaulle Airport in Paris, France. In Canada, the rail-truck intermodal business units of Canadian National and Canadian Pacific Railways are heavily involved in taking trucks off the road in the Quebec City to Windsor corridor. Rail's intermodal services are essentially roll-on/roll-off and piggy-back systems that also involve the introduction of high capacity, double-stacked container cars and multi-level auto carriers. The largest double-stacked intermodal/container train can take well over 200 trucks off our highways. On arrival at a rail intermodal yard, the freight is handed over to trucks for local delivery. Intermodal is now the largest line of business in the Canadian rail sector. It is also a key part of the equation in international movements, transporting import-export containers for ocean shipping companies.

Intermodal services have become attractive to time-sensitive businesses/shippers which are cognizant of the fact that intermodal trains have scheduled departure-arrival times, that they run over separate and dedicated corridors, and that rail's transactional times at border crossings are minimal. This has been particularly true in the wake of the September 11th attacks when commercial trucking sustained massive wait times at crossings. Companies in the retail sector (Canadian Tire, Hudson's Bay, Sears), in the automotive sector (Daimler Chrysler Canada), and in the courier market, to cite just a few, have all become regular users of intermodal services. That the Class 1 rail carriers have been able to capture this business testifies to their efficiency given the extent of the highway infrastructure subsidy to commercial trucks operating on Canada's roads and trade corridors, a subsidy that is reflected in the rates trucks may offer shippers. Bear in mind as well that railways must pay all of their own infrastructure costs and then pay property taxes on these linear corridors to provincial and municipal governments. After allowing for the truck fuel used to pick up and distribute loads, intermodal is about three to four times more fuel efficient than highway truck.[17] Rail's lighter "ecological footprint" is corroborated by the Organization for Economic Cooperation and Development in its study of Environmentally Sustainable Transportation. They write:

> Life-cycle assessments and eco-balance studies show that rail transport—including high speed rail—causes considerably less in the way of environmental impacts than road and air traffic.[18]

Governments can support goods transfer from our congested highways by investing in intermodal infrastructure. Such investments will have the added advantage of leveraging further private sector investment and reaping a range of public interest benefits, i.e reduction of congestion, pollution and accidents.

Urban Transportation

In Canada's largest cities there is a growing sense that present patterns of daily car-based commuting are no longer sustainable. The problem, though, is that existing public policy in relation to land use (low density) and highway financing and usage (no full-cost accounting) simply encourages individuals to drive. Building new roads or expanding existing ones is not the answer, as it merely induces new traffic. This is a public policy problem and a problem of individual incentives. No single individual will alter his commuting behaviour given the mix of explicit and tacit financial incentives facing him or her. Most motorists consider gas and parking as their only marginal costs. Pursuing your rational self interest as an individual commuter, though, leads to a "collective action" problem. Despite all of the advances in the science of traffic engineering we still inevitably confront what traffic engineers describe as the Wile E. Coyote effect:

> Just as the curve of maximum throughput—moving as many cars between two points on a road as efficiently as possible—reaches its peak, it abruptly falls of the cliff and is squashed flat against the baseline of the graph.[19]

With growing numbers of Canadians and new immigrants seeking to make their homes in or at the periphery of our largest urban areas, traffic congestion has become endemic. As the report from the Prime Minister's Task Force on Urban Issues put it:

> ...transportation is a major concern—from backlogged cars and trucks on major roads through Montreal, to pressure on the few routes that connect Ottawa and Gatineau, to congestion on major roads into Calgary's downtown core, to gridlock on the Lion's Gate Bridge into Vancouver.[20]

The answer lies in moving people by public transit and commuter rail. In Toronto, GO Transit carries 44 million passenger a year on its trains and buses and, in the process, removes 1.5 billion passenger kilometres of car trips each year from GTA roads. GO was taken back into provincial crown ownership in 2001 after operating for several years as an entity of the GTA municipalities. The difficulty is that GO is capacity constrained; its existing rail fleet is fully used during rush hour. The problem is one of insufficient financial resources. Many urban transit entities are funded by a mix of local property taxes, by direct (but irregular) transfers from more senior governments and by revenues from the farebox. The transit authorities in Vancouver (Greater Vancouver Transportation Authority) and Montreal (Agence Metropolitaine de Transport) also enjoy access to a portion of the provincial fuel excise tax revenue. On the whole, though, most transit/commuter rail systems, while covering about 60% of their operating costs from the farebox, are unable to expand their fixed plant (stations and trackage) because they lack the revenues. After all, they confront a heavily subsidized road and parking system which strongly favours car use. There is the added complication that commuter authorities lease track time from the freight rail companies and any subsequent expansion in the frequency of commuter service must make whole the adverse operating impacts on the freight business. Periodic injections of capital are not the answer and it is more clear now than ever that transit authorities require the kind of stable, long-term funding that will enable them to plan ahead and address their acute demand challenges.

The fact that Canada has no national program for investing in urban transit/commuter rail—the only major G-8 country in which this is the case—is a significant impediment to the preservation of the quality of life in our cities. This is doubly critical at a time when cities have assumed a new importance in both the demographic make-up of our own country and in the global economic pecking order. Several options have been advanced that would either involve direct federal involvement in the provision of urban transit infrastructure or result in a transfer of federal funds to municipal governments. They all presuppose a political will on the part of the Federal government to mobilize the financial resources at its disposal and a willingness to negotiate whatever constitutional restrictions exist on assertion of federal authority in what has previously been an area of provincial jurisdiction. The first option might be for the federal government to vacate tax room to the benefit of the municipalities so as to grant them the revenue base for dedicated funding of urban transportation infrastructure. The second might be to establish, at the national level, a permanent transportation infrastructure program, along the lines of the recently created Canada Strategic Infrastructure Fund, to which transit authorities would be eligible to apply. Neither of the first two options, however, passes the critical litmus test of incorporating full cost accounting or road user charges. The third would be to establish a New Zealand-type road fund of the kind recommended by the Canadian Transportation Act Review Panel using proceeds from gas taxes and road user fees. It is to this last option that I will turn my attention.

A Sustainable Solution to ending Gridlock

The solution to our surface transportation dilemma requires boldness and creativity and there is no doubt that, in the short term, it may offend some vested interests. However, the price of inaction is high, as the status quo in surface transportation in not sustainable in economic, environmental or social (quality of life) terms.

The model proposed below involves new policies for the funding and management of transportation infrastructure, including charges for its use. It would entail cooperation between federal, provincial and municipal governments. It builds, in particular, on Recommendation 10.1 of the Canada Transportation Act Review (CTAR) Panel, contained in their chapter on "Paying for Roads."[21] The CTAR Panel calls for the establishment of road and transport funding and management agencies. This approach is modelled on the World Bank/New Zealand Model of road and transport funding and management agencies. The model establishes a central fund allocation agency with revenues from three sources:

1. the federal and provincial governments would contribute their respective road and rail fuel excise tax proceeds;
2. existing provincial and municipal budgetary expenditures on transport would be rolled in; and
3. efficient road user charges covering congestion, infrastructure and externality costs.

The central fund would in turn disburse monies to a series of sub-fund agencies: a primary highway fund; an urban transport fund; a secondary road fund; and a municipal street fund. The central fund would decide on criteria for allocating funds to the four sectors. The central fund would be governed by the following set of principles:

- users should pay for roads by means of appropriate charges and fees;
- charges for roads should be based on costs imposed, differentiated so far as practical by nature of vehicle, type of road and amount of congestion;
- managers of the road network should have responsibility for both charging and spending decisions;
- users should be involved in decisions on both charges and expenditures; and
- alternatives to road spending in other modes should be allowed to compete for road funds.[22]

Exhibit 1 below gives an idea of how the model might be structured. Assigning rail fuel taxes to the central fund is consistent with the CTAR Panel's recommendation that alternatives to road spending in other modes should be allowed to compete for road funds. Funds would be disbursed to the most socially cost-beneficial projects on the basis of their contribution to a series of key public interest criteria (see Exhibit 2). The fund would have multi-jurisdictional representation (federal-provincial-municipal) with representation from user groups as well, reflecting the fact that revenue streams originate from registration fees, fuel taxes, road tolls etc. This model might also include some demand side incentives to encourage travellers and shippers to select more sustainable modes where feasible. An example of such a demand incentive would be making monthly transit or commuter rail passes a tax deduction. The advantages of the proposed model over the present system are several fold. First there would be more cost-effective investment decisions with respect to carriers and infrastructure as well as effective demand-side incentives. Roads would no longer be artificially favoured. Funding of the different modes would also be more balanced and adequate. Transparency of costs would become a permanent feature of the new model. The upshot is that by removing the systemic biases that presently distort the allocation of funds by mode, the market (travellers and freight shippers) would then decide on the most optimal mode for a particular movement or shipment.

In respect of roads that are not commercially viable (primarily local municipal and remote roads), the CTAR Panel suggests they "would continue to need some direct government funding but they too would benefit from separate management, use of objective evaluation criteria, and involvement of users in charging and spending decisions."[23]

Exhibit 1. Multi-modal transport funding agency model

Funding Sources	Short term: • Federal and provincial road and rail fuel taxes. Provincial license fees. • Provincial/municipal budgetary expenditures. Long term: • Effecient road user charges covering congestion, infrastructure & externality.
Applications of Funds	Infrastructure/innovation: • Roads, rail or alternative modes. • Passenger or freight. • Uni- or intermodal. • Most socially cost-beneficial projects.
Governance Requirements	Create multi-jurisdictional funding and management agencies. Federal/provincial/municipal cooperative arrangements. Major Institutional Reform.
Recipients of Funds	Roads and transport funding and managements agencies for subsequent disbursement.

Searching for the New Liberalism

Exhibit 2. Evaluation Criteria and Related Assessment Indicators

	Criteria	Assesment Indicators	
Dimensions of Suitability		Sustainability enhanced when, other things equal, policy leads to:	Indicator(s) employed:
Environmental	Climate change	Reduced emissions of greenhouse gases (GHGs) from transport.	Megatonnes of GHG emissions per year.
	Pollution prevention	Reduced production of criteria air contaminants (CACs) from transport.	Megatonnes of CAC production per year.
	Protection & conservation	Reduced use of fossil fuels in transport.	Litres of fossil fuels consumed per year.
Economic	Effeciency	Improved productivity of transportation services through the best use of all modes.	Freight tonne-km/ (track kms of rails + lane kms of road); Passenger kms/ (track kms of rails + lane kms of road).
	Cost interalization	Increased application of full cost pricing to transportation services, incl. social costs.	Degree and consistency of applications within and across modes.
	Affordability	Improved allocation of capital investment within and across modes.	Degree and consistency with which rigorous evaluation methods used.
Social	Safety & heath	Reduced probability and severity of accidents.	Accidents and fatality rates per capita per year.
	Access & choice	Greater availability of sustainable choices to users of transport.	Degree to which sustainable choices are increased.
Feasability	Design considerations	Fewer new design considerations.	Number and complexity of new design considerations.
	Institutional considerations	Less institutional change.	Degree and complexity of required institutional change.

Conclusion

This paper has sought to argue that Business-as-Usual (BAU) trends in transportation in Canada are no longer sustainable. If governments remain paralyzed by inertia and drift, the future that awaits us is bleak. Canada's competitiveness in the global economy will decline in the next twenty years because our transportation system won't be able to compete. Our major cities will be characterized by gridlock because there will be too much freight and too many people in too many vehicles with too few traffic lanes. Transportation sector greenhouse gases, already the single largest component of Canada's emissions, will continue to grow and the Kyoto targets of 6% below 1990 levels will seem illusory. Toronto, which is already 40% paved surface, will achieve the ignominy of Los Angeles, which is 60% paved. Traffic deaths and injuries, which cost society and the economy a fortune in suffering, insurance payouts, and lost productivity, will continue to grow. Overall ambient noise from roads will move from becoming a nuisance to an actual health hazard. These are just some of the very real outcomes that may arise if inaction and apathy remain the major policy responses to escalating private vehicle and truck use.

Bold policy changes are required. There is a clear need to marry land use to transportation policy. Low density development, and its corollary single use zoning, has given rise to a highly land-consumptive, gasoline-intensive and emissions-indifferent model. Greater densities, policies devoted to in-fill and brownfield redevelopment are the way forward. They will require resolve to implement as vested interests are bound to resist them.

Capturing the full cost of road use by private vehicles and commercial trucks is an urgently required step and the paper has sought to suggest how this might be achieved. As a recent OECD conference on sustainable transport put it, "ensuring that rail contributes its full potential towards achieving sustainable transportation will require the integration of financial and other decision-making tools for transport and environment so that sustainability criteria are applied in transport decision-making at all levels."[24] Intermodality must become the lens through which we view all future investments in the transportation sector. Urban transit and commuter rail will require a significant and stable funding commitment, a change that will probably necessitate the involvement of the federal government.

In essence, to return to the dichotomy of negative and positive liberty, which Berlin perceived as central to the debate about the nature of liberalism, some corrective must be introduced to limit the unbridled freedom that reigns on our roads and highways. The largely hidden costs that the BAU model imposes are too onerous for society to underwrite indefinitely. A new balance must be struck which recognizes that unconstrained mobility cannot continue to subordinate values such as quality of life, environmental sustainability and financial sanity.

* *The views expressed in this paper are those of the author alone and do not necessarily represent the views of the Railway Association of Canada. I would like to thank Robert Taylor for his help in refining some of the ideas contained in this paper.*

Notes:

[1] David Greenberg review of Michael Ignatieff's *Isaiah Berlin: A Life* in *Journal Civnet's Journal for Civil Society*, January-February 1999, Vol 3., No.1.

[2] Transport Canada, *Road Infrastructure Expenditures, Fuel Taxes and Road Related Revenues in Canada*, TP 12795E, June 1996, p.11.

[3] OECD, *Environmentally Sustainable Transport; Futures, Strategies and Best Practices,* (Paris: OECD, October 2000), p.28.

[4] *Ibid.*, p.21.

[5] Ontario Association of Chiefs of Police, *Media Communique,* 2nd December 1998, p.2

[6] OECD, *Environmentally Sustainable Transport,* p.28.

[7] Canada Transportation Act Review Panel, *Vision and Balance*, (Ottawa: Public Works and Government Services Canada, 2001), p.177.

[8] *Ibid.*, pp.180-81.

[9] *Ibid.*, p.185.

[10] Norman Myers and Jennifer Kent, *Perverse Subsidies; How Tax Dollars can undercut the Environment and the Economy,* (Washington: Island Press, 2001), p.97

[11] See IBI Group in association with Boon, Jones & Associates, *Full Cost Transportation and Cost-Based Pricing Strategies,* November 1995, Exhibit 4.12.

Canada's Domestic Expatriates:
the Urban Aboriginal Population

Mark Podlasly

WHY HAS IT BEEN so difficult for Canadians and aboriginal people to come to some sort of mutually agreeable understanding of what it means to share this land? How is it that after centuries of sharing this physical space called Canada, aboriginal and non-aboriginal people still know very little about each other's hopes, dreams and aspirations? One only needs to read newspapers in Canada to see that the tension between aboriginal people and the Canadian system is extreme. News reports of violent protests, court challenges, civil disobedience, treaty referenda, poverty, prison populations, and suicides characterize the poor relationship between Canada and its indigenous population.

Aboriginal statistics reveal a dismal picture. Aboriginal people in Canada are:
- 3 times as likely to die accidentally or violently
- 8 times more likely to commit suicide
- *have twice the infant mortality rates* than non-aboriginal Canadians
- 6.6 times likely to have of tuberculosis infections
- 2 times as likely to report a long-term disability
- in western Canada, four times as many Aboriginal people are below the poverty line[1]

- 3 times the rate of diabetes[2]
- 6 times higher incarceration rates[3]
- 50 % of aboriginal children, on and off reserve, live in poverty[4]

Policy makers have tried to craft policies to allow aboriginal people to define their place within Canada, but after decades of concerted effort and billions of dollars, aboriginal people continue to find themselves outside the governance system, and at the bottom of almost every indicator of social and economic progress.

There is a fundamental disconnect between policy makers and aboriginal people on the definition of aboriginality. Policy makers, for political and administrative reasons, have been unwilling to address what it truly means to be aboriginal in a modern and increasingly mobile liberal-democratic society.

To government policy makers, aboriginality exists primarily as a politically inspired, 19th century geographically based concept, namely: Indians living on isolated Indian Reserves to whom the federal government would provide all social services and direction. But this antiquated impression of aboriginality no longer exists. Over the past century, the indigenous concept of aboriginality has changed, evolved and outgrown the dated conceptions held by federal policy makers.

Forced by events and historical pressures, aboriginal people and their cultures are adapting to Canada's changing political, economic and social environments. The most visible aspect of this modernization is the growing urbanization of aboriginal people.

With limited economic opportunities and deplorable social conditions on reserve, an increasing number of aboriginal people have opted to seek better lives for themselves and their children in urban areas. The number of urban off-reserve native people in Canada has risen from a low of 7% in 1951 to just over 50% today.[5] Given the widespread availability of media influences, it is hardly surprising that aboriginal people, a youth-dominated population, are increasingly headed towards the big cities and bright lights. In many ways, this is part of a larger global trend towards urbanization.

Estimates as to the size of Canada's urban aboriginal populations vary widely.[6] Federal census data from 1996 indicates that the largest urban aboriginal population center in Canada is now Winnipeg with 45,750 residents. Other cities have similarly large and growing aboriginal populations. Edmonton and Vancouver each both have approximately 32,000 aboriginal residents, Saskatoon, 16,160, Regina, 13,605 and Toronto, 16,095.[7] Many provincial and provincial and aboriginal organizations believe that urban aboriginal populations are much higher than the federal estimates. For example, some groups estimate Toronto's aboriginal population to be between 40,000 and 60,000 as high as 60,000 in Toronto residents and 50,000 in Edmonton.[8]

And given the fact that Canada's aboriginal population is the fastest growing segment of the Canadian population increasing at almost twice the national average,[9] we can expect even more aboriginal people to migrate to cities and urban areas. But current federal practice largely ignores aboriginal people living outside Indian Reserves.

Life in the City

Overall, aboriginal life in urban environments can be equal to, if not more challenging than life on a reserve.[10] Government statistics reveal that urban aboriginal communities are generally younger, predominantly female and more impoverished than their non-aboriginal counterparts with overall health, employment and income indicators all lower than the Canadian average. The urban poverty rate for native people is 55.6%,[11] and the crime rate for off-reserve aboriginal people is higher than that of the non-aboriginal population—4.5 times higher in Calgary and nearly 12 times higher in Regina and Saskatoon.[12] But statistics don't reveal the diversity present in urban communities. Alongside depressing social conditions, there are other emerging expressions of aboriginal adaptation to urban life.

There are now over 150,000 aboriginal people across Canada who have completed or are enrolled in some form of post-secondary education, labor participation rates in urban areas are nearly equal to that of other Canadians and social problems such as suicide, rape and violence, although still higher than those of the non-aboriginal population, are generally lower off-reserve.[13] There are also anecdotal signs of growing cultural fusions, rising individual incomes, and increasing numbers of employed aboriginal people assuming places within urban society.

Even more importantly, across both on and off reserve communities, aboriginal people have quietly established informal networks outside of government that are important conduits of information, family support and cultural awareness. For those inside aboriginal networks, these informal channels are deepening and starting to spread. Tap into an urban aboriginal network and you'll find that native people are informally connected not only amongst themselves in city settings, but increasingly, to their home reserve communities.

Sadly, this growing urban aspect of modern aboriginality remains outside the purview of federal policy makers who remain hobbled by their past notions of aboriginality as an immobile and geographically remote concept. The current aboriginal policy focus on the more easily managed Indian Reserves ignores the reality of the growing multi-dimensional urban populations. As such, the federal government effectively overlooks the role the most educated and cross-culturally adroit portion of Canada's aboriginal indigenous population is playing in the overall development of First Nation modern aboriginals culture and society.[14]

The result of the reserve-centric perspective is that the federal government is missing an important opportunity to engage aboriginal people, both on and off reserve, to contribute to the overall development of all First Nations.

New Realities

Canada's current aboriginal policies are heavily influenced by past colonial interpretations of aboriginal people and cultures. At the time of Canada's founding, aboriginal people, their property, and all aspects of their lives, were deemed to be a federal responsibility as delineated by Section 91 (24) of the Constitution.

The Indian Act was created to consolidate administrative control over aboriginal people, their resources and property. Federal Indian Reserves were created across the country to restrict mobility and segregate aboriginal people from the land and the newly arriving non-indigenous populations. The Reserves were established as a federal jurisdiction. The federal government, or their designated agents, provided on-reserve services.

In 1951, Indian Act restrictions on mobility were removed and aboriginal people were allowed to move off federal reserves into provincial space in search of greater economic, education and social opportunities. But the constitutional provisions keeping aboriginal people and their lands in federal ward-ship have not been updated. As a result, aboriginal people off-reserve have found themselves in the peculiar situation of being federal subjects within provincial domains. Fifty years ago, when few aboriginal people lived off-reserve, this was a jurisdictional curiosity. But what began as a jurisdictional curiosity now causes real and immediate problems. Aboriginal people, by virtue of being a federal responsibility, are unable to easily access many of the provincially provided social programs that other Canadians take for granted.

Aboriginal people off-reserve are clearly a federal responsibility, but how should the federal government exercise its responsibilities to native people living extra-jurisdictionally in provincial space? How would this practically be accomplished? Faced with challenging constitutional and legal issues about federal incursions into provincial space, federal policy makers have chosen to largely ignore the issue and remain focused on the jurisdictionally neater federal reserves.

Provincial governments, not willing to encroach on a federal responsibility, offer aboriginal people limited and uneven social services. Cities and municipalities, as creations of the provincial government and in many cases limited in financial resources, are equally hesitant to assume an abandoned federal responsibility.

Aboriginal people thus find themselves trapped between federal and provincial practices that effectively limit them from the full benefits of the Canadian social net. Adding to their conundrum, by virtue of being off-reserve in provincial space, urban aboriginal people have limited ways of making their conditions known to federal policy makers. There are few, if any, effective urban political organizations that represent city-based aboriginal interests.

Federal Policy Application—The Situation

Where the federal government has taken an interest in a specific urban aboriginal area, it is usually in a limited capacity and almost always in conjunction with an existing provincial, municipal or First Nation government partner. The result is usually a conflicting labyrinth of overlapping and sometimes contradictory service offerings. A recent Canada West Foundation project found that gov-ernment services directed towards urban aboriginal clients differed from region to region. [15] The result is that social service offerings are often confusing, erratic and difficult to navigate.

Some municipalities have tried to fill in for an absent federal government, but their resources and capacities to deal with a highly mobile and transient population tax their limited resources. There are examples of municipal-aboriginal partnerships that provide services to aboriginal groups, but the majority of these agreements are with established First Nations groups that have existing reserve bases within city boundaries.

Pan-aboriginal social agencies, such as the Aboriginal Friendship Centres, offer some services to urban aboriginal populations, but funding for the Centres is often from multiple government funding sources and subject to annual review and cuts. Also, the Centres, when acting as social agencies, are not politically accountable to their urban aboriginal residents.

While all of these initiatives are admirable, they are each a poor substitute for a coherent on and off reserve federal policy. That said, it is not realistic to expect a major change in federal-provincial constitutional jurisdictions. Instead, what is needed is a new practical approach to address the problem imposed on a modern and mobile aboriginal population.

Aboriginal public policy needs to take into account not only the diverse geography, history, cultures and rights issues of aboriginal peoples in different parts of the country, but it must also embrace a growing modernity that comes part and parcel with urbanization and mobility. Creative insight on how to approach the social, education and development challenges that confound policy makers can be found in the cities.

A Missed Opportunity

In the move towards urbanization, city-dwelling aboriginal people have been forced to confront and, sometimes tragically, answer difficult questions about what it means to share Canada. This knowledge is remaking what it means to be aboriginal in an increasingly urban and global world. Some aboriginal leaders have heralded this increased urbanization as a loss of culture and birthright. Certainly the Royal Commission on Aboriginal Peoples reinforced this idea of geographic determinism, but there is another way in which to view this definitive migration.

I would like to posit that the on and off reserve components are not separate entities but are in fact, inexorably linked forming a communal moiety. All First Nations in Canada are now essentially bi-furcated communities with one part living on-reserve in the traditional territory, and the other living in urban centers. In urban environments, First Nation members from many different reserves interrelate with other aboriginal peoples to become an amorphous, loosely-affiliated meta-community that bears a striking resemblance to overseas expatriate communities.

When policy makers could broaden their view from a Canada-centric perspective to an international vantage, they will notice a remarkable similarity between off-reserve aboriginal populations and international émigré expatriate communities that exist apart from their homeland countries. [16] Global expatriate communities, similar to aboriginal urban populations, are not astray portions of their originating nations, but are increasingly important extensions of their homeland-based cultures. These foreign groups/individuals, like aboriginal people in Canada, have chosen to migrate in search of better opportunities for themselves and their families. Distant from their home nations and effectively residing extra-jurisdictionally in politically indifferent cities, expatriates adapt what is locally available and create self-reliant networks to meet their particular needs. The opportunities in including these migrant networks in home community development are staggering.

Thanks to increased mobility and lower telecommunication and travel costs, expatriates/émigrés who would have once been lost from their home nations continue to remain involved in their homeland's cultural, economic and political life. Development-focused nations with large émigré expatriate populations have begun to see this type of expatriate flow as a valuable resource in promoting societal and material development of their home-based societies. The Inter-America Development Bank reported that Latin America and Caribbean expatriate workers—sending relatively small individual amounts of US $250 to friends and family eight to ten times a year—contributed nearly US $20 billion in 2000 to their home countries. This amount exceeded the region's Official Development Assistance and is nearly equal to one-third of the region's Foreign Direct Investment. Worldwide, expatriates contributed more than US $100 billion in 2000 to their homeland communities. This amount is expected to increase to US $300 billion by the year 2010. [17]

To encourage their extra-jurisdictional nationals to participate in the development of their home societies, many countries have initiated creative public policies that allow their expatriates to contribute not only capital but knowledge to their home societies.

Mexico encourages its expatriates to contribute to their home communities by offering remittance development bonds and in some regional cases, matching three-for-one every dollar expatriates contribute to small-scale infrastructure projects.[18] In further recognition of the importance of expatriates, the Mexican government, working around the extra-jurisdictional issues of having its nationals out of the country, actively assists migrant associations of expatriates from the same region to form community networks in their host countries. There are now approximately 400 such community support organizations across the United States. Guatemala and El Salvador are now encouraging similar regional associations for their expatriate communities.[19] As an odd aside, El Salvador also helps its citizens in the United States apply for political asylum so that they will continue to send money back to their families. [20]

For the past ten years, Colombia has worked to build a knowledge network of expatriate researchers and engineers in 30 countries to contribute to nationally important joint research projects in areas such as biotech and robotics. Uruguay, recognizing the opportunity in its 400,000 increasingly educated overseas residents, has launched a similar program.[21] The Public Institute of California found that intellectual two-way flows between homeland and Silicon Valley expatriate communities, particularly in the Chinese and Indian communities, has resulted in entrepreneurial and commercial practices being "exported" back home. The supposed "brain drain" of these nations' highly-educated émigrés expatriates is being replaced by a "brain circulation."[22]

The United Nations (UN), has initiated the Transfer of Knowledge Through Expatriate Nationals (TOKTEN) program to encourage qualified expatriates to return home for short three to twelve week volunteer assignments as teachers, researchers and engineers.

The UN has found that TOKTEN participants transfer knowledge faster and easier than outside government officials as the volunteers do not require social and cultural context adjustment. The UN also reports that in almost all of the exchanges, valuable networks are created and follow-up between the home community and volunteer takes place. Expatriates interested in participating in the TOKTEN program can easily register their interest by registering on-line at a UN web site.[23]

Politically, homeland politicians are also increasingly seeking the support of their émigrés external expatriate communities. In recent Colombia national elections, a Miami-based Colombian won a seat in the Colombian Congress offering to represent his overseas compatriots and Mexican politicians regularly campaign and raise funds in Los Angeles, Houston and other U.S. cities.[24]

These nations and organizations have recognized the importance of crafting public policies that include expatriates in the overall development of their home societies. In fact, such an international outlook is absolutely vital to fulfilling the global human security agenda.

Within Canada, urban aboriginal communities are beginning to exhibit similar multi-directional education, knowledge and capital flows as their transnational counterparts. Like foreign émigré expatriate communities, aboriginal people off-reserve live in politically indifferent federal extra-jurisdictional politically indifferent environments where they are forced to develop networks to get around the constitutional limitations that stymie policy makers.

One only needs to look at the emergence of multiple pan-First Nation media, business organizations and cultural events to see that there is a burgeoning international-like cross-fertilization of thoughts and concepts occurring among on and off-reserve aboriginal people. Modern aboriginal media networks that service both urban and rural communities such as the Aboriginal Multi-Media Society, the Aboriginal People's Television Network, First Nation-oriented radio stations, and aboriginal newspapers such as Aboriginal Times, Raven's Eye or First Perspective, are all direct outgrowths of an increasing urbanization. Aboriginal business organizations and trade shows such as the Native Investment and Trade Association's NEXUS conference direct investors and capital to aboriginal entrepreneurs on and off reserve, and cultural events like the Toronto International

Pow-Wow and the National Aboriginal Achievement Awards are part of the growing non-geographic characterization of what it means to be modernly aboriginal.

Aboriginal youth in cities cross paths with indigenous youth from other First Nations and increasingly, other countries. Increasing numbers of aboriginal university students traveling to cities for education are exposed to new ideas and skills at urban institutions and work places and aboriginal wage earners returning to reserves for visits contribute gifts and financial remittances to friends and family. And Indian band election campaigns are increasingly being projected via the Internet to band members in cities far removed from their traditional territory.

This on and off reserve flow of people, ideas and goods between urban and rural communities is rapidly effecting a redefinition of what it means to be aboriginal in a modern Canada. Yet the possibilities and potential of the multi-directional flows of ideas, education, and capital is outside the purview of federal policy makers because the federal government limits its view of aboriginality to only one-half of aboriginal communities, the part that easily fits its needs.

Federal policy makers often continue to see aboriginality in terms of a historic 'top down' line structure with Ottawa supposedly directing all inputs into Canada's Indian Reserves. Requests to the Department of Indian and Northern Affairs for statistical data on the flow of people, goods and capital between on and off reserve populations are met with a perplexed silence. At present, the federal government does not collect the information that other émigré nations with large expatriate communities have realized is essential to their overall social, economic and education development. But the multi-directional, inter-communities and intra-reserve circulation of ideas, concepts and money is happening. And it is accelerating.

It seems that while Canada's concept of plurality has evolved, and indeed, our widespread acceptance of the idea of political correctness is positively 21st century, government attitudes and policies governing aboriginal people have not moved much past 1867. If we can shift our societal lens of the on-off reserve situation to an international-level perspective of urban expatriate communities, there is great reason for optimism. This is not to say that there are not still massive social problems to be resolved in urban aboriginal communities. The levels of overall aboriginal poverty, homelessness, unemployment and violence are extreme and undeniable. It would be heinously remiss of governments not to continue trying to help the most needy of our society. But in the quest for improving the lives of aboriginal people, policy makers need an inclusive view that assists aboriginal people both on and off-reserve.

New Directions

To move forward, here are some initial steps that the Federal Government could consider to improve the overall state of Canada's growing and rapidly modernizing aboriginal populations.

1. Replicate international examples of expatriate-to-homeland connections. Bolster the already existing informal channels.

Canadian aboriginal policy needs to adapt to the modern network reality of what it means to be aboriginal in this country. In formulating new aboriginal strategies, policy makers would be well advised to think "outside the constitutional box" and look at how other nations have successfully included extra-jurisdictional people in the development of their overall societies.

As was pointed out earlier, foreign governments have realized that they can best help international extra-jurisdictional communities by applying their expertise to enhance and strengthen the self-reliant networks that connect expatriates to their homelands. Successful governments have not tried to replicate—nor replace—the initiative of expatriates to better themselves or their communities.

It would be relatively easy, not to mention constitutionally polite, for the federal government to begin a process of bolstering aboriginal peoples' already existing on and off reserve multi-directional skills, ideas and community networks.

Next Steps

2. Enlarge the concept of aboriginality so that it matches the geographic diversity of a modern and highly mobile aboriginal population.

The Federal Government's focus on historic perceptions of aboriginality blinds it to what is really going on in aboriginal Canada. The 50% of aboriginal people who have chosen to relocate to the cities don't see themselves existing within the geographic reserve categories that are important to federal policy makers. The legal definitions of on or off-reserve have become hollow honorifics with little relevance to a modern, evolving and mobile aboriginal population.

There are very real constitutional restrictions on federal involvement in service delivery to urban expatriate aboriginal populations, but this box-like mentality of on or off reserve limits the government's ability to encourage the burgeoning intellectual, development and capital flows that exist between urban and reserve-based aboriginal communities. By using the constitution as a way to avoid considering unique ways to enable aboriginal people to contribute to their own development does all Canadians a disservice. There are no constitutional limits on creative thought.

3. Look globally for comparative examples.

As argued in this paper, Canada is not alone in having large numbers of disadvantaged populations relocating to urban centers. By broadening the perspective from a domestic focus to an international viewpoint, policy makers might see the on-off reserve situation in a very different light. By applying creative thought and looking outside our domestic perceptions, policy makers can expand their range of possible policy options. [25]

4. Collect data on the on-off reserve interaction.

The federal government's current on-reserve focus means that it does not maintain the essential intra-aboriginal community statistical data required to understand how urban expatriates interrelate among themselves and with their corresponding on-reserve components. The federally supported Canada Foundation for Innovation is currently funding a University of Saskatchewan Urban Aboriginal Database, which according to the university website, will start to document the location, dynamics, characteristics and change over time of Aboriginal people in urban centres. [26] The information being collected by the University is a good initial step to understanding the integrated nature of on and off reserve populations. Without full data on the nature of the interrelations between all aboriginal people, it will be impossible for policy makers to fully understand how to support aboriginal expatriate contributions to their home communities.

5. Create a politically neutral space for aboriginal people living in urban areas to speak.

Because the current aboriginal system is geared to a decidedly on-reserve perspective, off-reserve urban aboriginal people have few, if any, means to effectively communicate their views to policy makers. There is a great need for a politically neutral space for city-dwelling aboriginal people to convey their thoughts, experience and knowledge to the policy discourse. If a space can be created for urban aboriginal people to speak and be heard, not one but many voices will emerge from urban centers across Canada.

Conclusion

This paper is an attempt to inject a broader international perspective into what is occurring across all of Canada's aboriginal communities. Some of the concepts presented in this paper may be controversial. The aboriginal realm in Canada is a highly political, value laden and as such, emotionally charged environment. "To be aboriginal in this country is to be political. It has always been this way." [27] People, political parties and aboriginal organizations all listen and engage concepts from their particular political perspective. Government departments, aboriginal NGOs, academics and politicians have built careers based on the current nature of the federal aboriginal relationship. The idea of bolstering the non-attributable and distributive nature of Canada's existing aboriginal networks could be seen as a detriment to indigenous and political entities that depend on a centralized control of information.

This paper does not evade the fact that overall, aboriginal populations have desperate social and economic problems. The condition of aboriginal people in Canada is indefensible and inexcusable. Nor does this paper advocate that there is an emerging middle or elite aboriginal class that will save aboriginal Canada and soothe the conscience of non-aboriginal Canada, nor that successful aboriginal people should leave the cities and permanently return home to re-build their government-delineated reserve communities.

Reframing the urban aboriginal question from a constitutionally restrictive on or off-reserve problem to a wider, more expansive global view increases the range of possibilities policy makers might explore for improving the lives of aboriginal people wherever they live.

Sources:

Aboriginal Business Development Online. "The Power of Partnerships: New Opportunities for Aboriginal Peoples and Ontario Businesses." Ontario Native Affairs Secretariat. July 22, 2002. August 15, 2002. http:// www.aboriginalbusiness.on.ca/resource_kit/subhtml/chap04_05_06/chap04_1_right.html

Anderson, Daryl. Personal Interview. September 17, 2002.

"An Anthropology of Happiness – The Filipina Sisterhood." *The Economist,* December 20, 2001.

Bird, John et al. Nation to Nation: Aboriginal Sovereignty and the Future of Canada. Toronto: Public Justice Resource Center, 2002.

Cairns, Alan. Citizens Plus. Vancouver: UBC Press, 2000.

Cairns, Alan et al. Citizenship, Diversity and Pluralism: Canadian and Comparative Perspectives. Montreal: McGill-Queens University Press, 1999.

Cairns, Alan. "Aboriginal Peoples': Two Roads to the Future." *Policy Options,* Jan./Feb. 2000. October 13, 2002. http://www.irpp.org/po/archive/jan00/cairns.pdf

Conference Board of Canada. Aboriginal Report - Creating Value Through Corporate-Aboriginal Economic Relationships. October 2001. August 20, 2002. http://www.conferenceboard.ca/aboriginal/pdf/332-01rptandinsert.pdf

Conference Board of Canada. "Corporate-Aboriginal Relations Frequently asked Questions." 2002. August 20, 2002. http://www.conferenceboard.ca/ccbc/aboriginal/aboriginal_faq.htm

Cook, Curtis and Lindau, Juan, eds. Aboriginal Rights and Self-Government. Montreal: Montreal: McGill-Queens University Press, 2000.

Correctional Service Canada. "Backgrounders: Aboriginal Offenders." August 2001. September 15, 2002. http://www.csc-scc.gc.ca/text/pubed/feuilles/off-ab_e.shtml

Fidler, Stephen. (May 17, 2001). "Middle East, Latin American and Caribean: New migrants spur growth in remittances." *Financial Times.* August 2002 http://www.jubilee2000uk.org/finance Latin_america_migrants_growth_remittances.htm

Hanselmann, Calvin. "Urban Aboriginal People in Western Canada: Realities and Policies." September 2001. August 20, 2002. http://www.aboriginal-edmonton.com/PDF/CanWestUrbanRpt.pdf

Health Canada. "The Health of Aboriginal Women". April 16, 2002. August 30, 2002 http://www.hc-sc.gc.ca/english/women/facts_issues/facts_aborig.htm

Hylton, John, ed. Aboriginal Self-Government in Canada. Saskatoon: Purich Publishing Ltd., 1999.

Economic and Social Research Council. "Transnational Communities Programme." October 4, 2002. October 14, 2002. http://www.transcomm.ox.ac.uk/

Flanagan, Tom. *First Nations? Second Thoughts.* Montreal: McGill-Queens University Press, 2000

Francis, Daniel. *The Imaginary Indian. The Image of the Indian in Canadian Culture.* Vancouver: Arsenal Pulp Press, 1992.

Goulais, Bob "Fifty per cent of aboriginal children in poverty: report." Union of Ontario Indians. November 2000. August 20, 2002. http://www.anishinabek.ca/news/Past%20issues/2000/November%20issue/Nov00childpov.htm

Indian and Northern Affairs Canada. "Economic Development." June 21, 2000. August 20, 2002. http://www.ainc-inac.gc.ca/gs/ecdv_e.html

Indian and Northern Affairs. "Facts on Canada: Aboriginal People." June 28, 2002. August 20, 2002. http://www.ainc-inac.gc.ca/pr/info/info122_e.html

Indian and Northern Affairs Canada. "Social Development." June 21, 2000. September 15, 2002. http://www.ainc-inac.gc.ca/gs/soci_e.html

Kurien, C.T. "Brain Drain vs. Brain Gain." *Frontline.* Vol. 16, Issue 25. Nov. 27 – Dec. 10, 1999. August 20, 2002. www.flonnet.com/fl1625/16250880.htm

"Making the Most of an Exodus - Emigration from Latin America." *The Economist.* February 23, 2002. August 20, 2002. http://www.economist.com

Multilateral Investment Fund. "Remittances as a Development Tool: A Regional Conference - Remittances to Latin America and the Caribbean: Comparative Statistics." May 2001: pg. 6 –7. September 15, 2002. http://www.iadb.org/mif/eng/conferences/pdf/Comparativeremittan2.pdf

Naím, Moisés. "The New Diaspora." *Foreign Policy.* July-August 2002. September 15, 2002. http://www.foreignpolicy.com/issue_julyaug_2002/missing_links.html

Podlasly, Mark. "Are Aboriginal People Canadian?: An examination of what it means to be Canadian in a shared landAn Examination of What it Means to Share a Space." *Literary Review of Canada.* Nov./Dec. 2001. p. 22-23.

Public-Private Infrastructure Advisory Facility. "Tapping Financial Remittances for Infrastructure Development: The Case of Mexico." April 2002. August 20, 2002. http://wbln0018.worldbank.org/ppiaf/activity.nsf/files/MEXICO.pdf/$FILE/MEXICO.pdf

Public Policy Institute of California. "Silicon Valley's Skilled Immigrants Becoming Agents of Global Economic Change, Survey Finds Hi Tech Immigrants Fueling Entrepreneurial Networks in Home Countries." April 19, 2002. August 20, 2002. http://www.ppic.org/publications/PPIC159/ppic159.press.html

Royal Commission on Aboriginal Peoples. "Aboriginal Peoples in Urban Centes: Report of the National Round Table on Aboriginal Urban Issues." Nov. 15, 2001. August 20, 2002. http://www.ubcic.bc.ca/RCAP.htm

Ruggie, John Gerard. "Territoriality and Beyond: Problematizing Modernity in International Relations." *International Organization.* Winter 1993: 47, 1.

Stackhouse, John. "Assimilation is not something to fear." *The Globe and Mail.* December 15, 2001. August 20, 2002. http://www.globeandmail.com/series/apartheid/stories/20011215-5.html

Stackhouse, John. "Overhauling the reserve system." *The Globe and Mail.* Dec. 15, 2001. August 20, 2002. http://www.globeandmail.com/series/apartheid/stories/20011215-2.html

Stackhouse, John. "Welcome to Harlem on the Prairies." *The Globe and Mail.* November 3, 2001. August 14, 2002. http://www.globeandmail.com/series/apartheid/stories/20011103-3.html

Statistics Canada. "1996 Census: Aboriginal Data." January 13,1998. September 20, 2002. http://www.statcan.ca/Daily/English/980113/d980113.htm

Statistics Canada. "Population by Aboriginal Group, 1996 Census, Census Metropolitan Areas." September 15, 2002 www.statscan.ca/Pgdb/people/population/demo39b.htm

United Nations. "What is TOKTEN?" UNOPS. August 20, 2002. http://www.unops.org/textimageflash/default.asp?pmode=3&pno=122

University of Saskatchewan. "U of S News: $50,000 Awarded for Urban Aboriginal Database". Nov. 19, 2001. August 20, 2002. http://www.usask.ca/events/news/articles/20011129-2.html

Weiner, Myron. "Nations without Borders: The Gifts of Folk Gone Abroad." *Foreign Affairs*. March/April 1996. August 20, 2002. http://www.foreignaffairs.org/19960301fareviewessay4192/myron-weiner/nations-without-borders-the-gifts-of-folk-gone-abroad.html

Notes:

1. Indian and Northern Affairs Canada, —"Social Development," -June 21, 2000, September 15, 2002, http://www.ainc-inac.gc.ca/gs/soci_e.html.

2. Health Canada, . "The Health of Aboriginal Women," April 16, 2002, August 30, 2002, http://www.hc-sc.gc.ca/english/women/facts_issues/facts_aborig.htm.

3. Correctional Service Canada, "Backgrounders: Aboriginal Offenders," August 2001 , September 15, 2002 , http://www.csc-scc.gc.ca/text/pubed/feuilles/off-ab_e.shtml.

4. *Bob Goulais, Bob* "Fifty per cent of aboriginal children in poverty: report," Union of Ontario Indians. November 2000, August 20, 2002, http://www.anishinabek.ca/news/Past%20issues/2000/November%20issue/Nov00childpov.htm.

5. Calvin Hanselmann, "Urban aaboriginals rremain on the outside looking in," *The Calgary Herald,*. June 18, 2002, p. : A15.

6. In the 1996 Census, 799,010 Canadians identified themselves as aboriginal. How ever many aboriginal groups contend that due to enumeration errors and omissions, the number of aboriginal people in Canada is much higher than official federal statistics. Indian and Northern Affairs, "Facts on Canada: Aboriginal People," June 28, 2002, August 20, 2002, http://www.ainc-inac.gc.ca/pr/info/info122_e.html.

7. Statistics Canada , "1996 Census: Aboriginal Data," January 13, 1998, September 20, 2002, http://www.statcan.ca/Daily/English/980113/d980113.htm.

8. Aboriginal Business Development Online, "The Power of Partnerships: New Opportunities for Aboriginal Peoples and Ontario Businesses," Ontario Native Affairs Secretariat, July 22, 2002, August 15, 2002. http://www.aboriginalbusiness.on.ca/resource_kit/subhtml/chap04_05_06/chap04_1_right.html

9. Indian and Northern Affairs Canada, "Economic Development.," June 21, 2000. August 20, 2002, http://www.ainc-inac.gc.ca/gs/ecdv_e.html

10. The document Aboriginal Peoples in Urban Centes: Report of the National Round Table on Aboriginal Urban Issues provides a comprehensive overview of the off-reserve challenges faced by urban aboriginal populations. The document can be found at http://www.ubcic.bc.ca/docs/Urban_Centres.doc.

11. Indian and Northern Affairs Canada. "Economic Development."

12. Indian and Northern Affairs Canada. "Social Development." June 21, 2000. September 15, 2002. http://www.ainc-inac.gc.ca/gs/soci_e.html

13. Alan Cairns, Alan. "Aboriginal Peoples': Two Roads to the Future.," *Policy Options*. Jan./Feb. 2000, October 13, 2002, http://www.irpp.org/po/archive/jan00/cairns.pdf.

14. " I was struck in my own travels to see how so many of the most confident, and by mainstream standards successful, natives I met… had spent a good chunk of their leaders have built around their communities and reinforced with the steel of federal money." John Stackhouse, John. "Assimilation is not something to fear," *The*

Globe and Mail, December 15, 2001,. August 20, 2002, . http://www.globeandmail.com/series/apartheid/stories/20011215-5.html.

15 Calvin Hanselmann, "Urban Aboriginal People in Western Canada: Realities and Policies," September 2001., August 20, 2002, . http://www.aboriginal-edmonton.com/PDF/CanWestUrbanRpt.pdf.

16 There is a valuable lesson to be learned here from overseas development, where the best intentions for democracy and accountability have gone astray at times simply because they were imposed from the outside." John Stackhouse, John . "Overhauling the reserve system,." *The Globe and Mail.* , Dec. 15, 2001. , August 20, 2002, . http://www.globeandmail.com/series/apartheid/stories/20011215-2.html

17 Multilateral Investment Fund. , "Remittances as a Development Tool: A Regional Conference - Remittances to Latin America and the Caribbean: Comparative Statistics.," May 2001, : pg. 6 –7., September 15, 2002. http://www.iadb.org/mif/eng/conferences/pdf/Comparativeremittan2.pdf.

18 Public-Private Infrastructure Advisory Facility. , "Tapping Financial Remittances for Infrastructure Development: The Case of Mexico.," April 2002. , August 20, 2002, . http://wbln0018.worldbank.org/ppiaf/activity.nsf/files/MEXICO.pdf/$FILE/MEXICO.pdf

19 "Making the Most of an Exodus - Emigration from Latin America.," *The Economist*, February 23, 2002, . August 20, 2002, . www.economist.com.

20 Myron Weiner, "Nations without Borders: The Gifts of Folk Gone Abroad.," *Foreign Affairs*,March/April 1996, . August 20, 2002, . http://www.foreignaffairs.org/19960301fareviewessay4192/myron-weiner/nations-without-borders-the-gifts-of-folk-gone-abroad.html.

21 "Making the Most of an Exodus - Emigration from Latin America."

22 Public Policy Institute of California,. "Silicon Valley's Skilled Immigrants Becoming Agents of Global Economic Change, Survey Finds Hi Tech Immigrants Fueling Entrepreneurial Networks in Home Countries.," April 19, 2002., August 20, 2002, http://www.ppic.org/publications/PPIC159/ppic159.press.html

23 United Nations., "What is TOKTEN?," UNOPS. , August 20, 2002., http://www.unops.org/textimageflash/default.asp?pmode=3&pno=122

24 Moisés Naím, "The New Diaspora.," *Foreign Policy*,. July-August 2002, . September 15, 2002., http://www.foreignpolicy.com/issue_julyaug_2002/missing_links.html.

25 Trans-Communities Program at http://www.transcomm.ox.ac.uk studies provides numerous examplesof rise of successful global transnational labour, business and ommodity markets, political movements and cultural community social networks in labour, business and commodity markets, political movements and cultural flows.

26 University of Saskatchewan,. "U of S News: $50,000 Awarded for Urban Aboriginal Database," Nov. 19, 2001,1. August 20, 2002,. http://www.usask.ca/events/news/articles/20011129-2.html.

27 Mark Podlasly, "Are Aboriginal People Canadian?: An examination of what it means to be Canadian in a shared landAn Examination of What it Means to Share a Space,." *Literary Review of Canada.*, Nov./Dec. 2001, . p. 22-23.

Canada's Environmental Record:
The Case of (and for) the Kyoto Protocol

Désirée McGraw

IN JUNE 1992, over 100 heads of state and government as well as 30,000 activists and journalists gathered in Rio de Janeiro, Brazil for the first-ever "Earth Summit."[1] The meeting was widely heralded as the highest-level gathering in human history. Participants produced ground-breaking agreements to combat climate change and stem the loss of biological diversity, and in the process galvanized world attention on to environmental issues. The Rio meeting also created "Agenda 21," a global blueprint for implementing "sustainable development"[2]—which involves a balanced and integrated approach to ecological, economic and social concerns—into the 21st century.

Rio not only established a new regime of international law on sustainable development, it also institutionalized what Steven Bernstein labels the "compromise of liberal environmentalism"— i.e. "the predication of international environmental protection on the promotion and maintenance of liberal economic order."[3] This paper examines from a Canadian perspective, a key and current agreement on sustainable development and an instrument of liberal environmentalism, the *Kyoto Protocol*, under the climate change regime *UN Framework Convention on Climate Change* that emerged from the Rio Summit.

The United Nations designated the 1990s as the "turn around decade" on sustainable development; instead, the last ten years have been characterized by some as the lost decade in this regard. Since the 1992 UN Earth Summit, Canada is widely considered to have turned from environmental leader to environmental laggard—both at home and abroad.[4] Indeed, the Mulroney Conservative government is seen to have been much better on the environment than the Liberal government of Jean Chrétien.[5]

It is true that in Rio Canada readily signed on to general agreements on biodiversity and climate change—commitments which federal Environment Minister David Anderson later characterized as "immodest." There is no doubt that the main agreements of the 1992 Summit—*Convention on Biological Diversity, the UN Framework Convention on Climate Change, a Statement of Forest Principles* and *Agenda 21*—were lofty. Unfortunately, many of the outputs that emerged from the ten-year follow-up conference to Rio—the World Summit on Sustainable Development (WSSD) held in Johannesburg, South Africa in September 2002—appear to be headed for the same ineffectual fate as their predecessors. Indeed, many view the 2002 Earth Summit as constituting a step back from the 1992 one. Because Canadian negotiators were instructed by their political masters to resist specific targets and timelines on a broad range of issues, Canada bears some responsibility for this outcome. At the Johannesburg Summit, Canada earned a place alongside Australia and the United States to form what Greenpeace and other well-established NGOs dubbed the "Axis of Environmental Evil."

Although such rhetoric is undoubtedly excessive, it is clear that Canada no longer holds the mantle of international environmental leadership it once did. While Canada was one of the leading OECD countries to sign and ratify the original Rio conventions on biodiversity and climate change, it has subsequently stalled on stricter and more substantive sub-agreements, such as the *Biosafety Protocol*[6] to regulate international trade involving GMOs and, of course, the *Kyoto Protocol* to reduce greenhouse gas emissions globally.

At the domestic level, after commissioning an arms-length assessment of Canada's environmental performance since Rio, the federal government stalled on releasing the critical outcome: Canada's national report to the World Summit on Sustainable Development was made public only weeks before the conference started—several months past the due date set by the United Nations.[7]

A comprehensive review of Canada's environmental performance over the last decade[8] is well beyond the scope of this chapter. Instead, this overview will focus on a single case as an illustration of Canada's environmental record under the Chrétien government. The case in question is an environmental issue currently at the forefront of Canada's political agenda: the *Kyoto Protocol* to the 1992 *UN Framework Convention on Climate Change*.[9] Key concerns about the accord will be addressed according to five themes (or "5 Cs"): competitiveness, credibility, consultations, commitment, and consistency in public and foreign policy.[10]

The Kyoto Protocol

In 1992, under the Conservative government of Brian Mulroney, Canada was one of the first industrialized countries to both sign and ratify[11] the *United Nations Framework Convention on Climate Change*[12]—one of two treaties to emerge from the Rio Earth Summit. The *Kyoto Protocol*—named after the Japanese city in which it was adopted on 11 December 1997—constitutes the first substantive treaty aimed at reinforcing and operationalizing the principles embodied in the original framework agreement on climate change. Specifically, the accord calls for industrialized countries to reduce their greenhouse gas (GHG) emissions by at least 5% below 1990 levels within the period 2008-2012 (the first commitment period).[13] Under Kyoto, Canada is to achieve a 6% reduction below the 1990 base year. Kyoto represents the first critical step to meeting global climate change commitments. These entail a total reduction of 50-75% in global greenhouse gases in this century alone.

In light of its reduced environmental reputation in the decade since Rio, Canada did not go into the World Summit on Sustainable Development from a position of strength. Therefore, Prime Minister Chrétien's Summit pledge that Parliament would ratify the Kyoto Protocol by year's end came as a surprise to the UN community, to Canadians and, it would appear, to his own Cabinet.[14] Nonetheless, it was a critical announcement at a critical time. Kyoto now stands poised to become legally binding. To be operational, the accord requires ratification by a minimum of 55 countries responsible for at least 55% of the globe's GHG emissions.[15] Although Kyoto has long surpassed the first criterion for entry into force, the second has remained elusive, especially in light of the Bush Administration's refusal to ratify the agreement. While the U.S. contributes roughly 25% of total GHG emissions, Canada produces a mere 2%. But person-for-person, Canadians—along with Australians—are the biggest energy consumers in the world. Thus, the country has a unique opportunity and responsibility to contribute to the global fight against climate change. Our country should compensate for its vast size and extreme climate not with more GHG emissions, but with greater innovation and investment in efficient sources of energy.

Kyoto—A Question of Competitiveness

Opponents of Kyoto claim that Canada cannot afford to implement the accord because it would damage Canada's economic competitiveness. However, the policy uncertainty created by the government's protracted hesitation regarding ratification and the lack of a clear implementation plan has been most costly for corporate decision-making. Canadian corporations have a legitimate concern about the negative effects of uncertainty on their competitiveness and ability to attract investment. Ratification of the accord and efficient negotiation of details of the implementation plan, in conjunction with key industrial sectors in the provinces and territories, provides the best way to address such uncertainty. Clear and credible targets allow corporations to make more informed investment and other business decisions.

Kyoto will provide very substantial opportunities to make a transition to a more efficient and competitive economy. According to the Alberta-based Pembina Institute for Appropriate Technology, Canada's competitiveness is likely to benefit, not suffer, from a decision by Parliament to ratify the Kyoto Protocol.[16] Their report finds that by taking a lead on environmental policy, governments will position firms to be more efficient and competitive. In a survey of corporations in several key sectors (such oil and gas, electricity, chemicals, transportation and manufacturing) with major operations in Canada, those firms which took early action to improve efficiency and effect emission-reduction strategies in anticipation of

Kyoto ratification also increased their competitiveness. For example, from 1990 to 2000, *Dupont* reduced its GHG emissions by 60% while production increased by 10% and shareholder return quadrupled. Between 1995 and 2001, *Interface* (a flooring products firm) reduced GHG emissions (per unit of production) by 64% in its Canadian operations while the company's waste reduction program produced savings of over $185 million worldwide. In recent ads, *British Petroleum*, one of the world's largest oil companies, has dubbed itself "Beyond Petroleum." This is more than an advertising campaign: in 1997, the company committed to reducing its GHG emissions by 10% below 1990 levels by the year 2010. Not only has BP already achieved this target eight years ahead of schedule (March 2002), it has done so at no net economic cost (savings from increased efficiency outweighed expenditures) while more than doubling its basic earnings per share (from $0.17 in 1998 to $0.36 in 2001). Canadian policy now needs to recognize and credit this progress, and set clear and realistic targets for further improvements.

The editor of the Canadian business magazine *Corporate Knight*, Tony Heaps, in the November 2002 issue, described Kyoto as "an Innovation Agenda in Disguise"[10] with the following explanation:

> New technologies that make sense in a world that puts cost constraints on emitters of greenhouse gases will emerge. Firms that invest in cleaner ways of doing business will gain market share and reduce costs. By aligning firms with price signals that send a clear message (pollution costs), Kyoto will stir up a critical mass of activity establishing a business web of innovative firms that will act as a reinforcing network for developing ever-cleaner and more efficient processes. Those firms that continue to waste will waste away.[17]

Opportunities for trade in clean technologies are not limited to OECD countries. The emergence of markets in the developing world and economies in transition—China, India, Latin America and Africa as well as Eastern and Central Europe—will provide those who move quickly with tremendous economic opportunity. Indeed, over the next twenty years alone, the global market for climate-related technologies will be valued in the trillions of dollars. As developing countries continue to grow in the coming decades, Canada will be poised to export the very technologies that they will urgently need to develop in an environmentally sustainable way.[18] Thus, in meeting its Kyoto targets, Canada will not only be contributing to emission reductions and global sustainability, we will be at the forefront of an emerging world market that will represent a fundamental transition of the global economy.

Also prominent in the rhetoric of Kyoto critics is the notion that Canada cannot afford to implement the agreement because its largest trading partner has rejected it. This argument confuses lack of leadership by the Bush administration on climate change with lack of action by American states, cities, companies and citizens. Indeed, state and municipal governments in the U.S. are moving faster and further to reduce GHG emissions than their Canadian counterparts.[19] Moreover, despite the Bush team's opposition to Kyoto, Washington still administers a much more substantial body of GHG-reducing measures than does Ottawa. At every level of government, Canada lags behind its American counterparts in its efforts to curb climate change. If these trends continue, the U.S. may well shrink its GHG emissions in line with Kyoto targets despite not having formally ratified the accord. And although it is unlikely to do so under the Bush Administration's watch, the U.S. may well ratify under a future administration. With American ratification would come a stronger push for enforcement mechanisms, and thus potentially costly trade measures. So Canada has a choice: it can pay now or pay more later.

Although the U.S. appears to be making progress on climate change outside the Kyoto framework, Canada's track record remains very poor. In the absence of legally-binding targets, Canada invoked the voluntary Rio pledge to stabilize its GHG emissions at the 1990 level by 2000. Instead, despite a slew of federal and provincial plans purporting to address climate change, Canada's emissions levels grew by 20% in the last decade; and in 1997, it abandoned the voluntary target altogether. Given the country's ever-growing emissions levels, the federal government estimates that Canada will need to reduce its current levels by 25% in order to meet its Kyoto target by 2010.

In short, implementing Kyoto will not only allow Canada to contribute to the global effort to curb climate change, it will have the practical effect of narrowing—not widening—the gap with the U.S. Moreover, Kyoto does not preclude Canada from strengthening its global commitments with national or indeed regional (NAFTA-based) ones—provided these enhance rather than erase our Kyoto targets.

Currently, while the U.S. remains outside the global climate change regime, the demand for special emissions permits[20] (which Parties to Kyoto can purchase to offset their excess emissions) will be lower —thereby reducing the price of such permits and thus the cost of complying with Kyoto targets.

Kyoto — a Question of Credibility

Despite the initial praise it inspired in some international and environmental circles, the commitment made by Mr. Chrétien in Johannesburg was not clear-cut: for too long, Canada's position remained contingent upon two additional and improbable conditions—one national, the other international:

1. nationally, ratification seemes to depend upon the environmental and economic equivalent of a "Clarity Act on Kyoto" —a level of detail rarely, if ever, required by other international agreements Canada has signed; and
2. the international condition for ratifying Kyoto appeared to be credits for clean energy exports—Canada's appeal for special consideration due to the U.S. refusal to ratify failed to secure any substantive support during international negotiations on climate change.

This equivocation has undermined Canada's credibility on this critical issue both at home and abroad. Far from reestablishing the country's credentials as an environmental champion, the confusion following the Prime Minister's remarks in Johannesburg alienated important stakeholders on all sides of this issue:

1. *The international community*, especially the European Union, would likely block any additional amendments to Kyoto, particularly those proposed by a country widely seen to have already watered down the accord.[21] In this light, the position—held by several prominent political and business

leaders—that Canada should not ratify Kyoto because it is too feeble proves perverse. If Kyoto does not do enough to curb climate change, it is in part because countries such as Canada have consistently negotiated additional concessions (such as getting credits for its forests as "carbon sinks") which have served to weaken the Protocol's effect in terms of real reduction in greenhouse gas emissions. Having sucessfully softened the accord, Canada's walking away from it would have been viewed by the international community as an act of bad faith, if not betrayal. All too often, this is the American approach to international treaties—not the Canadian one.

Concretely, rejection of Kyoto would also mean that Canada would have little if any influence in future rounds of global climate negotiations, which are expected to bring key countries such as India, China and Brazil into the fold.[22] Thus, from an international perspective, non ratification is a non starter: it would damage Canada's reputation and its leverage in future international negotiations on critical issues beyond climate change.

2. *Environmentalists* who strongly support Kyoto viewed the Johannesburg announcement as a last-ditch, legacy-driven effort to reverse the country's decade-long slide from environmental leader to laggard. Many perceived the belated support for the accord as an act of "ecological opportunism" stemming from the Prime Minister's preoccupation with his legacy rather than from a real concern for the environment. Nonetheless, despite private musings regarding the motivation and timing[23] of the Johannesburg pledge, most environmentalists expressed public support for the decision.

3. *Business* may resent the added burden of having to now scramble to meet Kyoto targets within a much tighter time-frame. Had Canada not only signed but also ratified the protocol following its 1997 adoption, energy producers and consumers would have had more time to transition to a cleaner, less carbon-dependent economy. The policy confusion created by the

government's protracted hesitation regarding Kyoto has also proven problematic for corporate decision-making, which thrives in conditions of certainty. It is time to bring clarity and get on with the business of implementation. This is what the corporate community does well: set clear rules, and it will work to meet them.

4. Some provinces decried the federal government's "breech of public trust" in changing the focus of cross-Canada consultations on Kyoto from ratification to implementation. Alberta even threatened to legally challenge the federal government's authority in this regard. There is no doubt that the federal governent has circumvented a public consultation process that it had itself laid out. However, as noted above, this process was ill-conceived and over-extended from the start. Consent of the provinces is not required for ratification of international agreements; this authority rests strictly with the federal government. However, given the provinces' shared jurisdiction over natural resources, the federal government does have a responsibility to consult its provincial and territorial counter parts on how it arrives at implementing these treaties. It must work to involve the provinces, particularly in areas of action under their jurisdiction. Indeed, without securing the full cooperation of the provinces, a number of key instruments may be unavailable for implementation.

According to an international lawyer who has closely followed climate change negotiations since 1990:

> The federal government has clear jurisdiction to ratify the Kyoto Protocol. Only [it] can enter into international obligations on behalf of Canada, and no province can veto the ratification of an international treaty...[In addition] the federal government can act to address climate change and meet the Kyoto commitments on its own accord, without waiting for complimentary action by any or all of the provincial and territorial governments...While a federal-provincial-territorial and

municipal strategy is the most desirable route [both in political and practical terms], the reality of economic and environmental interests in the different provinces tells us that only if the federal government is prepared to act unilaterally is it going to be possible to effectively pursue a process of building a national consensus on implementation so that it does not have to act unilaterally...In short, the history of climate change negotiations within Canada shows that only if the federal government is prepared to use its authority unilaterally are the chances high of not actually having to do so. Conversely, taking this arrow out of the federal quiver, as was done in 1992 by the Mulroney government [in order to assuage provincial concerns], seriously reduces the chances of gaining a national consensus.[24]

Therefore, if one views ratification as a matter of foreign policy (to be exercised by the federal government for the common good) and implementation as a matter of domestic environmental and economic policy (to be exercised by the federal and provincial governments), the revised focus of the current deliberations—from consultations on whether to ratify, to real negotiations on how to implement—is not only more acceptable, it is preferable (again, notwithstanding as outlined above).

Kyoto – a Question of Consultations

Contrary to popular belief, Canada's commitment to ratify the Kyoto Protocol did not come with the Prime Minister's pledge at the Johannesburg Summit in September 2002. The Liberal government initially signaled its intent to ratify Kyoto when it signed[25] the accord on 29 April 1998. Why then, in the almost five years since first signing the accord, has Ottawa failed to produce a viable national action plan to implement the agreement? This failure is not, as some would have it, due to lack of consultations or technical know-how; Canada has some of world's best people in both the private and public sectors working on climate change issues. The failure to craft a clear, comprehensive and timely implementation program is due purely to a lack of political will.

Complaints regarding the federal government's failure to fully consult with the provinces, key sectors and stakeholders are disingenuous in light of the real record: Kyoto has arguably been more extensively consulted upon than any other treaty signed by Canada. Imagine the federal government consulting Canadians this much on whether it should adhere to international institutions, such as NAFTA or the WTO, which meet the approval of powerful sectors of the Canadian economy. The objection here is not to consultations *per se*, but to their selective use for purely opportunistic or PR purposes. As decisions once enacted by elected representatives in national legislatures are increasingly made by non-elected officials at international summits, it is critical that citizens and parliamentarians become more informed and involved at all levels and stages of the policy-making process. But tackling the "democratic deficit" in international decision-making should not be a discriminatory undertaking, nor should it be used as a delay tactic regarding matters on which the government would rather avoid taking decisive action.

Ottawa's mistake lies not in its failure to consult but, rather, in its failure to consult the right people on the right question: until recently, selective discussions with elites, experts and special interest groups have been framed by "whether to ratify" Kyoto; instead, the Chrétien government should have been consulting Canadians directly on "how to implement" the accord from the start. This is what Ottawa is poised to do in 2003—but only after years of policy confusion, procrastination and vacillation.

Kyoto—a Question of Commitment

As Canada commits to Kyoto, implementation of the plan that follows ratification is of central importance. With ratification, Kyoto becomes domestic law and Canada has six to ten more years to reach its targets. The country does not—as has been alleged by some government leaders —have another ten years to work out the plan. 2008-2012 is the deadline for achieving the plan, not developing it. This reality check leads some to want to abandon Kyoto altogether.

It leads others to the opposite conclusion: Canada must expedite ratification as a matter of utmost priority, and then actively engage the stakeholders on how—not whether—to achieve them.

Whatever side of the issue one espouses, one thing is clear: the federal government has mismanaged Kyoto from the beginning. No doubt, the Protocol is a political and technical minefield, but Ottawa has exacerbated the issue's inherent complexity and controversy through confusion. Instead of addressing Kyoto as a matter of public policy, federal and provincial governments have treated it as a matter of public relations—and it has done even this poorly. In the case of Kyoto, the federal government has so far broken every basic rule of crafting and selling public policy: define the problem and get the public to accept it; propose a solution and consult on it; develop and negotiate a plan to implement it, and accept the consequences.[26]

For Canada to meet its Kyoto targets, it must craft a national plan based on a truly national effort: a renewed federal, provincial, territorial and municipal undertaking that involves stakeholders from industry and labour as well as environmental and consumer groups. Demand for public information and stakeholder engagement is high. In the first three weeks since releasing its climate change plan, the federal government received over 1000 written submissions by individuals and its website had roughly 100,000 downloads. A cross-Canada "Commission on Climate Change" might be envisioned as a way of directly engaging concerned citizens and their elected representatives.

Reaching our Kyoto targets will require not only effective actions and measures to reduce GHG emissions, but effective governance systems to guide the implementation process. Building on core democratic principles such as leadership, transparency, accountability, enforcement and engagement, the first task in the post-ratification process will be to rebuild confidence among key stakeholders so that implementation is both credible and predictable. The president of *Strategies to Sustainability* (Stratos. Inc., an Ottawa-based consulting firm that facilitated the National Stakeholder Workshops on Climate Change[1] in spring 2002) proposed two key coordinating mechanisms:

1. An efficient, central focal point for the federal government. Given that responsibilities for climate change lie with many agencies, and that accountabilities need to be assigned to these same agencies, there is a need for a federal climate change coordination office which has the necessary authority and the technical knowledge to make this work.

2. An effective inter-jurisdictional body operating at both the political and bureaucratic levels. The National Air Issues Coordinating Committee had served this role until summer 2001. This body could be resurrected or a new one created, e.g. a "National Climate Change Action Committee."

During a special presentation to parliamentarians during the ratification debate, George Greene concluded:

> We need an effective governance system to implement Kyoto that provides: clear and transparent decision-making; accountability for delivering on commitments and obligations; and oversight and monitoring to ensure we are making progress. And we must always keep in mind the need for effective engagement of the public and key interests in moving forward.[23]

Any national initiative must also go beyond Kyoto *per se* to address global climate change. The continuing rise in Canada's GHG emissions places the country on a path that is far from sustainable. This trend must be reversed: the consensus of international scientists is that global emissions must fall by 50-75% in this century alone if we are to avoid dangerous man-made disruption of our climate. Such projections underscore the importance of Kyoto's modest 6% target as a vital first step in bringing Canada into the carbon-constrained world of the new millennium.

This Liberal Government has already proven it can muster the massive political will and resources to successfully tackle seemingly intractable problems: the fiscal deficit provides a compelling case in point. The rationale presented was short-term pain for long-term gain: it would be irresponsible to leave such a burden on future generations. The same logic applies, if not more so, to the ecological debt. If Canada can mobilize around something as seemingly mundane as a fiscal deficit, surely it can make headway on the environmental deficit.

In polls, the environment consistently ranks as a core value among Canadians. It is central to both our national economy and our national identity. Citizens are experiencing the effects of environmental deterioration—from increasingly volatile weather patterns to suffocating smog and poisoned water—all around them, and they want action. Among a broad range of worthy ecological issues and initiatives, Kyoto has become the litmus test on the environment. Any government, sector or individual seen to be stalling on Kyoto will be seen to be stalling on the environment.

In a survey of Canadian values conducted by Liberal pollster Michael Marzolini,[29] a majority of Canadians expressed strong support for state action on the environment and a preference for government's role in helping to equip them for the future. This challenge raises a question posed by Thomas Homer-Dixon in his award-winning book, *The Ingenuity Gap*: "Can we generate and implement useful ideas fast enough to solve the very problems—environmental, social and technological—we've created?"[30]

Ultimately, curbing climate change will constitute an unprecedented test not only of technical know-how, but of public will and political leadership. Kyoto will help determine whether Canada's citizens and leaders are up to the challenge of bringing our country and our economy into the 21st century. It will also provide very substantial opportunities to make a transition to a more efficient and competitive economy.

Kyoto—a Question of Consistency

Ratifying the Kyoto Protocol does not preclude Canadians from developing a Made-in-Canada action plan on climate change; it compels us to do so. Kyoto provides an internationally-agreed framework for meeting targets on greenhouse-gas reductions within a specified timeframe. It does not dictate how countries are to meet these objectives. In fact, through a series of global market-based mechanisms, the accord augments, not diminishes, the flexibility with which individual countries can meet their climate change commitments. In short, Kyoto sets the context for action on climate change, but does not dictate how a nation meets its international commitments.

The real issue is whether Canada will address climate change within a global framework, or whether it will adopt a strictly national (or, indeed, provincial or sectoral) approach to what is a global problem. Will Canada apply its general preference for multilateralism to climate change?

Canada has expressed strong support for a multilateral approach to solving international problems, such as Iraq and its potential use of weapons of mass destruction beyond its own borders. Just as our country has opposed a go-it-alone policy by the United States vis-à-vis Iraq, so too must it reject strictly unilateral approaches to curbing climate change. On both the issues of Iraq and climate change, anything short of globally-sanctioned action would represent not only diplomatic defeats, but sub-optimal solutions to what are ultimately global security threats.[31]

Within the hierarchy of international relations, "hard" security and trade matters have traditionally trumped "soft" social and environmental ones. The reality is, however, that ecological degradation is a growing source of conflict in the world, and thus represents a real threat to collective security. Pervasive climate change has been described as second only to nuclear war in terms of its catastrophic effects globally. In this sense, climate change is far more than a matter of environmental policy, it is increasingly a matter of national security.

The evidence underlying global climate change is objective, far-reaching and compelling. Indeed, few issues on the global agenda have galvanized such widespread consensus within political and scientific communities. The Intergovernmental Panel on Climate Change[32]—representing 1,500 of the world's leading atmospheric scientists, economists and technologists—has repeatedly concluded that: (1) the current scope, scale and pace of climate change are unprecedented, and (2) human activity—mainly through the production of greenhouse gases such as carbon dioxide—is increasingly influential in this regard. Canadian scientists from across the country have been active in their areas of expertise in the work of this international panel. And even sceptical nations find the science convincing. Thirteen national academies of science—including the American counterpart whose members were hand-picked by President George W. Bush himself—concur with these findings.

Still, international affairs are not susceptible to courtroom proofs beyond reasonable doubt. It is precisely for this reason that a "Precautionary Principle" underlies many environmental agreements such as the *Kyoto Protocol*. While the U.S. (and to some extent Canada) has sought to expel direct reference to this principle in international treaties, its intent is straightforward: where there is a threat of serious or irreversible harm, lack of scientific certainty should not preclude action. Otherwise, positive proof would come too late. The principle essentially asserts that it is better to err on the side of action that turns out to be unnecessary than to expose ourselves to preventable devastation through inaction.[33]

Conclusion

The *Kyoto Protocol* represents the most important international initiative to date for combatting rising greenhouse gas emissions. Indeed, Kyoto is the only global game in town for addressing global warming and other consequences of climate change. The result of ten years of tough negotiations[34] in which Canada played an influential role, the accord reflects trade-offs among more than 150 states with divergent interests at vastly different stages of their economic development. Significantly, Kyoto recognizes that it is industrialized countries that have been producing the majority of the globe's anthropogenic greenhouse gas emissions, and that it is these countries that must lead the global effort to reduce these emissions. Kyoto also acknowledges that developing countries must have room to grow their economies while preparing to assume their own targets in the future. As such, for critics of Kyoto to suggest that developing and least-developed countries are somehow getting a free ride is simply misguided.

Domestic disagreements within Canada about how to address climate change only serve to reinforce Kyoto's value as an international agreement. Indeed, the Protocol embodies innovative liberal principles,[35] such as "Intergenerational Equity," "Common but Differentiated Responsibility," the "Polluter Pays Principle" and the "Precautionary Principle," which may prove instructive for Canada as it seeks establish a fair and equitable national climate change regime that does not unduly burden particular provinces, sectors or stakeholders.

After more than a decade of international negotiations and national consultations on climate change, the federal government released a "Climate Change Action Plan for Canada"[36]—a matter of days before Parliament began debating whether Canada should be legally bound to Kyoto by ratifying the accord. There is no doubt that Canada's "ratification readiness" would have been greatly enhanced by a more comprehensive implementation plan to ensure we can meet our Kyoto commitments. However, the foot-dragging of the past decade made it clear that no such plan would materialize until ratification was assured. For better or worse, implementation is contingent upon ratification. By protracting the debate on ratification, the country has been running out the clock on implementation. The longer Canada postpones effective implementation, the more difficult—if not impossible—it will be to meet its Kyoto targets. Failure to meet our global climate change commitments could well become a self-fulfilling prophecy.

N.B. At the time of press, Parliament voted overwhelmingly in favour of ratifying the Kyoto Protocol on 9 December 2002. The Prime Minister of Canada signed an executive order-in-council which finalized the ratification process on 16 December 2002. The following day, Environment Minister deposed the instrument of ratification with the United Nations for formal international recognition of Canada's binding commitment to the *Kyoto Protocol*. With this act, Canada became the 98th country to become a Party to the Protocol; it provides positive encouragement to countries such as Russia which continue to waiver regarding their own ratification. Canada's international efforts should focus on securing support of this and other major greenhouse-gas producing countries—without which Kyoto cannot become fully operational. Domestic efforts should be devoted to building credibility and certainty into implementation initiatives. Although Canada's ratification of the *Kyoto Protocol* is now complete, the contentious nature of the debate surrounding this decision guarantees that the domestic implementation process will be dynamic, if not divisive.

Although the views expressed in this chapter remain the sole responsibility of the author, the advice and assistance of the following individuals are gratefully acknowledged: Jennifer Adams, Stephanie Cairns, Andrew Deutz, George Greene, Howard Mann and Clarisse Kehler Siebert.

Notes:

[1]   The Rio Earth Summit – known officially at the United Nations Conference on Environment and Development – marked the 20th anniversary of the United Nations Conference on the Human Environment held in Stockholm, Sweden. Canadian businessman and diplomat Maurice Strong spearheaded both summits.

[2]   The term "sustainable development" remains controversial: some perceive it as an attempt to legitimize economic growth within the concept of environmental protection. It was originally defined by the 1987 report of the World Commission on Environment and Development (or *Brundtland Report*) as "development that meets the needs of the present without compromising the ability of future generations to meet their own needs." In Canada, this definition has been integrated into federal legislation and into the amendments to the Auditor General Act (1995), which established the Commissioner of the Environment and Sustainable Development. For analyses of sustainable development in the Canadian context, see: O.P. Dwivedi, Patrick Kyba, Peter J. Stoett and Rebecan Tiessen, *Sustainable Development and Canada: National and International Perspectives* (Peterborough: Broadview Press) 2001; Environment Canada, *Sustainable Development Strategy 2001-2003*. (Ottawa: Minister of Public Works and Government Services Canada) 2001.

[3]   Steven Bernstein, "Liberal Environmentalism and Global Environmental Governance" in *Global Environmental Politics*, vol. 2, no. 3: 1-16 (August 2002).

[4]   Désirée M. McGraw, "Ten Years after the Earth Summit" in the *Montreal Gazette*, p.B7 (1 June 2002). See also Glen Toner, "Canada: From Early Frontrunner to Plodding Anchorman," pp.53-84 in William M. Lafferty and James Meadowcroft (eds.) *Implementing Sustainable Development: Strategies and Initiatives in High Consumption Societies* (New York: Oxford University Press) 2000.

[5]   Notwithstanding election pledges outlined in the Liberal Party of Canada's policy platforms. See in particular "Sustainable Development" (ch.4, pp. 62-70) in the Liberal Party of Canada's *Red Book*, formally entitled *Creating Opportunity: The Liberal Plan for Canada* (Ottawa, Liberal Party of Canada, 1993). See also policy platforms for 1997 (entitled *Securing Our Future Together: The Liberal Plan for Canada*) and 2000 (entitled *Opportunity for All: The Liberal Plan for the Future of Canada*).

[6]   Canada was the first industrialized country to sign the *Convention on Biological Diversity* (CBD) in Rio, thereby creating the "biodiversity bandwagon" which convinced most G7 countries to sign on – despite overt opposition by the Bush (41st) Administration. Canada has been viewed – by North and South alike – as a champion of the biodiversity issue-area. As a result, it managed to beat out countries such as Spain, Switzerland and Kenya in its bid to host the CBD Secretariat, which has been headquartered in Montreal since 1996. However, Canada's support for the CBD has slipped in more recent years. Most notably, Canada has signed but not yet ratified the first legally-binding sub-agreement to the CBD: the *Biosafety Protocol* addressing transboundary movement of genetically modified organisms (GMOs). During these negotiations, Canada served as the spokesperson for the so-called "Miami Group" of major agricultural exporters, which resisted any binding agreement regarding the trade in or labelling of products containing GMOs.
For an examination of the biosafety negotiations, see John Vogler and Désirée M. McGraw, "An International Environmental Regime for Biotechnology? The Case of the Cartagena Protocol on Biosafety" in John Vogler and Alan Russell (eds.) *The International Politics of Biotechnology: Investigating Global Futures* (Manchester: at

the University Press) 2000. For an overview of the biodiversity negotiations, see Désirée M. McGraw "The Convention on Biological Diversity – Key Characteristics and Implications for Implementation" in *Review of European Community and International Environmental Law*, vol. 11, no.1: 17-28 (Spring 2002). See also Désirée M. McGraw, "The Story of the Biodiversity Convention: From Negotiation to Implementation" in Philippe Le Prestre (ed.) *Governing Global Biodiversity: The Evolution and Implementation of the Convention on Biological Diversity* (London: Ashgate Press) 2002.

[7]   See Government of Canada, *Sustainable Development: A Canadian Perspective.* (Ottawa: Minister of Public Works and Government Services Canada) August 2002. http://www.wssd.gc.ca/canada_at_wssd/canadian_perspective_e.pdf

[8]   For a more complete analysis of Canada's environmental performance throughout the 1990s, see official reports by Canada's Commissioner on Environment and Sustainable Development (1997-2001) and a special report entitled "The Commissioner's Perspective: The Decade after Rio. Commissioner of the Environment and Sustainable Development" in *Report of the Commissioner of the Environment and Sustainable Development to the House of Commons of Canada* (Ottawa: Minister of Public Works and Government Services Canada) 2002. http://www.oag-bvg.gc.ca
See also non-governmental publications, such as "Rio Report Cards" by the Sierra Club of Canada (1993-2001) and "Shadow Reports" by the Canadian Environmental Network and One Sky (2002). Nikki Skuce (ed.) *Summit or Plummet: A Call for Canadian Leadership Ten Years after Rio.* (Ottawa: Canadian Environmental Network) July 2002 . http://www.cen-rce.org/wssd

[9]   UN Doc.A/AC237/18 (Part II, Add.1), 31, *International Legal Materials* 848. See also official climate convention website http://www.unfccc.int

[10] The "five Cs" framework was developed by the author during presentations to the following conferences: *Searching for the New Liberalism* (Munk Centre for International Studies, University of Toronto, Toronto) September 2002; the *Banff Forum* (Banff Conference Centre, Alberta) October 2002; and *NetImpact* (MBA program, McGill University Faculty of Management, Montreal) December 2002. The framework also appears in the author's: "How fast should we go on Kyoto?" in *Globe and Mail* , p.A19, 22 October 2002; and "The Case for Kyoto: A Question of Competitiveness, Consultations, Credibility, Commitment and Consistency" in *Policy Options*, vol. 24, no.1: 35-39 (December 2002-January 2003). See website of Institute for Research on Public Policy http://www.irpp.org

[11] Ratification is one of several formal processes (alongside acceptance, approval and accession) by which an international treaty becomes domestic law. For an excellent analysis of Canada's domestic application of international law, see Jutta Brunnée and Stephen J. Toope., "A Hesitant Embrace: The Application of International Law by Canadian Courts" (forthcoming publication) 2002.

[12] It has been argued that Canada's legal obligations to combat climate change stem not only from its adherence to the UNFCCC, but to other treaties in the fields of environment, human rights, trade and investment. See Lina Carlsson *et al*, *Canada's International Legal Obligations with Regard to Climate Change.* (Montreal: Centre for International Sustainable Development Law) November 2002. http://www.cisdl.org

[13] According to Article 3 of the Kyoto Protocol, Parties included in Annex I (i.e. industrialized countries and those in transition to market-based economies) "shall, individually or jointly, ensure that their aggregate anthropogenic carbon dioxide equivalent emissions of the greenhouse gases… do not exceed their assigned amounts…with a view to reducing the overall emissions of such gases by at least 5 per cent below 1990 levels in the commitment period 2008 to 2012." Moreover, "Each Party included in Annex I shall, by 2005, have made demonstrable progress in achieving its commit-

ments under this Protocol." Although Article 4.6 provides that those countries listed in Annex I which are transitioning to a market economy are accorded a "certain degree of flexibility" in meeting their commitments.

14   At the time of submitting this article for publication, Parliament had not yet voted to ratify the Kyoto Protocol. However, ratification was a foregone conclusion given that the majority of legislators (particularly MPs from the Liberal Party, NDP and Bloc Québécois) were expected to vote in support of the accord. Moreover, the Prime Minister reserves the right to ensure ratification through an executive order-in-council (requiring the signature of a few Cabinet Ministers).

15   According to Article 25 of the Kyoto Protocol, the rules for its entry into force require 55 Parties to the Convention to ratify (or approve, accept, or accede to) the Protocol, including Annex I countries accounting for 55% of that group's carbon dioxide emissions in 1990.

16   See Sylvie Boustie with Marlo Raynolds and Matthew Bramley, *How Ratifying the Kyoto Protocol Will Benefit Canada's Competitiveness.* (Ottawa: Pembina Institute for Appropriate Technology for the Canadian Climate Action Network) June 2002.

17   See Toby A.A Heaps, "Kyoto – An Innovation Agenda in Disguise" in *Corporate Knights,* 10-14 (November 2002).

18   Developing countries' demand for clean technology will significantly increase if they are required to grow in an environmentally-sustainable way, e.g. by decreasing their GHG emissions and other measures. By leading on Kyoto, Canada will have a greater say at the negotiation table as to whether and when countries such as Brazil, China and India come on board the global climate change regime. Ratification by industrialized countries such as Canada will also create an additional incentive for developing economies to commit to their own targets. In this way, Canada's commitment to Kyoto would support both its environmental and economic objectives. By ratifying Kyoto, Canada sends an important political signal which will strengthen future markets for its environmentally-friendly economic goods and services.

19   Matthew Bramley with Kirsty Hamilton and Leslie-Ann Robertson, *Comparison of Current Government Action on Climate Change in the U.S. and Canada,* Ottawa: Pembina Institute for Appropriate Technology and World Wildlife Fund Canada) May 2002.

20   The sale of emissions permits is one of several global market-based mechanisms under Kyoto that increase flexibility and reduce costs in terms of meeting targets. Other Kyoto schemes such as "Joint Implementation" and the "Clean Development Mechanism" also allow industrialized countries such as Canada to work with other countries so that not all implementation must be carried out domestically.

21   Canada played an influential role throughout the Kyoto and other global climate negotiations by successfully securing a number of concessions which reflect its national interests. One such example is the inclusion of "carbon sinks" in the Bonn agreement of November 2001: Canada helped to negotiate credits for expanding the size and carbon storage of its managed forests. The increased range and flexibility of mechanisms countries may employ to meet their commitments must be acknowledged as a diplomatic success for Canada. However, this same initiative has been criticized as a substantive weakness from an environmental perspective given that it effectively entails fewer real reductions in greenhouse gas emissions.

22   The most recent round of negotiations, held in New Delhi in November 2002, failed to commit developing countries to binding targets, but their inclusion will remain the focus of ongoing talks.

23   At a Liberal caucus retreat in Chicoutimi, Québec – just days before the Kyoto pledge in Johannesburg – Mr. Chrétien announced his intention to step down as Prime Minister in February 2004.

[24] Howard Mann, "Jurisdictional Issues," in notes for presentation to *Beyond Kyoto: A Win-Win Climate Change Action Plan or Canada* (Citizen-Government Dialogue, Parliament Hill, Ottawa) 4 December 2002.

[25] While a treaty is adopted collectively by the international community (e.g. via the United Nations), it is signed by individual countries. In international law, signature represents the first formal step on the road to ratification. Ratification by a requisite number of countries (normally specified in the treaty itself) ensures that a treaty enters into force, and thus becomes legally binding on all Parties (i.e. all countries which have ratified the agreement). Transforming an international agreement into domestic law is done differently in different countries. In Canada, this occurs through the adoption of legislation at the federal or provincial levels (and sometimes both levels) that creates domestic legal obligations consistent with the agreement. In some cases, the agreement as a whole can also be included in a statute that is adopted by the legislative or executive branch of government. Domestic implementation can also be accomplished in whole or in part by administrative acts of the governments of the individual Parties, such as the elaboration of national action plans.

[26] Perhaps Canada should follow the example of Norway and other parties to Kyoto. After assembling a team of high-profile and well-respected individuals to both champion the accord with domestic audiences and coordinate its implementation, Norway produced a solid national action plan in a matter of six weeks.

[27] These consultations were comprised of 14 day-long meetings in every province and territory of Canada, and involved over 900 stakeholders. Under consideration were four broad policy options for achieving climate change targets – as outlined in Government of Canada, *Discussion Paper on Canada's Contribution to Addressing Climate Change* (Ottawa: Minister of Public Works and Government Services Canada) May-June 2002.

[28] George Greene, "Putting in Place Governance and Engagement Processes for Implementation," in notes for presentation to *Beyond Kyoto: A Win-Win Climate Change Action Plan or Canada* Citizen-Government Dialogue, Parliament Hill, Ottawa) 4 December 2002.

[29] Michael Marzolini, "Polling Alone: Canadian Values and Liberalism," paper presented to *Searching for the New Liberalism* (Munk Centre for International Studies, University of Toronto, Toronto) 27-29 September 2002.

[30] Thomas Homer-Dixon, *The Ingenuity Gap: Can We Solve the Problems of the Future?* (Toronto: Vintage Canada) 2001.

[31] Just as there is little doubt that the U.S. – even acting alone - would prevail militarily against Iraq, a Made-in-the-USA alternative to Kyoto could undoubtedly help address climate change. But international relations are about means – not just ends. Both unilateral responses would represent not only diplomatic defeats, but sub-optimal solutions to what are ultimately collective-action problems on a global scale.
Let it be stated emphatically that there is no moral equivalence between the potential deployment of weapons of mass destruction by Saddam Hussein and the dangers posed by climate change. While the former would represent the deliberately evil act of a single despot, the latter reflects the seemingly benign actions of countless producers and consumers throughout the world (mainly in industrialized countries). Notwithstanding this important distinction, there is a clear double-standard in international affairs: the burden of proof for taking collective action against an environmental threat appears to exceed that required for responding to a military one.

[32] The World Meteorological Organization (WMO) and the United Nations Environment Programme (UNEP) established the Intergovernmental Panel on Climate Change (IPCC) in 1988. The role of the IPCC is to assess the scientific, technical and socio-

economic information relevant for the understanding of the risk of human-induced climate change. So far the IPCC has produced three key reports: the First Assessment Report, released in 1990, was instrumental informing the negotiations leading to the adoption of the UN Framework Convention on Climate Change in 1992; the Second Assessment Report, entitled *Climate Change 1995*, provided key input to the negotiations which led to the adoption of the Kyoto Protocol in 1997; the Third Assessment Report, entitled *Climate Change 2001*, publishes the results of findings on climate change in relation to three key areas – (1) scientific basis, (2) impacts, adaptation and vulnerability, and (3) mitigation. For more information, see http://www.ipcc.ch/about/about.htm

[33] According to this logic, Kyoto (as a first, albeit far more timid, global step) is, in a way, to climate change what an internationally-sanctioned pre-emptive attack might be to Iraq's use of weapons of mass destruction. Such an analogy will undoubtedly irritate environmentalists and military strategists alike, but it serves to highlight the need to apply a consistent standard of evidence as a basis for action across a range of international issues. Indeed, it could be argued that the burden of proof needed to justify a military action, which may involve loss of human life, should be higher than that required for a non-violent response to an environmental danger: implementing Kyoto may cost jobs (although it may also create some), but it will not cost lives (indeed, it may save some, particularly in small-island developing states that do not have the means to adapt to climate change).

[34] For an examination of these negotiations, see Irving M. Mintzer and J.A. Leonard, *Negotiating Climate Change* (Cambridge: at the University Press and Stockholm Environment Institute) 1994.

[35] Many of these principles are enshrined in the 1992 "Rio Declaration" contained in the *Report of United Nations Conference on Environment and Development*, U.N. Doc. A/CONF.151/6/Rev.1, 31 International Legal Materials 874. See also Philippe Sands, *Principles of International Environmental Law: Frameworks, Standards and Implementation, Vol.I* (Manchester: at the University Press) 1996.

[36] Government of Canada, *Climate Change Plan for Canada – Achieving our Commitments Together* (Ottawa: Minister of Public Works and Government Services Canada) November 2002.

The New Liberalism
and Canada's Public Service

Sandford Borins

Introduction

THE DISCUSSION TO this point has focused on developing a new liberal perspective on major policy issues. The public service represents a key component of Canada's infrastructure. Canada's politicians will turn to it, both for policy advice—which may either reinforce or contradict that given at this conference—on how to respond to these issues and for the implementation of their chosen policies. What then would a New Liberal perspective on the public service be?

This paper begins with recent history, looking at both the Mulroney-Campbell and Chrétien governments in terms of their ideological approaches towards the public service and their policy decisions affecting the public service. I then discuss three major challenges facing the public service: the need for integration, the opportunities presented by information technology, and strategies for being an effective employer in the evolving labour market. I sketch out responses to these challenges, and make the case that these must come not only from the public service, but from politicians as well.

During the heyday of neoconservatism, the received wisdom regarding the public service was encapsulated in public choice theory. This theory attempts to extend the economist's model of individualistic, self-interested, rational choice from markets to organizational hierarchies. Politicians are seen as simply desiring power, with policy as a means to that end. Bureaucrats—and I purposely use the pejorative term—want larger empires to run, leading to higher salaries and more prestige. Rent-seeking interest groups attempt to use the political process to insulate them from market competition. These incentives then lead to a three-way coalition in which politicians use the public purse to buy electoral contributions from organized interest groups and votes from their supporters, and public servants design and deliver the policies and programs benefiting the interest groups. The losers are large interests that are difficult to organize, for example, consumers and the general taxpayer, who bears the ever-increasing tax burden required to pay for growing government. This cynical analysis was delivered in its most amusing form in the television series *Yes, Minister* and *Yes, Prime Minister* (Borins, 1988).

The public choice prescriptions were clear. Reduce the size and power of the bureaucracy through program and staff cuts, market testing, and privatization. When delivering policy in a particular area, opt for market-based demand-side solutions (e.g., housing vouchers) rather than bureaucratic supply-side solutions (public housing). Control politicians' temptation to spend through legislated constraints, such as balanced budget laws, binding scheduled tax reductions, and laws obligating them to use surpluses to pay down the debt.

While Brian Mulroney was always more of a pragmatist than an ideologue, which gave rise to Margaret Thatcher's jibe that as leader of the Progressive Conservatives he put more emphasis on the adjective than the noun, his government often treated the public service in ways consistent with the public choice approach. In the 1984 election campaign, Mulroney talked about giving bureaucrats "pink slips and running shoes" and his ministers used similar rhetoric. The creation of ministerial chiefs of staff was intended to provide an alternative to the presumably self-seeking advice offered up by the bureaucracy. During this period Zussman and Jabes (1989) compared public and private sector manager attitudes and found increasing disaffection and declining loyalty as one moved down the ranks of the public sector managerial cadre—which was not the case in the private sector. Partially in response to these findings, the government launched its Public Service 2000 initiative. Ultimately, this initiative delivered little, in part because it did not engage middle managers and staff, and in part because the government gave it a low priority as compared with implementing the GST and bringing Quebec into the constitution. As the government's fiscal position worsened, it took a harder line in collective bargaining with public servants and froze salaries. A 1991 strike by The Public Service Alliance of Canada was ended by back to work legislation. The al-Mashat affair was a demoralizing instance of senior public servants being blamed by the government in order to protect ministers (Sutherland, 1991). Finally, while the Cabinet and departmental restructuring announced by Prime Minister Campbell was widely recognized as long overdue, one of its consequences was a dramatic reduction in the ranks of senior public servants (Lindquist and Paquet, 2000).

The overall record of the Mulroney years, then, was not particularly supportive of the public service. What Lindquist and Paquet termed the traditional cosmology of the public servic—a non-partisan public service, with promotions from within on the basis of merit, and with lifetime employment at decent salaries—had been called into question by the Conservatives (see also Kernaghan, 2002).

The Chrétien Years: Cosmology Restored?

In the last decade, a new way of thinking about the public service has begun to replace public choice. It has assimilated the most positive of the lessons of the New Public Management, such as its emphasis on user satisfaction and efficient production, with the injection of choice where possible as a means to those ends (Borins, 2002). An efficient, effective, and honest public service has now come to be seen as one of the factors responsible for a nation's economic competitiveness and social well-being. Conversely corrupt, ineffective, and overstaffed bureaucracy is seen as one of the causes of underdevelopment. This case is being made at an international level by organizations such as the World Bank and OECD. Evidence is often advanced through the creation of global league tables, and here non-governmental organizations such as Transparency International (www.transparency.org), which focuses on corruption, and international consultancies such as Accenture (2002), which focuses on e-government, have also played a role.

The most articulate Canadian voice in this movement is not a politician, but rather Jocelyne Bourgon, first in her capacity as head of the public service from 1994 to 1999, and now as President of the Canadian Centre for Management Development. She has put forward a Canadian model of public administration reform which rejects the minimalist state and envisions high-quality public services produced by a professional, non-partisan, career public service. That model is also consistent with one of the main political concerns of the Chrétien government, namely the survival of the federal government in the face of separatist and regionalist challenges. The federal government wants to remain visible to its citizens by continuing to deliver public services. In this view, career federal public servants can be expected to show greater loyalty to the Canadian state than loosely-affiliated networks of contractors and sub-contractors.

Many of the actions of the Chrétien government are consistent with this more activist approach (Lindquist and Paquet, 2000). Chrétien and his ministers have not engaged in bureaucrat-bashing. One of Chrétien's first actions was to remove the ministerial chiefs of staffs, signaling a greater reliance on the advice of public servants. As part of its Program Review, the Chrétien government did preside over the largest reduction in the history of the public service (45,000 positions—roughly 20% of the public service— over three years), but its early departure and early retirement initiatives were quite generous. The improvement in public finances and better economic performance of the latter years of the 1990's made more resources available for responding to the claims of the public service, and salary increases at all levels and merit pay for senior public servants were restored, with special adjustments made for some groups such as information technology professionals and the military. The public service and its departments rapidly increased their reward and recognition programs (Borins, 2000). Jocelyne Bourgon's La Releve initiative constituted a greater commitment to career development for the senior public service. On the question of letting public servants take the heat to protect ministers, the record is mixed, with the defense of the HRDC grants program handled mainly by public servants, while the Prime Minister himself defended advertising practices in Quebec as a necessity in the fight against separatism.

While the traditional cosmology that Lindquist and Paquet speak of has not in all respects been restored, the Public Service of Canada will be in better shape when Jean Chrétien leaves office than when he entered office. The radical surgery of Program Review affected the public service just as it affected public sector programs, but what emerged was viable and sustainable. We now have a smaller public service that is less under-resourced than a decade ago. It is more visible. It also has more public respect. The latter is partially the result of the Chrétien government's actions and partially the result of a changing environment. Terrorism has led to a recognition that the public sector bears the ultimate responsibility for ensuring citizen safety and security. The dot.com crash and the accounting scandals have led to a re-examination of the private sector's alleged superiority and a recognition that, here too, the public sector has a unique and unavoidable role to play in ensuring transparency and fairness in the marketplace.

While recognizing both the achievements of the Chrétien government in restoring the public service—and the influence of changes in the environment that made such a restoration possible—it is also necessary to look ahead. What are the key challenges and opportunities the public service faces? What is required to meet them ? I believe there are three major challenges—integration, information technology, and the labour market—each of which has a variety of aspects.

Integration

One of the popular New Public Management reforms was breaking much of the bureaucracy into smaller operating units, and giving them a few clear and measurable objectives and greater autonomy to pursue them. The Major Government in the UK pushed this farthest, reorganizing the public service so that roughly 70% of core public servants were working in 130 executive agencies by 1997.

The federal government's establishment of Special Operating Agencies (SOAs) is a comparable initiative, though not nearly as comprehensive in scope or autonomy as the UK's (Zussman, 2002). Executive agencies and SOAs have demonstrated efficiency gains in functions involving production that can operate at the margins of the core public service.

Unfortunately, the world is not neatly separable into discrete problems each of which can be parceled out to an autonomous SOA. The most important and most intractable ("wicked") policy problems are those that cross departmental and governmental boundaries, as was evidenced in our discussions of the cities, economic competitiveness, and aboriginal issues. Policy research indicates that progress will be made on these problems only if governments approach them holistically. Information technology facilitates horizontal communication—it is easy to keep a wide range of people in the loop through an email address list. As will be discussed below, the Internet creates a common platform for delivering many departments' services. Users of public services have made it clear in survey after survey that what they care about is quick and courteous one-stop service, while the identity of the level of government or department that owns the store is irrelevant. My own research on public sector innovation convinced me of the importance of integration; when I analyzed innovations in a variety of countries at different stages of economic development, the most common characteristic of the innovation, appearing in two-thirds of them, was that it was holistic, in that it crossed organizational boundaries, was based on systemic policy analysis, or provided a variety of services to users (Borins, 2001).

Information Technology (IT)

Information is intrinsic to government. Governments have the most comprehensive holdings of information regarding many important aspects of the lives of all Canadians. The application of IT to the public sector is becoming so extensive that it no longer makes sense to talk about e-government, e-consultation, or e-democracy; we will always have government services, consultation, and democracy, and IT will be applied to each, with impacts on each. The Internet may well be an ideal medium for many public sector trans-

actions because they are relatively straightforward and require neither physical examination of products nor face-to-face contact.
Indeed, the Internet may be more suitable for public sector transactions than for many of the products and services initially offered
through business-to-customer e-commerce (Porter, 2001). IT providers, for example IBM, have noticed that their fastest-growing
market is in the public sector.

Consider the following impacts of IT in the public sector.

- It can facilitate integration. Delivering service over the Internet
  is a clear example. The only logical way to organize a govern
  ment web portal is along client lines. The Canada site now
  has 35 service clusters (e.g., seniors, youth) and each cluster
  has a multi-departmental management board. While the
  management boards are initially tasked with managing the
  website, they facilitate discussions about program inter-relat-
  ionships, for example whether there is overlap among programs,
  or whether a common electronic form could be created that
  could serve a variety of programs

- IT changes the nature of the public sector workforce. Applying IT is what economists call capital-labour substitution. It
  reduces the size of the clerical and operating legions that once
  populated the public service. Fewer jobs remain, and those
  that do require higher skills, particularly the knowledge
  workers who operate the technology. The Public Service Commission (2002) reports that administrative support and operational categories fell from 49% of the federal workforce in
  1991 to 37%, while the scientific and professional and admi-
  inistration and foreign service categories rose from 37% to
  52%—in effect a mirror image. Technology made it possible
  for the public service to continue delivering services while
  undergoingthe downsizing mandated by Program Review.

- IT requires extensive outsourcing. In this capital-labour
  substitution, the public sector no longer builds the capital
  tal, but buys it from the private sector. The public sector has
  become a huge purchaser of hardware, software, and systems.
  The federal government is now spending $ 4 billion annually
  on hardware and software acquisition and operating costs,

which represents 10% of its budgetary expenditure on oper-rations. The big problems come in purchasing large systems and/or ongoing support services, and public servants must become effective contract or relationship managers (Auditor General of Canada, 2000).

- IT poses major challenges of security and privacy. Security means protecting systems and data from hackers; it has also meant removing from public sector websites information that could be used by terrorists to plan attacks. Public servants can envision a variety of reasons, such as better policy analysis, enhanced program design, and better service delivery, to justify linking public sector databases. Privacy legislation generally permits only voluntary link ages (e.g., the Permanent Voters List compiled annually from income tax records) and linkages justified by law enforcement, health, or security.

- IT has begun to effect public consultation and democratic dialogue. The Internet reduces the cost of communication, and hence makes it easier for marginal candidates like Jesse Ventura and John McCain to campaign (Kamarck, 2002) and for opponents of the WTO to organize (Deibert, 2000). Canadian governments have started experimenting with posting discussion papers on their websites and are wondering about protocols, such as whether to post all responses as well, and how to analyze what comes in. People are using the Internet to talk about politics, sometimes in banal ways, such as the wide circulation of jokes about the deadlocked US presidential election, but increasingly in more creative ways. A friend of mine, an Israel activist, has taken to emailing daily a wide range of media articles supportive of his view to several hundred friends and associates. I thought he was unique until I recently read a *New Yorker* piece about some one there doing exactly the same. This also illustrates, however, the Internet's tendency to facilitate the reinforcing of like-minded views rather than dialogue between differing views (Sunstein, 2001).

The Public Service Faces the Labour Market

In attempting to renew its workforce, the federal public service faces some equally daunting challenges. First, the public sector workforce is older than the Canadian labour force as a whole. The Public Service Commission forecasts that 45% of the public service, and 70% of its executives will retire between now and 2011-12. In addition, the retrenchment of the1990's meant that there is not a large cohort of experienced younger public servants ready to re-place them. As discussed above, an increasing percentage of the public service will consist of highly educated knowledge workers, and it is for this group that the competition with the private sector will be fiercest. Career aspiration studies show that this group is looking for interesting work and competitive wages, but not neces-sarily lifetime employment with a single employer (Public Service Commission, 2002). The public service has generally provided com-petitive entry level salaries, but does not keep up with the private sector at more senior levels (Gunderson, 2002). Hence, the quality and variety of the work and career development opportunities be-come extremely important to public sector retention.

One of the big difficulties in recruitment is that the application of the merit principle leads to lengthy competitions for permanent positions. As a consequence, managers have relied on short-term contracts to circumvent competitions. While this has the advan-tage of giving managers an opportunity to test new staff without making a commitment, it has the converse disadvantage that temps are equally uncommitted. Furthermore, short-term contracts are rarely advertised, and tend to be won by people known to the man-ager. Thus, the overly-exacting application of the merit principle has itself subverted the merit principle (Auditor General of Canada, 2001; Malloy, 2002).

The Canadian labour market is becoming increasingly diverse, particularly in the large urban centres. Despite making strong efforts to increase representation of designated groups (women, ab-original peoples, persons with disabilities, and visible minorities), all but aboriginals are sharply under-represented in the executive category (Public Service Commission, 2002).

Responding to These Challenges

If the Public Service of Canada is to make a major contribution to the well-being of Canadians and to participate creatively in solving the policy problems we have discussed, it has to make progress on confronting these challenges. The public service is not self-governing, and needs the support and assistance of its political masters to move forward. Consider some responses to each of the three challenges.

Integration

Integration poses several challenges for public servants. Will the careers of public servants who have been active in inter-departmental initiatives advance, or will they have been seen to have deserted their home department? Many departments or branches are dominated by a particular profession; integration often requires different professions having different cultures to work together. A classic instance of this is community policing, which has required police to move from a culture of "fighting crime" to a culture of collective problem-solving together with other professions. Generally, public sector budgets are allocated to departments, rather than inter-departmental projects or programs. Will departments be willing to make agreements with one another that would involve reallocating departmental funds to collective initiatives, and will such agreements be acceptable to the Treasury Board, the Auditor General, and Parliament? Despite these potential impediments, casual empiricism suggests that public servants in Ottawa are much more enthusiastic about participating in initiatives that cross organizational boundaries than they were twenty or thirty years ago. Being a strong defender of one's turf is not a good reputation to have these days.

How does integration play at the political level? The most important fact of life is vertical accountability to Parliament through a minister. The question always asked of inter-departmental initiatives is who is the minister accountable. The question becomes even more complicated if the initiative also involves a partnership with the private sector. The government-of-the-day and the government-in-waiting dislike inter-departmental partnerships for reason that are opposite sides of the same coin. If an inter-departmental initiative goes well, ministers ask who gets the credit and who cuts the ribbon—not an academic exercise when the prime minister has announced his intention to retire. If an inter-departmental initiative goes poorly, the opposition wants a scapegoat to blame and a ministerial career to destroy, rather than having responsibility diffused among several ministers.

Canadian politicians have not been particularly creative in delivering policy and program integration. Some think it unnecessary, hearkening back to a golden age—the St. Laurent years, perhaps—of strong ministries run by strong ministers, with little need for integration. Some governments have attempted to achieve integration by strengthening the central agencies, in particular cabinet office and the first minister's political office, and forcing ministers to get central clearance for virtually everything. Critics have alleged that Chrétien (Savoie, 1999) and Mike Harris have both followed this model. Another alternative used to deal with high profile inter-departmental problems is the creation of a temporary special purpose agency staffed by secondment, reporting to a ministerial committee, and represented in the legislature by the committee chair. This is the secretariat model used by Allan Blakeney (Blakeney and Borins, 1998) and, at the federal level, exemplified by the Trade Negotiation Office created by Brian Mulroney. The problem is that this structure works for problems of finite duration, while the policy issues of the cities, seniors, and economic competitiveness are ongoing.

Of all Westminster governments, Tony Blair's appears to have approached the problem of what it calls "joined-up government" with the most creativity. Some UK initiatives include

- directly funding inter-departmental initiatives and programs, with success measured on the basis of outcomes rather than outputs
- establishing central policy making units for cross-cutting problems (e.g., Social Exclusion Unit)
- establishing joined-up inter-ministerial service delivery units
- assigning a minister specific responsibility for a particular inter-ministerial program (Mulgan, 2002).

If New Liberalism is about bringing the power of government to bear on the major policy challenges, then Liberal governments of the future will be experimenting with more permeable boundaries within the public service, which necessarily entails more flexibility in the organization of Cabinet.

Technology

In the federal government, the impetus for IT appears to have come mainly from public servants. This has been the case from the outset, for example public servants in Industry Canada developing *Strategis* as a way for the department to meet its mandate of providing industry information within the constraints of Program Review and *SchoolNet* as a way to bring the Internet and the fed-eral government presence into the school system. Public servants are at work on integrating service delivery through the clusters on the Canada site. There are other integrative initiatives happening, such as closer cooperation between HRDC and CCRA. Together these two ministries deal with 85% of Canadian individuals and businesses. There is the potential for both front-line service delivery initiatives and back-office cooperation (e.g., shared server farms). Public servants can take service integration only up to the point where they require legislative change. Just as IT professionals talk about legacy systems, legislation enacted long ago for other needs is a legacy system. Just as updating legacy systems is costly (the Y2K fix), legislative change is costly. But we will achieve the full potential of IT in the public sector only with legislative changes, and the question is whether politicians will be willing to do what only they can do.

While the federal public service has embraced IT, there is a great deal more reluctance at the political level. We are just scratching the surface of e-consultation, with individual departments experimenting in the absence of any policy framework. There appears to be little political interest in IT, nor little use of IT by politicians, beyond perfunctory web sites (brochureware). The typical MP's reaction seems to be, "why should I concern myself with public sector IT when the voters aren't asking for it?" A somewhat more thoughtful MP's reaction might be, "why should I take email seriously when all that happens is I get spammed by vocal interest groups outside my constituency?" There are reasonable answers to both questions. To the first, I would point out that IT is a means of improving service quality and reducing costs, both factors that matter to politicians. There are many constituencies where IT firms are large employers. The public is concerned about policy issues involving IT, such as privacy, security, and intellectual property. Finally, demographic change is occurring. For many of my students, being in touch means their hotmail account and their cell phone. They are voters, too, and in ever-increasing numbers. To the second question, the answer is that the problem of MPs offices being spammed is not insuperable, software filters have been developed, and authentication software is on the way. On the other hand, MPs —especially those with policy interests that transcend their geographic constituencies—might decide that their constituencies include anyone who contacts them. Electronic voting is also at the experimental stage, but with the lowest voter turnouts among the youngest voters, there is clearly an incentive to politicians to move forward.

Competing in the Labour Market

The challenges the public sector faces competing in the labour market are not insurmountable, and substantial progress has already been made. Public service salaries have become more competitive. The Public Service web site (http://jobs.gc.ca) attracts a large number of applicants, but needs continued investment in screening software (Public Service Commission, 2002) to process effectively the large numbers of applicants. The Public Service Commission runs an elite entry-level internship program; that program will have to be expanded to prepare to replace the wave of executive retirements in the coming decade. The internship approach can be applied not only for general managers but in specific functional areas; the Ontario Public Service has launched an internship program in the IT area.

One way to tackle the problem of managers having an incentive to hire only on short-term contracts is to create pools of prequalified candidates for various areas, so that managers can quickly hire people for permanent positions from those pools (Malloy, 2002). The current managerial preference for short-term contracts is a function of both the lengthy hiring process and the difficulty of releasing people hired for permanent positions during their probationary period. The latter, too, will have to be addressed.

The biggest challenge will continue to be retention, which depends very much on whether work in the public service continues to be stimulating and to provide opportunities for career development. Here, too, there are some hopeful signs. If New Liberalism incorporates an active public sector agenda, there will be many opportunities for work in policy analysis and program development. One area where this appears to be the case is IT. Government IT applications are more challenging than those in the private sector—compare www.gc.ca and www.amazon.ca —and for those who want to work at the leading edge, the public sector is the place to be. The fact that there will be such rapid retirement at the executive level in the next decades means that there will be many more opportunities for promotion at all levels than in the last two decades.

I'll conclude this section with a word about public sector innovation, an area in which I have been doing research for the last ten years. My studies of the best applications to innovation awards in Canada, the US, and economically advanced and developing Commonwealth countries have shown that approximately 50% of innovations—a surprisingly large percentage—are bottom-up initiatives launched by middle managers and/or front line staff. This compares with roughly 25% by politicians and agency heads. I say this is surprisingly large because public sector organizations have traditionally been structured hierarchically and because their personnel systems have tended not to reward public servants for successful innovation, but to punish them for unsuccessful attempts (Borins, 2001).

Producing a climate supportive of bottom-up innovation is one of the ways that a government can provide stimulating careers for public servants. The Canadian Centre for Management Development recently sponsored an action-research roundtable on the innovative public service, and the group made a number of recommendations to the Clerk of the Privy Council on how to create a culture where innovation can flourish. These included:

- an annual report on innovation in the public sector
- a Chief Innovation Officer or Innovation Champion
- an innovation fund to support innovative new projects
- an innovation award

- teaching and developing innovation as a skill that is valued among public servants.

Conclusion

Liberalism is ideologically disposed to support the public service, certainly as compared to the skepticism of the neoconservative outlook that is so heavily influenced by public choice. Comparing both rhetoric and action, it is clear that the Chrétien government has compiled a better record than its Conservative predecessors.

In some areas, such as integration and the application of IT, the public service has already been moving ahead rapidly, and politicians are being challenged to keep up. The activist policy agenda that is likely to come out of New Liberalism will create opportunities for stimulating careers in the public service. The traditional public service cosmology referred to at the outset of this paper included nonpartisanship, promotion from within on the basis of merit, and lifetime employment with decent salaries. A New Liberal cosmology—and one that is more likely to appeal to young people now entering the labour force—may pay less attention to the expectation of lifetime employment, but will certainly put more emphasis on the quality of work by formulating and implementing the new policy agenda that emerges from discussions such as those we have held this weekend.

Sources:

Accenture (2002), *eGovernment Leadership – Realizing the Vision*, www.accenture.com

Auditor General of Canada (2001), *Annual Report*. Ottawa: Supply and Services Canada.

Auditor General of Canada (2002), *Annual Report*. Ottawa: Supply and Services Canada.

Blakeney, Allan and Borins, Sandford (1998). *Political Management in Canada*. Toronto: University of Toronto Press.

Borins, Sandford (1988). "Public Choice: 'Yes Minister' Made it Popular, but Does Winning a Nobel Prize Make it True?" *Canadian Public Administration* 31:1, 12-26

Borins, Sandford (2000). "Public Service Awards Programs: An Exploratory Analysis," *Canadian Public Administration* 43:3, 321-42

Borins, Sandford (2001). *The Challenge of Innovating in Government*. Arlington, VA: PricewaterhouseCoopers Endowment for the Business of Government. Available in its entirety at www.endowment.pwcglobal/pdfs/BorinsReport.pdf.

Borins, Sandford (2002). "Transformation of the Public Sector: Canada in Comparative Perspective," pp. 3-16 in Christopher Dunn, ed., *The Handbook of Canadian Public Administration*. Toronto: Oxford.

Deibert, Ronald (2000). "International Plug 'n Play? Citizen Activism, the Internet, and Global Public Policy," *International Studies Perspectives* 1, 255-72.

Gunderson, Morley (2002). "Compensation in the Public Sector," pp. 533-45 in Christopher Dunn, ed., *The Handbook of Canadian Public Administration*. Toronto: Oxford.

Kamarck, Elaine (2002). "Political Campaigning on the Internet: Business as Usual?" pp. 81-103 in Elaine Kamarck and Joseph Nye, eds., *Governance.com: Democracy in the Information Age*. Washington: Brookings.

Kernaghan, Kenneth (2002). "East Block and Westminster: Conventions, Values, and Public Service," pp. 104-19 in Christopher Dunn, ed., *The Handbook of Canadian Public Administration*. Toronto: Oxford.

Lindquist, Evert and Paquet, Gilles (2000). "Government Restructuring and the Federal Public Service: The Search for a New Cosmology," pp. 71-111 in Evert Lindquist, ed., *Government Restructuring and Career Public Services*. Toronto: Institute of Public Administration of Canada.

Malloy, Jonathan (2002). "The search for merit is killing Canada's civil service," *The Globe and Mail*, September 16, 2002, p. A17.

Mulgan, Geoff (2002). "Joined-up Government: Past, Present, and Future." Unpublished.

Porter, Michael (2001). "Strategy and the Internet," *Harvard Business Review* 79:3, 62-78.

Public Service Commission of Canada (2002). *The Road Ahead: Recruitment and Retention Challenges for the Public Service*. Ottawa: Public Service Commission of Canada.

Savoie, Donald (1999). *Governing from the Centre: The Concentration of Power in Canadian Politics*. Toronto: University of Toronto Press.

Sunstein, Cass (2001). *Republic.com*. Princeton, NJ: Princeton University Press.

Sutherland, Sharon (1991). "The Al-Mashat affair: administrative responsibility in parliamentary institutions," *Canadian Public Administration* 34:4, 573-603.

Zussman, David and Jabes, Jak (1989). *The Vertical Solitude*. Halifax: Institute for Research on Public Policy.

Zussman, David (2002). "Alternative Service Delivery," pp. 53-76 in Christopher Dunn, ed., *The Handbook of Canadian Public Administration*. Toronto: Oxford.

Commentary:

National Identity and the Cultural Covenant

Edgar Cowan

First let me admit to the sins and sinecures of a work-life straddling most of the cultural industry—from magazine and book publishing, to private and public television, sound recordings and finally the wired world of the internet. I've been there, and done most of that.

As you are all well aware, a nation's cultural output, a nation's identity and a nation's sovereignty are all very closely connected.

When I examined more closely the Canadian identity question, I decided to take a page out of Naomi Klein's writings in *No Logo*, and looked at Canada, as one would a commercial brand.

I asked myself, what really has happened to that brand called Canada over the last half century, a brand that has been under Liberal collective stewardship for almost 75% of that time.

It is clear to anyone who cares, this brand called Canada has been seriously devalued, and with it a huge mark down has occurred in our attitude toward, and support of our culture, which lies at the very heart of this particular brand.

Any brand that lacks nuture, soon becomes malnourished, then starved and finally succumbs to an inevitable end. Unfortunately, under our Liberal stewardship, we have, through neglect, carelessness, disrespect and insensitivity, condoned a pattern of slow starvation. And I would suggest this has been a serious dereliction of our duty as the voter-chosen supporters of our national identity and defenders of our national sovereignty.

Our devalued brand has suffered the indignity of lamely defended attacks, from outside sources, namely, a so-called friendly neighbour who has degraded and come dangerously close to humiliating us on various trade and cultural issues, while removing millions of disposable dollars from our cultural and entertainment pot at movie box offices, book cash registers and pay-per-view TV screens.

Also, it is becoming increasingly clear that the osmotic effect of the American led unprincipled globalization gallop has tended to water down traditional, home grown, private and institutional financial support for cultural endeavours. And increasingly has placed a pall over a wide range of cultural initiatives, as it continues to disenfranchise individuals and small businesses, and distort fundamental human rights endeavours in marginalized nations.

From the inside, we have presided over decades of political compromise, wanton neglect, and destruction through the financial starvation of so many of the pillars of our culture. Let me name a few.

Our book industry is currently in tatters, a severe devastation with all the infrastructure dominos falling as we speak. I wonder if any of our authors will ever see their hard-earned royalties and their only source of income.

Our gaunt NFB, and famished CBC have been starved by a succession of paranoid and insensitive political parties. Including ours.

Our film and television industries, especially on the English side, have spent hundreds upon hundreds of millions of direct taxpayer dollars, plus huge tax concessions to produce shows and films that most Canadians refuse, or are not encouraged to watch, that global markets will not buy, and that continue to make foreign co-production partners rich.

The amount of our money that goes into the pockets of caterers, location finders, technicians, drivers and foreign producers rather than into the pockets our own creators, interpreters and story tellers would make you sick.

We have created and funded a thriving commercial production industry that 'shines other peoples shit," and have turned our backs on why we created cultural funding mechanisms in the first place.

Our theatre, dance, orchestral and opera communities continue to run on empty-on deficit budgets, exacerbated by miserly annual federal grants and a mountain of bureaucratic interference. Most of these institutions are functioning on a day-to-day basis, constantly on the brink of bankruptcy, with creative people and processes squeezed to the point of near extinction.

In the absence of sensitive, responsive and responsible political leadership, layer upon layer of costly government bureaucracies and a plethora of cultural NGOs have emerged to adjudicate and represent the interests of these communities. Collectively, the staffs of theses NGOs, continue to haul down salaries and expenses that, if your not sick enough already, would make you gag.

And unbelievably, in order to access *our* public funds, these *same* cultural NGOs have been trained to justify to these *same* cultural bureaucrats, the existence and output of these *same* cultural communities. How? By rationalizing only the economic benefits and forgetting, for the most part, the role that a vibrant, caring creative cultural community plays in nation building.

We as Liberals have forsaken this community, and stood by watching them "from the wings" as they have slowly descended into this sorry state. What a humbling, degrading and humiliating experience for these educated, highly trained, caring, and creative Canadians. What a terrible black-eye for Canadian liberalism.

Somewhere along this weary road, we have shirked our responsibility and have gotten so committed to the economic payback equation, that we have stopped caring about the quality of the lives of our electorate, and the cultural imperative that continues to lie in wait, at the very heart of our identity as Canadians.

So what can we do? Here's one suggestion:

First get rid of the word, and very idea of "industry" as it relates to cultural products and replace it with "covenant." A new cultural covenant must be placed before Canadians, very soon. A covenant that strongly supports, respects and puts a priority on, and a challenge to, the Canadian cultural and creative community to assist us to expedite the strengthening of the fabric of our identity and fortification of our sovereignty.

On our part, we must now initiate a proactive posture on cultural policy, take a hard look at all our cultural assets, decide on what are our cultural priorities are as a nation, then do the unthinkable. Initiate a full audit of these cultural assets, and entertain the contemplation of a complete realignment of policy and financial resources in the funding of content, first and foremost, then the complete rebuilding of solid cultural infrastructures to fit a 21st century cultural future.

I am suggesting, as a start, that all the financial and tax policy resources be pooled, from all the government agencies that have any relationship to the culture. This means those overly protected fiefdoms, the shattered cultural pillars of the CBC, the NFB, Telefilm, the CRTC, External Affairs, Canada Council, Heritage Canada and the numerous Government of Canada promotion silos.

And then, as the government of the day, take the long-overdue, and sorely needed proactive leadership responsibility, and make refreshed, focused and progressive liberal policy decisions. Then clear away all the jurisdictional obstacles, and reapportion these pooled resources, and any rationalized new funding, directly into the appropriate Canadian creative and culture infrastructure community.

Yes, I mean, refocus these currently massive expenditures into where it will solidly support primary Canadian creators and interpreters, and their cultural advocate institutions, and where it will do the most good for our own cultural pillars, our identity, and finally, our nationhood.

Commentary:
Doing Business A Better Way: Some Comments

Hugh T. Cameron

Business advisors for universities

OTTAWA HAS MANY excellent programs, which supply the financial help
for research at our universities. We needed to support universities
and the great research that many of their professional staff is developing. A previous speaker told us that scientists at the University of
Toronto have a better diesel engine for the transportation industry.
Scientists at the University of Alberta have developed a method of
turning highly sulphurous flared gas into electricity. There are many
wonderful projects at Canadian universities that sit on the shelf
without ever getting to the market place.

My suggestion is that every university should have a volunteer
group of businessmen that will help take these great projects to
commercialization.

Support of cities

Earlier we had an excellent report on how Canadian cities' main
source of income is from property taxes compared to US cities that
derive more income from government grants. Financial support
must be given to our cities to prevent the deterioration of the central part of the cities.

Many projects need a small financial contribution and a lot of community volunteering. In the Town of Oakville and the Halton Region we have two health care centres, which are wonderful examples of what volunteers with help from local governments can accomplish. Oakville has The Wellspring Centre, which is for cancer patients and their families. With the financial support of Mary Anderson, and a wonderful citizens support group, Oakville has the Ian Anderson House for quality palliative care.

Both of these vital community facilities were built with large donations and the help of many volunteers and community supporters, with very little government funding. Canada has a great many people who donate many dollars and volunteer many hours of help to worthwhile projects and our governments need to provide seed money and encourage these worthwhile projects.

Get rid of the GST and use a limited transaction consumption tax

Every business transaction in Canada, except most food, requires every business to collect the GST and report all of these transactions to Ottawa.

Ottawa has an army of civil employees checking these transactions, collecting the GST owed or returning a cheque for overpayment of GST.

Revenue Canada checks all imported shipments and parcels into Canada for the collection of GST.

Foreign visitors who spend $100 per transaction on all goods, plus hotel and restaurants can claim a refund on the GST. This requires many hundreds of civil employees to check these refund requests

There is another government department that mails GST rebate cheques to low-income families.

Most Canadian cities now have a building and staff that are involved with collecting the GST. I wrote to my Member of Parliament asking what was the cost of collecting GST. How many civil employees were involved and what was the total cost including real estate, computers and communication such as telephone and postage.

The reply was, they didn't know!

GST has created an underground economy in Canada. I bet that every one of us knows someone who has paid cash rather then leave a paper trail, such as a cheque or credit card. Hence there is a good possibility of no GST being paid to Ottawa, plus a better chance that Income Tax is not paid on these cash transactions.

By changing the GST to a consumption tax, with no rebates, Ottawa can more effectively collect the tax and reduce the tremendous cost of following every GST transaction.

This new consumption taxes would be applied to a limited number of goods, where collection could be monitored with a minimum number of civil employees. The percentage of this new consumption tax would vary with different products and below are some suggested products. They would be no rebate or refund of this tax.

> *Cigarettes*: Apply at the manufacturers in addition to the current excise taxes.

> *Gasoline*: Consumption taxes would apply to all gasoline but not diesel fuel for trucks and railways or airplane fuels. This tax would be collected at the refiners or at the distributor or importer of gasoline.

> *Automobiles*: Apply the tax at the final selling price of all manufacturers and importers. In the past, importers had an advantage over domestic producers as the tax was applied at the point of importation and not on the final selling price to the auto dealers. This gave a tax advantage to the importer of foreign cars.

> This automotive consumption tax should be scaled to emissions. Hence vans and SUV's which now account for 75% of all automotive emissions, would pay a higher consumption tax of 12 to 15%. Smaller and hybrid gasoline electric cars would pay a lower consumption tax, because of their great efficiency of litres per 100 kilometers.

> *Boats, ski doos and all recreation vehicles*: Apply a consumption tax at the manufacturers or the final distributor of leisure craft.

Liquor distillers, breweries and wineries: Apply the consumption tax at the producing plant on all sales except export sales. Collect all consumption tax on imported wines, liquor and beers at point of sale to provincial liquor boards.

This consumption tax must be applied in such a way that it has a level field for Canadian manufactured products and would not unfairly, as the old excise tax, favour the importer. These are a few of the products where a fairer consumption tax could be applied instead of GST.

Start the economy with accelerated depreciation

In the 1974 budget, the Finance Minister allowed increased acceleration depreciation on the purchase of all new manufacturing equipment.

At the present time, we need to jump-start our economy and the best way is to give manufacturers who spend capital money on new production equipment a great first year write off of depreciation.

This accelerated depreciation would result in greater productivity and the introduction of new products.

There would be a short-term loss of revenue to Ottawa but this acceleration depreciation would not increase the total depreciation.

Commentary:

Does Canada Have an Innovation Strategy?

Kimon Valaskakis

LORNA MARSDEN'S PAPER on education was very perceptive and covered a lot of ground from the perspective of higher education seen as an end it itself—a worthwhile goal. Therefore, rather than restate her points, I will instead focus on the role higher education could play, in the context of the Canadian Economy. We must ask ourselves how learning and science in our universities can promote prosperity, growth and development for Canada as a whole. This must lead us into considering the question of whether Canada has an adequate innovation strategy, especially vis-à-vis its competitors in this new era of globalization.

My response to this question, as an educator, as the former head of a forecasting think tank, the Gamma Institute, and former Canadian ambassador to the OECD is No! Our innovation policy is lacking and compares unfavourably with what the other G-7 countries are doing. We are wasting our talent pool and missing major opportunities. In fact, as one OECD colleague put it, *Canada never misses an opportunity to miss an opportunity*.

What are the facts? The economic history of Canada reveals that we have always had good ideas, offered major intellectual breakthroughs to world thought but have been surprisingly weak in the follow up—*bringing these good ideas to successful economic fruition*. Over time, Canada has been a net exporter of ideas and a net importer of machines, software and other vehicles incorporating these ideas. We are considerably above average in citation indices. Our researchers are respected and quoted all over the world but when it comes to the next step—translating all this into meaningful economic projects—the system lets us down. The standard script for ideas originating in this country is: invented in Canada, patented in the United States, developed and manufactured in Asia and reimported in Canada!

Technological change goes through at least 5 stages. At the beginning is *scientific discovery*, a purely intellectual activity. Second comes *invention* the application of the new scientific discovery to a technological process. Third comes *innovation* which marks the passage to economic profitability in a competitive market. The fourth stage is characterized by national and the fifth, international *dissemination* of the said innovation.

In Canada's case we are very good at stage 1 and reasonably good at stage 2 but much less successful in the passage from invention to innovation and the two dissemination stages. Our history is replete of examples of such missed opportunities. In the mid-1950's Canada was poised to become a world leader in aerospace with the Avro Arrow fighter plane. The project was shelved due to lack of courage of our then political leaders coupled with strong pressure from the United States. In the 1970's Canada pioneered word processing. One of the first such machines in the world was manufactured by AES Data, a Montreal firm now defunct. Word processing was instead marketed by Wang in the United States until it became merged with other functions of multipurpose computers. Again in the 1970s Canada pioneered a videotext machine called the Telidon which was alpha geometric and was at least a generation ahead of its closest rivals the British and French versions. However it never came to market. Instead the French minitel system backed by the French government and an aggressive marketing strategy took over and reigned supreme until its current dethronement by the internet-capable general computers.

Why is Canada weak in the crucial passage from invention to innovation? My own view, based on years of studying the phenomenon, lays the blame on our multiple institutional adversary systems. First, the country is so decentralized (considered now to be the most decentralized of the OECD countries, ahead of Switzerland) that there can be no national innovation strategy without the consensus of the provinces. This consensus is difficult to achieve because of competing regional interests: everyone wants the same biotechnology and informatics labs, etc. When there were ministerial level meetings on education at the OECD, Canada was one of the very few countries without a national education minister to represent it. In fact, during my term of office, Canada was represented by the separatist Parti Québécois minister of education, advancing his own views and policies and not necessarily Canada's.

The second adversary system exists both between universities and real world actors and within the universities themselves. The gap between universities and real life challenges is still wide, although it's in the process of shrinking. Most contemporary challenges are interdisciplinary and intersectoral. Nature is not divided into a department of economics, a department of sociology, a department of environment. Unfortunately, universities are still divided along disciplinary lines. Although many efforts are made in the direction of interdisciplinarity, promotion criteria within universities remain very monodisciplinary. Every discipline has a short list of major journals for all tenure track professors to publish in if they want to be promoted. In most cases these journals are monodisciplinary. Consequently, the best minds focus on publishing in these journals, being cited abroad, etc. The interdisciplinary centres are often frowned upon by the line departments.With rewards going to mono-disciplinary output, there are fewer incentives to be an innovator in interdisciplinary ventures. As a result, cross-cutting issues, (like globalization itself, one of the premier challenges of our time), have been slow in penetrating the halls of academe. Consequently, universities—and to be fair this criticism does not only apply to Canada alone—tend to retreat into their ivory towers and do not keep up with rapid social and technological change. Their value added to society therefore diminishes considerably and leading edge innovation tales place elsewhere.

With its enormous talent pool, its excellent institutions of higher learning and its multicultural richness, Canada should be both a leading global *think* and *action* tank. If it is not, it is because we have not been able, so far, to come up with a true innovation strategy— one that not only shortens the passage from invention to innovation but also attracts global talent to come and work in our country as opposed to migrating to the United States, the recipient country of most of the top researchers in the world, as Lorna Marsden's has pointed out. One of the most important aspects of our innovation strategies must be to include serious *attractors* to entice global inventors and entrepreneurs to use Canada as their platform. To do so we must reduce to a minimum the present *repellents* which trap us into being a perpetual idea-exporting country.

The major challenge of a New Liberalism Innovation Strategy must be not just to cook the marshmallows, but to get them out of the fire for the benefit and advantage of all Canadians.

Commentary:

Health Care and the Search for New
Liberalism in Canada: Some Comments

Dan Andreae

As I BEGIN contemplating how best to respond to Antonia Maioni's
paper entitled "Health Care and the Search for New Liberalism in
Canada," I am reminded of Dr. Carolyn Bennett's admonition that
we need to be pragmatic in the implementation of our philosophical concepts—in effect, the operationalization of ideology. When I
reflect on Antonia Maioni's paper through this particular lens, the
crystallized essence is that we must adopt a proactive stance to protect and enhance publicly funded health care in Canada. This is a
crusade, if you will, that allows liberalism to seize the agenda and
define the debate rather than become relegated to a defensive, reactive posture. Certainly, as Dr. Maioni's paper suggests, health care is
considered to be the crown jewel in the armamentarium of our
social safety net system and symbolically, the lodestar that is pointed
to differentiating Canadians from Americans, alongside the model
of being a less violent society. As she points out, the ground was
made fertile for the implementation of nationally funded health care
arising from the enthusiasm and zeitgeist of the times following World
War II, a period of reconstruction when Canadians were prepared
to experiment with a new contract between the state and its citizens. This reflected an appetite for experimentation to avoid, in future, the calamities resulting from the Great Depression and the
Second World War. This new social contract was founded on the

conviction that sometimes people, through no fault of their own, become ill, unemployed and infirm and require some degree of governmental relief and support, and indeed are entitled to it. Of course, heated debates did ensue about the range and scope of what comprised "social welfare."

Also, as Dr. Maioni points out, our system of social welfare should not be taken for granted and one must recognize that the establishment of many seminal programs involved struggle and sacrifice. Indeed, social programs, including health care, are not an inevitability but, as she notes in her paper, statutes rather than constitutional provisions. Remember that Mackenzie King had to be pushed to implement some of these initiatives, prodded by the rising tide of the social gospel movement spearheaded politically by the Commonwealth Cooperative Federation (CCF) nationally, and the electoral advances achieved by the CCF's Joliette in Ontario in 1943. These pragmatic political realities hastened King to appoint Leonard March to prepare the Marsh Report, the blueprint for social welfare development and implementation in Canada based upon the work of Lord Beveridge in Great Britain, regarded as a key architect of the modern welfare state.

In her paper, Dr.Maioni also proclaims that poll after public opinion poll affirms that Canadians believe in certain values as embodied in public policy (recognizing that health policy, or for that matter, any policy, can never be value-free) and as Gregory Baum says, values comprising "compassion leading to collective responsibility." She notes that Canadians are essentially satisfied with the delivery of health care at least once they have entered the system beyond the waiting lists. Yet the image and perception of many is that of a health care delivery system in grave crisis, perhaps requiring radical surgery. Why is this dissonance occurring?

Certainly this is open to speculation and conjecture, but let me offer you some possible reasons. As has been discussed already at this Conference, the media portrayals of the health care "crisis" have raised awareness and have placed this issue squarely on the public policy radar screen. Unless one has not picked up a magazine, watched television, talked to neighbours and friends or listened to the radio, one is aware at least to some degree of the health care issue. Also, I point to the disconnection, felt in many ways as has already discussed in this forum, that exists between citizen aspirations and expectations and actions or lack of them by governments on certain key policies. It reminds me of Member of Parliament Dennis Mill's comment when he stated that constituents approach him with real concerns about critical issues such as the increasingly polluted environment, yet when he returns to Ottawa to raise these issues in Caucus, as expressed by the grassroots, he is told in essence not to worry, as the poll results remain highly favourable. Additionally, there is the accompanying disillusionment and impatience expressed by the populace over the constant wrangling, finger-pointing, positioning and posturing of different levels of government, who avoid taking responsibility which should be the focal issue as identified by another participant at this conference. The rising chorus from Canadians to these levels of government is an exasperated "get your act together!"

Looking at ideological underpinnings of public policy, I put forth to you that the most successful and effective ideologies in practice are those most able to foster a sense of optimism, to articulate an encompassing vision for the future—that if you follow a particular prescription, it is the path to a better life. And I contend that in the last two decades, the neoconservative movement has cornered the market on engendering hope. It may indeed be portrayed in overly simplistic terms such as Ronald Reagan's description of America as a shining city on a hill or George Bush's articulation of America's promise as a thousand points of light, but these catch phrases captured the imagination of people who were, in the early 1980s, looking for "new" solutions following the disillusionment of the late 1960s and 1970s hallmarked by oil crises and stagflation.

I am reminded of Axworthy's remarks, that a quintessential element for defining liberalism is the notion of choice for citizens and finding ways to increase its scope through public policies. Well, the neoconservative movement also focussed on choice— the choice leading to private gain and personal advantage and not choice leading to the collective good. I am reminded how neoconservatives have strategically framed this issue of choice such as when Ernie Eves, during his campaign for the premiership in Ontario, stated in effect, "If I can take my dog to the veterinarian at three in the morning, why shouldn't I be entitled to the same level of care?" This approach represents an example of the Americanization of the Canadian debate.

In terms of health care, neoconservatives have engaged in a host of strategies to dilute publicly funded health care, including by stealth. For example, by delisting services, they attempt to undermine universality, thus weakening support for publicly funded heath care. For when programs become targeted to one particular group in society (for example, those deemed the most needy, however defined), they stand to quickly lose support from the broader middle class who fund them but do not receive benefits, as has been articulately explained by author Linda McQuaig. Neoconservatives can also create the impression of a crisis such that people, desperate enough, will eventually be prepared to resort to any solution to "save" health care, even supporting two-tier health care. Their remedy is not systemic changes within the existing system but rather a radical overhaul; they have crafted the argument such that if one disagrees with their dominant neoconservative orthodoxy, we need to pare back government in order to reduce costs and bolster individual initiative (thus paving the way for the fragmentation of the social fabric of Canada); then one is deemed to be naïve or unrealistic to the real demands of the increasingly globalized world.

What does all of this mean for liberalism? Individuals advocating a liberal philosophy have to regroup and this will not be easy. They will be flying in the face of a dominant ideology which is expounded by much media, government itself, and influential sectors of academia. They face a fragmented and crowded public policy agenda whose priorities can shift like quicksilver. There is currently a lack of a concerted push from groups such as the NDP who seem to be suffering from an existential crisis—whether they are primarily anti-globalizationist or rather "liberals in a hurry." This lack of reform thrust within the electoral political system is not present today, as was the case fifty years ago, albeit several activist groups including nongovernmental organizations have mobilized outside this system, recognizing that effective change can occur through other fora. The political, economic and social climates have changed considerably since that bygone era. Finally, in our "24/7" world, there is an increasing cacophony of voices, each competing for attention and prominence with different public policy agendas.

But as Dr. Antonia Maioni implies, liberalism need not apologize in any way, shape or form for its position and must be proactive, not reactive in the public arena, and assertive, not subservient, in putting forward the case that politically funded health care is indeed in the public's best interests. To achieve this goal includes understanding specifically what strategies and tactics the neoconservatives and others, opposed to universally funded health care, have adopted while carrying out their campaigns through specifically crafted messages. Armed with this knowledge, those adhering to a liberal philosophy will be better able to develop effective rebuttals and meet their challengers head-on.

However, to have a chance of success, which is not guaranteed, there must be a mixing of empirically-based research content with emotional resonance. Solid research, though crucially necessary, is not sufficient. To debate strictly in the realm of ideas, without addressing the legitimate worries experienced by Canadians over the current plight of health care, is to place liberalism at a distinct disadvantage. Advocates of liberal philosophy must adhere to the quote referred to in the beginning of Dr. Maioni's paper by John F. Kennedy in 1960, that indeed liberalism involves "an attitude of mind and heart, a faith in man's ability through the experiences of his reason and judgment to increase for himself and his fellow men the amount of justice and freedom and brotherhood which all human life deserves." This advocating for a publicly funded universal health care system in Canada must be carried out with a conviction that recognizes that a good health policy is also good economics and good social policy.

Leaders may come and go and certain ideologies may be in vogue before cresting and eventually fading, but basic human needs remain unchanged. Liberalism must be grounded in its values while being prepared to be flexible in the quest for their implementation. This must be done with a visceral belief in the dignity of all human beings. The term "realpolitik" has been coined to refer to the need to be strategically pragmatic in the world as it really exists, and not be blinded by fixed ideological solutions to problems that require ingenuity and flexibility. What is required now is a "real liberalism" that seeks to advocate the tenets of liberal philosophy in a way that reaches people where they live. Accomplishment of this goal may be aided by incorporating what I refer to as the five "C"s. These include content, conviction, compassion, communitarianism, and coalitions, because the preservation and enhancement of publicly funded health care can never be achieved by any single group in isolation.

Commentary:

The Role of Governmental
Effectiveness in a New Liberalism:
Bridging the Four Key Gaps

C. David Crenna

Introduction

AN IMPORTANT CONTRIBUTOR to the political success of the Liberal Party
since 1993 has arguably been its ability to capture and hold onto
the "governmental effectiveness" agenda from the New Right.[1] Liberals have given real and deep cuts to government spending and
services a more progressive mantle than the rather limited trim-
ming of the Mulroney era.

Professor Borins notes that performing an active array of public
sector functions well—and with minimal waste—accords with the
values and wishes of the majority of Canadians, and also their British cousins under Tony Blair's leadership. The Republican thirst
for cutting back on almost everything but military spending south
of the border has never taken hold here, at least at the Federal
level, for a host of reasons. The Canadian economy and society are
much the better for it. Widespread acceptance and realization of
effective domestic government helps account for the fact that Canada
outperforms the United States on virtually every indicator of quality of life, save for per capita income.[2]

This paper makes four principal, interrelated arguments:

- Despite many positive corrective efforts, current policy-making processes in governments still suffer from a *fundamental weakness in integrating effort* across departmental and disciplinary lines. This is particularly so for addressing "wicked" problems and issues... those to which each solution seems to create more problems. Especially in these cases, which demand more rigour of analysis, Ministers and senior officials meet great difficulties in sorting systematically through evidence about the relative success and failure of current and past initiatives.

To mix metaphors thoroughly, the combination of flight to bureaucratic foxholes and papering over cracks can create a long-term image of a public sector vulnerable to the charge that it cannot shoot straight, at least on some major issues.

- A new Liberalism must also come to terms with the perilous task of *setting and sticking to priorities* for public interventions. This can be particularly difficult when substance rather than process is involved, e.g. when one must clearly stare down specific interest groups or say no. Of course, New Liberals want to engage the Canadian public in a process of formulating and implementing priorities. However, without a substantive knowledge base to inform priority-setting, the net of public policy can be cast so wide that all interventions are below "critical mass." Despite many valiant efforts over the years, under a variety of banners, there is more work to be done
- Another key element of the Liberal agenda since 1993 has been investment in science and technology. Many obvious benefits have resulted from the huge expenditures made in this field in a variety of ways. However, there may also be a *day of reckoning approaching*, when middle-income Canadians inquire about some of the results in tangible terms. They may even begin with the telecommunications sector. New Liberals need to gird themselves and the scientific community for some hard questions. Even if such questions never come, preparing for them will help to stimulate fresh think-

ing about the next agenda for investment in innovation.

- Flowing from all of these points, and on a global front, there is a need to *energize in very practical ways the Canadian committment to innovation for international development* to do more about bridging the "ingenuity gap," but defined in operational terms. This is the gap between what developing-county governmental institutions are doing and what they need to do to keep up with the problems their societies are facing.[3]

Bridging the Learning-from-Failure Gap

The "Red Books" that underpinned the Liberal election campaigns of 1993 and 1997 are, in many ways, masterpieces of policy integration and of learning from a range of previous government initiatives. They have proven the case for having a solid, fact-based but values-driven agenda to guide policy-making efforts and incidentally, to promote institutional learning and integration of effort across departments and agencies. Nor do the Red Books shy away from defining "wicked" or relatively intractable and cross-jurisdictional issues for Federal attention, e.g., prenatal and early childhood care, crime protection and urban quality of life.

Yet New Liberals are left with the question of what to do for an encore. They also need to assess whether and how to assume the political initiative on selected issues to which even resolute responses over the past decade are almost unblemished by success. Some of the challenges of renewing the fisheries and of reducing greenhouse gas emissions come to mind. In this connection, New Liberals are faced with the conundrum that the more policy-makers require integrated assessments of difficulties in applying the positive state, the less likely they are to find such assessments. There are, indeed, few rewards in government circles for contradicting in-group thinking about comparative performance of policies and programs, especially when that thinking is at odds with the facts on the ground. Each commentary about past failures may appear to be barbed with arrows aimed at specific rivals. Yet there is surely something better than standing still for periodic assaults on the public sector, topic by topic, from the Fraser Institute.

The credibility of New Liberals is likely to rest on their possession and use of superior knowledge about what is effective and efficient in government, and why, beginning with their response to some of the worst cases. The shibboleth about limiting governments to "doing what they do best" leads quickly to a rather short list in the view of the New Right at the national level—defence, foreign policy, taxation, and some critical infrastructure. It is essential to counter in depth the siren calls of those from the New Right who never met a simplistic idea they did not like.

Here is a specific proposal, advanced with some trepidation. New Liberals should establish a task force to address wicked problems perennially resisting public sector efforts. The aim would be to determine whether such problems could be broken open in new ways that learn from the past, but do not involve simply getting out, or preclude it either. In brief, New Liberals would systematically examine past, current, and emerging issues that seem to require government action, but for which existing solutions seem to range from actively harmful to feckless and wasteful of the credibility of the public sector.

There are two ways of going at this task: to start with the whole panoply of programs and sort them into baskets of relative success and failure, or to go straight to the ones in greatest distress. Given the interest and resources, the former strategy appears preferable, both in building morale and benchmarks, and in ensuring that scanning for deeply wounded but still standing interventions is complete.

Whichever substantive issues fall out as needing greatest attention in formulating Red Book III, the stickiest *process* problem—interagency integration of effort—should be at the top of the list. One way of organizing this inquiry is to consider problems according to a "life-cycle" approach. An option for addressing such problems could be permanently supported cross-departmental structures that reflect these full life cycles, as is done in some cases now for responding to crises such as border security after September 11, 2001.

As anyone who travels in Federal offices these days can see, a major generational change is occurring in the Federal public service. It is also essential, especially in the context of making promises to fresh and able young people, to determine how to stop stripping out of mainstream government institutions some of the most interesting and innovative work. More policy work needs to be organized according to life-cycle communities of practice inside its walls.

As Professor Borins advocates, New Liberals should look closely into the innovations that the Blair Government has been attempting in the United Kingdom, particularly in rewarding integrated and innovative public service effort.

Bridging the Evidence-Based Priorities Gap

Those who have worked in Cabinet minister's offices can attest that political life is a recipe for Attention Deficit Disorder (ADD). In this context, there is strong resistance to setting and holding to real and sustained priorities for public policy in many quarters. Endless meetings can still produce laundry lists that avoid the central issues. This, in turn, often translates into support for the status quo in allocating attention and resources, except in crisis situations. On the other hand, a set of evidence-based priorities within a learning organization is a tremendous tool for both defending what is being attempted, and for getting the job done. Think of a Health Minister able to point constantly to a widely-accepted list of major causes of death, injury, and days off work, and of cost-effective public health solutions. Such a Minister would be well armed to focus on the most critical drivers shaping the health of the nation.

The still-fragile state of a culture of evidence-based priorities makes even policy fields in which there are clear ways of ranking prospective solution—such as reducing greenhouse gas emissions—more difficult to address. Indeed, public debate about signing and implementing the Kyoto Protocol illustrates rather well the challenges that policy-makers can face in setting effective priorities. Global climate change is one instance in which there is a simple and ineluctable common metric against which to assess relative impacts of different potential actions, as well as their "collateral damage". That is: amounts of greenhouse gases prevented or consumed. Hence, "soft options" are much more limited. Yet effective public sector action also demands that there be "buy-in" to making difficult choices in the face of uncertain ultimate results.

What is needed is *not* ways to eliminate political calculation and coalition-building or to move them to the margins. These are the main meat of politics, and will remain of central importance. However, sound policy advice must surely be based on bringing together in a few pages the best available knowledge of what causes major problems and how effective, based on the evidence, different types of proposed solutions are likely to be. An analogous methodology animates the Finance Department in shooting holes at departmental proposals. It would be preferable to have evidence-based decision-making spread, with appropriate modifications, to proposing departments and agencies so that the dialogue is less lop-sided.

In brief, better scientific knowledge and better information technology now make it feasible for New Liberals to learn from efforts to apply "evidence-based decision-making" in the health care field, and to adapt and move this concept up to the policy-making level, and to other fields as well. The aim would be to formulate an agreed priority-ranking system in each major policy field based on a coherent workshop-based process to develop it. This in turn would provide the bedrock knowledge upon which Cabinet tests proposed new initiatives against criteria that go beyond their cost, but are not just the result of harried policy analysts coming up with the requisite three or four "options." Moreover, if a proposed solution clearly addresses an evidence-based priority problem, and emerges from more systematic scanning of what is likely to work, the risk appetite of governments should increase.

Bridging the Prospective Gap Between Promise and Performance of Science and Technology

The foundation of all science is evidence found by following certain protocols of research and analysis. Yet taking scientific findings and translating them into successful ventures is a matter of bold leaps of faith, whether in business or in politics. Building the Internet was such a leap of faith, based on solid advances in physics, engineering, and mathematics. Observers watched in awe as the way opened to tap and put to work what appeared to be all the knowledge in the world, and a tremendous research and communication tool was created. At the same time, users and prospective investors were engulfed by one of the largest waves of sheer nonsense and outright prevarication that has come along since people went mad over tulips.

Building across North America is a deep anger at the combination of sales pitches and corporate planning mistakes that has resulted in the loss of billions from almost everyone's life savings. At the moment, this anger may be focused on specific individuals, such as the glib stockbrokers who urged one to hold the shares bound to go even higher. However, it is almost inevitable that the anger will be mobilized and focused by someone on a political plane. President George W. Bush may have some limitations, but lack of attentiveness to public mood is not one of them. Whoever succeeds in mining the deep vein of anger among the middle-income Canadians at the staggering losses of savings over the past two years is likely to have a rosy, though turbulent, political future.

The specific case of Federal support for innovative telecommunications ventures now gone somewhat awry is only one example. Through direct engagement with them over decades, the author has found that quite a number of scientists in government laboratories grow impatient at being asked to offer evidence of the contribution they are making to the public good. Alternatively, they may offer anecdotes when patterns are required. At one level, this prickliness is entirely understandable, since questions along these lines can be, or can appear to be, the thin edge of the wedge of political interference. On the other hand, as federal reinvestment in science and technology activities continues, it will be natural to strengthen mechanisms for obtaining assurance of results, outcomes and impacts that go far beyond simple indicators of outputs like R&D expenditure as a proportion of GDP.

This is not a blinding new insight. However, it is becoming ever more urgent to reinforce the move toward comprehensive performance measurement systems for federal science and technology investments. With this fully in place, New Liberals and members of the public alike can inquire sensibly about the comparative returns from different fields of inquiry, about the overall portfolio of public support for scientific and technological activities, and also about what values are driving such activities.

Bridging the Global Ingenuity Gap

The International Development Research Centre is a remarkable Canadian invention, of which too few examples still exist: a true organization for "citizens of the world." Nonetheless, it remains a research centre and must contribute to international development innovation indirectly through practical knowledge, demonstration projects, and persuasion with investors and donors.

The "basket-case" developing countries have a triple deficit to overcome: lack of democracy, political and economic equity; the elevation of corrupt sociopaths to many positions of high office; and their consequent lack of interest in creative solutions to the problems of their own people. On the other hand, notable exceptions in relatively smooth political transitions such as South Africa, the Baltic States, Uruguay and Thailand demonstrate that these deficits can be overcome and that the groundwork for ingenuity in developing solutions can be laid.

The Government of Canada needs to "put wheels" under innovations from IDRC and from Canadian entrepreneurs struggling to stay in business by serving poor people in difficult and dangerous places. Important models along these lines are being developed, for example, by Industry Canada via the Canadian Sustainable Cities Initiative, and via the Department of Foreign Affairs and International Trade participation in International Aid & Trade events. However, almost by definition, these initiatives must hold out the prospect of rather immediate commercial benefits to Canada. A second track is needed for recovery, reconstruction, mitigation and sustainable development in the countries that pose the greatest threats to the security of the world as well as being in unconscionable misery, or else that simply need us badly. They include: Afghanistan, Sudan, Rwanda, El Salvador, and East Timor, among others.

Here are some specific examples of how Canadians can make a dramatic impact on people's lives, all based on real innovations developed in this country that have yet to receive concentrated or sustained support:

- low-cost brick-making technology;
- low-cost water purification technology;
- low-cost solar cooker technology;
- low-cost interactive telecommunications technology.
- low-cost methods of incorporating disaster resistance into small buildings.

In pursuing creative solutions to urgent global needs, for example, Canadians still lack the kind of flexible tool for supporting investment in developing countries that Americans have in the Overseas Private Investment Corporation (OPIC).

New Liberals would do well to embrace a rejuvenated strategy for Canadians as citizens of the world; not just as suppliers of more foreign aid.

Conclusion

Since 1993, Liberals have enjoyed tremendous political success through a combination of good management and good fortune. Wise sailors as well as political planners like to "trim sail while the wind is high." In this period of preparation for the next election, New Liberals need to dig into four key problems that bedevil more effective government. They need to take stock of what has been learned about failures in government-initiated solutions as a basis for strategies toward "wicked" problems in the next mandate. They need to define some key priorities according to the evidence of perils and benefits to the well-being of Canadians, e.g., to reforming health care in relation to largest causes of death and injury. They need to support a more rigorous demonstration of the results from science and technology investment, e.g., based on indicators of contributions to quality of life as well as the economy. And they need to apply their talents for innovation in a more concerted way to the needs of the developing and transitional economies, beginning with some of the worst situations first.

Notes:

1   See: "The New Liberalism and Canada's Public Service" at www.newliberalism.ca.

2   See United Nations Development Programme, *Human Development Report*, (New York: Oxford University Press, annual). Of course, for the New Right, this is a very important "but".

3   See www.ingenuitygap.com. While Dr. Homer-Dixon defines the gap as one between ideas needed and ideas available, there is also a gap between having sound ideas, and acting upon them.

Commentary:

The New Liberalism and Canada's Public Service

Elena Mantagaris

I WOULD LIKE to make some comments focussing upon the themes of information technology and integration, e-consultation, and the public service labour force raised by Professor Borins in his paper "The New Liberalism and Canada's Public Service."

For the first theme, the following is a specific example of how linking information technology with the concept of information integration (clustering) can, in fact, provide significant benefits to the public, transform how the public service works, and respond to the needs of Canadians.

In the face of crisis on September 11, 2001, federal public servants rose to the occasion by using the Internet as a vehicle to bring together (or cluster) accurate and up-to-date information for Canadians regarding the events in the United States, the arrival of airplanes in Canada, security measures being implemented, etc. Where previously, information would have resided in various locations, departments and areas of authority, the public service clustered and organized relevant information on behalf of Canadians. Through a single link entitled "Fighting Terrorism," located on the Canada Site (www.canada.gc.ca), the public service demonstrated that it could work horizontally by pulling together information from various jurisdictions, that it could provide information and services that responded to immediate and specific concerns amongst Canadians, and that it could provide that information and service in a timely manner. Previously, Canadians would have had to navigate the maze of departmental jurisdictions to get complete information related to the crisis.

Whereas television coverage was focusing on how our security was being compromised, the federal public service was working to demonstrate how it was securing our country and, thus, still *relevant* in the lives of Canadians. This was no small feat in an era of cynicism towards the public service and when governments are constantly being accused of not moving quickly enough to respond to the priorities of Canadians. Technology provided the means to integrate *authoritative* information from across jurisdictions under the heading of a single electronic link.

International delegations seeking to learn how the federal public service uses technology to provide better service to Canadians were impressed with the speed with which the "Fighting Terrorism" link was launched and the fact that the public service broke through traditional departmental silos to bring together relevant information in a holistic manner. While this innovative approach may have contributed to raising confidence in government amongst the public, it also proved to the public service itself that technology and the concept of information clustering across jurisdictions could present an opportunity to work in new ways and provide better service delivery to Canadians.

On the issue of e-consultations, there are some broad cautionary points worth raising. While many of its proponents have touted the benefits of using the Internet to engage in electronic consultations with the public on any number of policy issues, e-consultation differs significantly from information clustering and service delivery in terms of potential cultural impact. E-consultation has been described as a modern form of direct democracy, one that responds to the demands of populists seeking direct public response as guidance. However, technology will not fix the democracy deficit and waning interest in public institutions we are experiencing in this country. Nor will it necessarily improve the quality of debate surrounding any contemporary issue of interest to the public. It must always be remembered that the Internet is primarily a communication and information tool. IT may expedite service delivery and information integration, but it does not automatically result in a better democratic interaction or inevitably bring clarity to the policy-making process.

We can establish as many online consultation sessions as we want between government and the people. However, the consultation process will be all but meaningless if, as a society, we fail to first educate and encourage citizens to pursue the knowledge with which to make informed and reasoned contributions to public debate. A liberal democratic society must constantly promote a culture that encourages and values responsible public engagement as a worthwhile activity, particularly if technology is going to allow citizens to grow even closer to the political and policy decision-making processes. More simply put, e-consultation is not an enlivening of democracy, but it is in fact a tool that demands a public clarification concerning the very values of democracy. This would include the necessary rights and responsibilities of all citizens. Only then will e-consultation begin to meet the idealistic expectations it is built upon.

Another point to be considered with respect to e-consultation is the potential impact on our parliamentary system. What we need to ask ourselves at this juncture is the following: If the public service is going to directly engage Canadians in the development of public policy, what is the purpose of the MP or MPP? An MP/MPP is supposed to represent his or her constituents, but the Internet allows for direct interaction between the public and the public service. In that context, why have an MP/MPP at all? The potential for a more robust e-consultation process in the future raises crucial issues about the very structure of a parliamentary democracy and requires that we re-examine roles, responsibilities, authorities and accountabilities between the citizen, and our elected and non-elected government officials.

Section Three

Prospects

Some Structures to Think With:
Interconnectivity and Network Possibilities

Candis Callison

LIBERALISM AS AN IDEOLOGY holds the individual, and freedom of choice for the individual to be its supreme values. Yet in practice, our Canadian system of governance, informed by liberal values, has created a set of institutions that at best, serve the individual, and at worst, dedicate their energies to monolithic institutional self-preservation. The past several years of telecommunications-fueled economic boom and bust have demonstrated, quite painfully for some institutions, that despite best efforts at adaptation or a protective stance, individuals incorporate new ideas, technology, and tools for communication in both predictable and unexpected ways and means. What becomes obsolete, virtual, or important is dependent on a multi-faceted process involving interaction, exchange, and utility. It is this lesson, based, in part, on observing how new technology has been adapted, that has begun to shape modes of analysis, and structures for thinking more broadly about how individuals are connecting, making choices, and tapping into political, commercial and governing institutions. Here, I would like to introduce some of these structures to think with and investigate where they might be applied in a Canadian and liberal policy-making context.

To start, I would like to contrast traditional ideas about connectivity with the concept of interconnectivity. Connectivity implies a line between two points. Interconnectivity implies bi-directional and multi-dimensional links and overlaps between issues, objects, individuals, and groups. As a conceptual structure, it has been applied by theorist Manuel Castells most notably and others to describe what is being hailed as the rise of a network society. Network society is most closely associated with the unrealistically sanguine cyber-rhetoric associated with the Internet. But as Castells pointed out, technology can be seen a point of departure, rather than an end in itself revealing more complexity in patterns of change and interaction. By its hybrid nature, a network society has the potential to redefine notions of cohesion, cultural interactions, identity and representations.

To help understand what I mean by interconnectivity and networks, imagine if you will, something like the root system of a persistent set of weeds in the garden. The way these roots connect, sprout, extend, branch, and persist matches a structure very much like a rhizome. It is fragmented and conjoined unpredictably through nodes of access that lead to yet more nodes and branches of access. This is essentially the description of a rhizomatic network that contains overlapping structures and, unlike the weed system, invites all kinds of connections regardless of type or form as long as they heed basic and sometimes shifting protocols for connection.

Interconnectivity within a rhizomatic network is not merely the joining of individual boxes by lines in a kind of line or staff hierarchical vision. Rather, substitute a finite box with many small boxes, and groups of boxes with multiple lines crossing and criss-crossing one another coalescing at various points, dispersing at others. Interconnectivity is not a constant, but rather a fluid notion of cohesion involving movement, varying momentums, and moments of stability. It also allows elements and connection between elements to shift in terms of allegiances and connections creating a sense of temporary equilibrium.

This model of social interaction and cultural development permeates and interconnects every aspect of society reflecting a much more rich and diverse assemblage version of reality. Yet, our modern state functions by way of separating lines of connectivity and stabilizing or formalizing elements.[1] Our institutions rely on the ability to represent and disseminate legibility and stability. More clearly, our institutions rely on what heorist Alberto Melucci calls a "reduction of complexity" to maintain order and secure the tenants of a political system.[2] In other words, the convenience of the state attempts to determine the capacity of our productivity, efficiency, and mobility. Network society has effected a quiet succession from this mode of organization by employing interconnectivity and rhizomatic structures that include formalized lines of communication and control, but often augment, twist, and generally complexify to the point of slippery non-compliance.

Networked information technology has been posited as the materiality of this networked society, a society we as Canadians are fast becoming and joining.[3] It could, and is, being argued that we have always been a society of networks that span the globe.[4] What's different about developments in the past century is that we have watched as information technology and media have insinuated themselves into many aspects of our life. The telegraph, radio, television, and now the Internet—being the most recent—came with all the hype of a cultural revolution. Particularly, in recent memory regarding the Internet, a whole body of rhetoric sprang up promising more connection, new community, exciting culture. The Internet both subsumed and exploded the singular direction of older broadcast media making interactivity an assumption rather than a passing fancy. It is actually not so different than the previous media in this respect (radio started out as a two-way ideal as well), but the Internet's capacity to combine, envelop and mimic the other forms of media as well as its individuation and inherent bi-directional capabilities invite a broad realm of networking possibilities.

While a revolution may or may not have occurred in your living room or office cubicle, information technology in many forms including the Internet has arrived and affects how we connect to the bigger world beyond our everyday lived experience. I want to be clear that I am not upholding the hype of "information technology as wunderkind," merely that it is present and here to stay much like the television, refrigerator, motorized engine—technologies that were earlier heralded as revolutionary.

In our highly developed country, we have created a playground for culture and technology to collide, interact, and nurture growth. But what do we hope to create with this technology? Cities devoted to the technological elite enabling the growth of enterprise? A break with the stranglehold of broadcast/corporate media geared to the lowest common denominator? Cultural destinations online? Wider access to wireless Internet? All possible, but not probable unless there is some active coalescence from both Canadians and Canadian institutions towards this common goal. We, at this juncture, where the dot-com economic bust has intersected with what some fear to be the erosion of faith in technology, have an opportunity to consider reflexively our relationship with technology and our growing status as and in a networked society.

Thinking with the Internet

Technology, culture, politics, and economics determine the development and indeed, the materials of each other. The interconnectivity between these elements can be framed this way: our values are as important as, and a determinant of technological invention and the use of technology. As Dutch theorist Wiebe Bijker, Bruno Latour and others have posited: we are shaped by our tools, and they are shaped by us.[5] The Internet is not the network society I am referring to—rather, it is the materiality in the sense that is a powerful object to think with and about, embedded and situated in a society that itself is a network. The Internet, then, is a reflection of the transformations inherent in the combination of our cultural, political, technological, and economic aspirations and entrenchments.

Perhaps this is why the US debate about Napster remains such a contentious moral issue. Napster is a peer-to-peer network that connects individual computers in a rhizomatic pattern for the purpose of sharing media files. The debate about its abilities and existence can be framed as (1) a betrayal of artists, (2) the rise of militant consumers, (3) theft from the recording industry, and (4) depending on which side of the value-laden fence you're on: a poor or brilliant use of networked technology. If you don't download music online, then you probably aren't aware that clones exist everywhere and the legacy of Napster continues without front-page coverage. And importantly, the reach of peer-to-peer networking extends far beyond the domain of music to include all forms of media and software. If something can be digitally recorded or transferred to a digital format, there is a very good chance it already exists online.

This kind of system defies institutionalization in many ways. Certainly as a construct for thinking about culture, there is no gatekeeper or control mechanism like a Canadian Radio-television and Tele-communications Commission (CRTC). The overlaps and individual ability to shape and reshape the network defy borders and adherence to ideology. Some countries have tried to set up virtual walls, but these values do not line up with Canadian principles of freedom and democracy. More important for Canadian institutions is the fact that networks invite evasion of some of the sacredness of modernity. There are no strict lines of division for organization, instead there are fragments connected by points of bi-directional contact. Identity is defined in terms of multiples rather than singularity. There is little cohesion except in the fact that the possibility for more interconnection exists. In a world where enterprise is based on profit and the state on a certain amount of control, these aspects of networked society threaten to destabilize and remake the fabric of our Westphalian society.

This is not to say that a network society is without its own limiting sets of controls and inhibiting standardizations. Coding and algorithms, as well as representational capacities, determine and direct content in an online environment. Similarly, a networked society introduces new protocols for control, information, and connection on an ad hoc basis—most of which are never formalized, and most of which react or act in relation to our prevailing values. For example, Napster created what MIT Professor Joe Dumit calls "anonymous on-the-fly alliances for sharing information outside any known channels" and, in the process of this creation, embedded its own terms of engagement that range from sharing to fanatical control of mini-domains in the electronic environment.[6] Rather than strict lines of modernity bisecting at regular intervals, rules and capacities rest on the user preference combined with technological abilities, cutting across authoritarian inscribed homogeneity and stability.

Enabled by information technology, inter-institutional forays are doing much the same crossing cultural, governmental, corporate institutional lines.[7] Theorist Bruno Latour posits that the way things are studied in a scientific or academic setting do not stem from the actual problem to be solved, but more closely reflect entrenched relations between disciplines, subject areas and data.[8] This same kind of analysis could be applied to government and corporate departments, as well as cultural institutions. It is these kinds of entrenchments that prevent issue or data oriented coalescence, erecting boundaries that risk making those groups irrelevant by design. Entities whether created inside or outside an institution that challenge this organization around administrative function have the potential to effect change in both process and issue resolution.

And yet, our post-9/11 world, especially on this continent, has seen the rise in importance of physical borders running counter to the idea of a network society. Importantly, this touches on issues of surveillance or what I like to call the 'soft underbelly' of the network society. When alleged terrorist Richard Reed's email from a public Internet terminal in Paris was recovered within minutes or hours of him being discovered on a plane to Miami with a bomb in his shoes, which part did you focus on? His shoes, or the ability to track down the contents of his email outbox so quickly and precisely? A little closer to home, there are more parallels still: how did Canada send or share its immigration and other internal files with the Americans? Did we send a large crate of paper files or easily indexable electronic files that allowed the FBI—or whichever agency investigates Canadians—to find, link and trace identities and movement of individuals?

We live in a postcolonial reality where colonialism as the standard bearer of modernity constructed boundaries for nationhood and identity concealing the fragmentary nature of our existence.[9] And importantly in Canada, we live with the constant presence of another pseudo-empire whose network in terms of media and policy influence could constrain the boundaries of our imagination. Now more than ever as members of a global network society, our existing institutions are incapable of barricading us against the onslaught of these transborder influences, nor can they easily adapt to fragmented rhizomatic interconnectivities. Individuals and movements of fluid coalesced individuals construct identities and form allegiances that are multiple, often temporary. One only has to look at the emerging social movements around the world to see these kinds of allegiances being formed and translated into action.[10]

Social movements, however, have not always had the corner on these kinds of formations and transformations. Regardless of what institutions are created or adapted, individuals will and do develop strategies and tactics for dealing with constraining order in everyday life. This process of what theorist Michel deCerteau calls "making do" becomes another mode of interconnectivity outside the realm of the state.[11] Many cultural and governance institutions exist as emminent repositories with inhibiting systems of rules and parameters of usage geared to an imaginary homogenized public.[12] The processes individuals face of often struggling and finally making do with imposed systems are not acknowledged or captured within the precepts we substantiate through policy-making. Yet, the rise of the Internet has made avail of entities like Indymedia.org, an organization devoted to "open-publishing," styling itself as a "decentralized autonomous network" formed as a result of what has been characterized as the unbalanced media coverage of the 1999 World Trade Organization protests in Seattle.[13] In this mode of analysis, Indymedia.org can be framed as a process of making do that has become both an externalized public reality and a social movement making it difficult to ignore the constraints of media institutions, and the ability to create another network.

A conceptual shift: Canada in, and as, a (global) network

To concretize what I am describing and in the spirit of using objects and issues to think with, I will advance several examples of how we might effect a conceptual shift in approaching distinctly Canadian issues. Beginning with the most prominent: we might reframe the "brain drain" to the United States as an extension of network and an example of flows between nodes within the network which may in turn lead to unexpected networking eventualities and probabilities.[14] And maybe in some respects, we should look at these types of cultural phenomena as a measure and criteria for adaptability in areas like taxation, education, health, media, and culture. More importantly, can we not find a way to foster and support mobility without it threatening our identities, which are hardly singular anyway?[15] Is it just possible that international experience is essential to the various networks we as individual Canadians find ourselves a part of in terms of work, familial ties, belief associations, and other areas of our lives?

A second example lies even closer to home. It is abundantly obvious that the stories we tell ourselves as Canadians often do not take into account the complex realities of our networked history: Aboriginal, French, and Anglo-Canadians can barely settle on the ontology or epistemology of our shared history let alone complexify the unrealistic solidity of these artificially amassed groups. Certainly the stories we hear from our grandparents, embedded as they are with Canada's development and policies, differ based on our individual heritage. And indeed, we know ourselves to be a diverse lot, whether we hail from one of over 600 Indian Reserves, thousands of rural communities, or several of the urban environs. Yet, somehow we must settle for a sanitized nostalgia of a glorious past or some other kind of binding narrative. Is it any wonder our identity as Canadians seems to constantly be in flux or at least, under scrutiny and question? We would do well to imitate a rhizomatic pattern seeing areas where we connect and coalesce around these in all our complexities, or at the very least, aim for an agreement about our taught history that is decidedly un-American in its lack of nostalgia, heterogeneous narratives, and sense of veracity. Is this not what a liberal commitment to a multicultural agenda, past and present, entails?[16]

Thirdly, our environmental policies do not take into account the synthesis of human and organic actions and relations, nor the constriction of artificial boundaries enforced by nation-states. Information about environmental issues coming from institutions is purposely streamlined rather than being cross-linked and overlapped, preferring standardization rather than a messy mix of the reality surrounding natural resources we know to exist. Standardization often comes part and parcel with mini-domains within governmental divisions and departments who resist combining information and decision-making. Outside of governmental information dockets lie further realms of corporate information, community perspectives, and organized environmental movements each with there own modes of gathering, sifting, and presenting data. Is there a way to account for and combine oral histories, alternative views of land, land usage and values outside of the statistically precise metrics enforced through agencies often dedicated to administrative efficiency rather than overall efficacy? For example: if there was a way to understand the rhizomatic existence of a transborder watershed —its inhabitants' connections to each other and the land—how would that change our policies regarding that watershed?[17]

Importantly in this view of the environment, we can begin to think beyond Canadian borders to what is harming the global and importantly for us, continental environment. Rather than merely signing the UN Kyoto Protocol, what about using our position in the global network to lead climate change concerns towards inventing a new mechanism for enforcement of environmental treaties?[18] The Canadian legacy in establishing peacekeeping as viable international security solution stands as a testament to this kind of innovative thinking—now that the threat involves global climate change, our attention may need to shift from past glories to present danger. In this case, it is not just the idea that we are a network but a situated knowledge of our existence in larger global networks. These concepts move beyond what is embodied in the Internet and embrace that of social movements where individuals coalesce around ideas and beliefs—in this case, the idea and belief in Canada as a unit through which we can interact on a world stage to protect what is of great shared importance to us all: ensuring the sustainability of our global ecosystem.

Finally, I touched on the issue of surveillance earlier. US policy is setting the pace for discussions, boundaries, and themes in this area and many others related to information technology (most notably, copyright infringement). Not only official policy and bills before the US Congress, but US-based multi-national corporations are poised to dictate world standards based on their bottom line needs and the needs of the US government.[19] These issues affect Canadians in many realms: how we do business, how we govern, how we create and make works of art and production, how we communicate on email and mobile phones. Our presence in a network of shifting alliances and developing technologies is not felt in terms of our influence over US corporate or political developments, yet we are often direct recipients of the results of these decisions. How can we address the flows of information technology policy, software, and products that follow network protocols and lines of access? If traditional forms of nation-state intervention are not adequate or adaptive enough, what other forms of intervention will work to ensure a free flowing stream of information that ultimately benefits Canada as a network society?

Conclusion

The rhizomatic concept I am forwarding here stretches across the standardization of information and relations. It is radical in its suggestion of what lies outside the bounds of institutionalization and control, but perhaps it is not so far from the way we relate to one another outside the modes of officialdom—certainly the lesson of Napster as an alternative mode relies on this kind of connection exterior to official channels, but goes further in its inherent anonymity, lack of centrality, and constant flux. What a networked society, as I am proposing it here, necessitates is a shift in our ways of conceptualizing what is shared, connected, central, and cohesive, and where boundaries matter and/or cease to exist. It is also a challenge to how information is disseminated, structured, and used by individuals who are mobile, and multiple in allegiances. The resulting interconnectivity envelops all forms of connectivity, going beyond, above, outside, and through the formalized hierarchy of structured relations to create a rhizomatic whole in a constant mode of adaptation—a series of temporary equilibriums.

The challenge for policy makers is to think not in terms of departments, provinces, or even Canada, but to utilize a rhizomatic structure to think with—a structure that acknowledges the fact that installing new institutions, protecting or ensuring the survival of elusive and sometimes non existent cultural boundaries, investing in the development and use of new technology are interventions into an existing network of buzzing interconnectivity. The fluidity of a network redefines some of our static ideals of identity, cohesion, and even security or privacy, but it is also these ideals that will define our use and placement of networked technology. Adaptability and frameworks for adaptability that take into account mobility and unpredictability are the skills and goals defined by a network society. And it is this resulting co-production of technology, culture, and politics that is and will continue to define Canadians' future relationship with each other and our role in a global network society.

Sources:

"About Indymedia," 30 April 2000, Independent Media Center, 14 Oct 2002 http://www.indymedia.org/about.php3.

Anderson, Benedict. *Imagined communities: reflections on the origin and spread of nationalism.* London and New York: Verson, 1983.

Babiker, Mustafa, et al. "The evolution of a climate regime: Kyoto to Marrakech and beyond." Report No. 82, February 2002. MIT Join Program on the Science and Policy of Global Change. http://web.mit.edu/globalchange/www/MITJPSPGC_Rpt82.pdf.

Beck, Ulrich. *What is Globalization?* Trans. Patrick Camiller. Cambridge, UK and Malden, MA: Polity Press and Blackwell Publishers, 2000.

Bijker, Wiebe E., Thomas P. Hughes, and Trevor Pinch, Eds. *The Social Construction of*

Technological Systems: New directions in the sociology and history of technology. Cambridge, MA: MIT Press, 1987.

Bradford-Wilson, Shauna and Michael. Email to the author, 29 Sept. 2002.

Callison, Candis. "A Digital Assemblage: Diagramming the Social Realities of the Stikine Watershed." Master's Thesis, Program in Comparative Media Studies, Massachusetts Institute of Technology 2002.

Castells, Manuel. *The Rise of the Network Society,* 2nd Ed. Oxford: Blackwell Publishers, 2000.

Center for Democracy and Technology. Website. http://www.cdt.org.

de Certeau, Michel. *The Practice of Everyday Life.* Trans. Steve Rendall. Berkley and Los Angeles: University of California Press, 1984.

Dumit, Joseph. Email to the author, 26 Sept. 2002.

Deleuze, Gilles and Felix Guattari. *A Thousand Plateaus: Capitalism and Schizophrenia.* Trans. Brian Massumi. Minneapolis: University of Minnesota Press, 1987.

Foucault, Michel. *Discipline and Punish: The Birth of the Prison.* Trans. Alan Sheridan. New York: Random House, 1977.

Freidberg, Jill and Rick Rowley, dir. *This is what Democracy looks like.* Seattle Independent Media Center and Big Noise Films. http://www.thisisdemocracy.org.

Hardt, Michael and Antonio Negri. *Empire.* Cambridge, MA: Harvard University Press, 2000.

Jenkins, Henry. *Textual Poachers.* New York and London: Routledge, 1992.

Latour, Bruno. *Science in Action,* Cambridge: Harvard University Press, 1987

Latour, Bruno. *We Were Never Modern.* Trans. Catherine Porter. Cambridge, MA: Harvard University Press, 1993.

Melucci, Alberto. *Challenging Codes: Collective Action in the Information Age.* Cambridge: Cambridge University Press, 1996.

Myers, Natasha. Email to the author, 26 Sept. 2002.

Povinelli, Elizabeth A. *The Cunning of Recognition: Indigenous Alterities and the Making of Australian Multiculturalism.* Durham and London: Duke, 2002.

Saxenian, Anna Lee. "Brain Circulation: How High-Skill Immigration Makes Everyone Better Off." *The Brookings Review* v.20 (1), Winter 2002, pp. 28-31.

Scott, James. *Seeing Like a State.* New Haven and London: Yale University Press, 1998.

Susskind, Lawrence. *Environmental diplomacy: negotiating more effective global agreements.* New York: Oxford University Press, 1994.

White, Richard. *The Organic Machine: The Remaking of the Columbia River.* New York: Hill and Wang, 1995.

Notes:

1. James Scott, *Seeing Like a State* (New Haven and London: Yale University Press, 1998); Michel Foucault, *Discipline and Punish: The Birth of the Prison,* trans. Alan Sheridan, (New York: Random House, 1977); Jonathan Crary, *Suspensions of Perception* (Cambridge, MA: MIT Press, 1999).

2. Alberto Melucci, *Challenging Codes: Collective Action in the Information Age,* (Cambridge, UK: Cambridge University Press, 1996), p. 177.

3. Manuel Castells, *The Rise of the Network Society,* 2nd Ed.

4. Ulrich Beck, *What is Globalization?* Trans. Patrick Camiller, (Cambridge, UK and Malden, MA: Polity Press and Blackwell Publishers, 2000).

5. Wiebe E. Bijker, Thomas P. Hughes, and Trevor Pinch, eds., *The Social Construction of Technological Systems: New directions in the sociology and history of technology,* (Cambridge, MA: MIT Press, 1987); Bruno Latour, *We Were Never Modern.*

6. Joseph Dumit, "Re:draft cdn conf," Email to the author, 26 Sept. 2002.

7. Ibid.

8   Bruno Latour, *Science in Action*, (Cambridge: Harvard University Press, 1987), p. 16.

9   Benedict Anderson, *Imagined communities: reflections on the origin and spread of nationalism* (London and New York: Verson, 1983).

10 Melucci, *Challenging Codes: Collective Action in the Information Age.*

11 Michel de Certeau, *The Practice of Everyday Life,* trans. Steve Rendall (Berkley and Los Angeles: University of California Press, 1984), pp. 29-31.

12 Henry Jenkins, *Textual Poachers* (New York and London: Routledge, 1992). Jenkins uses de Certeau's theory to look at the way fan communities adapt and use fictional narratives like *Star Trek* that are disseminated through broadcast media. There are arguments to be made about copyright issues and authorial inscription that pertain to Napster and other phenomena based on this analysis of creative work. It is incumbent on us to ask what fair use is in a digital world of reproducibility, layered imagery, artistic and hobbyist works related to popular culture that find an audience and community online – how much are we willing to curtail creativity in the interest of corporate profitability, copyright protection, and eminent relations of production?

13 "About Indymedia," 30 April 2000, Independent Media Center, 14 Oct 2002 http://www.indymedia.org/about.php3. For more on the media coverage of 1999 WTO protests, see: Jill Freidberg and Rick Rowley, dir.,*This is what Democracy looks like*, Seattle Independent Media Center and Big Noise Films, http://www.thisisdemocracy.org.

14 Anna Lee Saxenian, "Brain Circulation: How High-Skill Immigration Makes Everyone Better Off," *The Brookings Review* v.20 (1), Winter 2002, pp. 28-31. What I am describing is not dissimilar to the 'brain circulation' ideas espoused in this article, and other current discussions surrounding India's diaspora.

15 Scott, *Seeing Like a State,* details the ways in which the mobility of individuals has been oppressed through state regimes.

16 Elizabeth A. Povinelli, *The Cunning of Recognition: Indigenous Alterities and the Making of Australian Multiculturalism*, (Durham and London: Duke, 2002). Povinelli's study of Australian liberalism has striking parallels for Canada and liberal ideology in exploring questions like: "… how a state and public leans on a multicultural imaginary to defer the problems that capital, (post) colonialism, and human diasporas pose to national identity in the late twentieth century and early twenty-first centuries… how they recreate a superordinate monocultural referent, chase a transcultural if not transcendental desire, a flickering *something* beyond our differences, even as they purport to be recognizing the cultural subjects standing before them…," pp. 29.

17 Candis Callison, "A Digital Assemblage: Diagramming the Social Realities of the Stikine Watershed" Master's Thesis, Program in Comparative Media Studies, Massachusetts Institute of Technology 2002. This thesis looked at combining standardized and non-standardized information regarding the environment, specifically a transborder watershed, to reveal a complex and wholistic perspective of cultural and communal values, resource extraction, land use planning, and historical developments.

18 Lawrence Susskind, *Environmental diplomacy: negotiating more effective global agreements* (New York: Oxford University Press, 1994); Babiker, Mustafa H., et al., "The evolution of a climate regime: Kyoto to Marrakech and beyond" (Report No. 82, February 2002, MIT Join Program on the Science and Policy of Global Change, http://web.mit.edu/globalchange/www/MITJPSPGC_Rpt82.pdf).

19 For US discussions on the subject, see the Center for Democracy and Technology website at http://www.cdt.org/wiretap.

A "Brand Canada"
For the Connected World

Wayne Hunt

ONE OF THE MOST significant divisions of the 21ˢᵗ century will be the way in which societies adapt to new technologies. The Internet Revolution and later, the Bio-Tech Revolution, offer different challenges for our societies. Biotechnology will profoundly transform agriculture. It will also transform public attitudes toward food safety. But it promises to do far more than this. Bioengineering could, in future, change the very basis of what it means to be human. We can move from an "End of History" to an "End of Humanity," or as the popularizer of the first expression has it, to a "Posthuman Future."[1] But the Internet has already forced a fundamental transformation upon us. It is a distribution channel for ideas and information, a communications tool, and a marketplace; and it is all of these things at the same time.

The present institutions of public decision-making are ill-adapted to the new demands being placed upon them. Our parliamentary institutions were designed for the nineteenth century, and urgently need to be reexamined in a comprehensive manner. Our present electoral system is in need of reform. Other countries have usefully combined different types of electoral systems. Germany, for example, uses a combination of proportional representation and a first-past-the-post system of the type with which we are familiar in this country. It is the argument of this paper that there has to be a democratic renewal of our public institutions. It will be further argued that one of the best avenues for this renewal is through the creative use of Internet-based debate. Behind these arguments, however, lies a more important consideration. It has become a commonplace to point out that a younger generation prefers to engage with the world through nontraditional mechanisms. They prefer to work through Non-Governmental Organizations rather than through political parties. This is not a situation which is unique to this country. It has an impact on Germany, as much as Britain, or the United States, or on non-Western societies. The overall thesis of this paper is simple: that the most important way in which the generational gap can be narrowed will be to put ethics at the heart of public life.

The need for innovation can be put forward in an open and direct way but it needs to be directly associated with ethical concerns. Communications technology can be viewed from this perspective.

The Case for Innovation

Monopolies have the capacity to stifle more than their competitors—they can stifle new ideas. This is as true for the Internet as for other areas of commerce. One of the most widely cited authorities on this is Lawrence (Larry) Lessig, a Professor of Law at Stanford Law School. Lessig could be called the John Kenneth Galbraith of the 21st century. Also like Galbraith, Lessig eschews the strictly analytical approaches to public policy. Again like Galbraith, Lessig champions the forces that will act as a counter-balance to the power of big business. He lacks the Harvard economist's telling sense of satire, but his capsular analysis of the wider processes are masterful. He asks, "Who owns the Internet?" and answers with the obvious reply—"Until recently, nobody."

The Internet offered a design that was totally unique. As a resource it was open to all. The spirit of the wild west animated the entire enterprise. This changed. Courts and corporations are walling off portions of cyberspace. Lessig maintains that lawyers are killing the Internet. His argument is that Americans have a notion of private property as a core element of their political culture. He quotes with approval Carol Rose, of the Yale Law School. Rose explains that Americans are captivated by the idea that the world is best managed "when divided among private owners," and when, as a corollary, the market regulates that relationship. The state is there to protect property and to supply a rule of law. So far, so fundamental. But this worldview breaks down when applied to the Internet. As Lessig makes clear, the Internet may have been born in the USA, but many of the innovations now taken for granted were the product of "outsiders" with the World Wide Web being one case-in-point. (The Web was developed by a researcher in a Swiss laboratory who fought to bring it into being. Neither was web-based email an exclusively American invention. It was cocreated by an immigrant to the United States from India, Sabeer Bhatia. It gave birth to one of the fastest growing communities on record—Hotmail.) The core resources of the Internet were left to what Lessig calls the "commons." Innovators could freely roam this "commons." Policy-makers, he insists, have to understand the importance of this architectural design because, in the developing world in particular, many "real space" alternatives for commerce and innovation are neither free nor open.[2]

Fencing Off the Informational Commons

Also quoted with approval by Lessig was a maxim of Machiavelli's, that innovation "makes enemies of all those who prospered under the old regime (while)... only lukewarm support is forthcoming from those who prosper under the new." The "commons" during its initial phase was not controlled. It was a resource to which everyone had equal access. When the Internet took off, narrow-band service across acoustic modems enabled millions of computers to connect through thousands of ISPs. Local telephone service providers had to provide access to local wires, they were not allowed to have differential fees or to discriminate against Internet service. The physical platform on which the Internet developed was regulated to remain neutral. This changed.

The dominant broadband technology in North America is currently cable. Cable providers have no obligation to grant access to their facilities. Cable has pressed for a different set of regulatory principles and have employed new technologies which allow them to act in a "strategic" manner. Cisco, to use one example, has developed "policy-based routers," which allows them to decide upon the flow of content. Some content will move quickly, others less so. They can block content, such as advertising from competitors, that is not consistent with their business model—to use a felicitous phrase. As Lessig puts it, this network "will increase the opportunity for strategic behavior in favor of some technologies and against others." The principle of neutrality will have been lost and the potential for innovation on a world-wide scale will have been compromised.[3]

Copyright regulation has had a parallel effect. In his recent book, *The Future of Ideas*, Lessig shows how "an army of high priced lawyers, greased with piles of money from PACs" have forced Congress and the courts to "defend the old against the new." Patents also invoked sceptical response. Lessig points out that this has had a long history. Thomas Jefferson—the first patent commissioner—had a fear of monopolies, as did Ben Franklin. In fact, the latter thought them immoral. Science, he further observed, "has traditionally resisted patents." And even Bill Gates ("no patsy when it comes to intellectual property protections") has expressed scepticism about patents.[4]

The cumulative effect of all these changes is to move the cyber world from an architecture of innovation to an architecture of control.[5] How will we react as a society to the forces of monopoly capitalism? When radio was the dominant communications technology of the era, Graham Spry famously declared that Canadians were faced with a choice: "the State or the United States." Spry was the leading figure in a group that was formed in the fall of 1930 to promote Canadian broadcasting. Calling itself the Canadian Radio League, the new pressure group brought together a wide, constantly-shifting coalition of personalities and group interests. Included in the latter category were several premiers, women's groups, university presidents and university women's groups, organized labour, agrarian groups like the United Farmers, western interests, and francophone groups. Theirs was a communitarian spirit. Graham Spry was the chief spokesperson. Appealing in an unambiguous way to the romanticism of a national project on this scale, Spry constantly made the point that radio was "a majestic instrument of national unity and national culture." Its potentialities were too great, "its influence and significance too vast" to be left "to the petty purposes of selling soap."[6] The results of these efforts became a storied part of this country's heritage. In 1932 Parliament passed its first

Broadcasting Act, establishing the Canadian Radio Broadcasting Commission (the CRBC). This was the forerunner to the Canadian Broadcasting Corporation (the CBC), which was formed in 1936. The Canadian Broadcasting Corporation supplied a public voice for radio and, later, for television. Will there be a Canadian presence in the new information order? And more importantly, will the same communitarian ethos animate events?

Creating a Canadian "Brand" in the New Information Order

The first question is the easier to answer. The federal government has placed an emphasis on access. The latest communication technology should be available to rural Canada, to the places that suffer out-migration, as well as to the north. This is the link to the outside world in these places. There has to be an equality of *educational* opportunity so that all can share in the civic benefits of the Computer Revolution. Health care provision is one important example of the ways in which new technologies can help teams of specialists bring the benefits of their expertise to people who do not have mobility. More innovative use of long distance education is another. Pippa Norris, of Harvard University, has examined the social impact of the digital revolution on a global scale. She has pointed out that farmers in the developing world can use community centres to learn about future price changes in crop values and to have an analysis of weather forecasts. In those places where there is a lack of access to the media, the convergence of communications technologies means that the Internet has the potential to deliver virtual stories from local newspapers, as well as stream real-time radio and television video.[7]

In Canada, decision-makers in the public sector are in broad agreement about the potential of this new technology. But much of the will to harness this potential has been lost. Why? The fascination with leadership politics within the Liberal party of Canada goes a long way toward providing an explanation. In a remarkably public fight, then Industry Minister Brian Tobin fought with then Finance Minister Paul Martin over a national broadband program. Mr. Tobin's enthusiasm for the project went down as quickly as his leadership ambitions, however, when he was on the losing side of that fight. But this was not the only reason the project was put aside. Public enthusiasm was beginning to cool. The damage that was done in the equity markets to tech stocks left an impression that this was a revolution that had already peaked. In fact, this is manifestly not the case—but the impression was there nonetheless.

Access to this new technology remains a crucial issue. Use of the Internet has dramatically increased in the last two decades. Its potential has only begun to be appreciated.[8] The wonderment and majesty so elegantly described by Graham Spry at the time when one new technology was appearing is there with this next generation of communications technology as well. Still, the question remains: *How do you put a Canadian face on this phase of the technological revolution?* And it is here that we must go back to the question of a communitarian ethos. Depopulation is a problem for small-town Atlantic Canada, as it is for small-town northern Ontario or northern Quebec or northern Saskatchewan. Technology can bring a better quality of life to these locales when there is a political will to find innovative ways to put the infrastructure in place.

The Government of Canada has to be ahead of the curve when it comes to change. There are important issues of content on the Web. The search engines which you use are an important lens on the world. Take one representative example. Type in "aboriginal policy." The first nineteen sites are likely to be American. The same results can be obtained with other examples. It is important to understand that this situation can be changed. The Canadian government has a critically important role in this area. The government could sponsor the creation of a search engine which would provide a frame of reference consistent with the values, the ethos and the issues which are central to the nationhood of this country.

Canada is not alone in this initiative. In other parts of the world there have been governmental attempts to develop innovative strategies for dealing with the unstoppable advance of Gap, Starbucks and other corporate interests. Consider the French strategy. With the creation of a new public diplomacy department, the government of that nation developed a novel approach. Instead of pushing the losing case of French exceptionalism, the Government of France positioned itself as the front of a coalition of nation-states which promoted a new sense of nationalism in culturally-significant areas such as telecommunications and information technology. In a similar move, when it became apparent that French could not compete with English as the language of commerce, the French took up the cause of multilingualism. Other nation-states have followed a parallel course of action. The British use a number of cultural programs to show that they too are open to cultural diversity.[9] For its part, the United States has recognized the importance of the private sector in its efforts to fight the war on terrorism through the agencies of public diplomacy.[10] How does our country fit into this? We protect the sovereignty of our country through a system of counter-balances. At present, the United States dominates the channels of communication to the outside world. Television images are broadcast to the world through CNN and other news gathering agencies. But when one society monopolizes a medium of communication, a society at the margin may seek other mechanisms. This is an insight that dates to the work of Harold Innis.[11] A pan-Canadian presence in the cyber world that develops an informational commons for the public good would be a critically important innovation. Canada can lead the world not just in ideas, but in finding new mechanisms and new platforms to express these ideas.

Directing the Social Activism of the Cyber Generation

The Canadian government has to have a bold, new approach to generational change. At present, a large percentage of state support goes to older people. The subsidies can be direct, through pensions, or indirect, through the health care system. The state has an important moral obligation to provide cradle-to-grave care. This obligation will only remain if a younger generation of Canadians can be encouraged in their efforts to discover a sense of civic engagement. It can begin with an inter-generational initiative. Consider this option. Technology diffusion can be promoted through a program which allows young people to teach seniors how to use computers. Computer facilities can be established in retirement homes as part of the program. Link-up programs can be established with facilities in the developing world, so that this can be an idea without borders. It would require a massive redeployment of state resources. These resources will be redeployed along age lines (for 18 to 24 year olds) rather than the traditional lines of socio/economic class. Parenthetically, it should be noted that the private sector has already discovered that developing tech solutions to allow an aging population to enhance their independence and live in their own homes is a growth industry. Or as one American magazine put it, "considering that every seven seconds another of the nation's 75 million baby boomers turns 50, there's clearly gold in helping the old."[12]

It is important to place these initiatives in the broader context of changing political cycles. The era of private interests is being called into question. Corruption and accounting scandals in the private sector have taken much of the romance out of a career in that area. A new political era is beginning to take form. At present, it only exists in an indistinct form, but the general pattern is clear. There is a dialectical play of forces at work. The American historian, Arthur Schlesinger Jr., famously described two cycles in American politics. One was identified with public purposes; the other, with private interests. Bursts of energy, enthusiasm and experimentation with public programs followed from the first cycle.[13] We are now at the cusp of a cycle in which the need to place public interests above private interests is becoming more apparent. It is time to act upon it. But before we do so, it would be wise to retrieve what is best from the past and to build upon this heritage. An earlier generation of Canada's youth put its energies into programs such as the Company of Young Canadians. This was not the only innovation to come out of our nation's capital. Opportunities for Youth was designed "to combine the resources of government with the resources of youth."[14] And there were other noteworthy examples. Katimavik and Canada World Youth were two parallel programs that were proposed by non governmental organizations and funded by government. Each provided early examples of a successful partnership between the voluntary sector and the public sector.

The present generation needs a broadly-based governmental initiative which will demonstrate how communications technology can serve a social purpose. What is the role of the state in this? A state presence was needed to counter market forces for radio and television. Now it must be there to perform the same function for the next great communications revolution. *This means a CBC for the Internet.* State-sponsored inducements can create exciting sites which celebrate Canada's past, and its future, as a society that is open to the world. Why not allow Canadians to tell their stories through the latest communications technology? The federal department of

Heritage Canada should place a priority on software development and access to information in the way that Industry Canada does for business.

There are reasons why we should do this. We can start with the size of the country. The physical geography of Canada has always been a shaping influence on our lives. We have a huge landmass with a relatively small number of people. The communication of shared experiences has been the central point of our nationhood. Alexander Graham Bell was at the forefront of technological change. Harold Innis and George Grant brought their own visions, and their own academically-trained imaginations, to a conceptual understanding of the role of the nation-state in these changes. Marshall McLuhan's eclectically-delivered insights dealt with the intrinsic nature of the new forms of communications. The phantasmagoric rambles of the Canadian media guru were said to be part of the spirit of the emerging age of television. They were grounded on the notion that a medium of communications like radio—or television —was an extension of our physical senses. His most lasting contribution, however, was something far greater: he offered a fresh perspective on a world in which the representation of human experience was essentially mediated by electronic pulses. His fluid insights burst the boundaries of existing categories of analysis.

From an Informational Defecit to a Democratic Defecit

A McLuhan is now needed for the Age of the Internet. The next generation of theorists are exploring new platforms and formats for empirically-grounded research. One pattern that can be discerned at present: Internet communications are at the core of human rights movements. A diverse range of advocacy networks and new social movements use this mechanism. The Internet is not a driving force behind these groups but it does help them to organize and to mobilize.[15] The data that is available suggests that cyber culture does encourage a suspicion of big government (a natural sentiment since much of the Internet mania was centred in Silicon Valley) but that it is sympathetic to alternative social groupings (again, natural, since the same area was associated with these lifestyle movements in the 1960's, Gay rights groups, pro-choice advocates and environmental and feminist movements have a following in cyber culture. European data confirms this general trend.[16] The Internet had a dramatic impact on the business world. It reduced the transaction costs of companies. Innovative e-strategies were developed by groups like Amazon.com (Amazon.ca when it travels north) and eBay to create flexible market niches. In the same way, as Pippa Norris has pointed out, "digital politics has shifted the balance of resources away from large-scale professional bureaucracies...and toward technical knowledge and skills" in the partisan political world.[17] In retrospect, most of the tendencies associated with the New Economy were as much about style as content. Open decision-making, flatter hierarchies, flexible work hours and alternative dress codes—all were associated with the era of cyber enthusiasm.

In Canada, this style clashed head-on with the management ethos of the Chrétien government. His is a decidedly paternalistic government. Its managerial approach is also decidedly old-style.[18] Ministers are given a certain amount of leeway within their own sphere but they are always held to account by head office. Under these circumstances, it is no accident that the Office of the Prime Minister has gained a higher profile, as has its sister agency the Privy Council Office.[19] Regional desks, modelled on the 1968 to 1972 period of the Trudeau government, gained a higher profile. This is said to be a top-down government where backbenchers, in the dismissive Trudeau phrase, continue to be "nobodies". When Chrétien puts his public face to this, it is also said to be a "friendly dictatorship."[20] (This is a phrase which has resonance. It recalls Lord Hailsham's description of prime ministerial government in Britain as an "elective dictatorship.") A number of people who felt passed over by the Prime Minister were able to turn the tables on their master in the summer of 2002 but this is—and was—another story. At that time, another term was also imported from across the Atlantic—"democratic deficit." It was originally applied to the European Union to mean that too much time was given over to the process of governance, too little to actual accomplishments. The priorities and concerns of a cumbersome federal structure in Europe did not match the concerns of a majority of the population. These concerns find an echo in this country.[21]

The pent-up demand unleashed by such forces is likely to result in limited structural change. More free votes in Parliament is one likely result, the election of parliamentary committee chairs by the committee itself rather than by the Prime Minister is another. These can only be regarded as stop-gap measures, however. More fundamental change is necessary, starting with reform of our upper house and reform of the electoral system. The party system must evolve to accommodate these reforms. Relations between parties in different countries have to be fostered. State funding should be made available for this. One model is Germany's Konrad Adenauer *Stiftung* — a politically oriented Institute loosely associated with the Christian Democratic party. It has a comparatively huge on-the-ground organization which facilitates exchanges between countries. The aim is to maintain an ongoing policy debate. German taxpayers fund parallel Institutes with links to the Green party, the Liberals and the Social Democrats. Benefits include a clearer appreciation of the political problems faced by neighbouring countries and countries with parallel political ideologies, a policy exchange that enhances the intellectual capital of parties between elections, and a more progressive and international outlook.[22] Each of these considerations are hugely significant in themselves. In the Canadian instance, they point to the fact that Canadian parties should work to place an institutional foundation upon their links with their counterparts south of the border. A key area is private sector involvement. Partnerships with the private sector are to be encouraged but they have to be placed on a permanent foundation. Partnerships with the not-for-profit sector are also essential.

The Liberal Party of Canada should have an ongoing relationship with progressive political forces in all parts of the Americas—and all parts of the world. The closest relationship has to be with the Democratic Party in the United States. Political parties in the United States are moving away from old-style "wedge" issues that play off one ethic group against another.[23] Parties in Canada have to move in the same direction, being careful not to play off one region against another. But the ties between political parties should not be confined to one level of government. The Ottawa-Washington corridor has to be broadened. Important developments are taking place at the state level, and in urban politics. A broad constellation should be actively encouraged and allowed to take shape. It should be one that makes open and accountable government at the municipal, state and national level its first priority. Canada should take the lead in pressing for campaign finance reform and "clean" money within its own jurisdiction. Only then can it have the moral authority to lead by its own example. It is an undisputable fact that big money is grotesquely distorting politics. The question is: how do you deal with it? Practical measures are urgently needed.

This is not the only reform that needs to be pursued. The Liberal Party of Canada needs to restore its role as the voice of the community. This means bringing an activist agenda to another level of governance: municipal politics. Political parties have an important role to play here. They bring an organization and they bring ideas to bear on problems at the local level. A Liberal slate of candidates for urban office (and for rural office) would allow municipal governments to have a sustained presence in the affairs of the nation. It would also underline the growing political sophistication of these structures.

In order to understand how this fits together it is necessary to go back to what has been called "the big picture."

The Ideapolis

Canadian politics have, by history and by tradition, turned on three fundamental axes. They involved relations between the centre and the periphery, relations between francophones and the rest of the country, and Canada-US relations.[24] There were a number of assumptions to this. Assumed, for example, was the fact that the system could only focus on one relationship at one time. Also assumed was the view that other relationships would be subsumed to the dominant axis. Thus it is now with the Canada's position in North America. Canada-US relations have, by tradition, been compartmentalized as a component of foreign policy. This meant that it was dealt with in a vertical fashion rather than in a horizontal manner. A comprehensive examination is required. Political parties, it should be emphasized, have to be the key agents of change in this process. Links have to be (re)established.

The base of Liberal support in national elections tends to be in "smart city" areas. The results of the 2000 general election confirmed this. The Democrats in the United States have a base of support in what have been called "ideopolis counties." By definition, "ideopolis counties" are those parts of metro areas which have high tech economic activity and a front rank research university. Most of the people in these areas voted for Republican presidential candidates in 1980 and 1984. But in the 2000 election, Gore garnered 54 % of the vote while Bush came in at 41%. A compelling case has been made for an increasing association between the Democrats and the "ideopolis." It is argued that this connection will give progressive forces an electoral hold on the future. The demographics are moving in this direction. Women with college degrees voted 57% for Gore. For women with advanced degrees the number was 63%. Added to that is the fact that the "ideopolis" is home to the fastest-growing segment of the American population, the Latinos. The "ideopolis" is the locale that knowledge workers call home. Credentialed, professional and network-friendly, these knowledge workers have added value not just to their workplace, but to the political party that places emphasis on the lifestyle issues that matter to them. Thus they tend to favor libertarian social policies but they also believe that capitalism can, and should, be regulated. (This last point marks a change from the Reagan era.) The fastest-growing areas of support for the Democrats are in "ideopolis" counties, around San Francisco Bay or metro Chicago. These are areas that tend to have spin-offs from university research facilities. They provide "soft technology" services—dealing with the media, public relations, legal representation, fashion, design and advertising. They work at the intersection of technology and creativity—but most of their efforts are directed toward the marketing of concepts and ideas.[25]

The Liberal Party of Canada has to harness these forces in this country and they have to adapt to them in a creative way. The party has to restore its intellectual capital. This means that it must be open to new ways of looking at the world. This also means that communication has to be more than a one-way affair. To date, political parties have taken a passive approach to the Internet. It has been used by the Prime Minister's Office in a mechanical manner. Much of the information which is sent out is also available in a more traditional form, in hard copy or via fax. This is not the way it should be. At a conference on reviving democracy on April 10 2002, the Honourable Robin Cook maintained that:

> There is a connection waiting to be made between
> the decline in democratic participation and the

explosion in new ways of communicating.We
need not accept the paradox that gives us more
ways than ever to speak, and leaves the public
with a wider feeling than ever before that their
voices are not being heard. The new technologies can strengthen our democracy, by giving us
greater opportunities than ever before for better
transparency and a more responsive relationship
between the government and the electors.[26]

The Internet's potential lies in creating new avenues for dialogue.
It would be a policy failure not to develop an Internet "commons"
that carries a distinct Canadian "brand." Still more it is a policy
failure not to take on big corporations when they use a monopoly
position in a manner that stifles innovation. The reform of parties
must be tied to the reform of political institutions. But the overall
design of the project has to restore the unimpeachable link between morality and politics.[27]

Conclusion

In the last year, the Liberal Party of Canada has been torn apart
by internal divisions over leadership. These divisions reflected a
deeper divide. It was often described as a chasm that existed between right and left with "business" Liberals adhering to the former
designation, and "social" Liberals being attached to the latter category. As a party of the centre, the Liberals were able to move from
one camp to another as circumstances allowed. Pragmatism took
precedence over ideology.[28] "Innovation" was the buzz-word of the
first camp, of the group that placed an emphasis on raising Canada's
standard of living through the raising of levels of productivity. "Social justice" was the concern of a second group which placed, in
another phrase, "people before profits." Matters of ethics were relegated to the second category, as were efforts to create a sustainable
environment for Canadians. The right to safe water and to clean
air was to be included as a basic human right. A simple point
emerges from this: *morality cannot be placed in a category*. We need a
principled reminder that markets require morality. The Liberal Party
of Canada needs to strike a new balance between "enterprise" and
"social cohesion."

The fate of Tony Blair's version of a Third Way is instructive in this regard.[29] Promising to move beyond the Old Left nostrums of "state control, high taxes and producer interests," the British Prime Minister announced that he could join entrepreneurial zeal and social objectives. New technology, he added, "represents an opportunity, not a threat."[30] This fascination with technological advance placed Blair on the wrong side of public opinion in the debate over genetically-modified foods. The strength of the opposition surprised the British leader, obliging him, eventually, to genetically-modify his own position on the issue. By endorsing technological change in a wholesale manner, the Third Way demonstrated its indifference to ecological damage. Big business was driving these developments. Many ecological authorities pressured the government to adopt a more precautionary outlook toward change, saying that we should rein in scientific advances until we are more certain as to their social and environmental impact.[31] There is a lesson to be taken from the British experience. We cannot make the mistake of equating technological advance with social advance. But as Vaclav Havel said on another occasion, there is "no way back." "Only a dreamer," he continued,

> can believe that the solution lies in curtailing the progress of civilization in some way or another. The main task of the coming era is something else: a radical renewal of our sense of responsibility. Our conscience must catch up with our reason —otherwise we are lost.[32]

Political parties are the only instrument which can bring together conscience and reason in a sustainable manner. That is the message which has to be brought to the Liberal Party of Canada. And that is the message, in turn, that the party has to take to the nation.

Notes:

[1]   Francis Fukuyama was confounded by the argument that "there could be no end of history unless there was an end of science." Hence his interest in the ethical and socio/politico dilemmas posed by bio-engineering. He believed that "the most significant threat posed by biotechnology is the possibility that it will alter human nature and thereby move us into a 'posthuman' stage of

history." He further argues that human nature exists as a meaningful concept and that this concept has given stability to us as a species. Conjointly with religion, it has defined our most basic values. Human nature shapes our politics and our political structures. It follows from this that "a technology powerful enough to reshape what we are will have consequences for liberal democracy and the nature of politics itself." Quoted in Francis Fukuyama, *Our Posthuman Future, Consequences of the Biotechnology Revolution* (New York: Farrar, Straus and Giroux, 2002), xii, 7.

[2] Lawrence Lessig, "The Internet Under Siege," *Foreign Policy* (November/December, 2001), 56.

[3] *Ibid*, 62.

[4] Lawrence Lessig, *The Future of Ideas, The Fate of the Commons in a Connected World* (New York: Random House, 2001), 199, 206.

[5] The words, again, belong to Lessig. He concludes that we have moved to the architecture of control "without noticing, without resistance, without so much as a question." He concludes that those who are "threatened by this technology of freedom have learned to turn the technology off. The switch has been thrown. We are doing nothing about it." *Ibid*, 268.

[6] Quoted in Paul Nesbitt-Larking, *Politics, Society and the Media: Canadian Perspectives* (Peterborough: Broadview, 2001), 60-61. The author draws upon an original source by Graham Spry, *Queen's Quarterly*, 1931.

[7] Pippa Norris, *Digital Divide, Civic Education, Information Poverty, And The Internet Worldwide* (Cambridge: Cambridge University Press, 2001), 7.

[8] *Ibid*.

[9] See the arguments put forward by Mark Leonard, "Diplomacy by Other Means," *Foreign Policy* 132 (September/October, 2002), particularly 52-53.

[10] For an extended argument about the merits of this approach see Peter Petersen, "Public Diplomacy and the War on Terrorism," *Foreign Affairs* 81: 5 (September/October, 2002), 74-93.

[11] The classic analysis is Harold Innis, "The Bias of Communications," in Innis, *The Bias of Communications* (Toronto: University of Toronto Press, 1951 (1975 ed), 33-60.

[12] Joan Raymond, "Gray Market For Gadgets—Technologies to Help the Elderly Live on their Own," Next Frontiers, *Newsweek*, 23 September, 2002, 52.

[13] Arthur M. Schlesinger, Jr., *The Cycles of American History* (Boston: Houghton, Mifflin, 1986), 47.

[14] Quoted by Jacques Herbert, "Legislating for Freedom," in Thomas Axworthy and Pierre Trudeau, eds., *Towards A Just Society, The Trudeau Years* (Markham: Viking, 1990), 140, ff.5. Herbert draws upon the House of Commons, *Debates*, 16 March, 1971.

[15] Norris, *Digital Divide*, 9, 19. Norris makes the point that some analysts see the Internet as an intervening rather than a driving variable for transnational advocacy networks. She cites Margaret Keck and Kathryn Kikkink, *Activists Beyond Borders – Advocacy Networks in International Politics* (Ithaca: Cornell University Press, 1998) as a representative example of this view.

[16] *Ibid*, 215.

[17] *Ibid*, 239.

[18] Managerialism comes at a cost. Two decades ago, Robert Reich delivered an indictment of what he called the managerial era. This era, he wrote, put an undue emphasis on "efficiency." "Managerial government was adept at finding efficient solutions, but not at engaging the political process by which they were made." Too much reliance was placed on the courts, meant that America's

political system "was incapable of ranking demands or choosing among them because it had no legitimate mechanism for deciding how the burdens and benefits of public decisions were to be allocated." Robert Reich, *The Next American Frontier* (New York: Times, 1983), 268-269.

19   For an extended analysis see Wayne Hunt, "The Prime Minister Today," Paul Fox and Graham White, eds., *Politics: Canada*, Eight Ed., (Toronto: McGraw-Hill Ryerson, 1995), 258-269.

20   Jeffrey Simpson, *The Friendly Dictatorship* (Toronto: McClelland and Stewart, 2001). Simpson writes that his purpose is to make sense "of what is happen ing in three areas vital to Canadian democracy: the parliamentary system, the political parties, and the electorate." What has occurred in each of these spheres "has directly influenced developments in the others, and the combined effect has left Canadian democracy in a weakened state." See *The Friendly Dictatorship*, xiii.

21   A pollster who works for the Liberal party has warned that the Liberal "soap opera" is eroding support. "Canadians," Michael Marzolini finds, "have suffered too much process, and not enough policy". Quoted in Jane Taber, "Liberal 'soap opera' eroding support," *Globe and Mail*, 20 September, 2002, A4.

22   See Leonard, "Diplomacy by Other Means," 55.

23   Refer, for example, to the findings of William A. Galston and Elaine C. Kamarck, "Five Realities in US Politics," in Anthony Giddens, ed., *The Global Third Way Debate* (Cambridge: Polity, 2001), 107-109.

24   The classic account of this comes from D.V. Smiley, *Canada in Question, Federalism in the Eighties*, Third ed., (Toronto: McGraw-Hill Ryerson, 1980), 252-281.

25   See John Judis and Ruy Teixeira, "Majority Rules," *The New Republic*, 5 and 12 August, 2002, 18-23. It is excerpted from their book, *The Emerging Democratic Majority*, 2002.

26   Quoted in Grant Kippen and Gordon Jenkins, " The Challenge of E-Democracy for Political Parties," Sponsored by the Community Connections Project of the Institute for the Study of Information Technology and Society, H.J. Heinz III School of Public Policy and Management, Carnegie Mellon University, 2002. Mimeo.

27   It is worth recalling the original words of the 1993 "Red Book":
The most important asset of government is the confidence it enjoys of the people to whom it is accountable. If government is to play a positive role in society, as it must, honesty and integrity in our political institutions must be restored.
Creating Opportunity, The Liberal Plan for Canada (Ottawa: The Liberal Party of Canada, 1993), 90.

28   A standard account of this movement is contained in W. Christian and C. Campbell, *Parties, Leaders and Ideologies in Canada* (Toronto: McGraw-Hill Ryerson, 1996), 66-111.

29   For an extended critique see Wayne Hunt, "The Importance of Being Tony", *Queen's Quarterly* 109: 2 (Summer 2002), 264-271.

30   Tony Blair, *The Third Way, New Politics for a New Century*, Fabian Pamphlet 588 (London: The Fabian Society, 1998), 1-4.

31   See Anthony Giddens, *The Third Way and Its Critics* (Cambridge: Polity, 2000),

32   Vaclav Havel, "Harvard University," *The Art of the Impossible, Politics as Morality in Practice, Speeches and Writing, 1990-1996*, transl. Paul Wilson (New York: Knopf, 1997), 221-222.

Canada Unbound:
Redefining Citizenship for a Borderless World

Alison Loat
Gord Moodie
Robyn Tingley
Naheed Nenshi
John McArthur

GLOBALIZATION.
CONTINENTAL INTEGRATION.
A BORDERLESS WORLD.

Young Canadians have grown up with these concepts. We entered the adulthood alongside glum predictions that our dollar, our economic sovereignty and in the wake of the 1995 referendum, even our country, may not be around by the time we retire. But we don't buy it.

Despite our traditional Canadian reticence to blow our own horns, we believe Canada has a lot to offer the world. When we think about our Canada and the world, it is not enough that our Minister of Foreign Affairs champions treaties on our behalf, that we send delegations to international summits, or that we supply military support in places of conflict. Although these are excellent, necessary and laudable goals, we can do more.

As a nation, we need to support our citizens, particularly our young people, in bringing the best of Canada to the world, and in investing in the networks that will link these experiences and people with Canada to bring the best of the world back home. We have the talent. We have the solutions. We need to reclaim our place.

This paper outlines the forces that have shaped the thinking of young Canadians (roughly 25 to 35 years old), and presents our plan on how we can better help Canadians to help the world. Our goal is the largest imaginable: Canada and Canadians solving the most difficult problems of the world. We must be bold enough to take up the challenge.

Defining a Generation: A Brief History

We are a group of individuals born during the 1970's all over this country. We share no common past other than belonging to the same time in our nation's history and have come together to share ideas about a subject that matters deeply to us: Canada.

We represent just a small few of the hundreds of young Canadians we've shared ideas with over the past two years through our work with Canada25.[1] Through the course of this work, we have learned much about the influences that have shaped the perspectives and concerns of young Canadians. More important, we have learned that young Canadians, far from being insecure about the role of Canada in the world, are proud of their national heritage, continually look abroad for opportunities, and are willing to champion and embrace their identity on a global stage. The challenge for us all is to make sure they have the venues and opportunities to do so, and the motivation and means to use experience gained abroad to contribute back home. Young Canadians want Canada to be more than a place, and citizenship to mean more than a passport. By embracing internationalism and responding to these desires, we can ensure Canada achieves its potential at home and in the world. The challenge for us all is to make sure they have the venues and opportunities to do so, and in doing so, support Canada in achieving its potential at home and in the world.

As a small country next to the world's only superpower, Canada may always struggle to find its place. Recent history, which has defined the experience for many young Canadians, has been no exception. Domestically, the past 15 years have been punctuated for many by a general feeling of worry and uncertainty about the future of the country as a coherent, vigorous whole. National unity and constitutional concerns dominated for a time, followed by federal and provincial budgetary cutbacks. And while the Canada-US Free

Trade Agreement and NAFTA ushered in waves of continental integration, our national conversations appeared increasingly regionalized, polarized between the West, Ontario, Quebec and Atlantic Canada.

Internationally, instability and turmoil also dominated with famines, floods and internecine conflicts. Although we were raised with the legacy of Canada's peacekeeping efforts, and took pride in the accolades of a the United Nations human index survey Human Development Report, we have seen far too many other instances where Canada had an opportunity to lead internationally but appeared unwilling to chart a unique course.

At times, this failure to lead has put younger Canadians directly at odds with the actions of our politicians. Consider the environment as one example. We were the first generation to be raised Green. We reduce, reuse, recycle, and try to live our lives in a way that is environmentally friendly. Despite this, we have seen little political leadership on the environment, either in Canada or abroad, despite increasingly clear signs that things will start going downhill quickly. This inaction only produces further alienation and cynicism among young people about government—and promotes cynicism about the public sector as a place to make change. This is —exactly the opposite of how we believe our feelings ought to be moving.

This phenomenon is not limited just to the environment. The technology frenzy of the later 1990's that shifted us from dark pessimism to dizzying optimism had an unexpected impact. Although it pulled us out of a period of recession and government cutbacks, it also made the private sector, at home and around the world, the most attractive career option for young Canadians looking to leave a mark. This feeling was even more pronounced as it coincided with a period when government was firing, not hiring. During these times, public service the sector that has defined what it is to be Canadian didn't lacked the cachet it may have held for our parents and for other generations that came before them.

Despite this continued struggle for place, Canada have a more international population than ever, and this stretches further than simply immigration. Canadian cultural exports, from Margaret Atwood to Celine Dion to Margaret Atwood to Atom Egoyan, are commanding international attention, and our academics are in leadership positions at some of the world's top universities and research facilities. Economics and culture are more fluid than they used to be, and young people appear comfortable with that fluidity. The Internet and its incredible democratizing effect on information has given young Canadians a sense that the world is at their doorstep, either through direct travel or via electronic passageways. The notion of moving thousands of miles nationally or internationally for a job opportunity is not a foreign concept, and, in fact, is often sought as an end to itself.

Despite this increased mobility, we still see a love of, and a passion for Canada, but less of a feeling that one must always live here to serve it. In some quarters, there may actually be a sense that one must leave, at least for a time, to really serve Canada well, and to properly bring new world experiences home. Terms like "brain drain" and "brain gain" don't adequately describe this evolution, and miss out on the opportunities of international mobility. "Brain circulation" better underlies our wish to integrate varied lifestyles and familiarities into Canada's daily social and economic experience, and to take these experiences and apply them to the most rigorous domestic and international challenges.

Revisioning Canada in a Borderless World

The energy of young Canadians and their desire to contribute meaningfully to the public good has been one of the most uplifting discoveries in building Canada25. We yearn for a Canada that truly "punches above its weight" in global economic and political affairs. That is the legacy of our history, yet we find our traditional relevance even in North America is diminishing. For a generation blessed with skills and mobility in a country rich in peace and prosperity, we see national complacency and deeply unexploited opportunity.

Before proceeding, it is worth asking why this matters. Why does this matter? Why talk about Canada's role in the world when pressing domestic issues demand attention?

First, since we carry neither colonial baggage nor the dominant superpower influence of the United States, we have tremendous potential to bring together unusual bedfellows and get things done. Canada has a history of playing honest broker between America and

Europe, and our success at building a multicultural, pluralist society ("an amazing global human asset" according to the Aga Khan) affords us a particular strength to influence global counterparts and mediate and lead in international affairs.

Second, the simple fact is that our global role matters to Canadians. Many Canadian corporations engage in significant business overseas, and individual Canadians work and invest all over the globe. And international activity is by no means confined to business. Canadians care about helping the poorest of the poor, about finding solutions to global health care crises, about peace.[2] Although our federal government makes significant contributions in this realm, numerous others are engaged in similar issues through university research, non-governmental organizations and independent advocacy. We need to encourage these concerns, and make sure Canadians have the opportunity to be involved in them.

Finally, and most fundamentally, an internationally engaged population is a matter of enlightened self-interest. The quantity amount of learning occurring around the globe as on the same sorts of problems that are tackled at home offers an unparalleled opportunity to share knowledge and apply new insights to accelerate social progress. Major contemporary issues—poverty, the environment, health, illiteracy—can unfortunately be seen in any country in which one chooses to look for them, and increased global interdependence only serves to reinforce this point further. How much more vigorously could we solve domestic challenges with a real sense of how others abroad have approached similar the same issues? How much more strongly can could our we contribute internationally contribution be with success to speak of at home? To tackle such problems in the isolation of national confines just doesn't make any sense, and limits our ability to create and apply the best solutions.

Reasserting our Role

In reasserting our world role, we must not be blind to the forces that led to its decline. Historical notions of "Canada as Peace-keeper", or "Canada as Health Care Leader" offer a base to work from, but carving out a role in the next century will involve much more than government choosing a cause or program on which to focus. The government is one actor among many, uniquely positioned to invest in and catalyze the growth of the others.[3]

In his 2002 Speech from the Throne, Prime Minister Jean Chrétien promised a discussion with Canadians on their country's role in the world. While defence policy, military spending and border security are all important components to a successful assertion of Canada on the international stage, a true conception of Canada and the world involves a broad space for action and activity outside of government, and government policy that builds on our international population to ensure we exercise it to its full potential.

To do this, we need to not only to enhance *Canada's* role in the world, but also to enhance *Canadians'* role in the world. The way that government works with individuals and groups—both within and outside our borders—is as important as the government's own behaviour in actively participating in global affairs. Globalization has closed the door to trying to assert a global role top-down through government decree; but it has opened the door to allowing an authentically Canadian presence to emerge by empowering citizens to achieve their goals on a world scale, and incorporating the experiences of Canadians living around the world in our domestic and international affairs.

If we do so, we have an opportunity to reassert our role in the world as an internationally recognized platform for tackling major problems and getting things done. Rather than conceptualizing ourselves in the world solely by our military or foreign aid expenditure, we can do so in a way that takes the strengths and experience of our citizens to enhance our position and influence abroad, and at the same time, builds on our domestic potential and capability.

Wither the "Brain Drain": Citizenship without Walls

The term "knowledge economy" is thrown about with such frequency and panache that we risk it losing value in its ability to describe Canadian society. We can almost accept it as so. Yet regardless of titles, our successes increasingly depend on our ability to create and implement ideas. Knowledge, however, can be gained and ideas can be developed in many places, however, and the size of Canada our country necessarily precludes the best of every field from existing in Canada. If we truly want to create a country nation that is recognized as the best place to effectively tackle major contemporary domestic and global challenges, we need to build a thirst for this knowledge, an ability to seek it out on a global level, and the desire and mechanisms to bring it back home.

For this, we propose a three-part prescription. First, we need to build a culture in which the development of great ideas is second only to our ability to implement them. Second, we require real opportunities to expose our young people to the realities of other countries and cultures, and where possible, to offer those opportunities under the auspices of the Canadian flag. And finally, we need to find real ways to motivate those Canadians living abroad to bring their experiences to bear on issues of national concern, and play a supporting role to Canada in their countries of residence. While there are undoubtedly thousands of small initiatives that can help to build our platform, these three meaningful steps would certainly propel us in the right direction.

1. Inspiring Citizens to Think Big By Celebrating Innovation

The first step is to support a culture that *recognizes and celebrates ideas and innovation in all its forms.* To reach our potential both domestically and internationally, we need to test our ingenuity across all sectors of society: social innovation to build a fair and equitable society; economic innovation to foster investment; policy innovation to solve the challenges of our demographic profile; and cultural innovation to strengthen our national pride. To do so requires a culture where all Canadians feel empowered to constantly find new methods of addressing and improving upon the challenges they face in their particular sphere of life, whether that be scientific research, business, politics, community affairs or any other realm. In short, Canada must strive to be a community of creative thinkers, one where we develop a culture where our ability to generate ideas is second only to our ability to implement them, and one where we have a commitment to developing minds, not just skills.

Canada has a strong history of innovation in its public policy, its academic research and its private enterprise. In an economy where success depends so strongly on generating ideas, the culture that enabled invention in the past is even more important to nurture today. Part of this involves making investments in universities, and in our researchers, so they continue to create internationally competitive and accessible educational opportunities for Canadians. This requires tactical investments, such as infrastructure funds, scholarship and granting programs,[4] and incentives to increase individual philanthropy to our institutions, as well as strong public leadership that conceptualizes health care and education as crucial investments in our economy and our society, and not as competing cost centres.

This could also involve exploiting opportunities for interdisciplinary education and learning by creating and entrenching links to ensure mobility and idea-sharing among our universities, public and private sectors to help create and nurture new ideas, and help break down existing silos. Private sector companies, for example, could provide incentives for their employees to take positions in related government departments. Universities could more actively appoint nonacademics to teaching or research positions for short or longer-term contracts. Additionally, a "Prime Minister's Fellows' Program" could be instituted to recognized 30 of Canada's top innovators, providing them with opportunities to act as "innovation advisors" to the government for one year, and by doing so, providing a channel of new ideas into the highest level of public service. Such a program would, at low cost, invigorate the concept of working on issues in the public interest among those for whom a career in the civil service is not a current option. Finally, universities could more actively appoint nonacademics to teaching or research positions for short or longer-term contracts. Such a broad commitment to innovation throughout all sectors of Canadian society is a necessary next step to our international leadership in the development of human capital,[5] and to the attainment of our vision.

2. Promoting Internationalism From an Early Age

The second big stage is to *make international experiences an integral and realizable component of every education.* Canada should make it easier for students to build an international understanding through exchanges and the development of internship programs.

A very simple way to start down this path would be to vastly expand and promote international programs for young Canadians. Government can work toward this end by better facilitating affordable exchanges for students, particularly as international experience becomes recognized as important to success in the workplace and in life. Universities have already made great strides in offering exchange opportunities to students, and organizations such as the World University Service of Canada and the AFS International Canada have been facilitating hundreds of thousands of international exchanges for more than the past 50 years. In today's environment, however, international experience needs to be made a realistic option for all students, not just those with the resources to afford it. As a commitment to developing global leaders, the federal government could establish a fund to provide small grants of several thousand dollars to help offset the costs of studying abroad for those in financial need. To further endorse international awareness, government could also increase the amount available through student loan programs for young Canadians interested in pursuing international affairs or exchange.

Canada could also build international understanding by creating a national internship program that deploys our young people on international projects on a much larger and more accessible scale than exists today.[6] Given the significant evolution of foreign affairs from state-managed relations to one of increasing personal engagement, it's no longer enough to have our political delegations meet with the heads of state of countries in need of relief and support. If such a program were to be established, government could significantly enhance its contribution by mobilizing several thousand interested students, for example, and sponsoring them to travel abroad to provide aid and to share their skills for a period of several months.

Promoting a society of internationalist Canadians has two main benefits. The first is that Canadians, with all their strengths, have a great deal to contribute to the world and its most pressing problems. These are problems that will only be solved through knowledge based on direct experience in and deep understanding of other parts of the world. For example, the Millennium Declaration,[7] adopted in September 2000 at the United Nations Millennium Summit, offer a rare framework in which Canada, as one of the world's most privileged countries, can play a leading role in prompting its citizens to take some responsibility for solving the problems of the world's most disadvantaged people. Central to such an era will be the engagement of young people in global development challenges, both as advocates of change and as problem-solvers in their own right. Canada needs to stimulate its own citizens to think of themselves as resources who can contribute to the achievement of the goals outlined in this declaration.

The second benefit is of more direct benefit to Canada itself. As international experience becomes more popular among young Canadians, and as an increasingly important quality among employers, it must become seen as an investment, something that is not only available and encouraged, but also something that is affordable and accessible for any Canadian who cares to pursue it.

3. *Motivating Expatriates to Contribute Back and Strengthen our National Fabric*

The third step is to *view our expatriates as an asset.* It is nothing short of incredible that Canadians have risen to be leaders in so many fields—from business, to medicine, to journalism, to academia—and in so many institutions around the world. Our need to tap into their experiences only becomes more significant in a world where the cost and ease of global travel and communications are increasing, and in a world where Canadians continue to seek international opportunity. We must redouble our efforts to build a network of Canadians abroad, and leverage this asset to enhance our world role, and to bringing their experiences to bear on our domestic challenges.

A practical example of how one country made this work comes from India, where expatriates have made invaluable economic, business and academic investments, advised on tough domestic policy challenges, and created opportunities for future generations of Indians. Indian citizens living in the United States are responsible for many of the investments behind the high-tech firms based in Bangalore and Hyderabad, and have also shared their international knowledge to advise their home government on a number of important issues, from developing venture capital laws to deregulating the country's telecommunications sectors. Furthermore, they have made generous donations to India's elite universities and have provided internship and exchange opportunities for Indian students looking to expand their perspectives and knowledge.

China and Taiwan, while certainly not perfectly analogous to the

Canadian experience, are further examples. In China well over half of foreign direct investment in that country was made by Chinese expatriates in 1999, with Taiwanese returnees responsible for the development of tech companies that accounted for over 10% of Taiwan's GNP at the turn of the 21st century.[8] If these links can be forged in a developing economy setting, they can definitely be forged for Canada.

Specifically, Canada we could make similar efforts across a number of forums. Our embassies could make it a priority to provide outreach to Canadians living in countries where they are located, rather than focusing extensively on foreign companies or individuals wishing to relocate to or visit Canada. Government and business leaders should give serious consideration to building a Congress of Canadian World Leaders composed of expatriates in top positions abroad. This board could serve as a senior advisory body to Canadian governments and businesses to aid international outreach, provide direct input into policy, trade or investment strategies, and be the bridge between Canadians at home and abroad. Similarly, networks of expatriates could be developed around particular fields or industries, providing a ready base of international knowledge and contacts. Finally, universities should track graduate students who decide to study at international schools, and work with them to facilitate continuing study, collaborative research projects and exchange opportunities in the future. Extending the notion of citizenship in such ways would strengthen our presence, and provide space and opportunity for broader participation in the development of Canada in the world.

Conclusion

These are only a few small steps for what is fundamentally a broad and bold vision for the future of Canada in the world; but they are small enough that we can start taking them now. In our increasingly competitive and changing world, time is not a luxury afforded to many, least of all to a country trying to reclaim its place as a global leader of peace, plurality and prosperity. When we look back over the past recent years, we can see clearly that the time for action is upon us. Indeed, it is urgently beckoning. Amid our achievements, we have seen our influence diminish in North America, our

UN ranking as the best place to live slip, an inward focus on political leadership affect our already-weak dollar, a wait-and-see attitude toward environmental accords, and our role as international mediator challenged by Norway.

It is time to claim a new place for Canada. An international policy that involves all Canadians, living at home and abroad, speaks to our assets and aspirations. Although Canada's history in peacekeeping is inspiring, it doesn't suggest much of a role for civilians, and doesn't speak to the experience of many of our most successful citizens. Additionally, an international policy that identifies a clear link to a strengthened domestic space reminds us all of the importance and opportunity of international investment. Throughout all this, we should look to government as an eager partner for the energetic Canadians, for groups of Canadians, and for institutions seeking to make a difference; a partner that can set an example itself at the same time as bringing the ambitious dreams of others within reach, even when it may not play the central role. A partnership between Canada and its citizens—among the state, groups, and individuals of this nation—is the only way to apply our full complement of resources to positively impact world change.

Every time a Canadian does something positive in the world, it is a victory for our society. Our challenge is to help more Canadians do more good things and help them remain integrated with Canada while doing so. Canada must become more than a cocoon to be sloughed away before real achievement begins. By promoting innovation, embracing internationalism, and viewing expatriates as an asset, Canada can take the first steps to becoming a country that people thank first for helping them to achieve their dreams, and that draws strength from Canadians everywhere in reasserting a distinctive global role.

Notes:

[1] The authors of this paper came together as part of an experiment called Canada25, one predicated on the assumption that young Canadians wanted to become involved in public policy debates, but through an alternative vehicle to youth wings of political parties or student government. Two years later, this has undoubtedly proved true. The organization (www.canada25.com) has brought together hundreds of Canadians between the ages of 20 and 35 and living around the world, and has learned that young Canadians have a deep desire to think critically about, and

engage in solving, important challenges for the future outside of their professional commitments. While this document represents the views of the authors only, not not of Canada25, we would like to thank all members of the organization for their indirect help in making it possible.

[2] For instance, over 95% of Canadians responding to a survey urged the country to continue its activism after it spearheaded the formation of a treaty outlawing anti-personnel land mines.

[3] As but one example of this shift, the recent United Nations World Summit on Sustainable Development in Johannesburg focussed attention not only on agreements between governments, but on forging 230 new "Type 2" partnerships between governments, corporations, and non-governmental groups. These partnerships offer a combination of resources, expertise, and accountability that would be difficult to duplicate in agreements between governments alone.

[4] There is no shortage of options. Options could include increased funds to existing programs, grants for international exchange, or "Graduate Student Hiring Grants" that provide funds for young, up-and-coming professors to award fellowships to leading graduate students who may otherwise be unwilling to take a risk with a young professor, enabling our new academics to accelerate their careers, and in turn, the research opportunities they can offer.

[5] Organization for Economic Co-operation and Development, "Canada's Growth Scorecard." A presentation by Hon. Donald Johnston, Secretary General, OECD, October 8, 2002.

[6] The Government of Canada facilitates international internships and exchanges through several of its departments, either directly or through the funding of other agencies.

[7] This landmark document for international cooperation in turn led to the UN's Millennium Development Goals (MDGs), clear targets for reducing poverty, hunger, disease, illiteracy, environmental degradation, and discrimination against women by 2015. Under the leadership of the Secretary General, the UN system is now working with members of civil society, academia, and public and private sectors around the world to mobilize support for these goals and to develop practical policy measures to achieve them. These goals are listed at http://www.un.org/millenniumgoals/index.html

[8] Devan, Janamitra and Parth S. Tewari, "Brains Abroad." *McKinsey Quarterly*, 2001, Number 4, pp. 51-60.

[9] For example, of the six Canadians who have won the Nobel Prize in economics in recent years, only one lists his nationality as Canadian.

The Challenge of e-democracy for Political Parties

Grant Kippen
Gordon Jenkins

THERE IS A CONNECTION *waiting to be made between the decline in democratic participation and the explosion in new ways of communicating. We need not accept the paradox that gives us more ways than ever to speak, and leaves the public with a wider feeling than ever before that their voices are not being heard. The new technologies can strengthen our democracy, by giving us greater opportunities than ever before for better transparency and a more responsive relationship between government and electors.*

The Honourable Robin Cook
London Conference on Reviving Democracy,
April 10, 2002

1. Introduction

The connection referred to by Mr. Robin Cook is still waiting to be made. However, it is not just the relationship between government and citizens that appears to need strengthening. Recent elections in the United States, Canada and the United Kingdom also point to a weakening of the relationship, as demonstrated through declining voter participation rates, between political parties and voters. While there may well be an explosion in new ways to communicate, the question is whether anyone is really listening, much less participating.

Over the past several years considerable effort has been made by governments world-wide to transition their old command and control style operations to a new more citizen centric e-government approach. Influenced in part by globalization but mainly fuelled by the surge in e-commerce, these important changes are still in their infancy yet citizens are beginning to see meaningful improvements in the delivery of public sector services and in the information available to them from all levels of government. However, as consumers become more educated and demanding in this new globalized economic and social space, the desire grows for greater involvement and accountability between themselves, their governments and their elected representatives. More recently, there has been increasing study and discussion around the concept of e-democracy as one possible approach to gaining greater citizen engagement in the governing process.

As interesting and important as these developments are, political parties are also struggling with similar issues. Thomas Friedman in his book, *The Lexus and the Olive Tree*,[1] draws the conclusion that in order for globalization to succeed and prosper, the democratic systems and processes must be vibrant and strong. Government, business and political parties are cornerstones to a healthy democratic system. While businesses and governments are responding to the challenges and opportunities of globalization, political parties appear to be lagging in responding to the changes that are occurring. Over the past decade or so, signs have appeared that point to the erosion of political parties as dynamic and positive change agents. Some of these factors include:

- the rise in the number and the influence of single-issue interest groups. Have political parties ceased to maintain their position as "integrators" or "honest brokers" of the diverse economic and social interests of their members?
- the increasing percentage of voters who decline to participate in national, state/province and local elections. Regrettably, this phenomenon that now exists in most western democracies.

- less loyalty to traditional political parties. Voters are more "flexible" when casting their vote meaning parties cannot necessarily rely on traditional bases of support.
- lack of transparency relative to the improvements that have been made with information and communications technologies (ICTs) and what citizens expect. Parties have been characterized as closed organizations guided by back room advisors. Within business and government, current trends point to greater transparency, openness and accountability through appropriate governance structures. Can political parties respond to this change and still remain viable organizations?

With the advent of e-government as a means through which citizens have greater access to services and information, there has been considerable interest in and study of how e-democracy could transform the way we are governed. While e-democracy appears to offer the potential of enhancing or possibly redefining the relationships citizens have with various levels of governments, the same potential would also appear to exist for political parties.

But what does e-democracy really mean? Steven Clift, Publisher of Democracies Online Newswire defines e-democracy as:

> representing the use of information and communication technologies and strategies by democratic actors (governments, elected officials, the media, political organizations, citizen/voters) within political and governance processes of local communities, nations and on the international stage. To many, e-democracy suggests greater and more active citizen participation enabled by the Internet, mobile communications, and other technologies in today's representative democracy as well as through more participatory or direct forms of citizen involvement in addressing public challenges.

For the purposes of this paper, e-democracy is viewed as an approach that provides governments, politicians, political parties, non-governmental organizations and other related groups with alternative consultative models facilitated through the use of the Internet and other ICTs.

But how are political parties responding to the challenges and opportunities of e-democracy? As Friedman points out, political parties are an essential ingredient of a healthy democratic system, yet political parties and their elected representatives are just coming to terms with the concept of e-democracy and its potential impact on their particular organizations.

There are those that see e-democracy as the ultimate enabler or next iteration of democratic representation, which has been primarily brought about by the pervasiveness of Internet in today's society. Others see this as simply another means for already engaged politically astute groups to further communicate their messages and influence decision-makers. To date, though, the interest in e-democracy appears to have been driven by the fact that this new form of consultation and engagement has the potential to be a powerful legitimizer in helping to shape future government policy and enriching the political process.

Indeed, e-democracy is a relatively new concept and its appearance seems to have coincided with the advent of e-business and e-government in most developed countries. In order to assess the challenges of e-democracy to political parties, our intent is to explore developments in the e-business and e-government sectors and see if they offer any clues to the challenges e-democracy places on political parties. The fact that e-business and more recently e-government are more tangible aspects of the e-conomy might provide us with a more realistic perspective from which to view the challenges and opportunities that e-democracy offers political parties.

While governments today appear eager to explore the potential of e-democracy, political parties do not seem to have embraced this new opportunity with quite the same enthusiasm. From interviewing elected representatives and party officials in both Canada and the United States for this paper, there appear to be a limited number of individuals attuned to this particular issue. E-democracy, it seems, has not yet entered into the mainstream consciousness of political parties. Why is that? In the era of the 24-hour per day news cycle and changing voter expectations, are parties and politicians simply overwhelmed with the myriad demands placed on their time? Or, has the role of political parties changed over time? One might argue that political parties are so focused on the next election cycle that more pervasive, longer term issues such as e-democracy do not capture the attention of elected and senior officials responsible for setting the agenda of the parties. Put another way, why should political parties commit valuable time resources responding now to a phenomenon that may or may not have some future impact on their core business objective—getting elected?

As the Robin Cook quote indicates, it is somewhat ironic that as political parties and candidates have increasingly relied on information and communications technologies to assist their electoral campaigns, there has been a general decline in voter participation. While these new technologies offer considerable potential to enrich the political process, one can not help but wonder if political parties have not chosen to focus on the medium instead of improving the content.

A great deal of attention has been paid to how political parties use new information and communications technologies within the electoral arena. However, little attention has been given to the potential of these same technologies to fundamentally alter the structure, organization and functioning of parties responding to the challenges of e-democracy. While political parties have been quick to adopt new technologies to influence voters, perhaps politicians and party officials need to be more convinced of the merits of e-democracy before committing themselves to this new approach. Just as e-business and e-government are hardly mature sectors, e-democracy can best be described as a rapidly evolving space.

Phil Noble, Founder and Publisher of PoliticsOnline, and an internationally recognized expert on the use of technology in politics, perhaps summed up the e-democracy challenge facing political parties best by saying that "E-democracy will radically change politics, however no one knows where this will lead or the time it will take to change."

The intent of this paper is to explore the challenge e-democracy poses for political parties. It draws two principal sources of information: first interviews conducted with elected representatives, political party officials in Canada and the United States, the Chief Electoral Officer of Canada, senior officials within the Parliamentary Centre and Congressional Management Foundation, and individuals involved in providing Internet campaign services to candidates in the United States; and second source, a review of books, studies, articles and other related publications that explore the issue of e-democracy, the impact of the Internet on political parties as well as e-business and e-government. Our hope is that, by exploring some of the trends and developments surrounding e-business and e-government, we might be able to identify the challenges and opportunities that e-democracy poses for political parties.

2. *Political Parties: The new environment*

Political parties today are very different entities than they were 100 years ago. At the beginning of the 20th century, political parties were seen as efficient mechanisms able to broker the many different and competing interests of social, cultural and economic groups within society. Industrialization was the driving economic force with nation states competing to build their own indigenous industrial bases. Global trade was limited, as was participation in the political process, for it would be years before universal suffrage would be the norm. Newspapers were the only forms of mass communication, and these often had specific political perspectives, which impacted the way in which news was reported.

Today, the efficiency of political parties as honest brokers and champions of social and economic change is being challenged on a broad range of fronts.[2] At the turn of this new century, globalization is the dominant economic system, which in its purest form aims to integrate the economies of countries around the world. The rise of single-issue interest groups has demonstrated, to a certain degree, the inability of parties to effectively broker a more diverse set of economic and societal interests than existed a century ago.

The environment that political parties operate within has also changed. Diamond and Gunther state that "throughout the established Trilateral democracies—Japan, North America and Europe—confidence in government is in decline. Citizens are cynical about their representative institutions, political parties, and most of all, their politicians."[3] The authors make the point that:

> In almost all the advanced industrialized democracies... the proportion of the population identifying with a political party has declined in the past

quarter century, as has the strength of party attachments. This appears to been driven not only by objective political developments but also by generational trends, as younger, better educated citizens have lower levels of party loyalty, even though they have higher levels of political interest and engagement.[4]

A recent study by the Canadian Policy Research Network supports this view. The report concludes that for all the talk, money and time spent on "public consultations" and "citizen involvement," Canadians aren't having a real say in federal policies. And if they do get a say, they're rarely listened to. The report's coauthor, Susan Phillips of Carleton University's School of Public Administration, states that "what's needed is a cultural change that provides an atmosphere of open access to information, because if you've become so afraid of getting information out that you won't commit to paper, then you can't do effective consultation—and that's the environment in the public service right now: restricted access, fear of sharing information and the need to control." [5]

The demand for greater access to information has been driven in part by the existence of the Internet and the proliferation of new information and communications technologies. Coincidentally, it has been the advent of ICTs that has presented modern day political parties with some of their biggest opportunities and challenges. From the radio, telephone, television, fax machines and computers these technologies have served to shape over time an iterative progressive construct in engaging citizens within the political process, primarily around the election cycle. Yet, it is within this most recent and some might argue the most powerful technological manifestation—the Internet, that the notion of electronic democracy has emerged.

The brave new world of e-democracy is only now starting to emerge, yet there is already confusion around the definition of this new concept. To some, e-democracy represents a future state, almost utopian in some respects, where the broadest possible consultation with citizens can take place within the on-line environment. The pervasive technological infrastructure coupled with an increasingly informed and engaged population provides the potential for an open, inclusive and transparent state in contrast to a political process that is not well understood, and often characterized as secretive and subject to manipulation.

To a politician, e-democracy can represent another channel through which they can more effectively dialogue with their constituents, thereby enhancing the more traditional citizen engagement and communications activities such as town hall meetings, telephone conversations, letters etc., irrespective of geography or time. To a political party or campaign consultant focused on the next election campaign, e-democracy can represent the next iteration of website development, the use of mobile wireless devices or sophisticated email campaigns that offers even greater interactivity with cyber-voters. For electoral commissions charged with the responsibility of overseeing the voting process, e-democracy offers the potential to reverse the decline in voter participation by providing greater choice in the way a vote can be cast, whether that be by kiosk, over the Internet or through an individual's cellular phone.

To understand both the potential opportunity and challenges that e-democracy poses for political parties, one first needs to look at the *raison d'être* of its existence. Schmitter states that "electoral structuration is the primary function for parties, in the sense that it is this activity that constitutes their strongest claim to a distinctive political role." [6] While political parties do carry out other important functions (i.e., providing linkages between citizens and state, setting the policy agenda and formulation of policy, recruitment of elites, etc.), [7] by and large, the overriding focus is to ensure the success of the party, its leader and candidates during election campaigns.

The debate on e-democracy is beginning to frame a dilemma for political parties. On the one hand, e-democracy offers the potential of engaging a much broader group of citizens in the political process than is currently the case. Intuitively, one would think that this would be an important priority for any political party interested in its long-term future and viability. In the present electoral environment, engaging a greater number of voters in the political process has the potential to translate into votes and perhaps even money. However, political parties appear to be less than enthusiastic about e-democracy, because the linkage between e-democracy and success at the polls has not yet been clearly established. Where is the political value (votes and dollars) in building a sustainable e-democracy approach if the return may or may not pay off at the polls?

The e-democracy debate also appears to be one of responsibility. Should political parties be concerned about ensuring the broadest possible group of citizens participate in the political process? Or should they simply be focussed on reaching those voters (albeit a declining number) that will cast their ballot? If this is not a responsibility of political parties then whose responsibility is it? The unfortunate predicament is that citizens now appear, more than in the past, to be increasingly frustrated by a system over which they have little apparent influence and control.

In a report by the Institute for Public Policy Research (IPPR) entitled *New Democratic Processes: better decisions, stronger democracy,* author Robin Clarke states that "people are not disengaged from political issues, they are frustrated by a political process which does not seem to value their opinions (and that) a solution may lie in revisiting the nature of the democratic relationship." He goes on to state that "the search for an answer would need to involve a commitment across all public organisations to experiment with deepening the democratic relationship. Politicians and other decision makers need to view their legitimacy as resting on a closer relationship with citizens." [8] Indeed part of the appeal of e-democracy is that it offers a potential solution to the problems that are plaguing the political process presently.

But it's not simply about changing the democratic relationship between parties and voters. It is also about how parties respond to these changes and make the necessary adjustments to their internal processes and structures that will pose the greatest challenge for the adoption of e-democracy. Political parties are by their very nature fluid organizations given the variety of functions they perform and the nature of the environment they operate. As much as parties are having difficulty engaging members of the general public within the political process they also face these same challenges internally. The desire by party members for greater involvement in internal party processes such as decision-making and policy development is also causing conflict within political parties. In *Rebuilding Canadian Party Politics,* Carty, Cross and Young state that party activists in the old-line parties showed a high degree of discontent over their (limited) role in party decision making. [9] The authors also point out "that grass-roots involvement in party policy making is meaningful only if there is some connection between the policy positions of the party and the positions taken by its parliamentary caucus. This is a tension that is as old as organized political parties." [10]

The interesting point here is the contradiction between the short-term realities of parties and candidates preparing for the next election campaign and the need to tackle a problem that can only be solved, it appears, over a longer period of time. How will parties respond to this struggle and what alternatives will they have to consider? If e-democracy is, to a certain extent, a political manifestation of the developments in e-business and e-government, let's first begin by examining these two issues further.

3. E-Commerce: building the foundation amid changing consumer relationships

The introduction of rail and the steam engine to North America in the 19th century changed the economic and geopolitical landscape of the continent. Communities and nations were built and self-identified along the iron lines stretching from coast to coast. The telegraph wire followed the iron rails, then the telephone, until today the Internet has become as important and almost as ubiquitous as the phone.

Now, at the beginning of the 21st century, the availability and widespread adoption of advanced communications technologies on a global scale is once again transforming the ways and means in which individuals, groups, companies and governments are sharing information and conducting business.

While the origins of the Internet came about as a result of US Department of Defense funded research, it was the business sector that, not surprisingly, was the first to seize on the commercial potential of the Internet. This led to a burst of entrepreneurial creativity as the economics of communication and distribution were altered and accelerated by the declining costs of hardware and software relative to the performance of these components. As a result Electronic Commerce or Electronic Business was born (NB—the two terms are used interchangeably throughout this paper).

There are several aspects to the development of e-business that, we believe bear on the genesis of the e-democracy movement and which also factor into the way in which political parties address e-democracy. These include the following:

- the rise in Internet usage in business and at home, as well as ICT knowledge and skills among the general populations within developed and developing countries;
- the increasing importance of e-business, both business-to-business (B2B) and business-to-consumer (B2C), to the interconnected globalized economies of industrialized and developing countries;
- the profound shifts from hierarchical, command and control to flattened, horizontal organizational structures within most businesses; and
- the changing relationships consumers have with companies in the e-business space.

Internet usage worldwide

Barely a week goes by without a new study or report detailing the increase in Internet usage. When the World Wide Web came into existence in the early 1990's there were approximately 800 separate computer networks and 160,000 computers attached to the Internet.[11]   Today Internet users can be found in just about every country in the world. According to a recent report by Nielsen NetRatings, more than 553 million people worldwide now have Internet access. As usage increases so too does the robustness of the Internet. According to a recent eMarketer forecast, the number of broadband subscribers worldwide is expected to rise from just over 15 million in 2000 to over 117 million in 2004. As impressive as these statistics are, the issue of the digital divide is still a reality and is likely to remain one for some time.

Internet usage patterns are also becoming more established. In the early years of the World Wide Web, users spent large portions of their time simply surfing the Net to satisfy their own curiosity. As users began to increase and business responded to this new medium, the Internet transformed from a purely informational space to one where personal business, entertainment and a variety of other activities, including politics, could take place.

Rise of e-business

While e-business has had an enormous impact on developed economies globally it is still a relatively recent trend when compared to the industrialization era over a hundred years ago. The research company IDC predicts that within a five-year period the e-commerce sector (B2B and B2C) will have grown from $131 billion (USD) in 1999 to over $5,300 billion (USD) by 2004. There are few industrial sectors today where e-business has not had some transformative effect in terms of operations or markets.

The real story of e-business is that as transaction costs fell, entire industry supply chains became disaggregated and reaggregated. The resulting supply chains began to take on forms ranging from hierarchical to self-organizing and in turn created new value propositions for the end-customer. Investments not just in infrastructure but in applications such as supply chain management (SCM), enterprise resource planning (ERP) and customer relationship management (CRM) contributed to driving down costs, creating increased efficiencies and revenues for most companies.

While the B2B sector accounts for the vast majority of total e-commerce revenues it is the B2C sector that is often the "face" of the Internet to most online consumers. Given the increasing percentage of individuals connecting to the Internet it is not surprising that the B2C sector is experiencing impressive growth with more and more retailers offering consumers the opportunity to conduct business on-line.Clearly the impact of e-business, both B2C and B2B, will become even more pronounced over time.

Organizational changes

The impact of new technologies and the Internet on e-business also contributed to fundamental restructuring of business organisation and processes. Dell Computer is often singled out as one of the most successful examples of a company that completely redefined the role of a computer manufacturer by rewriting the book on supply chain management. With a flatter organizational structure Dell was able to become more responsive to customer requirements, thereby enjoying a distinct competitive advantage over its competitors.

The power behind this new model was that it allowed Dell to develop sophisticated databases populated with detailed consumer information on which they could anticipate future purchasing patterns. This customer-centric approach has now permeated just about every aspect of the business today and is evolving to a point where highly sophisticated customer relationship management models are being used to strengthen the on-going relationship between companies and their customers.

The importance of CRM applications to the B2C space is expected to increase dramatically over the next few years. According to a report published by IDC, *Customer Relationship Management Market Forecast and Analysis, 2000-2004*, worldwide CRM revenues are forecasted to reach $12 billion (USD) by 2004.

The changing consumer relationship

One of the profound changes precipitated by the Internet has been the shift in power that consumers now have with retailers. Today customers can literally, to paraphrase a popular commercial, have it their way. For businesses and consumers it is not so much about the product or service as it is about the relationship that exists between them. Frederick Newell states that the basic principle is "to add value to the customer relationship in the customer's terms to maximize the value of the relationship to the customer for the customer's benefit and the company's profit."[12]

The importance of the customer relationship is now viewed as an intrinsic business asset. In the book *Digital Capital*, authors Don Tapscott, David Ticoll and Alex Lowy position the notion of relationship capital as follows: "The wealth embedded in customer relationships is now more important than the capital contained in land, factories, buildings and even big bank accounts. Relationships are now assets. A firm's ability to engage customers, suppliers and other partners in mutually beneficial value exchanges determines its relationship capital."[13]

In order to nurture this new type of relationship both businesses and, more recently, governments are investing in the necessary systems and services. It is the lure of reduced operating costs and the opportunity to improve services to clients within the business sector that caught the eye of government. But the real opportunity for e-government efforts is the potential to develop a stronger, more responsive relationship between citizen and state with the emergence of e-democracy.

4. e-Government : realigning the public sector

Over the past several years, e-government has become the focal point of public sector initiatives in most industrialized countries. While the roots for a more responsive client-centred government can be traced to the beginning of the previous decade, e-government is a more recent phenomenon and shadows the success of e-business within the corporate sector.

Following on the success of e-business initiatives, the public sector began looking to and experimenting with new technologies with the objective of radically changing the paradigm of program delivery, both in terms of cost and service. Spawned to a degree by the "Reinventing Government" approach as articulated by Osborne and Gaebler[14] in the early 1990s, the Clinton/Gore Administration championed this fresh new thinking by introducing the National Performance Review (NPR) during its first term in office. Driven by the opportunity for greater cost efficiencies and the potential to meet (and perhaps exceed) changing customer/voter expectations of public service programs, the NPR signaled a major shift in public policy thinking. The unique concept here was to try and match citizen expectations for service delivery by establishing performance standards across government departments and agencies in much the same way as consumers expected private sector companies to respond to their particular needs.

While reliant on information technology to drive many of the reengineering efforts brought about by the NPR, it was with the advent of the World Wide Web in the early 1990's that both businesses and governments began to look at this new infrastructure as an efficient delivery and communications channel.

The first steps were to put government services online, a step that remains a "work-in-progress." To date, most technology-enabled government efforts have been less dramatic than private sector initiatives. Rather than disaggregate and rebuild entire supply chains (a.k.a. Dell), many governments have transferred their internal information and systems to the Web. To be sure, this has had a dramatic impact on service costs and efficiency. But replicating existing systems by transferring documents from a filing cabinet to a web page seems to be an intermediary step. This approach ignores one of the powerful tools of the Internet—the ability to create new forms of value by focusing on and transforming core competencies and creating partnerships for non-core activities, new extensions to public services with fewer inhibitions and greater speed.

These initial activities appear to be having resonance with citizens. Like other industrialized countries around the world, the Government of Canada has placed a priority on its e-government activities that have been driven primarily through the Government On-Line (GOL) initiative. In a survey conducted last year the Canadian public signaled its awareness of and appetite for increased government services online with the majority of the respondents having a very positive impression of GOL. [15]

Consistent with the trend in e-business, e-government initiatives are now beginning to focus on making the necessary changes that will allow for a strengthening of the relationship between state and citizen. According to the 2002 Accenture report on eGovernment Leadership:

> Governments that adopt Customer Relationship Management or rather Citizen Relationship Management principles (client/citizen involvement) early in their eGovernment initiatives are improving at a much faster pace. Portals are becoming far more prevalent, but their true potential continues to be unrealized due to the barriers to cross agency cooperation. There is some evidence that these barriers are starting to be dismantled, as governments, businesses and citizens acknowledge that the benefits of common platforms and information sharing outweigh the perceived costs.[16]

Another recent Accenture report entitled *Customer Relationship Management: A Blueprint for Government* [17] makes the case that next generation advances in e-government will come about through the adoption of CRM. The report states that:

- Commercial messages surrounding CRM may not all apply to government, although the principles are generally found to quite relevant;

- Improving customer service is a driver across all government agencies; however, current business processes and infrastructure act as barriers;
- Opening up new government channels for customer interaction is critical to enhancing customer service;
- Government agencies are focusing on technology to address their service access priorities, but they have yet to embrace CRM as a whole-of-business approach;
- Agencies are receptive to the possibilities of partnering with each other and with private-sector organizations to facilitate information sharing and relieve human capital and cost pressures; however, they lack the capabilities to make it happen.

The fact that the e-government trend is towards more direct and closer relationships between citizen and state is a positive development from an e-democracy perspective. However, as businesses and governments pursue these consumer/citizen-centric engagement models, this situation could have important consequences for political parties if these initiatives contrast dramatically with a lack of political efforts in this area.

5. The e-democracy challenge

In *The Electronic Republic,* Lawrence Grossman quotes Marshall McLuhan as stating that "as the speed of information increases the tendency is for politics to move away from the representation and delegation of constituents toward immediate involvement of the entire community in the central acts of decision." [18] Indeed, the debate around e-democracy and the need for more meaningful citizen engagement suggests that McLuhan's comments are again proving prophetic. Developments in the e-business and e-government sectors have contributed to increasing the speed of information, however, certain actions of political parties and elected representatives have also contributed to the public's urge for greater involvement in the political process. Bill Cross makes the point that "the aftermath of Canadians' rejection of elite-brokered constitutional deals in the 1980s and 1990's... (contributed) to a strong desire by voters to be active, ongoing participants in public affairs." [19]

The speed of information appears to be increasing in even faster increments as the Internet has given rise to an entirely new means of reaching voters outside of traditional media channels. Coupled with other new technologies such as cell phones and wireless personal digital assistants (PDA's), political parties now have the ability to sustain virtually instantaneous two-way communications between campaign organizers and the news media as well as voters themselves on a 24/7 cycle. [20]

While parties and elected representatives have dabbled from time to time with new technological approaches to improve citizen engagement, [21] it appears that the continued short term focus on the electoral cycle has caused political parties to lose sight of the fact that the ongoing engagement of people within traditional party structures has been diminished in value. One example of this is the small percentage of citizens who are active in political parties. In Canada, this problem is particularly acute as a recent study examining political party membership points out. Authors Bill Cross and Lisa Young indicate that with 2% of voters belonging to a political party, Canada ranks near the bottom in a comparative list of countries.[22] Whether the adoption of e-democracy by political parties can turn this situation around remains to be seen.

More evidence and time needed

Political parties have traditionally been aggressive users of new technologies (Selnow, 1998; Axworthy, 1991; Swerdlow, 1988). Since the emergence of television in the 1950's as a mass communications medium, political parties have increasingly relied on both technological tools and increasingly sophisticated market research and advertising techniques to reach and influence voters as well as to raise money during electoral campaigns. One of the reasons these adaptations have proved so successful is the fact that clear evidence existed, based on private sector experience, that party officials and elected representatives could reference in deciding whether these new tools and techniques were applicable to the political arena. The result of these initial successes meant that a mutually beneficial and symbiotic relationship developed over the past four to fifty years between political parties and companies providing communications, marketing, fundraising and advertising services. With the advent of the World Wide Web in the early 1990's new players emerged offering Internet-based electoral services.

However, as important as Internet based services and solutions are to present day electoral campaigning, there are indications that the relationship between these new players and campaign officials is still evolving. Jonah Seiger, Cofounder and Chief Strategist for Mindshare Internet Campaigns, states that part of the current resistance towards the greater use of the Internet in campaigns is the fact that most professional campaign consultants, who are the decision-makers in terms of campaign expenditures, are of the old school and therefore tend to favour the use traditional approaches. If this view is prevalent among senior party officials, then it could well signal an inherent bias against the potential of ICTs and e-democracy within political parties.

Indeed, Luddites would find some support for their beliefs in research conducted by Bruce Bimber, who suggests that "the idea of the Internet transforming patterns of citizen-to-government communication or increasing overall participation seems unlikely." [23] Bimber also concludes that "communications technologies themselves have very little effect on citizen participation and political communication...and is more likely that the Internet is a new and complementary resource for those persons who are already engaged in public affairs...which may enlarge the gap that already exists between the politically active and inactive in U.S. society." [24]

In speaking with a number of elected representatives and party officials from federal political parties in Canada, it appears that the issue of e-democracy is far from a mainstream one. Of the party officials interviewed, none felt that e-democracy was priority issue facing their organizations. One Canadian Member of Parliament (MP) felt that out of a total of 301 elected representatives, only between 10-20 of his colleagues were interested or somewhat knowledgeable about e-government and that an even smaller group were interested in the issue of e-democracy. Other MPs expressed frustration with the lack of attention and support by the party on this issue and in hopes of providing better representation to their constituents have simply forged ahead on their own.

As such there seem to be two issues influencing the appetite for e-democracy within political parties: a lack of hard data extolling the benefits of e-democracy; and the hesitation of senior party officials who are more familiar with traditional election approaches than new Internet based solutions. If there is reluctance to embrace

Internet-based solutions aimed at increasing citizen/voter participation during elections, then one can only imagine the resistance to
using similar technologies to redefine traditional political structures
and processes.

The dilemma for political parties appears to boil down to an issue
of diffusion, as e-democracy really has not been around long enough
to have an enduring impact on the political process. Pippa Norris
points out that "the process of technological diffusion remains in
transition and, just like parties and governments, organizations are
still learning how to use the potential of the Web to do more than
act as a static form of electronic pamphlet or poster."[25]

How quickly can we expect the diffusion of e-democracy within
political parties? If the findings of Bill Woodley are applicable politically, we may be in for a long wait. In a paper published by the
Institute of Governance, Woodley examined the impact of four technologies (printing, steam engine, electricity and atomic energy) on governance and noted that from the time when these technologies were
first introduced until diffusion took place ranged from 15 years for atomic
energy to 50-100 years for the other three. [26]

As rapid and transformative as e-business and e-government
initiatives have been, then they are still relatively young on the diffusion scale when contrasted with other technologies. The same
can be said of e-democracy. While studies are beginning to delin-
eate its potential, e-democracy has not yet reached the point where
it is known and accepted not just by political leaders but by the
population as a whole. For political parties the need to demonstrate
the linkage between e-democracy and success at the polls will be of
paramount importance. E-business and e-government approaches
are often as unique as the industries and countries that employ them.
However, e-democracy has not yet evolved to a point where com-
parisons can be made between different e-democracy approaches
made by governments, let alone political parties, and this may in-
hibit the adoption rate of e-democracy.

Refreshing the old paradigm

One of the challenges e-democracy poses for political parties is
the perception that the Internet would become the primary channel for citizen engagement. This may well be too big a jump too

soon for many political players. Perhaps it's not just a question of changing something old for something new but rather a question of doing a better job with the system in place and incrementally adding the benefits of e-democracy as it becomes better defined. As Pippa Norris points out, political parties undertake a variety of important activities. These activities have taken place for centuries without the benefit of the Internet, and digital technologies can only be expected to supplement, not replace, the many functions and activities of political parties. [27]

Important as these new opportunities are, some authorities suggest that political parties and politicians perhaps have not been as effective with the tools they currently have. Canada's Minister of Finance and M.P. for Ottawa South, John Manley suggests that being an effective representative is analogous to being an effective small business owner. There are a number of key activities an elected representative must undertake that are as fundamental to politics as accounting would be for a successful business owner. For example, ensuring that the riding association is of sufficient size and reflective of the community at large and personally meeting with constituents in order to gauge public opinion are extremely important for an elected representative. In Mr. Manley's opinion there are those MPs who have forgotten the fundamentals and have therefore failed to protect the brand of the party. Consequently, voters have become disengaged from the political process and parties are now paying the price in terms of voter dissatisfaction.

Relying too much on new technologies causes problems of validity. With large numbers of emails arriving in the offices of elected representatives, it is sometimes difficult to authenticate the owner(s) of emails. Mark Walsh refers to this as "astroturf," where online activities can sometimes fake a grassroots initiative.

Perhaps one of the more challenging aspects of political parties adopting e-democracy will be the way in which they incorporate new approaches with the more traditional methods. This is the approach that has been taken by the Canadian Alliance Party, where the Internet is used in a variety of ways to support, but not replace, the more traditional processes. For example, Canadians can join the Party or make a donation over the Internet, but can accomplish the same tasks by walking in to an Alliance office or using the telephone. For the Canadian Alliance, this blending of traditional and modern approaches is extremely important given the demographics of their membership. The party recognizes that a digital divide exists within the membership and, in order to keep members engaged, they need to offer choice.

That being said, political parties should be thinking bigger. As we have seen from the e-commerce sector, political parties should be looking beyond the election campaign to how their back offices and internal processes can be improved through the application of new technologies as well as through experimenting with and cataloguing their e-democracy efforts. Some politicians and political parties have already begun this journey, but parties need to internalize the discussion and experimentation before any substantial progress is likely to be made. The fact that political parties have not internalized the discussion on e-democracy also means that party members have not yet had the opportunity to engage with this issue. This situation could prove to be a detriment to advancing the e-democracy agenda as members will want to have an input on any substantive changes that will occur in the policies and direction of the party.

Political parties should focus less on the product they are selling during election campaigns and instead concentrate more on research and development when it comes to e-democracy as Robin Clarke suggests. Changing the nature of the democratic relationship will require a lot of trial and error.

Tom Riley has written that "what is being prognosticated here are not revolutionary change but rather evolutionary change through which the current and emerging information and communication changes hold within them the promise of change. The change will depend on the degree to which people want to be more engaged in government and on the emergence of new political thinkers who will think through to the next evolution of democracy." He suggests too that "as with e-government for e-democracy to grow it is going to need vision, strategy and political leadership." [28]

Riley makes an interesting and important point regarding vision, strategy and political leadership. These factors have been present in successful e-business and e-government initiatives and will also be required if e-democracy is to find a home within political parties. Prime Minister Tony Blair has been a champion on this issue with respect to the United Kingdom's e-government efforts. However, it has been hard to find an elected leader who will articulate how e-democracy, at a party level, will provide the vision for the party moving forward.

Self -interests versus the benefit to society

Dr. Tom Flanagan, Director of Operations in the Office of the Official Opposition in Ottawa states that in many respects the debate around e-democracy shows the warts of our present day democratic system. On the one hand, the self-interest of the parties and candidates to be elected is paramount. Yet, there also appears to be a more egalitarian goal of raising the bar on democracy by encouraging greater voter participation within the political process, not just at elections but in an ongoing way.

There are those who would argue the fix is in on e-democracy already because it poses a serious threat to the order and structure that drives the present day political system.

Mark Walsh, Chief Technology Advisor for the Democratic National Committee, believes that there is no natural migration path of political parties in terms of e-democracy as there has been for the corporate sector in terms of e-business. One of the main problems is that the demand for openness, accountability and transparency that drives e-business works against the processes that run political parties. There are too many groups with self-interests that dominate political parties who see no reason to change even though e-democracy might potentially benefit the party as well as society at large.

Carolyn Bennett, MP, sees e-democracy as a way to address the issues of transparency and accountability with political parties — something that she believes is very important in today's environment. Dr. Tom Flanagan feels that e-democracy is not going to transform democracy, certainly not overnight. It doesn't offer utopia either. As has been proven in the past, it will be used by people to further their own agendas as opposed to being a great democratization vehicle.

If e-democracy forces political parties to become more open, accessible and transparent, then it is bound to have an impact on party structures and processes such as policy development, organization, fundraising, membership etc. Even with political leadership and commitment, to undertake changes on this large a scale will likely take years to achieve given the consultation and input that will be required once party members become engaged.

In other words there really does not appear to be any incentives for political parties to move beyond the status quo, election focus, at this point in time. That is not to say that at some future date political parties might not give e-democracy greater attention, but right now the number of elected officials experimenting with this approach are still few in number.

Educating elected representatives and party officials

The effectiveness of the Internet as a communications and organizational medium has been played out many times in terms of mobilizing citizens and interest groups in lobbying legislators. But these examples are mostly short term in nature—here today, gone tomorrow. However, what is the potential of e-democracy as a long-term sustainable citizen engagement approach? Developments within the e-business and e-government sectors may be able to offer us some insight. The increasing attention toward and investment in customer/citizen centric approaches and solutions, such as CRM, by business and government would appear to demonstrate that there is potential pay-off for political parties and elected representatives to develop a more direct and responsive relationship with citizens.

In fact, some elected representatives are already thinking along these lines. Reg Alcock, MP (Winnipeg South Centre), who is well known for his pioneering approach to using technology, has already developed a CRM-type system that allows him to better serve his constituents. Carolyn Bennett, MP (St. Paul's), firmly believes that e-democracy allows her to dialogue with constituents outside of the traditional means of communications and further strengthens the relationship she has with voters. In the United States both the Republican and Democratic parties are experimenting with CRM-type applications, although the focus appears to be on fundraising as opposed to citizen engagement-type activities.

While these MPs intuitively know that e-democracy offers value to their constituents, there is very little substantive evidence that would make an effective case to other legislators and party members.

A recent report by The Hansard Society in the United Kingdom indicated that one in four Westminster MPs had no functioning email account in their parliamentary office and that 60% have no personal website. Representatives in the devolved assemblies (Scotland,

Wales and Northern Ireland) have even lower profiles on the Internet. The report also rated the content and design of existing web sites and found that "all the sites failed to address the issues and problems of visitors in favour of explaining how each legislature works and had search tools that deliver too much undifferentiated information with little interaction."

A similar survey conducted by the Centre for Collaborative Government that examined the use of the Internet by Canadian Parliamentarians identified that only 58% had official websites. Furthermore, only 27% of those with websites used any sort of interactive tools, such as feedback forms or online surveys.

Perhaps these numbers are not too surprising given that we are really in the early adoption stage within the overall diffusion cycle. However, if elected representatives are to become champions for change then a greater emphasis on education, knowledge and skills development will be required in order to make them more comfortable in this new medium. If e-democracy is to make a breakthrough within political parties then it will require a critical mass of elected representatives experimenting with this approach.

Currently, elected representatives in the United States and Canada rely on two important nonpartisan, not-for-profit organizations that provide research, training and tools to assist them in managing technological change. The Parliamentary Centre in Ottawa and the Congressional Management Foundation in Washington assist elected representatives in meeting the challenges brought about by the increasing reliance on technology within their office environments, but challenges still remain.

Kathy Goldschmidt, Director of Technology at the Congressional Management Foundation indicates that while Capitol Hill staffers need technology to do their job, most offices now are using technology as a business tool and not as a constituency tool. The fact that a resource and skills gap exists in most offices means that elected representatives are not optimized to adopt and use these new technologies in more fundamental ways as has been the case with e-business and e-government initiatives.

This view reflects the experience of the Liberal Party of Canada (LPC) which has developed, sold and supported (through a partnership with a private sector company) a suite of software called ElecSys. The first product (AdminElect) assists Members of Parliament in managing their constituency cases. The second product (ManagElect) is used by LPC candidates during election campaigns to track voter identification and GOTV (Get Out The Vote) activities. Despite the investment made by the LPC in this software suite and the fact that it could assist MPs in managing their constituencies more effectively, it is used by less than 9% of the caucus.

For the Liberal Party of Canada this is clearly a disappointing return on investment. But, aside from the issue of MPs being comfortable with the technology, the problem with the lack of usage by the rest of the Liberal caucus may also be a question of inadequate resources (financial and personnel) being available for citizen engagement activities. The average MP receives less than three dollars per year per constituent to staff their offices, cover travel and communication expenses.

However, one of the issues that will determine the move towards greater e-democracy type efforts by parties and politicians seems to be the issue of that cost. Realistically, if parties are focussed on the electoral cycle and funds are used to support activities that directly contribute to the election effort, there occurs a competition for scarce resources. If e-democracy is not seen as supporting the election effort, the likelihood of financial support is slim.

Lower operational costs have been a driver in many e-business and e-government initiatives as has been demonstrated by e-business and e-government and ICT costs have continued to drop from a price/performance perspective. In recent years, campaign spending in the United States has increased dramatically, yet fewer voters actually end up casting a ballot. This same trend holds true in most other western democracies, including Canada. In many respects we have a situation where there are more dollars chasing fewer voters.

The cost of e-democracy

Previous sections of this paper have detailed how the customer/citizen-centric relationship has transformed e-business and e-government initiatives. To implement these initiatives both public and private organizations have had to make significant investments in their technology infrastructures, not to mention changes to their organizational structures and processes.

Political parties and elected representatives appear to be at a distinct disadvantage when compared to governmental efforts to provide more citizen-centric services. Government departments have considerably more resources available to them than do political parties. Should political parties be concerned about these developments? The short answer is yes. If political parties are too focused on the electoral process and ignore the citizen engagement efforts of e-government initiatives, how can they realistically hope to provide alternative views or approaches to the development of policy? It really is a question of investing in a process that will be a key differentiator from an electoral perspective but also one that provides legitimacy to elected representatives. For political parties, what is the price of losing legitimacy in the policy development process in terms of its members and voters?

While business and government funding models can support these new investments, one has to wonder whether political parties will ever have access to the same levels of funding that would be required to implement similar large scale, citizen-engagement infrastructures.

In previous sections of this paper, other cost issues have been identified. These include the costs of transitioning to an e-democracy approach. Some costs would be fairly straightforward—the cost of hardware, software, support, training etc. The more intangible, and perhaps significant, costs would involve the required changes to political party structures and processes that have been institutionalized over time. More importantly, changes would need to be ratified by party members, which would likely mean a substantial effort over a long period of time. A more likely approach would be to see a more gradual adoption of e-democracy type activities within both electoral and party related activities. This is a perspective that Tom Flanagan shares. Any change in terms of e-democracy or use of technology within the Canadian Alliance will be incremental as opposed to overhauling their traditional processes.

The question then becomes what will be the cost for political parties should they want to move towards a more voter centric e-democracy model? We know from e-business and e-government efforts that these approaches are expensive. At this point, the costs of such a system can only be guessed at. In the United States both the Republican and Democratic parties are starting to bring CRM to the political process. However, efforts here are focussed more on fundraising than they are on citizen engagement.

But it appears that political parties are gradually increasing their IT expenditures. According to a survey conducted last year by the E-Voter Institute, IT investment is predicted to increase over the next few years. The report stated that:

> Leaders predict that by 2008, Internet budgets will represent one in four dollars spent in a campaign budget, nearly double what they expect in 2004. Until then, leaders expressed hesitation about being able to reach desirable voters because of the limitations of the Internet for targeting constituents, the Digital Divide and the resistance of their clients to try new approaches.[29]

The issue for political parties is one of financial sustainability. Parties can't afford to ignore the long-term repercussions of declining voter participation. They are becoming increasingly reliant on corporate donation as the number of donations from individuals is declining.

If the issue is greater engagement of voters in the political process, then perhaps the time has come to consider rewarding political parties and politicians for their efforts in this regard. If we are at the beginning of a new era of greater citizen engagement, whether it is through e-democracy or traditional methods, then maybe we need to consider building in financial incentives in order to move to the next step. More incentives are required for political parties and candidates, not disincentives.

Metrics of e-democracy

Robin Clarke makes the point that e-democracy's "starting point is that public involvement should be about both achieving better quality decision and democratic renewal. Public involvement for better decision-making offers instant returns, though a firm body of evidence is urgently needed to win over doubters. Public involvement as a means to democratic renewal is a trickier and, in reality, a long-term goal." [30]

If the consensus is that e-democracy is an approach worth pursuing then would it not make sense to develop a set of metrics to determine its success or failure? Robin Clarke's point is a good one, that if public involvement is about achieving better quality decision making and democratic renewal then it will be important to develop a set of criteria by which practitioners can determine the success or failure of their efforts. From a political party perspective how will success be defined? If the decline in voter participation can be reversed, is that an appropriate indicator of success? More importantly though, what does e-democracy mean from the perspective of voters/citizens? Will it mean they view the political process as more open, transparent and accessible? Or will citizens place a greater emphasis on the ability to cast a vote on major issues facing governments at all levels?

For elected representatives it will be important to have an evaluative framework that can be used to determine the effectiveness of their citizen engagement activities, whether they are traditional or Internet based. The important thing is to be able to measure, evaluate and then respond with corrective action if needed. Presently, elected representatives are evaluated on their efforts only at election time. The challenge for political parties utilizing a more citizen-centric, e-democracy approach will be developing effective evaluation frameworks that can be used on an ongoing basis.

What does e-democracy look like?

What will e-democracy look like within the political environment? If e-business and e-government initiatives are any indication, it will be increasingly like the CRM model. But this is merely a guess. Building on the base that has been started by their elected representatives, political parties need to start experimenting on a more systematic basis with e-democracy approaches. As the previous section mentioned, parties also need to start evaluating what works and what doesn't and building an inventory of what their elected representatives are undertaking in this area.

One evolutionary path might be the adoption of a more life-cycle approach to managing member and voter relationships. Automobile manufacturers use this life-cycle approach in developing and marketing their various product lines. For political parties, moving to a more responsive party model could be accomplished through use of databases and adaptive CRM models. The downside would be the inherent cost to such as system, the disruption it might cause to existing processes and the impact the new approach might have on individuals' privacy and security. Given the low regard in which political parties are held by the general public, this might be a difficult hurdle to overcome.

It isn't a case of one e-democracy model or approach working for all but rather building an e-democracy model that works for them. Political parties vary in their structure, the constitutions that govern their activities as well as the environment they must operate. Therefore, how parties respond to e-democracy challenges and opportunities will likely be both unique and reflective as they are today.

Where does this lead us with respect to e-democracy? It points to the need for more sustained citizen engagement by political parties than has been the case to date. The fact of the matter is that parties have stopped interacting with voters in a sustained way and perhaps have turned to technology as one way (perhaps seen as the easiest way) to reengage citizens. The IPPR study points to the fact that local councils in the UK who have taken a long term approach to citizen engagement have found that the participation rate in elections tended to be higher than in areas where this approach was not taken. This suggests that parties and elected representatives who make a priority of engaging citizens on a regular and sustained basis will reap the rewards at election time.

6. Where do political parties go from here?

How should political parties respond to the challenges and opportunities offered by e-democracy? The following is one suggestion on how political parties could be encouraged to become more aggressive in their e-democracy efforts.

Financing citizen engagement—encouraging parties to think longer term

One of the principle e-democracy challenges for political parties is finding the right balance between financing the electoral needs of the party, the ongoing organizational, communications and policy development processes, and reaching out to encourage greater participation of people the political process. Currently, parties are only rewarded for winning elections, which poses a problem from a citizen engagement perspective, as there is no incentive for them to engage in e-democracy activities on a broader scale.

If political parties were to be rewarded financially for undertaking broader citizen engagement activities, some positive changes might be possible. There is some precedence for this approach where political parties in Germany have received government funding for undertaking education and citizen engagement activities. While the details would need to be worked out, the idea in the Canadian context would be that recognized political parties would receive a funding allotment from government (i.e. Elections Canada) that would go to citizen engagement, education and outreach type activities. These citizen engagement funds would provide parties with the incentive to invest and experiment in new approaches and mediums. From an e-democracy perspective, this funding could potentially be used by parties to fund innovative online citizen engagement approaches either through their elected MPs or at the constituency level. It also means that parties would not have to make a choice between financing their election efforts or funding e-democracy initiatives. These new funds would give parties the flexibility and capacity to undertake both activities.

Political parties could augment this allotment with funds of their own, but all parties would be expected to account for this funding through appropriate disclosure mechanisms. This would hopefully provide an incentive for parties to develop a useful evaluation mechanism that would reduce public skepticism over political parties receiving additional public funds.

Public funds are an indication that greater citizen engagement in the political process is the responsibility of other organizations, not just political parties. It also recognizes that political parties need to strike a balance between the need for electoral success and the requirement for greater engagement of the general population in the decision making and policy development processes.

7. Conclusion

The potential of e-democracy as an important and complementary citizen engagement process is just beginning to be realized now by political parties. To date, a small but growing number of elected representatives are experimenting with e-democracy approaches and, as a result, are beginning to challenge the status quo within their various parliaments and political parties.

The pervasiveness of e-business and e-government with most western democracies is driving fundamental economic and societal changes that are also in turn having ramifications on the political landscape. The traditional political engagement models do not appear to be as sustainable as they once were.

While e-democracy appears to pose some interesting and compelling challenges for political parties, this phenomenon is still relatively new and therefore hasn't been subjected to the full test of time. If history is any indication, change will likely occur at an evolutionary as opposed to revolutionary pace before e-democracy and its various iterations will be assimilated into the mainstream political engagement processes we are familiar with today.

However, since the ICT revolution was born, the pace of change has increased substantially on year over year basis, as borne out by the proliferation of e-business and more recently e-government initiatives. In order to counteract the recent decline by citizens in the political process, political parties should seize upon the opportunity offered by the e-democracy movement and begin spending more time and energy experimenting, molding and adapting this approach in order to reinvigorate the political process.

Political parties are pragmatic. E-democracy is not the panacea that will alone revitalize declining voter turnout and antipathy towards parties and politicians. Parties should acknowledge the publics' appetite for change in the political process as an opportunity to re-examine their own internal processes and structures. This examination should, at the minimum, evaluate how these existing processes and structures could be improved or enhanced through the judicious application of technology and new e-democracy type approaches.

Just as e-business and e-government customer/citizen-centric initiatives are different, the evolution of e-democracy will likely be dependent on a number of factors. These include the state of the local technology infrastructure, the level of knowledge and use of the Internet by elected representatives, and, perhaps most importantly, the financial ability of the political system and parties to respond to this opportunity.

It is not that political parties have not kept up with the Internet revolution—they have when it comes to using it for electoral purposes. Where they have missed the boat is in internalizing that knowledge to create a more dynamic and citizen centric political engagement process. There is still time—but those responsible for the stewardship of political parties have to realize that change is required and that they must take the necessary steps to do something about it.

Bibliography:

Alexander, Cynthia J and Pal, Leslie A. ed. (1998) *Digital Democracy: Policy and Politics in the Wired World.* Toronto, Ontario: Oxford University Press.

Allison, Juliann Emmons ed. (2002) *Technology, Development, and Democracy: International Conflict and Cooperation in the Information Age.* Albany, New York: State University of New York Press.

Axworthy, Thomas, S. (1991) Capital Intensive Politics: Money, Media and Mores in the United States and Canada. In *Issues in Party and Election Finance in Canada,* ed. F. Leslie Seidle, Toronto, Ontario: Dundurn Press.

Barney, Darin (2000) *Prometheus Wired: The Hope for Democracy in the Age of Network Technology.* Vancouver, British Columbia: UBC Press.

Blumler, Jay G. and Coleman, Stephen (2001) *Realising Democracy Online: A Civic Comons in Cyberspace.* London, England: Institute for Public Policy Research/Citizens Online.

Carty, R. Kenneth, Cross, William and Young, Lisa (2000) *Rebuilding Canadian Party Politics.* Vancouver, British Columbia: UBC Press.

Centre for Collaborative Government (2002) *Canadian Federal Members of Parliament Online Website Prevalence.* Ottawa, Ontario.

Clarke, Robin (2002) *New Democratic Processes. Better Decisions, stronger democracy.* London, England: Institute for Public Policy Research.

Coleman, Stephen ed. (2001) *2001: Cyber Space Odyssey. The internet in the UK Election.* London, England: Hansard Society.

Coleman, Stephen ed. (2001) *Elections in the age of the Internet: Lessons from the United States.* London, England: Hansard Society.

Cross, William Cross and Young, Lisa (2001) *Contours of Political Party Membership in Canada.* Paper presented to the 2001 annual meeting of the Canadian Political Science Association.

Davis, Richard (1999) *The Web of Politics: The Internet's Impact on the American Political System.* New York, New York: Oxford University Press.

E-Voter Institute (December 2001) *E-Voter 2001: Dawning of a New Era – Measuring the Initial Impact of the Internet on Political and Advocacy Communication.*

Friedman, Thomas L. (2000) *The Lexus and the Olive Tree.* New York, New York: First Anchor Books.

Gartner Dataquest Guide (2002) *Infrastructure and Applications Worldwide Software Market Definitions.* Stamford, Connecticut: Gartner.

Grossman, Lawrence K. (1995) *The Electronic republic: Reshaping Democracy in the Information Age.* New York, New York: Penguin Group.

Gunther, Richard and Diamond, Larry ed. (2001) *Political Parties and Democracy.* Baltimore, Maryland: The Johns Hopkins University Press.

Hague, Barry N. and Loader, Brian D (1999) *Digital Democracy: Discourse and Decision*

Making in the Information Age. New York, New York: Routledge.

Hanselmann, Calvin (2001) *Electronically Enhanced Democracy in Canada.* Calgary, Alberta: Canada West Foundation.

Hill, Kevin A. and Hughes, John E. (1998) *Cyberpolitics: Citizen Activism in the age of the Internet.* Lanham, Maryland: Rowan & Littlefield Publishers, Inc.

Kamarck, Elaine Ciulla and Nye Jr., Joseph S. ed. (2002) *Governance.com: Democracy in the Information Age.* Washington, D.C.: Brookings Institution Press.

Lenihan, Donald G. (2002) *Realigning Governance: From E-Government to E-Democracy.* Ottawa, Ontario: Centre for Collaborative Government.

Lenihan, Donald G. (2002) *Survey on Canadian Federal MP Website Prevalence.* Ottawa, Ontario: Centre for Collaborative Government.

Newell, Frederick (2000) *Loyalty.com: Customer Relationship Management in the New Era of Internet Marketing.* New York, New York: McGraw-Hill.

Norris, Pippa (2001) *Digital Divide: Civic Engagement, Information Poverty, and the Internet Worldwide.* New York, New York: Cambridge University Press.

Office of the e-Envoy (2002) *In the Service of Democracy: a consultation paper on a policy for electronic democracy.* London, England: Cabinet Office.

Osborne, David and Gaebler, Ted (1992) *Reinventing Government.* Reading, Massachusetts: Addison-Wesley.

Pammett, Jon H. and Dornan, Christopher (2001) *The Canadian General Election of 2000.* Toronto, Ontario: Dundurn Press.

Riley, Thomas B. (August 2002) *E-Democracy in the Future: Will We See Significant Change?* Ottawa, Ontario: Riley Information Services.

Phillips, Susan D. (2002) *Mapping the Links: Citizen Involvement in Policy Processes.* Ottawa, Ontario: Canadian Policy Research Networks.

Selnow, Gary W. (1998) *Electronic Whistle Stops: The Impact of the Internet on American Politics.* Westport, Connecticut: Praeger Publishers.

Shine, Sean (2002) *Building Customer Relationship Management in Government.* Dublin, Ireland: Accenture.

Swerdlow, Joel L. ed. (1988) *Media Technology and the Vote.* Boulder, Colorado: Westview Press.

Tapscott, Don, Ticoll, Alex and Lowy, Alex (2000) *Digital Capital: Harnessing the Power of Business Webs.* Boston, Massachusetts: Harvard Business School Press.

Thorburn, Hugh G. ed. (1996) *Party Politics in Canada.* Scarborough, Ontario: Prentice Hall Canada Inc.

The Government Executive Series (2002) *eGovernment Leadership – Realizing the Vision.* Chicago, Illinois: Accenture.

Wilhelm, Anthony G. (2000) *Democracy in the Digital Age: Challenges to Political Life in Cyberspace.* New York, New York: Routledge.

Woodley, Bill (2001) *The Impact of Transformative Technologies on Governance: Some Lessons from History.* Ottawa, Ontario: Institute of Governance.

Notes

[1] Thomas L. Freidman *The Lexus and the Olive Tree* (New York: First Anchor Books, 2000)

[2] See Philippe C. Schmitter *Parties Are Not What They Once Were* in Political Parties and Democracy, Larry Diamond and Richard Gunther ed.

[3] ibid.

[4] Page ix *Political Parties and Democracy* Larry Diamond and Richard Gunther ed.

[5] ibid.

[6] Philippe C. Schmitter, *Parties Are Not What They Used To Be* in Political Parties and

Democracy, Larry Diamond and Richard Gunther ed. (Baltimore: John Hopkins Hopkins Press, 2001), 74.

[7] John Meisel and Matthew Mendelsohn, *Meteor? Phoenix? Chameleon? The Decline and Transformation of Party in Canada* in Party Politics in Canada, Hugh G. Thorburn ed. (Scarborough: Prentice-Hall, 1996), 179.

[8] Robin Clarke *New Democratic Processes: better decisions, stronger democracy*, (London: IPPR, 2002), 1-2.

[9] R. Kenneth Carty, William Cross and Lisa Young, *Rebuilding Canadian Party Politics* (Vancouver: UBC Press, 2000) 117.

[10] Ibid, 121.

[11] Thomas L. Freidman *The Lexus and the Olive Tree* (New York: Anchor Books, 2000), 65.

[12] Frederick Newell *loyalty.com* (New York: McGraw-Hill, 2000), 2.

[13] Don Tapscott, David Ticoll, Alex Lowy *Digital Capital* (Boston: Harvard Business School Press, 2000), 192.

[14] David Osborne and Ted Gaebler *Reiventing Government* (Reading: Addison-Wesley, 1992)

[15] Communication Canada – Fall 2001; Listening to Canadians 2001 as cited in Government On-line and Canadians (Ottawa: Government of Canada, 2002).

[16] Accenture Report *eGovernment Leadership : Realizing the Vision* (Chicago: Accenture, 2002).

[17] Accenture Report *Customer Relationship Management: A Blueprint for Government* (Chicago: Accenture, 2001).

[18] Lawrence Grossman *The Electronic Republic* (New York: Penguin Books, 1996), 119.

[19] Bill Cross *Teledemocracy: Canadian Political Parties Listening To Their Constituents* in *Digital Democracy* Cynthia J. Alexander and Leslie A. Pal ed. (Toronto: Oxford University Press, 1998), 133.

[20] See Richard Davis *The Web of Politics* (New York: Oxford University Press, 1999) and Stephen Coleman ed. *Elections in the age of the Internet: Lessons from the United States* (London: Hansard Society, 2001)

[21] Bill Cross *Teledemocracy: Canadian Political Parties Listening To Their Constituents* in *Digital Democracy* Cynthia J. Alexander and Leslie A. Pal ed. (Toronto: Oxford University Press, 1998), 133.

[22] William Cross and Lisa Young *Contours of Political Party Membership in Canada* (2001), 6.

[23] Bruce Bimber *The Internet and Citizen Communication with Government: Does the Medium Matter* in Anthony G. Wilhelm, Democracy in the Digital Age (New York: Routledge, 2000), 27.

[24] Bruce Bimber *Toward an Empirical Mapping of Political Participation on the Internet* in Anthony G. Wilhelm, Democracy in the Digital Age (New York: Routledge, 2000), 27.

[25] Pippa Norris *Digital Divide* (New York: Cambridge University Press, 2001), 190.

[26] Bill Woodley *The Impact of Transformative Technologies on Governance: Some Lessons from History.* (Ottawa: Institute of Governance, 2002), 5.

[27] Pippa Norris *Digital Divide* (New York: Cambridge University Press, 2001), 167.

[28] Thomas B. Riley. *E-Democracy in the Future: Will We See Significant Change?* (Ottawa: The Riley Report, 2002), 6.

[29] *E-Voter 2001: Dawning of a New Era – Measuring the Initial Impact of the Internet on Political and Advocacy Communication* (E-Voter Institute, 2001), 2.

[30] Robin Clarke, *New Democratic Processes* (London:IPPR, 2002), 53.

Political Reforms in Canada:
Strengthening Representative Government[1]

W.T. *Stanbury*
John L. *Howard*
Sean *Moore*

1. *Introduction*

THE PURPOSE OF THIS paper is to propose a number of reforms to the
way government operates in Canada and the manner in which it
relates to the citizenry. Our focus is on the institutions and processes of the federal government, though we believe the proposals
we're forwarding also have direct relevance to provincial governments as well.

We believe that this is a critical juncture in the history of this
nation. The three oldest political parties in the country are all at
various stages of selecting new leaders. Such times are typically
pivotal in the consideration of new approaches to leadership and
public policy and in attracting public attention to such matters.

We believe that any political party—or individual candidate for
national leadership—which wants to impress the electorate with
its vision for the future of this country needs to address the fundamentals of how this nation is governed and the role citizens can
play in the governing.

We believe a series of reforms should be implemented as soon as
possible because Canada has been in the throes of a crisis of legitimacy with respect to its political institutions and processes for some

years (see Simpson, 2001). There is considerable evidence that an increasing number of people are being "turned off" by politics and have "lost faith in the system." As we note below, Canadians' traditional respect for government has declined notably over the past decade. A study for the Canadian Policy Research Networks (2002) found that Canadians rank the matter of democratic rights and participation first among nine quality of life indicators, that between 1990 and 2000 their willingness to vote declined,[2] and so did their satisfaction with the electoral process and their belief that citizens have input into what government does.

Political reforms such as those proposed below are not usually what pollsters call "top of mind" issues with many Canadians: but we believe they are more important than has yet been realized by most politicians.[3] And by any objective measure, they are, in fact, *very* important.

The substantive content of public policies and the ways in which they are created and implemented are in large part a reflection of the design of the political *system*. The reforms proposed below are intended to make substantial changes in the system. We are confident that by changing key characteristics of the system it is likely that the federal government will be more representative and more responsive to citizens—those in whose name the system is supposed to work. It is also likely that the federal government will become more efficient and effective because of improvements in the ways of holding it accountable.

In preparing the proposed list of reforms, we have made two assumptions: a) that Canada will remain a constitutional monarchy for the foreseeable future, and b) what is described as "a reform" consists of several components necessary to achieve the effects desired.

The first assumption is purely a matter of pragmatism. To push for a republic would likely arouse strong emotional opposition which would effectively block highly desirable substantive changes. We recognize that some of the changes we strongly desire cannot be made within the framework of a constitutional monarchy, which implies that the Westminster model will remain in place. That model, however, can be modified to achieve important reforms. This is another case of perfection being the enemy of the good.

All of the reforms described below can be implemented by either a) the simple order of the PM, or b) by amending an ordinary statute. None require a change in the Constitution. All could be put in place in one session of Parliament.

The reforms have been grouped under eight headings.
- Strengthening Parliament
- Reducing Concentration of Power in the Hands of the Prime Minister
- Improving Access to Information
- Creating New Rules Governing Political Parties
- Changing the Laws Governing Financing of Political Parties
- Improving Accountability of Ministers and Deputy Ministers
- Creating More Opportunities for Direct Democracy
- Improving Public Consultations and Citizen Engagement

In each section, before listing the proposed reforms, we sketch the rationale or justification for such changes under the heading "discussion."

2. Canadians' Attitudes

Two recent polls provide new and, in one case, surprising evidence on Canadians' attitudes toward politics. A national poll by Leger Marketing conducted in early April 2002 found that 69% of respondents believe the federal political system is "corrupt" or "somewhat corrupt." Only 26% said it was "not very corrupt" or "not at all" corrupt. The comparable figures for the provincial level were 68% and 26% respectively. Some 53% of respondents described municipal political systems as highly or somewhat corrupt (Canadian Press, 2002a). Further, 80% wanted to see a major reform in the methods of awarding of government contracts. And 24% of respondents said that they believe that the political system was either not very democratic or not democratic at all (Ibid).

The more surprising data—in light of the decades of accepted wisdom that Canadians have *greater* trust in their governments than do Americans—were those generated by a national poll of about 1,000 Canadians and Americans in May 2002. These polls found that 51% of Canadians said that they have little, if any, trust in the federal government; for Americans the comparable figure was 30%. While 65% of Americans said they have a great deal of trust in their state governments, only 51% of Canadians had a great deal of trust in their provincial governments (Lawlor, 2002). Andrew Parkin, assistant director of the Centre for Research and Information on Canada, co-sponsor of the two polls, said that Canadians' lack of trust in government started in the early 1990's at the end of the two-term Mulroney Government and has continued since then. This helps to explain the decline in voter turnout over the last handful of federal general elections, he said.

Electors vary greatly in their level of knowledge[4] or even interest in public policy.[5] About one-third of electors do *not* vote in federal general elections in Canada (compared to about 50% in the U.S.). Columnist Jeffrey Simpson (2002a) reports on a recent study on the reasons why voter turnout has declined in Canada over the past few decades (to 61% in the November 2000 general election). Canadians who come to voting age after 1988 accounted for much of the decline. They are less engaged in both politics and other kinds of civic activity such as joining interest groups. They pay less attention to politics, are less well informed, and a smaller fraction vote. We believe that the political reforms we propose could increase Canadians' sense of personal efficacy with respect to politics and participation would increase. They will certainly increase the efficacy of both Government backbenchers and opposition MPs.[6]

3. Strengthening Parliament
3.1   Discussion

Currently, both the Legislative and Executive branches of government are now "integrated" under the control of the Prime Minister as long as he heads a majority government. In effect, the PM has a monopoly over the supply of new bills and also has the means to see they are enacted with no change he does not want.

In general, the independence and power of both houses of the legislature must be increased. But it cannot be increased so much that the essential design characteristics of cabinet/responsible government (that is the Westminster model) are threatened.

At present, the Senate[7] is largely a patronage vehicle for the PM, although some Senators do produce useful committee investigations and reports (e.g., see the reports by Senator Kirby). We argue that the Senate should regularly pose a disciplined challenge to the Government which will continue to effectively control the Commons if it has a majority. Thus the Senate should not be a clone of the House in terms of party standings. Different timing and methods of election are necessary to achieve that goal.

The role of opposition parties needs to be strengthened. Successive governments have put in place a series of measures over time apparently aimed at limiting and channeling the role of opposition parties which has helped to make them into what they are today, e.g., a) treating all committees as miniature replicas of the House with the whips on. This limits their ability to improve new legislation—unless the minister responsible adopts proposed changes as his/her own; b) giving opposition parties very little money with which to develop a research base necessary for the development of informed and reasoned alternatives; c) blocking virtually all private member's bills (although the PM said recently that he will allow them to be given First Reading!);[8] d) making it impossible for the opposition to modify the annual expenditure budget (i.e., the Estimates); e) seeing that Parliament reviews subordinate legislation only long after it has become law; and f) setting the time allotted to debates and the use of closure, notably major new bill, the Estimates and revenue budget. The result is to make Parliament the slave of a schedule determined by the Government.

The Government could do much to enhance the role of opposition parties in Canada's Parliament, while retaining its authority to govern and to be responsible for how it governs.

If the opposition is to have greater weight in the House of Commons, however, it must start with the injunction "physician, heal thyself." Sean Moore (2002c) put it this way:

> The answer, or at least one element of it, rests in part with the notion of devising and presenting alternatives, looking and sounding like a government-in-waiting. For opposition members, that means a new level of discipline, sophistication, focus, creativity, political courage and just plain hard work.

It is not enough for the opposition to criticize. It must put forward remedies or even broad alternatives. The latter is impossible to do in legislative terms.[9]   It is possible for opposition parties to develop their policies in some detail so that a) the bases for their criticisms and proposed changes are clear, and b) voters in the next elections will know for what the party stands and is likely to implement.

The current "first-past-the-post" or more formally, "single member plurality" method of electing MPs has some notable weaknesses: a) Much of the electorate is not represented in the House of Commons in any way at all; in the last general election, all opposition parties garnered 59.2% of the popular vote, but gained only 42.5% of the 301 seats; b) entire regions may be incompletely represented, e.g., in the November 2000 general election, only one-half of Ontario voters chose the Liberal Party, but that party obtained 100 of the 103 seats in Ontario; c) following a general election, only Government MPs can have much influence provided there is a majority government. Even then, only cabinet ministers have any real power—and they are appointed, shuffled or fired by the PM.[10] Over the last three decades, an increasing amount of power has been exercised by the Prime Minister assisted by officials in the PCO and PMO (see Savoie, 1999). Prime Minister Trudeau once said that when they were off Parliament Hill, MPs were "nobodies." Sadly, when they are in their offices or the Commons chamber backbench MPs are almost nobodies.[11] Party discipline in Canada is exercised more stringently than in the U.K., for example. Successive PMs have made it clear that what they want Government MPs to be cheerleaders for any initiative the PM proposes.[12] Because the PM has a large number of carrots and sticks, almost all ambitious backbenchers—those seeking a cabinet post—are very careful to mute any criticisms and never to voice them in public. Sean Moore (2000) describes the problem as follows:

> [There is] a conviction that's becoming infectious on Parliament Hill – that the legislative branch of Canadian government has come to exist only in theory. "We've created an illusion that Parliament works," says [Toronto MP Dennis] Mills. A prime ministerial aide and business executive before be-

lic-policy process up close and personal for much
of his adult life. "The reality of Ottawa is that
senior officials in departments and PCO, along
with ministerial staff and lobbyists are the people
who make the policies." According to Mills, MPs
just aren't in the game. "By the time something
gets to Parliament, it's baked."

The most frequently recommended "solution" to the problems
sketched above is some form of "proportional representation" of
which "there are literally dozens of variations," as Gordon Gibson
(2002b, p. 26) points out.[13] Note that in 1984 Jean Chrétien said
that if he were Prime Minister he would implement at least partial
proportional representation (see Johnson, 2002). Proportional representation is not without its own problems, so it might be best to
apply it on a limited basis—starting with the Senate.

3.2   Proposed Reforms

- Create an elected Senate.[14] The PM could *begin* the shift to
  an elected Senate by announcing that all future appointees
  shall be elected by voters in the relevant province.[15]
- Ensure that more votes in Parliament will be "free votes"
  and that there will be fewer votes when party discipline
  will prevail (aside from those which involve a true matter of
  confidence).
- Ensure that there is a realistic opportunity for more private
  member's bills to become law. For example, set aside 25%
  of the time devoted to debating Government bills for
  private member's bills. Require at least two hours debate
  on private member's bills that are endorsed by the two
  largest opposition parties.
- Provide more money for opposition parties to do research
  and develop policy options.
- Strengthen the role of committees in reviewing legislation
  and increasing their independence (e.g., requiring that an
  opposition member be the co-chair). This will also include
  giving them more money, some of which may be used to
  hire permanent, professional staff.

- Require voting by secret ballot for the election of chairs of House of Commons committees (see John Reynolds, 2002).
- Require near perfect equality in the size of electoral districts (except for previous constitutional deals such as four MPs for PEI).[16]
- Require that new statutes or major amendments be accompanied by the related regulations so both can be considered in the House, Senate and committees at the same time.
- Specify time limits for *ex post* review of subordinate legislation (currently by the Joint Standing Committee for the Scrutiny of Regulations).

4. *Reduce the Excessive Concentration of Power in the Hands of the Prime Minister*
   4.1 *Discussion*

Very simply, the Prime Minister (PM) is by far the most powerful person in Canada (see Savoie, 1999). Corporate titans are far better paid (at least ten times as much, not counting stock options), but they are pikers when it comes to the amount of power they possess relative to that which can be exercised by the PM (see Stanbury, 2002b). Yet Canadians seem rather comfortable with this fact— perhaps because they do not appreciate the full extent of the PM's power.

The Westminster model developed in England over more than three centuries concentrates power in the person of the PM. It does so by giving the head of the Executive (the PM) control over the Legislature so long as the PM retains the confidence of the House of Commons. When his party has a majority of seats in the Commons,[17] the PM has almost complete control over that body. The PM controls both the supply of legislative initiatives and the votes to enact them. Should the Senate object because it is dominated by the appointees of previous Prime Ministers of another party, the current PM can create more Senators who will see things his way.[18]

Here is a summary list of the powers of the PM.[19]

- The PM sets the legislative priorities of his Government (to the extent he desires to do so). The PM can almost always obtain the legislation he wants so long as his party has a majority of the seats in the House.

- The PM appoints, shuffles and fires cabinet ministers who collectively lead the Executive. It is the prospect of becoming a minister (hence exercising some power) that gives the PM great control over ambitious MPs. The PM also apppoints all the parliamentary secretaries—the men and women being tested for appointment to the cabinet. The PM decides on the number, responsibilities and relative authority of cabinet committees.
- The PM appoints all members of the Supreme Court of Canada and, through the Minister of Justice, he controls the appointment of all other federal judges (see Tibbetts, 2002). The PM also appoints all Deputy Ministers, all heads of federal Crown corporations (as well as their directors) and regulatory agencies, and also the head of the RCMP.
- The PM appoints all senators (and so he can put key bagmen and political organizers on the public payroll).
- The PM appoints the chief of defense staff, although the Governor General is the titular commander in chief of Canada's armed forces. It appears that the PM has the authority to declare war and later have his decision ratified by Parliament.
- The PM effectively controls the flow of subordinate legislation[20] whose sheer volume is greater than that of legislation passed by Parliament.
- If he wishes, the PM can substitute rule by PMO officials for true cabinet government. According to Gordon Gibson, "Jean Chrétien's ministers are just plain vegetables when it comes to great decisions of state. Such things are decided by the PM and his senior advisors—who are rarely ministers" (quoted in Fisher, 1999).
- The PM is *primus inter pares* within the cabinet. He can "out vote" all of his ministers at any time, although if he does so regularly he may precipitate some resignations or even a full-scale revolt.
- The PM effectively controls several thousand order-in-council appointments (and an increasing number of these are of the "at pleasure" variety, as opposed to "during good behavior").

- While the Queen appoints the Governor General (her representative in Canada and head of state in Canada), it is the PM who advises the Queen whom to appoint.
- The PM decides on the dates of by-elections and the next general election (subject to the five-year limit in the constitution).
- He controls the flow of patronage (to the extent desired). And the PM has unique ability to target his (her) riding with pork barrel "goodies" (see Cameron, 1995).
- The PM can spend any amount of taxpayer's money on scientific public opinion polls (see Feschuk, 1998) and keep the results secret for sufficient time to exploit their strategic advantage.
- The PM can decide on the design/responsibilities of executive departments to the extent he is interested in the machinery of government.

Against this plentitude of powers, is the British tradition of providing leadership while practicing the virtues of self restraint and moderation. These virtues have generally been in short supply in Canadian Prime Ministers. The *actual* amount of power exercised by the PM directly depends more on his (her) energy, style, values (e.g., willingness to delegate), confidence in colleagues, subordinates, etc. than what is set out in the law. Over time, Canadian PMs have increased their direct exercise of power by greatly expanding the staff in the PMO and PCO (see Savoie, 1999).

Diane Francis (2002), editor of the *Financial Post,* argues that corruption within the federal government is largely due to the concentration of power.

The biggest single reason behind corruption in this country is that the Canadian version of the Parliamentary system is a poor excuse for democracy. There are no checks and balances. The Prime Minister dictates to Cabinet, Cabinet to party whips and party whips to backbenchers. It's a genteel dictatorship, punctuated by elections planned timing-wise to benefit the incumbent. Little wonder the vast majority of the electorate don't bother to participate.

4.2   Proposed Reforms
These reforms must be taken together with those
listed in section 3.2 above.

- Establish fixed (4 year) election dates (except when the Government loses the confidence of the House).[21]
- Reduce the number of Order in Council Appointees from over 3,000 to, say, about 1,000 (to reduce opportunities for patronage). Thus the others would be Public Service Commission appointees.
- Establish criteria in regulations specifying which order-in-council appointments are "at pleasure" and which are "with tenure subject to a good behavior standard."
- Require that all senior order in council appointees (deputy ministers, heads of regulatory administrative agencies and Crown corporations) be confirmed by a standing committee of the House of Commons.
- Amend the *Supreme Court Act* to require that a newly-created independent advisory committee generate a list of candidates for appointment to the Supreme Court of Canada from whom the Prime Minister would nominate. The nominee would then have to be confirmed by Parliament after a public hearing by a committee (see Ziegel, 2002). Gordon Gibson (2002) argues that Supreme Court of Canada judges "should be appointed only with the advice and consent of the *provinces* [because] the Court arbitrates between the federal and provincial governments. Who ever heard of an arbitral panel appointed by one side?"

5. *Improve Access to Information*
   5.1   *Discussion*

One of the main characteristics of Canada's version of the Westminster model of government is a high degree of administrative secrecy. In whose name is this practice maintained? The official answer is "the people." Their elected representatives, selected by the Prime Minister to form the cabinet (which effectively controls both the Executive and Legislative branches), function largely behind a heavy veil of secrecy in order to more effectively conduct the public's business. Or so we are told. In fact, the main beneficiaries of pervasive administrative secrecy are the PM, his ministers, the public service, and the PM's unelected advisors outside the public service.

In any system of government claiming to be a democracy, citizens need relevant, truthful and authoritative information if the system is to work properly for several reasons. First, citizens need such information to assess the performance of their representative and also that of the Government of the day. This is the first step in holding the Government accountable, and accountability is at the core of democratic government (see Stanbury, 2002c).[22] Second, citizens need to be well informed so as to be better able to participate in debates about public policy—including assessing the proposals of opposition parties. Information is the currency of politics. Third, citizens need information to try to understand how the world works, i.e., knowledge for its own sake. An individual's sense of affect depends heavily upon the knowledge they possess. Fourth, citizens need relevant and unbiased information to act as an antidote against the heavily manipulated flow of information supplied by government.

In his final report, Information Commissioner John Grace (1998, p. A5), argued that "a culture of secrecy still flourishes in too many high places even after 15 years of life under the *Access to Information Act*."[23] Grace indicated that many senior public servants do not trust the public with the information created by their taxes and this has important implications for accountability.

The insult is equal only to the intellectual arrogance of it all. The commitment, by word and deed, to the principle of accountability through transparency has been too often, faltering and weak-kneed. It should not be a surprise that some of those who wield power also recoil from the accountability which transparency brings. (Grace, 1998, p. A5)

The current Information Commissioner (John Reid) indicates that he has found considerable evidence that senior public servants are "trying to avoid accountably by failing to create and keep appropriate records" (Reid, 2002, p. 2). Further, within days of passage of the *Access to Information Act* in 1983, "the Privy Council Office attempted to extinguish a substantive right [access to Discussion Papers going to cabinet] merely by changing the name of a record [calling them memoranda to Cabinet]...(Reid, 2001, p.3). A judge of the Federal Court Trial Division agreed with him (Federal Court, 2001).

Canada has few and only weak tools with which to fight government secrecy. First, access to government information is *not* a constitutionally protected right. But freedom of expression is so protected in the 1982 Charter of Rights and Freedoms. Second, there are obvious design flaws in the *ATI Act*, e.g., as John Reid (2001) points out, the exclusion of cabinet confidences (not merely subject to exemption—hence reviewable by the courts) amounts to a "loophole" big enough to drive an 18-wheeler through. Why should the *Access to Information Act* provide that cabinet documents are automatically kept secret for 20 years after which time they may be requested under the Act—thus putting the onus on the person requesting they be made public. It is only after 30 years that cabinet documents are made widely available through the National Archives. But this practice is hardly the same as posting them all— with a good index—on a website hence providing truly easy access at low cost for almost anyone.

Third, the *Canada Evidence Act* allows a cabinet minister to refuse to disclose information in both civil and criminal actions on the grounds that it is a cabinet confidence. Note, however, that the Supreme Court of Canada has recently put some limits on the cabinet's discretion in these situations—see Makin (2002). Fourth, why should current or former senior officials be able to "clam up" and refuse to answer questions of a parliamentary committee on matters on which it is authorized to hold hearings? See Le Blanc (2002).

Both officials and ministers very strongly resist any proposal to reduce secrecy because that is tantamount to an effort to, diffuse power, or constrain the power of the cabinet or Prime Minister. Secrecy is used to contain critical analyses, to curb the diffusion of inconvenient facts, to cover-up errors both large and small, and to disguise the crassest examples of the political calculus that informs so many of the decisions by ministers. Perhaps, most important, secrecy is used to bury the alternative policy recommendations that were considered and rejected.[24] Improvements in accountability to citizens begin with a major reduction in institutionalized secrecy.

5.2 Proposed Reforms

- Limit the exemptions and so broaden the coverage of the *Access to Information Act*.[25]
- Require all Crown corporations and the new quasi-govern mental agencies like Canada Customs and Revenue Agency be subject to the *ATI Act*.[26]
- Increase the financial resources given to the Information Commissioner.
- Shorten the period of confidentiality for cabinet documents (say to 10 years instead of 30!).[27]
- Speed-up challenges in the courts (both sides).
- Section 8 of the *Privacy Act* should be amended such that the discretionary power respecting release of information in the hands of any government institution is removed to an official reporting directly to Parliament, ideally an amalgamated office of the Information and Privacy Commissioner.[28]
- Create rules which encourage "whistleblowers" to disclose evidence of illegality or of improper administration of government programs after seeking to correct the problem through the hierarchy have failed (see May 2002). Further, legitimate whistleblowers must be protected from reprisals and any other form of punishment (see Winsor, 2002).

6. *Create New Rules Governing Political Parties*
   6.1 *Discussion*

Recent experience with party leadership races and particularly the unofficial leadership race to succeed Jean Chrétien as leader of the Liberal Party (which eventually forced him to announce his planned retirement) provides a great deal of evidence for the proposition that the federal government should propose new rules governing political parties, and leadership races in particular.

Very briefly, the case for the regulation of leadership contests of federal political parties appears to be as follows: First, leadership races are of great public importance because the leader of one of the parties is or will become Prime Minister (PM). Second, as noted above, the Westminster model of government concentrates truly enormous power in the hands of the PM. Thus it is logical to ensure that the means by which he or she comes to power are appropriate for democratic society. Third, in general elections, the electors in only one electoral district can vote for/against a party's leader and potential PM. This fact of the Westminster model increases the desirability of electing party leaders in a fair and proper manner. Fourth, some private entities are too important to society not to intervene in their governance. Corporations are the dominant form of organization engaged in economic activity. They are primarily private bodies, but their *internal* governance is subject to extensive government regulation through corporation acts. This is done to achieve public policy goals. A similar argument applies to political parties. Hugh Segal (2002), head of the Institute for Research on Public Policy, has argued cogently that, "In the end, political parties are not the property of their membership or leadership to be used as electoral machines only. They are public instruments, financed by Canadian taxpayers, and primarily for the purpose of facilitating democratic expression, economic performance, social progress and real engagement on issues." Fifth, the regulation of leadership races by the parties themselves has proven to be varied and of limited effectiveness.[29] Columnist Andrew Coyne (2002) noted how loose those rules were in the Liberal Party.[30]

> Wait, wait: You're saying Cabinet ministers could take money from the industries they regulated, indeed from the very companies they might have subsidized out of public funds? And that, as far as party leadership campaigns were concerned, ministers of the Crown could rake in all this private cash without even having to declare it? This is a joke, right?

On June 12, 2002, the Prime Minister established some new "Guidelines to Govern/Ministerial Activities for Personal Political Purposes" that deal with fundraising for leadership races: a) Ministers may opt to put contributions in a blind trust (after consultation with the Office of the Ethics Counsellor) that will be disclosed no later than 30 days before a leadership convention, or b) Donations to a minister's leadership campaign including contributions in kind, collected outside a blind trust or which otherwise become known to a minister, must be disclosed every 60 days (Prime Minister's Office, 2002). Further, all contributions to a minister's leadership campaign received *before* the publication of the new Guidelines must be disclosed with 30 days (i.e., by July 11, 2002). Finally, the new Guidelines do not apply to "campaign expenditures," nor to "funds raised for a political party." Andrew Coyne (2002g) explains the weaknesses in these proposals.

The new *Guidelines* focus on "funds raised for personal political purposes," and they also refer funds raised for a leadership campaign as if they are the same thing. Not so. When a minister raises funds as a candidate he is obviously doing so for "personal political purposes." Indeed, some of the money for some ministers' leadership campaigns came from the surplus they generated during the November 2000 general election. For example, John Manley's riding association contributed $96,000 to his campaign, out of a total of $171,950 raised (Trickey, 2002). Allan Rock's riding association collected $236,592 in 2001 (not an election year!) from corporations and individuals. The association could give it to Rock's leadership campaign (Laghi, 2002b).

6.2   Proposed Reforms
These reforms should be considered along with those in section 7.2 below.

Disclosure:[31] Require full and prompt disclosure (i.e., monthly) of all contributions and expenditures by leadership candidates whether there is an official or unofficial leadership race in progress. The timing of disclosure should be quarterly prior to official race (see below) and monthly during the official race (both one week after the end of the period). For each donation of $200 or more, the same disclosure requirements as now apply to registered parties and candidates in the *Canada Elections Act (CEA)* should be applied to leadership races.

Unofficial Races: Require prompt and extensive disclosure of all revenues and expenditure by any person (natural or legal) who spent say $25,000 or more in any quarter on any activity aimed, directly or indirectly, at making a person leader of a registered political party or made with the purpose of assisting the incumbent leader to retain his/her position. With respect to the identification of donors of $200 or more, the same rules would apply as now apply to registered parties and candidates under the *CEA*. Here is another alternative: require a potential leadership candidate, prior to the announcement of an official leadership race, to appoint a trustee to maintain a confidential trust whose sources and uses of funds would have to be publicly disclosed at once when an official leadership race begins.[32] This approach should help potential candidates avoid the problem of being undermined by the incumbent leader. Presumably, the blind trust would only be created once a potential candidate raised and/or spent, say, $25,000 in any quarter.

Definition of Eligibility to Vote in a Leadership Race: Require each registered party[33] to promulgate a set of rules defining eligibility of persons to vote in the next leadership race within one year of the selection of a new leader. (Parties should give serious consideration to having MPs vote first and have the result made public *before* the rest of the members vote on the next leader.) These rules could *not* be changed without the approval of the Chief Electoral Officer or an umpire appointed by him (following a public hearing) until *after* the next leadership race. The objective is to eliminate the strategic manipulation of the rules to influence the result of a leadership race. These rules must include the "cut-off" date for signing-up new members, the supplying of the official list of party members eligible to vote in the leadership race, and specify the method of voting (e.g., by telephone, by mail, at polling places, at a Convention, etc.)

Leadership Review: Require each registered party to promulgate rules under which the periodic review of the incumbent leader must occur.[34] These rules would have to be established within one year of the election of a leader and they could not be changed without the approval of the Chief Electoral Officer (who would be requested to hold a public hearing in the matter) until after the next general election.[35]

Membership Lists: Require parties to maintain a central, computerized list of all members that is updated at least once per year and is available to the public[36] and to leadership candidates at nominal cost. Require party's to report annually in January to the CEO on the number of members as of December 31st.

Foreign Sources: The rules would specify that no foreign money or foreign volunteers are entitled to participate in the leadership contests of federal parties.

Expenditure Limits: Parties would be required to establish limits on expenditures during both official and unofficial leadership races. They would have to establish adequate methods of enforcing such limits (i.e., subject to review by the CEO at a public hearing).[37]

Income Tax Credit: Leadership candidates would not be permitted to use, directly or indirectly, the income tax credit currently available for political contributions to registered parties and candidates. (This practice is tolerated by the CEO at present.)

Party Membership: Eligibility for membership in a registered party would be subject to the person and party being able to meet the following criteria:

- The person does not hold membership in any other party. Since each party would be required to publish its list of members annually in an electronic form this would be easy to check.
- The individual fills out the application form.
- The information requested by the party on the application form is substantially correct.
- The person pays the required fee.
- The person is a Canadian citizen who is also an elector.[38]

7. *Change the Laws Governing the Financing of Parties, Candidates, etc.*
   7.1   *Discussion*

Since the mid-1970s, Canada has sought to greatly limit the role that money plays in election campaigns (generally, see Stanbury, 1991, 2000a). The general approach has been to limit campaign expenditures, but not contributions. Disclosure of both is also central to the regime. Although amendments were made to the *Canada Elections Act* effective September 1, 2000, extensive changes are needed.

What is wrong with the rules governing party and candidate finances in the *Canada Elections Act*, effective September 1, 2000? Here is a brief summary:

- There is no federal regulation of leadership races (except by parties and these may not be enforced).[39]

- There is an excessively long delay in reporting by *parties*. It is six months after the *end* of the calendar year for parties, electoral district associations and trust funds. However, it is only four months after the election for candidates to file data on their revenues and expenditures.
- The penalties are inadequate, e.g., Canadian Alliance was over a month late in filing its report for 2001, but no penalty was imposed; CUPE failed to report spending $150,000 as a "third party" but paid a fine of only $1,000 (see Waldie, 2002).
- There are questionable uses of the tax credit, e.g., contributions to leadership races;[40] for contributions to the federal party that are later transferred to the provincial or local level (by NDP); to cover convention fees (see Stanbury, 1991; Stanbury, 2000a).
- Donors can hide the source of contributions by donating to provincial bodies which are later transferred to various reporting entities, e.g., federal party or candidate. The source of the donations behind the transfer is not disclosed.
- EDAs can receive large surpluses from candidates at the end of a general election (or by-election). This creates a discretionary "slush fund" for whoever controls the EDA—usually the sitting MP.
- EDAs can receive donations (but not issue tax receipts) in non election years. The money can be used to benefit the incumbent MP. See Laghi (2002b).
- The regulation of EDAs is obscure and convoluted[41] and needs to be simplified along the lines as in Ontario.
- Individuals or corporations can donate fairly large sums with out the party or candidate having to disclose the donor's name via multiple cash contributions under $200.
- There is excessive regulation of "third parties." The expendi ture limits are too low. The reporting burden is too great for those spending small amounts (see Stanbury, 2002d).
- At present, the *Canada Elections Act* requires that the official candidates of each party be endorsed by the party leader. Thus it is not sufficient to win the nomination at the local constituency level even with the strong support of many members of the party at the local level. This rule obviously gives the leader great control over dissidents or potential dissi

dents.[42] If MPs are to be representatives of the persons living in a local area, then they should be selected by locals, not the party leader. At the same time, it seems reasonable to suggest that where a candidate is not endorsed by the party leader, that this fact be required to be disclosed on all the candidate's literature, signs, commercials, and on the ballots.

• At present, there are almost no government rules dealing with nomination races—except that the expenditures by the winner are deducted from the allowable "election expenses" for candidates in that riding in the general election. David Marley (2002) argues that nomination and leadership races are the "fulcrum of the democratic process. They are where one gets maximum leverage per unit of effort or money expended. As the late, former Mayor of Chicago, Richard Daley, was apparently fond of saying, "I don't care who does the electing, just let me do the running."

In the June 12, 2002 News Release, the Prime Minister's Office (2002) said that there will be changes to the rules governing the financing of parties and candidates "to ensure that all contributions and expenditures are fully and clearly disclosed."[43] The changes will specify that:

• All transfers of funds from provincial political entities as well as from trust funds and local electoral district associations (EDAs) name the original contributors to these bodies;[44]
• Stronger enforcement provisions;[45] and
• All contributions be receipted (those under $200 are now exempt).

There will be other disclosure requirements of contributions and expenses incurred by a) contestants for the leadership of a party, and b) contestants for party endorsement.

Bryden (2002b) states that the Government is planning legislation (to be announced in the Throne speech) that will a) require full disclosure of donations to riding associations and to leadership candidates,[46] and b) limit the amount that may be contributed by any contributor (there are no limits at present).

Note that the PCO (2002) document spoke of a) developing tax-based approaches to further facilitate the making of contributions by individuals (currently the maximum tax credit is $500 and is reached when annual contributions total $1075); and b) developing, if necessary, other governmental subsidies of the electoral process to compensate for the smaller pool of contributors and/or smaller amounts given. (It is estimated that, over a complete electoral cycle—usually four years—that taxpayers finance about 40% of the total expenditures by candidates and parties—see Stanbury, 1991).[47]

We recognize that even if the reforms we propose below are adopted, that we have not dealt with symmetrically with all the entities which seek to influence public policy in Canada. We refer to the growing importance of interest groups in Canadian politics (see Stanbury, 1993). The crucial point is to recognize that much more money is spent *between* elections to influence public policy than is spent on election campaigns to do the same thing indirectly by influencing who gets into power. While we believe that their revenues and expenditures also merit disclosure, we have not had sufficient time to formulate appropriate rules in this paper.

7.2   Proposed Reforms

- Limit the total amount of contributions to any political entity during the course of a calendar year to, say, $10,000 and adjust it annually for inflation. (There is no limit at present, although the maximum tax credit is $500.)[48]
- Consider limiting the *source* of contributions to electors.[49] (This would eliminate corporations and unions as donors, and has been the law in Quebec since 1976.)
- Increase the income tax credit for contributions from individuals, i.e., electors. (The amount of the increase will depend on whether donations are limited only to those by electors.)
- Require more frequent reporting by all political entitities (one month after the end of each quarter—except when a general election occurs).
- Make party or candidate trust funds, electoral district associations, leadership candidates, so-called "third parties, etc. *reporting entities* which are obligated to use the same form de-

scribing their revenues, expenditures and transfers provided by the Chief Electoral Officer.[50] If it is used, all monies will be tracked and all donors identified. There will be no more "black holes."

- Require parties to establish rules re financing leadership races (e.g., limits), but mandate detailed and frequent disclosure for all such races. (Recall section 6.2)

- Limit amount/value of contributions in kind in the form of efforts by volunteers. (At present, lobbyists can effectively "donate" $50,000 in time and not be recorded.) In general the rules governing volunteers in the *Canada Elections Act* need to be revised to close the loophole which permits certain professionals to, in effect, make large contributions in kind which are not reported.

- Eliminate the requirement that the party leader must sign the nomination papers of each candidate running under the party's banner. If the leader does not endorse a candidate, the candidate would be obliged to disclose this fact on his/her advertising materials and on the ballot.

- Establish a *separate* limit on individual's expenditures in nomination races equal to 20% of the allowable "election expenses" in that district in the previous federal election. (This would result in a limit of about $13,600 in the next general election.)

- Require all persons seeking nomination as a candidate who spends over $1,000 to file a statement of their revenues and expenditures within three months using the form specified by the Chief Electoral Officer.

8. *Improve the Accountability of Ministers
    and Deputy Ministers*[51]
    8.1   Discussion

The concept of accountability is essential to what we mean by democratic government. The need for accountability flows from the delegation of authority, the exercise of discretion and the possibility that such authority will be used in ways not anticipated or approved by those persons who delegated authority in order to achieve the benefits of division of labour. In a popular democracy, citizens, collectively, are the ultimate principal; elected representatives are their agents. These agents are also principals who, through the legislature, delegate authority to a host of departments and agencies that make up the sprawling executive branch of government.

It is the necessity to exercise power[52] in the context of a democracy that generates the need for accountability. Power is a conundrum. It may be necessary to get things done and to do so efficiently.[53] It is necessary to use coercion to ensure peace and order for the vast majority in the face of the disruptive behavior of the few. The central problem for all political systems is to reconcile government's use of coercion with the citizens' right to liberty. So while power is necessary, it can be used improperly. The clear evidence is that power tends to corrupt and, as Lord Acton so famously put it, "absolute power tends to corrupt absolutely." Power without accountability is likely to lead to tyranny. Thus it is necessary to (a) justify the moral basis for the existence of power (might does not make right), (b) constrain the use of power, and (c) hold those who exercise power responsible for its exercise. "Accountability is what makes delegated authority legitimate; without accountability, there is nothing to prevent abuse" (Monks & Minow, 1991, p. 75). Even with good accountability regimes, however, abuses can still occur, although they tend to be smaller and less frequent.

The correlative of power in the context of a democracy is the responsibility to exercise it effectively and honestly. The correlative of responsibility is *accountability*. This requires, at the least, the specification of performance standards and provision of information regarding the agent's performance to the principal, together with the opportunity for the principal to reward or sanction the agent to whom authority was delegated.

The *realpolitik* of accountability to citizens under the Westminster model as it operates in Canada at the federal level can be summarized as follows:[54]

a) In the Westminster model, the key mechanism by which elected representatives (and parties) are to be held accountable to citizens is the next general election. But its date is up to the PM within the constitutional limit of five years.

b) Periodic general elections are a remarkably poor mechanism for making elected representatives accountable to citizens. While citizens vote to elect an MP, it is merely the first of several steps (effectively aggregation rules) in which voters collectively choose the governing party and its leader chooses the three dozen men and women (the cabinet) who will control both the executive and the legislature for the next few years.

c) From the perspective of many citizens, the sanction of "voting the bastards out" must seem puny indeed. Most defeated MPs will receive an indexed pension (so long as they were elected twice) and all receive transitional assistance out of the public purse. Defeated cabinet ministers do lose a large set of perks, e.g., limo and driver, a host of assistants, the status of being a Minister of the Crown, and a varying degree of real power over public policy. But this is the harshest punishment defeated MPs of the previous party in power will face. Some of the former ministers—even manifestly poor ones—may even receive a patronage appointment from the new party in power. No matter how badly the previous Government performed, no real punishment will be inflicted on those responsible. Worse, some of the MPs hardest hit by the election results may have had almost nothing to do with the debacles created by those MPs who were ministers.

d) Within the federal government, individuals and organizations are subject to varying accountability regimes which are, in most cases, likely to be more effective than that under which citizens are to hold their elected representatives accountable (see Priest & Stanbury, 1999). The most arrogant ministers, when challenged to explain/justify his/her actions, often fall back on the following argument: the voters will be able to pass judgment on my performance and that of the Government at the next election. This argument tends to be used far less frequently as the date of the next general election approaches.

e) The doctrine of collective responsibility is frequently used to shield individual ministers from being held accountable. In any event, ministers are not accountable to Parliament, as the theory claims, but to the Prime Minister. So long as it has a majority, the Government (and the PM) is not accountable to the Commons because it can't be defeated on a non confidence motion so long as strict party discipline is imposed by the PM, and accepted by the MPs.[55]

In summary terms, the Westminster model's main claim to fame, that it holds the governors (i.e., ministers) accountable to the governed (i.e., citizens) is largely a myth, and potentially a dangerous one at that. Stanbury (2002c) shows that the regime for holding elected representatives accountable (the general election) to citizens is grossly deficient: It is infrequent, crude, indirect, lacks the means to inflict serious punishment no matter how bad the performance, and it usually prevents voters from targeting those largely responsible for both superior and bad performance.

8.1 Proposed Reforms

- Require Deputy Ministers to appear annually before the Public Accounts Committee to explain his/her department's performance and to justify the requested Estimates.[56]
- Require ministers to appear at least twice before committees reviewing new legislation: when a bill is first considered to explain the rationale for the proposed changes, and to respond to the committee's draft recommendations for changes to the bill.
- Establish clear conflict of interest legislation (not "guidelines").[57] This problem was *not* remedied by the Prime Minister Chrétien's proposals of June 11, 2002. See Prime Minister's Office (2002). However, Bryden (2002b) states that in the throne speech, the Government will announce a new draft code of conduct for MPs and Senators under which they and their spouse will be required to disclose their assets and liabilities to a new parliamentary ethics officer on a confidential basis. It is not clear if the new requirements will be put into legislation.
- Make it much easier for private organizations or individuals to sue the government for violations of its own laws, regulations (see Abbate, 2002).
- Require departments/agencies to report annually on certain standardized measures of performance specified by Parliament (see Auditor General, 2002).
- Require that all departments' contracts reviewed at least once every two years by an independent agency such as the Auditor General (particularly in areas known to be subject to abuse, e.g., advertising contracts).[58]
- Institutionalize an *independent* review (at least once every

five years) of *every* government organization using a set of standard criteria plus those for that specific organization.[59] The reviews must be published quickly.

9. *Create More Opportunities for Direct Democracy*
   9.1 *Discussion*

Canadians need more opportunities to participate in their governance directly. One of the weaknesses of the Westminster model is that the Prime Minister is not elected by all voters directly, but only by those in his/her electoral district.

Some elements of direct democracy would be a very use complement to our traditions of responsible or cabinet government. No serious commentator argues the extensive use of the recall, initiative or referenda.[60] But on a limited basis each of these tools could make government more accountable to voters. Gordon Gibson (2002a, p. 23) explains:

> As a practical matter, direct democracy is little used and even little discussed in the Canadian context, it has a small but essential place in our system. Beyond the election of representatives directly, the direct approval of constitutional amendments is required by law in B.C. and Alberta, and by quite strong precedent elsewhere. The nation-wide vote on the Charlottetown Accord (which of course rejected that constitutional plan notwithstanding its support by the federal government, every provincial government, most local governments and essentially the entire "establishment" of the country from business through unions, churches and the media) has probably set a pattern which governments will be unable to ignore in the future.

It is no secret that many people in Canada are frustrated by the way the present political system works. They want some new and powerful signaling devices to force their federal government to be more responsive to them. This is the case for using the tools of direct democracy as a "safety valve." Gibson (2002a, p. 23) explains: "the 'safety valve' consists of machinery that can be activated by an outraged public against government action or refusal to act. The two main instruments here are the 'Initiative' and 'Recall'. The Initiative allows a group of citizens of a stipulated minimum size to force a vote on any given proposition of public policy. The Recall provides for a vote that can potentially prematurely end the term of the local representative."

These tools are commonplace in the U.S. And they were put in place most reluctantly in B.C. by the NDP government following a referendum by the previous Social Credit government in which there was over 80% support for an Initiative and Recall procedure. The problem is that the requirements established by the NDP are so restrictive that these tools are effectively impossible to use, e.g., an Initiative can be activated only by obtaining the signature of 10% of the persons on the voters list in every electoral district! (Gibson, 2002a).

We want the tools of direct democracy to require considerable effort to be put into operation—but we also want them to be practicable when a fair amount of discontent builds up and the Government needs to hear stronger signals.[61]

9.2 Proposed Reforms

- Initiative: When the valid signatures of 10% of electors are collected in each of the following five regions (the Maritimes, Ontario, Quebec, the Prairies and B.C. and the far North), the Government of Canada shall be obligated to hold a national referendum on the policy issue (or issues) advocated by the proponents of the initiative within four months of the validation of the necessary signatures. The Government will be obligated to implement the policy (policies) that receive at least 50% of the votes cast.
- Recall: When the valid signatures of 20% of the electors are collected in any electoral district calling for a recall election, the Government of Canada is required to hold a by-election within three months.
- National Referenda:[62] A national referendum shall be held on any non-technical amendment to the Constitution of Canada. The proposed amendment shall be adopted if it receives at least 50% of the votes cast on a national basis.

10. Improving Public Consultations and Citizen Engagement
10.1 Discussion

While we believe that the role of legislators in canvassing the views of citizens is important, so too is the role played by the executive branch in its public consultations on public policy matters. However, despite the substantial human and financial resources expended annually by governments on consulting the public at large and stakeholders in particular on a vast array of issues, there is widespread dissatisfaction with both the processes and the results, on the part of participants both inside and outside government.

One of the biggest challenges for government is what to do with the information and the ideas presented to it during consultations. Too often, for many in government, consultations involve going through the motions, fulfilling an obligation (often set out in law or regulation) to consult stakeholders representing consumer and commercial interests. Yet, too often, such consultation processes are cooked from the beginning with key premises defined, options specified and—frequently—conclusions predetermined by those for whom consultations is largely an exercise in social marketing and communications rather than an open engagement on ideas.

There is no lack of creative means for eliciting the views of citizens and stakeholders. Over the years, a substantial cadre of skilled facilitators and public consultations professionals have emerged in Canada with lots of ideas about how to elicit views on complex issues. The remaining challenge is what to do with this information and how it should be factored in to the deliberations of decision-makers. Given the considerable diversity in scope, complexity and relevance of the various issues which are subject to public consultations, we will make no attempt here to propose how the information should be used in policy-making. However, in the interests of transparency, accountability we believe it is essential that much more attention by paid by governments in responding to what it hears in such consultations.

Too often, those who make representations to government on public policy issues do so without adequate information on background associated with the matters at issue (including key assumptions being used by policymakers, their definition and parameters of the issue and the policy options under consideration) and are unaware of the decision-making apparatus, process and timetable in place to deal with the issue. It's no wonder then, that such citizen or stakeholder representations are then judged by public servants to be not very helpful or germane.

There is often too little diversity in the information and proposals provided to government. There are too few organizations in Canada which have the financial means to do the research and policy development required to play a meaningful, constructive role in public consultations on policy matters. Yet, Canada's substantial civil society network is eager to expand its role in this regard.

There seems no doubt that citizens want new and more effective ways of signalling their political preferences to governments in Canada. Voting once every four years or so is not sufficient (see Stanbury, 2002c). Over the past three decades at least, the volume of lobbying activities has increased and a far wider range of organizations are actively seeking to influence public policy.[63] But the tax treatment of donations and/or expenditures aimed at influencing public policy is not the same for all entities engaged in lobbying in any of its many forms. Perhaps the easiest and more general approach is to permit individuals to have a tax credit for direct expenditures on lobbying (defined broadly as any effort to influence public policy) or for donations to any "registered political entity." The latter would simply be any entity that spent over, say, $25,000 per year on lobbying. It could only issue receipts for tax purposes provided it was registered with the federal government, and filed the required annual report on its revenues, expenditures and issues/policies it sought to influence. The tax credit might be structured like that for donations to parties or candidates. Thus the maximum tax credit would be $500.

Andrew Coyne (2002h) argues strongly against the proposition that registered charities (i.e., those entitled to issue a receipt for tax purposes for the contributions they receive) be permitted to spend as much as 49% of their revenues on advocacy. The current limit is 10% (although enforcement is hardly uniform). The crux of his argument is that by increasing the limit, "the government [will be] paying people to lobby it to pay them to lobby it to pay them to lobby it. And so on and so forth, per ardua ad astra." Further, "the right to speak your mind does not extend to the right to a subsidy to do so."

The crucial weakness in Coyne's analysis is the fact that he fails to note that profit-making businesses deduct tens of millions each year for lobbying expenses. Such activity is expressly designed to influence public policy in ways favourable to the firms (trade associations) doing the lobbying. In other words, other taxpayers indirectly subsidize the free speech of any tax-paying corporation that spends money on lobbying. Unions, on the other hand, not being taxable entities, cannot obtain a comparable subsidy for the money they spend on lobbying either directly, or through dues paid to the Canadian Labour Congress or other central body.

10.2 Political Reforms

- Require government departments or agencies which under take public consultations to publicly provide a summary of what it heard during the consultations and indicate, at least in general terms, its response to the proposals (i.e., whether they are being reflected in public policy or, if not, reasons as to why).
- Require that some written explanation be provided before, during and following public consultations of the options and associated trade-offs which must be considered by policy-makers. (This in contrast to the typical practice of government merely providing an explanation, defence and rationale for the single policy option chosen in the end.)
- Require government organizations sponsoring public consul tations to provide more detailed information on the decision-making processes in place to make decisions on the issues at hand, the timeframes governing the decision-making process, the premises used by government in initially framing the is sues and the preliminary range of policy options for discussion along with some assessment of the trade-offs associated with each.
- Amend the *Income Tax Act* to enable registered charities to expend up to 25% of their resources on "advocacy" activities. (They are currently restricted to a maximum of 10%).
- Permit "registered political entities" (i.e., lobbying organizations) to issue tax receipts for contributions to individuals. Then individuals would be entitled to a tax credit on the same basis as they now receive for contributions to registered parties or candidates under the *Canada Elections Act*.

11. Conclusions

Georges Clemenceau (1841-1929) observed that "war is much too serious a matter to be entrusted to the military."[64] So it is with political reform. It would be foolish to leave it up to the incumbent politicians, although it is the party in power which must legislate the reforms. For example, Paul Martin (2002) has recently promised a number of reforms aimed at strengthening the role of backbench MPs as has the Canadian Alliance (2002). In any event, we note that the Glorious (but peaceful) Revolution of 1688-1689 in England did not come about under the leadership of James I, who was deposed and went into exile. If Canadians want the reforms outlined above, they must communicate their wishes strongly to all parties and all leadership candidates.

Democracy in the form we have today is the product of a long slow process first in England and then in Canada beginning in the 1840s when responsible government first came to the colonies.[66] Recall that it was not until 1918 that women could vote in Canadian federal elections.[67] As important, democracy is a process in which citizens must take an active role—or it tends toward oligarchy. If the Prime Minister has vastly too much power, it is because citizens have failed to curb the increasing concentration of that power in the hands of successive PMs. In short, Canadians have been far too trusting of their elected representatives and far too uncritical of the gradual evolution of the Westminster model of government in Canada. The performance of Canadian democracy is far, far from satisfactory on any of the key criteria: representativeness, responsiveness to electors, limitation of the inevitable abuse of power, and citizens' access to sufficient reliable and authoritative information necessary to make sound decisions about their elected representatives.

The claims in the mind of the current Prime Minister with respect to the last general election are proof that—as a signaling system—general elections in Canada are highly deficient. Prime Minister Chrétien has repeatedly referred to the "mandate" he received from Canadians in light of the larger majority of seats the Liberal Party obtained in the general election of November 2000.[68] Recent research seriously questions his claim:

Only 15% of people polled by SES Canada Research Inc. said they think the Liberals won the last election because of Mr. Chrétien leadership. And only slightly more—17%—said the 2000 election results were a shared victory for the "team" of Mr. Chrétien and former finance minister Paul Martin. Just seven per cent said the Liberals won because the party had the right vision for Canada.

Meanwhile, though a whopping 40% of Canadians said the Liberals won their third majority government 20 months ago because there was no appealing alternative among the opposition parties. And 21% said they were simply "unsure" why the Liberals won. That's almost two-thirds of Canadians who seem to believe that this country is being governed by default. (Delacourt, 2002).

Unfortunately, the political reforms most likely to benefit citizens —like those described above—are also what economists call pure public goods. That is they have two essential characteristics: a) increased consumption by one or any number of persons does not reduce the amount available for others; and b) efforts to create such goods are subject to "free riders," i.e., there is apparently no incentive to help pay the costs of creating such goods because—if they are created—no one can be *excluded* from their benefits. They need not pay to get them. Thus it appears that citizens will not gather together to see that the political reforms they want will, in fact, be put in place. This phenomenon has been described as the "logic of collective inaction" (see Stanbury, 2002e).

But there are two crucial facts which belie this analysis: a) citizens can only ride for free if the public good in question (i.e., political reform) is, in fact, produced; and b) citizens recognize that their calculation of the benefits and costs of taking political action should not be a narrow one. They must reckon with the possibility that what was a democratic regime could become transformed into a tyranny.[69] Ironically, a democratically elected government could, by a majority vote, effectively establish a dictatorship. This threat may seem remote—but it is that prospect which greatly increases the potential benefits of making political reforms. Or, put another way, the costs of *failing* to act to institute reforms could result in extraordinarily high costs to Canadians.

Most economists recognize that the calculus of choice involving the basic elements of participation in a democracy is not like that for ordinary economic goods and services. It is a fact that a bountiful economy requires very extensive reliance on effectively competitive markets. But the existence of such markets is closely correlated with the existence of a popular constitutional democracy. Ensuring the health of that democracy is critical to an abundant and growing economy. The health of Canada's democracy requires that most of the reforms set out above be implemented promptly.

References/Bibliography:

Abbate, Gay (2002) "Civil servants get go-ahead to sue Ottawa," *Globe and Mail*, August 9, 2002, p. A7.

Aubry, Jack (2002a) "Speaker says he's above the law," *Ottawa Citizen*, in Canada.comNews, July 30, 2002. [*re Official Languages Act*]

Aubry, Jack (2002b) "Senate : 69 days of work of work is enough," *Ottawa Citizen* in Canada.comNews, September 20, 2002.

Aubry, Jack (2002c) "Agency got $330,000 in deals: 81 BDC contracts were each considered too small for competitive bidding," *Ottawa Citizen* in Canada.comNews, August 6, 2002.

Auditor General (2002) News Release, "The Auditor General identifies weaknesses in accountability chain," (Ottawa: OAG, April 16, 2002).

BC Freedom of Information and Privacy Association (2002) "News Release Backgrounder: Quasi-Governmental Bodies Created by the Federal Government" (Vancouver: June 12, 2002).

Bliss, Michael (2002a) "Bottom line: Chrétien did not play fair," *National Post*, July 12, 2002.

Bliss, Michael (2002b) "Southern republic, northern dictatorship," *National Post*, September 6, 2002, p. A18.

Bryden, Joan (2002a) "Backers urge PM to skirt rules," *Ottawa Citizen* in Canada.comNews, June 29, 2002.

Bryden, Joan (2002b) "Liberals to open donation books," *Ottawa Citizen* on Canada.comNews, September 23, 2002.

Cameron, Stevie (1995) *On the Take: Crime, Corruption and Greed in the Mulroney Years* (Toronto: Seal books/McClelland Bantam Inc.).

Canadian Alliance (2001) "Leadership Election 2002 Rules," Edition #1 – October 24, 2001, 16 pp. (obtained from the Alliance's website: www.leadership2002.canadianalliance.ca).

Canadian Alliance/John Reynolds (2002) *Building Trust II: Making Parliament More Responsive to Canadians* (Calgary, Canadian Alliance website, www.canadianalliance.ca, September 24, 2002.

Canadian Policy Research Networks (2002) Press Release, "Quality of Life in Canada: A Citizens' Report Card," September 2, 2002. [www.cprn.org]

Canadian Press (2002a) "Politics essentially corrupt, most Canadians believe," *Globeandmail.com*, April 2.

Canadian Press (2002b) "Rules set for Liberal leadership review," Globe and Mail online edition, June 9, 2002.

Clark, Campbell (2002a) "Leadership contenders told to return some cheques," *Globe and Mail*, online edition, July 12, 2002.

Clark, Campbell (2002b) "Martin's blind trust gets ethics approval," *Globe and Mail*, July 10, 2002, p. A4.

Cobb, Chris (2002) "Canadians confused by left & right: 18% put Alliance on wrong side of NDP, 32% haven't a clue," *Ottawa Citizen*, April 29. (www.canada.com/national/features/mandate/story.html?).

Cooper, Barry & David Bercuson (2002) "The inevitability of Liberal rule," *National Post*, September 18, 2002 (originally published in the *Calgary Herald*).

Cosgrove, Gillian (2002) "Key Liberals to thrash out new vision for party," *National Post*, September 14, 2002.

Coyne Andrew (2002) "How can they take the money?", *National Post Online*, February 4, 2002.

Coyne, Andrew (2002a) "Democracy for sale," *National Post*, February 11, 2002.

Coyne, Andrew (2002b) "He dared expose our sham Commons," *Nation Post Online*, April 18, 2002.

Coyne, Andrew (2002c) "Disclosure is not enough," *National Post*, May 31, 2002.

Coyne, Andrew (2002d) Campaign finance: The answer," *National Post*, June 12, 2002.

Coyne, Andrew (2002e) "Indecent disclosure," *National Post*, July 13, 2002.

Coyne, Andrew (2002f) "Stop me if you've heard this." *National Post*, July 27, 2002. [re parliamentary reform proposals by Paul Martin]

Coyne, Andrew (2002g) "The system will…produce the same results," *National Post*, June 12, 2002.

Coyne, Andrew (2002h) "To be charitable, this is a scam," *National Post*, April 3, 2002.

Curry, Bill (2002) "Federal ethics plan may cover spouses," *National Post*, September 19, 2002.

Dalby, Simon (2001) "Electoral Reform: Lessons From the Irish?" *Policy Options*, November, pp 77-79.

Delacourt, Susan (2002) "Poll undermines notion of PM's mandate," *Ottawa Citizen*, in Canada.comNews, August 8, 2002.

Democracy Watch (2002) News Release, "Democracy Watch Raises Serious Ethical Concerns About Canadian Alliance and all Other Leadership Races," March 8, 2002.

Dunfield, Allison (2002) "Opposition tackles mighty PMO," *Globe and Mail*.online edition, September 24, 2002.

Federal Court of Canada (2001) Trial Division Judgment T-1125-99, "Information Commissioner of Canada and Minister of Environment Canada and Ethyl Canada Inc.," (April 2, 2001).

Feschuk, Scott (1998) "Ottawa spends $12 million for your thoughts" *Globe and Mail*, May 20, pp. A1, A6.

Fife, Robert (2002a) "Executives to pay $10,000 to meet PM," *National Post*, May 23, 2002.

Fife, Robert (2002b) "Tobin won't disclose donors, aide says," *National Post*, July 11, 2002. [He resigned on January 14, 2002]

Fife, Robert (2002c) "Liberals tout in-house solution to slush funds," *National Post* online, May 27, 2002.

Fisher, Douglas (1999) "The Prime Minister reigns supreme," *Toronto Sun*, August 15, 1999.

Francis, Diane (2002) "Ottawa's moral deterioration and public accounting," *National Post Online*, May 30, 2002.

Freeman, Aaron (2002) "Transparency and political donations: parties still don't get it,"

The Hill Times, August 12, 2002.

Gibson, Gordon (2002a) "The Fundamentals of Democratic Reform—Part IV," *Fraser Forum*, January 2002, pp. 22-23.

Gibson, Gordon (2002b) "The Fundamentals of Democratic Reform—Part V," *Fraser Forum*, pp. 25-26. [re PR].

Gibson, Gordon (2002c) "Democratic Reform—Part VI: Internal Party Governance," *Fraser Forum*, May 2002, pp. 23-24, 27.

Gibson, Gordon (2002d) Personal communication, e-mail to the authors September 23, 2002.

Grace, John (1998) "Memos to bury, files to destroy," *Globe and Mail*, June 5, p. A22.

Greenaway, Norma (2002) "Sheila Copps: Ministers and the money," *National Post*, July 12, 2002.

Johnson, William (2002) "Time to remember an old promise, Mr. Chrétien," *Globe and Mail*, September 19, 2002, p. A25. [re PR, made in 1984]

Joyce, Greg (2002) "B.C. treaty referendum question on native self-government starts fiery debate," Canadian Press on Canada.comNews, July 7, 202.

Kennedy, Mark (2002) "Allan Rock: Ministers and the money," *National Post*, July 12, 2002.

Laghi, Brian (2002a) "Mulroney says leaders must take good care of caucus," *Globe and Mail*, August 20, 2002, p. A1.

Laghi, Brian (2002b) "Rock has built up leadership war chest" *Globe and Mail*, July 4, 2002, p. A6. [$236,592 donated to his riding association in 2001]

Laghi, Brian (2002c) "Alliance blasts Martin's pledge of House reform," *Globe and Mail*, September 25, 2002, p. A5.

Lawlor, Allison (2002) "Canadians less trusting of government than Americans," *Globeandmail.com*, June 20.

LeBlanc, Daniel (2002) "Bureaucrat in ad furor stonewalls," *Globe and Mail*, July 10, p. A1.

LeBlanc, Daniel & Campbell Clark (2002) "Angry auditor slams Ottawa on ads," *Globe and Mail*, May 9, 2002, online edition.

Loenen, Nick (1997) *Citizenship and Democracy: A Case for Proportional Representation* (Toronto: Dundurn Press).

Loenen, Nick (2001) "Selecting Representatives" (Paper presented to the Fraser Institute Conference "Finally! Reforming Politics: The B.C. Blueprint," Vancouver, November 22, website: fraserinstitute.ca/publications/politics_reform/Loenen.html).

Mackie, Richard & Murray Campbell (2002) "Tory race cost rivals $8.5 million," *Globe and Mail*, September 24, 2002, p. A1.

Makin, Kirk (2002) "Tenets of cabinet confidentiality upheld," *Globeandmail.com*, July 12, 2002.

Mancuso, Maureen, M.M. Atkinson, A. Bliss, I. Greene, Neil Nevitte (1998) *A Question of Ethics: Canadians Speak Out* (Toronto: Oxford University Press Canada).

Marley, David (2002) Personal communication, e-mail to the authors September 23, 2002.

Martin, Paul (2002) "Proposals for reform of the House of Commons" (Speech at Osgoode Hall Law School, York University, Toronto, October 21, 2002.

May, Kathryn (2002) "Whistleblowing is PS duty: ethics czar," *Ottawa Citizen* in Canada.comNews, August 12, 2002.

McCarthy, Shawn (2002a) "Martin refuses to name financial backers," *Globe and Mail*, July 12, 2002, online edition. [Martin was fired on June 2, 2002]

McCarthy, Shawn (2002b) "Shut campaign, PM orders Finance Minister," *Globe and Mail*, online edition, May 31, 2002.

Michalski, Joseph H. (2002) *Quality of Life in Canada: A Citizens' Report Card* (Background Report for Canadian Policy Research Networks, July 2002).

Monks, R.A.G. & Nell Minow: (1991) *Power and Accountability* (New York: HarperCollins).

Moore, Sean (2000) "Parliamentary Reform: The Big Kahuna," *The Hill Times*, May 29, 2000.

Moore, Sean (2002a) "A Made-in-Canada Model for Democratic Government," *The Hill Times*, April 15, 2002.

Moore, Sean (2002b) "Confronting Canada's 'Democratic Deficit'," *The Hill Times*, June 10, 2002.

Moore, Sean (2002c) [re opposition parties] *The Hill Times*, August 5, 2002.

National Post (2002) [Editorial] "The backbench gets its due," *National Post*, June 20, 2002.

National Post (2002) "Dumont: It is the patriotism of responsibility that I am proposing," *National Post*, September 24, 2002.

PC Party of Ontario (2001) "Leadership Election Rules," November 10, 2001 [from the party's website: ontariopc.on.ca].

Phillips, Susan & Michael Orsini (2002) "Mapping the Links: Citizen Involvement in Policy Processes" (Canadian Policy Research Network: www.cprin.org).

Priest, Margot & W.T. Stanbury (1999) "An Accountability Framework Based on the Principal-Agent Paradigm" (Unpublished paper, June, mimeo).

Prime Minister's Office (2002) "Prime Minister Announces New Ethics Guidelines for the Ministry and New Appointment Procedure for Ethics Counsellor" (Ottawa: PMO, June 11, 2002).

Rana, F. Abbas (2002) "Political donations to Canadian Alliance on downward spiral," *The Hill Times*, August 12, 2002.

Reid, John (2001) "Remarks to COGEL – 2001," December 3, 2001 (Ottawa: Office of the Information Commissioner website: www.infocom.gc.ca/speeches).

Reid, John (2002) "Remarks to ARMA – Canadian Conference 2002," June 4, 2002 (Ottawa: Office of the Information Commissioner website: www.infocom.gc.ca/speeches).

Reynolds, John (2002) "Step right up folks and see 'corrupt' House committee elections," The Hill Times, July 29, 2002.

Roberts, Alasdair (1998) "Losing accountability: Governments across Canada are quietly undermining freedom of information laws," *Ottawa Citizen*, April 24, p. A7. [http://qsilver.queenu.ca/-foi/].

Rubin, Ken (2002) "Federal Government plans to keep more public records secret, including documents on advertising sponsorship," *The Hill Times*, June 24, 2002.

Savoie, Donald (1999) *Governing From the Centre. The Concentration of Power in Canadian Politics* (Toronto: University of Toronto Press).

Scofield, Heather (2002) "Martin woos backbenchers with talk of reform," *Globe and Mail* online edition, July 10, 2002.

Segal, Hugh (2002) "Unique period in history for our political leaders," National Post, August 8, 2002.

Simpson, Jeffrey (2001) *The Friendly Dictatorship: Reflections on Canadian Democracy* (Toronto: McClelland & Stewart).

Simpson, Jeffrey (2002a) "No 'X' on the ballot for this generation," *Globe and Mail*, May 18, p. A19.

Simpson, Jeffrey (2002b) "Hey, Tories, how 'bout a delegated convention?" *Globe and Mail*, August 13, 2002, p. A17.

Southam News (2002) "Restrict political memberships to citizens," *National Post*, March 7, 2002.

Stanbury, W.T. (1991) *Money in Politics: Financing Federal Parties and Candidates in Canada* (Research Study No 1 for the Royal Commission on Electoral Reform and Party Financing; Toronto: Dundurn Press).

Stanbury, W.T. (1993) *Business-Government Relations in Canada: Influencing Public Policy* (Toronto: Nelson Canada).

Stanbury, W.T. (2000a) "Regulating Federal Party and Candidate Finances in a Dynamic Environment" in H.G. Thorburn & A. Whitehorn (eds.) *Party Politics in Canada*, 8th ed. (Scarborough, Ontario: Prentice Hall Canada).

Stanbury, W.T. (2000b) *Environmental Groups and the International Conflict Over the Forests for British Columbia, 1990 to 2000* (Vancouver: SFU-UBC Centre for the Study of Government Business.)

Stanbury, W.T. (2002a) "Should government regulate federal party leadership races?" *The Hill Times*, August 5, 2002.

Stanbury, W.T. (2002b) "PM wields too much power; PM wields far more power than any king," *The Hill Times*, September 16, 2002.

Stanbury, W.T. (2002c) "Accountability to Citizens in the Westminster Model of Government: More Myth Than Reality" (Vancouver: Fraser Institute for Digital Publication November 2002.)

Stanbury, W.T. (2002d) "Third party spending in Canada is small bananas," *The Hill Times*, August 12, 2002.

Stanbury, W.T. (2002e) "The Politics of Milk in Canada," (Vancouver: Fraser Institute Digital Publication: August 2002).

Stanbury, W.T. (2002f) "Concentration of power leads to 'not invented here' phenomenon, PM's vast powers not understood by voters," *The Hill Times*, September 23, 2002.

Sullivan, Paul (2002) "A Gordian fight for democracy," *Globe and Mail*, September 25, 2002, p. A19.

Taber, Jane (2002a) "Martin releases list of donors," *Globe and Mail*, September 12, 2002, online edition. [but only amounts in July and August 2002 outside his blind trust established four years ago]

Taber, Jane (2002b) "Chrétien is leaving us out, Grit MP complains," Globe and Mail, September 19, 2002, p. A4.

Thorne, J.O. & T.C. Collocutt eds. (1974) *Chambers Biographical Dictionary* (Edinburgh: W & R Chambers).

Tibbetts, Janice (2002) "PM leaves lasting mark on top court," *Ottawa Citizen* in Canada.comNews, August 9, 2002.

Trickey, Mike (2002) "John Manley: Ministers and the money," *National Post*, July 12, 2002.

Valpy, Michael (2002) "Affection for Queen remains strong in Canada," *Globe and Mail*, September 3, 2002, p. A3.

Victoria Times Colonist (2002) "Treaty referendum a futile exercise; There's no point in voting on negotiating principles if First Nations don't accept them," *Times Colonist* editorial, on Canada.comNews, July 7, 2002.

von Mises, Ludwig (1966) *Human Action: A Treaty on Economics*, Third Revised Edition (Chicago: Contemporary Books, Inc.).

Waldie, Paul (2002) "CUPE reaches settlement for violating election law," *Globe and Mail*, August 30, 2002, p. A7.

Winsor, Hugh (2002) "Punishing whistle blowers is wrong message," *Globe and Mail*, September 20, 2002, p. A4.

Ziegel, Jacob (2002) "A Supreme democratic deficit," *National Post*, August 12, 2002.

Notes:

[1]	This paper was submitted to the conference called "Searching for the New Liberalism," organized by Tom Axworthy on September 27-29, 2002 in Toronto. See Cosgrove (2002). We have benefited greatly from the thoughtful and some times provocative comments by David Marley and Gordon Gibson. Even when we did not make a change they suggested, we often modified a point or tried to

improve our explanation. In short, their advice has been invaluable.

2 The turnout in federal elections fell steadily from 75% in 1988 to 62% in 2000. Turnout fell by at least 10 percentage points in all provincial elections in the 1990's, except New Brunswick.

3 Two notable exceptions must be cited—the proposals of the Canadian Alliance party (see Dunfield, 2002) and of Gordon Campbell, Premier of BC (see Sullivan, 2002).

4 See Cobb (2002) who reports on a study showing that a large number of Canadians are confused about the left-right position of the NDP and Canadian Alliance parties.

5 Indeed, David Marley (2002) argues that, "There is an alarming level of political, not to mention economic, illiteracy in this country, as well as ever-increasing citizen apathy, largely due to a widespread decision by electors, especially among the young, to practice a variant of rational ignorance respecting the political system."

6 Because Congressmen have far greater efficacy, the committee system in the U.S. often produces very fine analyses of policy issues.

7 Aubry (2002b) notes that the Senate is expected to sit only 69 days in 2002 and that senators gave themselves a pay raise of 20% in 2001 to $106,400.

8 Columnist Andrew Coyne (2002b) had this to say about private member's bills: "In the current Parliament, some 229 such bills have been introduced in the Commons. Most of these die then and there: A small fraction win a lottery —literally—which entitles their sponsors to go before a committee to plead why their bill should be brought to a vote. A small fraction of these—just five out of the original 229 – succeed in persuading the committee, a majority of whom are government MPs, to make them "votable." And that's just the start of the many legislative hoops through which they then pass. Exactly two of those five bills have even made it as far as Mr. Martin's bill did [to second reading] and none have made it to committee: the clause-by-clause examination that bills receive after passing second reading."

9 Note that in 1783 William Pitt, as Leader of the Opposition in Great Britain, "brought forward an elaborate scheme of Parliamentary reform. He was defeated by 293 to 149....His other measure for the reform of abuses in the public offices passed the Commons, but was rejected in the Lords." In December 1783, Pitt took office as Chancellor of the Exchequer and first lord of the Treasury, i.e., he became Prime Minister (Thorne & Collocott, 1974, p. 1015).

10 And note that Donald Savoie (1999) quotes a Chrétien minister as saying that the cabinet is largely a focus group for the Prime Minister.

11 Jean Chrétien is also reported as having said, on viewing the terra cotta soldiers at Xian, that "They look just like backbenchers!" See also Taber (2002b).

12 Paul Martin states that he wants to strengthen the role of backbenchers, but columnist Andrew Coyne (2002f) is skeptical.

13 For more detail, see Leonen (1997), (2001).

14 Our ideal is a Senate which has the following characteristics: a) all members are elected, b) the single transferable ballot would be used (see Dalby, 2001; Simpson, 2001), and c) the number of seats would be allocated among six regions so that those regions outside central Canada (Quebec and Ontario) obtain more seats than their respective proportion of the national population. Obviously, this matter will be highly controversial, but here is an allocation with which to begin the discussion: Atlantic 12; Quebec 21; Ontario 28; Prairies 22; B.C. 16; and North 1 for a total of 100.

15   We adopt this "phased approach" because what we really want (outlined in the previous footnote) will require changes in the Constitution and we indicated at the outset that none of the reforms proposed in this paper would require such changes.

16   Supreme Court of Canada decisions permit large variations (the average ±25%) in the size of electoral districts. There is still a substantial bias favoring rural voters in Canada.

17   From 1949 to 2000 there were six minority federal governments (three Liberal and three Progressive Conservative) which held power for a total of about 10 years. The rest of the time, majority governments prevailed—usually that of the Liberal Party.

18   Recall that Prime Minister Mulroney did this when the Liberal-dominated Senate was holding up his legislation dealing with the Goods and Services Tax.

19   Adapted from Stanbury (2002b). See also Bliss (2002b) for a shorter list.

20   It is made into law by a cabinet committee, the Special Committee of Council.

21   This change has been made in British Columbia by the Liberal Party under Gordon Campbell.

22   David Marley (2002) argues that, "Without essentially unfettered and timely access to information held by government, it is virtually impossible for citizens, acting on their own initiative, or through either their elected representatives or the media, to hold officials, elected or otherwise, to account."

23   One former senior official argues that, "Mr. Grace overstates the conspiracy of silence notion. In fact, high level servants tend, in order to protect and enhance their own careers, to be very careful about exposing the minister to embarrassment, hence the tendency not to divulge sensitive information. Also, ministers do not like to be upstaged by bureaucrats."

24   The routine disclosure of the alternatives considered is one of the great strengths of the committee system in the U.S.

25   Perhaps the *ACI Act* should be transformed by starting with the assumption that all public documents should be in the public domain except those categories which are specifically exempted in the statute.

26   See B.C. Freedom of Information and Privacy Association (2002).

27   Gordon Gibson (2002d) argues that Cabinet Minutes should be confidential for a very long time, but not submissions to Cabinet nor Records of Decision.

28   Some time ago, John Reynolds introduced a private member's bill to this effect, according to Marley (2002).

29   For example, Paul Martin and Brian Tobin refused to reveal the names of donors and amounts given to the leadership campaigns. See Fife (2002b), McCarthy (2002a). However, John Manley, Allan Rock and Sheila Copps did so. See Trickey (2002), Kennedy (2002), Greenaway (2002) respectively. See also Bryden (2002a).

30   Since Coyne wrote the column quoted below, the Prime Minister's Office established some new rules for ministers involved in leadership races. See section 7.2 below.

31   Most of these proposals were put forward in Stanbury (2002a).

32   See section 7.1 below and Clark (2002b).

33   David Marley (2002) does not want to leave such matters up to the parties: "I don't believe it should be left to political parties to establish eligibility criteria for voting on intra-party matters, be they leadership races, candidate nominations, party executive selections (national, regional or local), or policy resolutions. The elections law of the country should apply to any and all intra-party voting. To be eligible, one must a Canadian citizen who meets the other criteria for voting in a general or by-election. To have it otherwise, as is the case today in Canada, makes

a mockery of election law and connotes a marked lack of self-respect on the part of the society concerned."

[34] Re the Liberal Party, see Canadian Press (2002b).

[35] The objective is to stabilize the rules and prevent them being changed to benefit a particular individual—recall how Paul Martin's people "captured" the executive of the Liberal Party and then changed the rules. This was a key factor in Jean Chrétien's announcement of his planned retirement.

[36] Gordon Gibson (2002d) asks, "Why should party membership lists be available to the public? Suppose I want to join the Communist party—isn't that my business?" We reply that if parties are to recognized as important public institutions their operations must be largely transparent. Further, public corporations must maintain a registry of all shareholders accessible to the public. That too could be considered an invasion of privacy.

[37] Note that the Ontario PCs set a limit of $1.5 million for each candidate in the leadership race in early 2002 although it appears that this was violated. See Mackie & Campbell (2002). The Canadian Alliance, however, did not set a limit for the race won by Stephen Harper in May 2002.

[38] Southam News (2002) proposed that only citizens be eligible to vote for party leaders and that they be age 18 or over. We appreciate that this will conflict with the existence of "youth wings" in parties.

[39] For example, after his first run for the leadership of the Progressive Conservative Party, Brian Mulroney refused to disclose his expenditures as required by the party. Party leadership races can involve large sums. For example, in the last one in *Ontario* the five candidates spent $8.6 million. The winner spent over $3 million. By comparison, the PCs spent $6.2 million to win the 1999 provincial election (see Mackie & Campbell, 2002).

[40] To gain this benefit, it is necessary to flow contributions through the party which then issues a receipt and forwards the contribution to the leadership candidate— usually after retaining a portion of the donation. This was done by the Canadian Alliance during its last leadership race, for example.

[41] See section 424 of the *Canada Elections Act* which requires the national party to report the names of donors of $200 or more. Thus one cannot tell how much money was donated by whom to which EDA. Each EDA should be required to report publicly annually separately from the party (see Stanbury 2000a).

[42] After John Nunziata voted against the Liberal Party on a budget bill, Mr. Chrétien refused to sign his nomination papers before the next election despite the strong endorsation of his constituency members. Thus he could not be the Liberal Party's official candidate. He did get re-elected as an independent in 1997 but not in 2000.

[43] Andrew Coyne (2002g) summarized them as "partial disclosure, sham enforcement, lots of artful loopholes."

[44] It is not clear how this can be done. Suppose a provincial association raises $100,000 for which it has a complete list of donors. Then it transfers $40,000 to a federal party or candidate, how does it decide which persons contributed the $40,000? One might assume a rateable allocation.

[45] Note that CUPE effectively paid a $1,000 "fine" (in the form of a donation to charity) for failing to report spending $150,000 as a "third party" in the November 2000 general election. See Waldie (2002). On third party spending in that election, see Stanbury (2002d).

[46] But donations to "third parties" will not have to be disclosed apparently.

[47] See Stanbury (1991). Note this excludes leadership races and the actual cost of administering general elections by the Chief Electoral Officer (some $120 mil-

lion!). The main direct subsidies are the rebates on party "election expenses" (22.5% of total), and 50% rebate on candidates' "election expenses." The indirect subsidy consists of the income tax credit for contributions by individuals and corporations.

[48] David Marley (2002) argues, "there ought to be reasonable contribution limits placed, on an annual basis, respecting political parties, candidates for office, public or party, and third party advocacy campaigns, I've come to the conclusion that limits on spending are inappropriate. Rigorous disclosure rules, seriously enforced, will likely cure any abuses in this respect. The public can then see and judge for themselves the role of money in any given contest. Besides, in my view, the impact of money in the determination of political battles is overemphasized. Classic examples being both Brian Mulroney's 1976 campaign for the federal PC Party leadership and the 1992 referendum on the Charlottetown Accord."

[49] Coyne (2002d) and Marley (2002) strongly support permitting only electors to contribute to parties, etc. Marley (2002) states, "I believe that only individual Canadian citizens ought to be entitled to make contributions, monetary or in-kind, to political parties or candidates. Entities such as industry associations, professional firms, corporations, or unions ought to have no ability to influence either electoral contests or public policy by means of financial or coerced 'volunteer' muscle. Subject to stringent disclosure rules, they ought to be limited to participation in 'third party' issue advocacy campaigns only."

[50] The best model here is Ontario.

[51] The discussion in this section is adapted from Stanbury (2002c).

[52] In a democracy, government has a monopoly on the legitimate use of coercion— in the name of preserving order in the face of disruptive individuals/groups who threaten the peaceful cooperation that generates the benefits of division of labor (see von Mises, 1996).

[53] Efficiency also requires specialization and the division of labour. Thus authority must be delegated by principals to agents. Further, as noted above, the process involves a hierarchy of principals and agents in which all but the top and bottom entities are *both* principals and agents. See Priest & Stanbury (1999).

[54] This section is adapted from Stanbury 2002c).

[55] Gordon Gibson (personal communication, July 4, 2002) points out to the curious truth that a rebellion by a majority of the party's MPs could change the system at any time. An incipient rebellion of Liberal Party MPs, led by Paul Martin, helped to bring about the announced retirement of Jean Chrétien on August 21, 2002 to be effective in February 2004.

[56] A former senior official noted that, "The present system requires the DM and/or ADMs to make such a presentation if the committee requests it, but it is a futile gesture. The committee chairman's role is to muzzle any question that might lead to embarrassment of the minister or government. And, under our system, no MP has the knowledge or the analytical resources to get to the bottom of financial issues, never mind expose financial misconduct. Far more useful would be the creation of Budget bureau, as in the U.S., which can do the analysis and feed the hard questions to the committee for real debate." It appears, however, that such actions may be inconsistent with the Westminster model.

[57] The evolution and content of the various "guidelines" is discussed in Mancuso et al. (1998). They were first introduced in 1964. On the effectiveness of the Ethics Counsellor, Coyne (2002g) states: "We know of the many ways in which the current ethics counsellor falls short of independence this requires. He is, as the name implies, neither an investigator nor a commissioner, but an advisor, hired by the Prime Minister and answering to him. He has no power to compel evidence, or to enforce his findings. All of this remains the case today. He may not be quite so

58   tongue-tied, now that he has the promise of five years' job security, but he is just as toothless."

58   Diane Francis (2002) argues "...the moral deterioration in Ottawa spread the minute the Liberals gained power in 1993, when they imposed a blackout in the public accounts as to how money was spent, how much was spent and by whom. All contracts over a certain small amount used to be a matter of public information, annually posted, which kept the politicians and civil service more or less honest. But now absolutely nothing stands between our money and sticky-fingered friends of the Liberals except leaks by principled persons, whistleblowers from inside government or investigative journalists." See also, Aubry (2002c).

59   We recognize that such an approach is best suited to routinized functions. For professionals, the problem is much more complex and other, more flexible, ways of measuring performance are necessary.

60   One of the commentators on an earlier draft made the following point: "It was the plebiscite which, according to the historian Mommsen, led to the death of the roman Republic, for it finally collapsed under the influence of demagogues like Julius Caesar. A recent example of what can happen with initiatives is the notorious tax ceiling initiative in California. In any case, I would never recommend that an initiative be permitted to be invoked in connection with a money bill."

61   We agree with Gordon Gibson (2002a, p. 23) notes that "Direct democracy is not the voice of God, merely mass opinion on one issue at one point in time." See also Joyce (2002), Victoria Times Colonist (2002).

62   We use the term referenda not plebiscite. The former are binding on the legislature; the latter is not—it only gathers the opinion of electors.

63   And, Canadian policies are being influenced by groups funded abroad and by the efforts of interest groups in other countries. See, for example, Stanbury (2000b).

64   The saying is also attributed to Charles Maurice de Talleyrand Perigord (1754-1838)

65   Nova Scotia is usually said to be the first colony to achieve responsible government in 1847 largely due to the efforts of Joseph Howe. The Province of Canada soon followed.

66   Note that even after the Reform Bill of 1832 in the U.K., only 20% of adult males were able to vote. Note that in France, women did not get the vote until 1946!

67   The Liberals obtained 173 seats in 2000 versus 155 in 1997.

68   This point was recognized explicitly by the U.S. "founding fathers" who (following the ideas of John Locke) stated in the Declaration of Independence that "when a long train of abuses and usurpations [by government], pursuing invariably the same object, it is their duty [i.e., of citizens] to throw off such government, and to provide new guards for their future security."

Leadership Now*

Deborah Coyne

WHAT IS CANADA'S purpose in the 21ˢᵗ century? Will we achieve great things as a country or will "Canada" simply refer to a geographic space, and little else but a semi-autonomous appendage to the United States in the attic of North America?

The 20ᵗʰ century witnessed the completion of Canada's transition from colony to nation. Our country has continued its evolution into a peaceful multicultural state with two official languages and a reasonably healthy tradition of respect for human rights, of openness to others' differences, and of the pursuit of social and economic justice, solidified in an entrenched *Charter of Rights and Freedoms*. As a result of our domestic accomplishments and despite our relatively small population, Canada became a respected voice in world affairs. Canada continues to participate in most significant international forums and is regarded by both developed and developing countries as having something meaningful to say on issues of peace and security, economic and social development, environmental protection, and worldwide migration. Our Charter has inspired constitution building in a number of emerging liberal democracies such as South Africa.

Our hopes and dreams for the 21ˢᵗ century may not be as extravagant as those of Sir Wilfrid Laurier in 1900.[1] But Canadians would like to believe that we can provide an example for others to follow, as we maintain an open, peaceful, progressive society in the increasingly integrated global community of the 21st century.

We would like to believe that despite our relatively small size, we can continue to play a meaningful role in building effective international governance structures and a better, safer world for future generations. Scope for public action, as well as a distinctive identity in the community of nations.

But will we be able to achieve any of this in the future? Despite clear signs of a resurgence in civic and local activism and volunteerism, our leaders are failing to mobilize this to build a greater common good, and articulate a clear ethical vision to guide our civic lives.

Public discourse, whether expressed by those in public life or through the filter of the media, rarely contributes to understanding the larger goal of citizenship and the mutual responsibilities that accompany the rights and privileges of citizenship. Instead, public discourse is dominated by clinical reports of the decline or disintegration of the instruments for maintaining an open, progressive society, most notably, good public education, adequate health care for all, and environmentally sound development. There is little analysis or constructive debate about the importance of public action in maintaining an open, progressive, just society.

We demand little of our leaders and they demand even less of us. Feel good? Don't worry; be happy! This is the predominant message. No one is challenging us to imagine the future, to devise ways to strengthen our sense of social responsibility for each other, and to maintain and expand our contribution to world affairs and the stewardship of the planet.

With the end of the Cold War, the world and Canada had a holiday from serious business. We were able to address trivial issues: who would win "Survivors" or "Who wants to be a Millionaire?" The nuclear generation now of political age—the first generation to grow up in the shadow of nuclear Armageddon—seemed content to live with the permanent threat of annihilation, as they and their children measured their achievements primarily by their level of consumption.

With a record low voter turnout in the 2000 federal election, the issue that aroused the liveliest public response was the poll by the brilliant satirists of "This Hour Has 22 Minutes" on whether to change

Canadian Alliance leader Stockwell Day's name to Doris Day. Over half a million Canadians responded and punched out their ballot on the Internet. Governments and our elected representatives seem remote and unresponsive to genuine and deeply felt concerns of the electorate.

Even before the terrorist attacks in New York on September 11th, enormous pressures were building on democratic societies' commitment to respect individual rights and freedoms, and to articulate acceptable new limits to those rights and freedoms. This is because the complexities of globalization and technological advances require public action in a whole range of new areas. The scope for public action in areas where free markets or unfettered individual consumption have inequitable or unacceptable impacts has widened, and will continue to widen, especially as the potential for even greater terrorist threats, environmental disasters, unmanageable migration flows, and greater inequality of wealth and income intensifies. Public action will be required that, among other things, will: intrude even more on our privacy; limit our civil rights at least on an emergency basis; adjudicate delicate ethical issues such as abortion, euthanasia and socio-biological issues of genetic engineering; moderate consumption which degrades the environment and our quality of life; strongly encourage public and community service; and reduce the debilitating and growing gap in wealth and income.

Canadians are not alone in witnessing the emergence of a global economy and global society on a scale and complexity without real historical antecedent. As September 11th demonstrated, we are unprepared, both intellectually and materially, for the risks and new dangers as well as the great opportunities that lie ahead. We must have a clear idea of what we want and where we are going, or we risk being swept along with the tide towards an uncertain and turbulent future.

Our leadership is unprepared for a world in which Canada's representatives will be spending much, if not a majority, of their time participating in international forums where more and more decisions will be made that will affect every aspect of our daily lives: environmental, economic, trade, health, security. Unless we fully understand the world context within which we function and unless we encourage leaders with a global perspective, Canada may soon have no other "purpose" than to attempt to wall ourselves off from global challenges such as environmental disasters, new viruses and diseases, aggression by rogue states and terrorists, ethnic conflict, increasing global inequalities of income, and the migration of people trying to escape desperate conditions elsewhere. At the same time, we will be powerless to prevent at home the emergence of a neglected underclass, permanently unemployed and living at the margins of an increasingly uncivil and unjust society.

All Canadians of conscience must boldly stake out new ground, and analyze the nature of the challenges that confront them. We must regenerate the power that resides in our sense of public purpose and public responsibility for bringing about enduring societal change. We must turn once again to public action and to public service as a means of advancing the democratic values of equality, freedom, social responsibility and concern for the general well-being of the people. We must think about, and articulate more precisely, what we expect our leaders and our governments to do, to ensure that we continue to evolve as an open, progressive, just society, and maintain meaningful influence internationally.

It is time to demand much more of our political leaders. They are the animators of the state, elected to positions of public trust. We need them to articulate and pursue the broader public interest and be much more than managers of a budget and brokers for special interests. We need them to be principled and genuinely committed to public service. We need them to be forward thinking and innovative, and above all able to project a clear ethical vision of our future as a political community. We need them to inspire the equally essential leadership required at all levels and in all sectors of society, whether individual, the community, business.

The Six Challenges

- The first challenge or our leaders is to provide a clear ethical vision of our political community, and provide greater opportunity for the public expression of social solidarity, and our mutual responsibility for the well-being of our fellow citizens and the community as a whole.
- A second challenge for our leaders is to respond more effectively to the needs and concerns of Canadians, and to find

new tools with which to accomplish our social and economic goals: reducing the widening gap in income and wealth between more affluent and poorer Canadians; ensuring a good education and meaningful work for all; and to the greatest extent possible eliminating poverty, hunger and homelessness.

- The third challenge for our leaders is to understand fully the international context within which we operate and to ensure a meaningful voice for Canada in international affairs.
- A fourth challenge for our leaders is to ensure that Canada plays an active role in the pursuit of greater international peace and security.
- The fifth challenge for our leaders will be to manage our increasingly close relationship with the United States, while continuing to pursue our own socio-economic goals as well as participating effectively in international affairs.
- The final challenge for our leaders is to encourage the widest possible debate on public policy and allow much more space to individual citizens and citizens' groups to participate in and influence policy decisions.

Conclusion

The late 20th century will be remembered, in part, for the tremendous advances in the protection of human rights and freedoms. We presumably learned something, however imperfectly from the destructive wars and economic depression of the first half of the century and the emergence of the nuclear balance of terror in the second half. But the last decade of the 20th century will also be remembered as the time when the ethical vision of the secular state was challenged. The cold war (communism versus democracy) was replaced by a global market economy that weakened national sovereignty and was conspicuously devoid of political ideals. The public sense of insecurity intensified, as our public authorities seemed unwilling and unable to prevent, or even to mitigate the emergence of ever-greater inequalities of income and opportunities. Those with wealth and power seemed to become simply richer and more powerful, while the ranks of the underclass expanded rapidly.

The early years of the 21st century are already scarred by the catastrophic events of September 11th and their aftermath. Yet, as we have in the past, we can turn challenges into opportunities and move forward once more. Let the early 21st century be remembered as the period of reflection, when global forces were harnessed to promote a more equitable world order, when we focused on discharging the human responsibilities which accompany our human rights and without which we would be unable to live together in peace and humanity. In the face of serious challenges from religious extremists, the secular authority of the state, either acting alone or in concert with other states, must regain its moral as well as legal force. The Osama bin Ladens of the world cannot be allowed to claim that religious forces alone, (albeit viewed from their distorted perspective), are able to sustain public order.[2]

Perhaps it is comforting in these rather bleak times to hear some powerful voices of moderation speak out in the Islamic world. The president of Iran, Muhammad Khatami, in a speech to religious leaders in New York in November 2001 said as follows:

> Vicious terrorists who concoct weapons out of religion are superficial literalists clinging to simplistic ideas. They are utterly incapable of understanding that, perhaps inadvertently, they are turning religion into the handmaiden of the most decadent ideologies. While terrorists purport to be serving the cause of religion and accuse all those who disagree with them of heresy and sacrilege, they are serving the very ideologies they condemn...

> The role of religious scholars has now become even more crucial, and their responsibility ever more significant. Christian thinkers in the 19th century put forward the idea that religion should be seen as a vehicle for social solidarity. Now that the world is on the edge of chaos...the notion of Christian solidarity should prove helpful in calling for peace and security. In the holy Koran, human beings are invited to join their efforts in *ta'awon,* and *ta'awon* means solidarity, which can be translated into co-

operation to do good. We should all cooperate in
the cause of doing good.[3]

It is encouraging to realize that this speaker is the elected leader
of the same state that, in 1988, refused to protect the author Salman
Rushdie after he was condemned to death by the religious leadership for daring to write *The Satanic Verses*. But we must not forget
that Canadian authorities actually halted the distribution of *The
Satanic Verses* on the grounds that it might be hate literature, a sad
commentary on the strength of our own commitment to the basic
tenets of liberal democracy and an illustration of why we must be
constantly vigilant.

Our leaders must project a clear ethical vision of a strong Canadian political community if we want to continue to promote greater
social and economic justice both nationally and internationally.
Canada is a reasonably well educated and wealthy nation, and continues to be a magnet for immigrants around the world, whether
those escaping desperate poverty or utterly polluted environments,
or those highly educated immigrants who decide that Canada is a
better place to live and from which to establish strategic family networks. As a result, Canadian society is becoming more and more a
microcosm of the global society and if we can continue to build an
open, progressive society, respectful of both rights and responsibilities, our voice will carry significant weight in global forums.

Our leaders must engage in open, constructive debate about the
nature of the world we live in, and what sort of society and political
community all Canadians, regardless of backgrounds and identities, are trying to build together. To implement the necessary reforms requires principled leaders who will bring together and work
with the wide range of interests in the pursuit of the greater public
interest. It requires a more activist government, particularly at the
national level, to establish the broad policy frameworks and the necessary national standards (or assured outcomes) that will ensure
that we harness the technological revolution for the benefit of all
Canadians. It requires more responsive, productive government to
meet more effectively the needs and demands of all Canadians for a
just and caring society.

Our leaders must now bring a global as well as a national perspective to bear on the challenges that we face in common and the

joint action required to overcome them. They must talk about the purposes for which we want to use government powers, and our shared values and goals as Canadians. They must talk about how we have built, and must continue to build, a great country that ensures equality of opportunity for all, and respect for basic rights and freedoms, human dignity, and self-worth. They must also talk about the mutual civic responsibility each Canadian has toward his/her fellow citizen and society as a whole to enable us to live together in peace and humanity.

Our leaders must draw us beyond the short term and make us think about how the world is changing and how irresistible forces are sweeping us into a more cosmopolitan age. They must then be able to transmit a vision of Canada to Canadians, a description of the projects we must accomplish together, and an understanding of how we can reconcile a strong national government with sensitivity to community and regional concerns, of how to ensure Canadians both enjoy the rights and respect the responsibilities of civic life. The role of the government may be different in an age of globalization, but it is no less important if we are to avoid the emergence of a neglected underclass, permanently unemployed and living at the margins of an increasingly uncivil and unjust society. The possibilities for public action are limited only by our imagination, and these, in turn, provide the domestic examples and credibility to guide our efforts at the international level.

Notes:

*   an abbreviated version of the paper, written in December 2001 which is available in its entirety at www.newliberalism.ca

1   Among other things, Laurier said that the 20th century would belong to Canada.

2   Mark Juergensmeyer, *Terror in the Mind of God. The Global Rise of Religious Violence.* University of California Press, 2000.

3   Quoted in *The Economist,* November 24, 2001, p. 16.

Commentary:

Reconnecting the People and the Politics
Through Renewal

Nathon Gunn

THERE ARE TWO themes that have repeatedly surfaced here that strike me as critically interrelated. The first is the restatement today that liberalism is the belief in the supreme importance of the individual and their freedom of choice, in balance with the same freedom for others. The other recurrent theme is that there is a profound disconnect between the people and the politicians, the issues that matter to us and our government policies. The first observation therefore is that from the perspective of the citizen, the philosophy as it is currently realized fails to establish the desired freedom of choice.

I wonder if the other very important issues of the day that we have been discussing, including diplomatic influence with our hyperpower neighbour, finance reform, health care, environmental issues, and many others, are to some degree all a subset and are subject to this greater concern. Notwithstanding political polls and the gradual filtering up of certain issues, there seems to be very little in the system that has been designed to facilitate a connection between the individual and the policy of government. Where is the deliberate outreach to and inclusion of new energy, ideas and people? If the overriding sentiment is that the individual does not have any consequential impact on the decisions of their government, then there is no real perception of choice. If liberalism seems irrelevant to the citizen as a philosophy then it is likely that they will abandon it as a political vehicle. This appears to be borne out by the trend of decreasing participation in all political parties.

The disconnect is echoed in my daily conversations with my peers and colleagues in the arts, business and academic realms who feel that the core issues of our day are not adequately addressed by our government and that neither government nor political parties provide any kind of an entry point for new constructive energy to get its hands on the levers of power. Within the context of this "access" vacuum has arisen a new class of entrepreneurial activists who no longer feel that parties represent relevant mechanisms for the expression of their desire to make a difference. For my colleagues who find themselves ready to contribute, the only viable options at the moment have been the creation of foundations, organizing protests and entrepreneurial stabs at usurping the established media.

As Désirée McGraw mentioned, "Parties do not have a monopoly on political power." To a generation of people who have figured out they can recreate IBM instead of working for it, this is a powerful notion. Let's not underestimate who we are referring to. This is a wave of talented, driven, focused, successful folks who have created youth organizations of hundreds of thousands, entrepreneurs who have made billions of dollars and contemplate starting micro banks along with artists and writers who reach the world through their work. These people are bursting at the seams with pent up energy for the same purposes that parties and government were formed. These interests are largely in alignment and as the established mechanism for involvement, I put it to you that it is the parties and governments that have failed to connect with this abundant source of energy in a meaningful way.

We have to seek ways to make the current mechanisms relevant to the individual. By developing and implementing a set of systems by which parties and governments can encourage involvement and partnerships with each new wave of active, impassioned, socially constructive citizens we could ensure a rich influx of talent. The promise of opportunity to use the government as a tool for our own authorship of good is surely a lure that will attract the best and the brightest problem solvers. Clearly it can not be an empty promise, as Andrew Heintzman said, "People are looking for authenticity with an emphasis on practical idealism." Interest in endless panels, focus groups and youth conferences hold little appeal to this class of activist, who view their energy and time expenditures with an eye towards return on investment.

What if traditional groups such as the Liberal party deliberately became increasingly porous while offering access to real power? This would be a powerful incentive for the growing tidal wave of untapped political energy to reengage the party as a political mechanism.

Instead of "new" liberalism and "reinventing" the system, let's reconsider the fundamental precepts of the philosophy and focus on active renewal through involvement. Simply put: a reconnect with the individual, not by polls but through choice and access.

We've heard arguments against the current US-style unilateralism in global politics, and I would suggest that we should demonstrate similar concern with the discrepancy between the agenda of our parties or governments and our citizens. In reconnecting there is a great opportunity to tap the pent up desire to participate. This is the resource that will finance our political future and help us address the other questions, concerns and issues that inevitably and persistently arise.

In a system which does not renew itself, positive change is beholden to glacially incremental improvement. Ideas critical to our survival like holistic healthcare, integrative medicine, the global village and sustainability are all subject to a gradual, feeble trickling up, hampered by old paradigms and established interests. In a world where we have the power to destroy the economy, the environment or life itself in a mere matter of minutes or days, our capacity for regression outstrips our ability to improve.

We need to equip ourselves for the challenges ahead by making fundamental changes to how we involve people. It is going to take everything we have to address the important questions that have been raised at this conference and we can't afford to exclude anyone. I am reminded of the story of Copernicus who advanced astronomy with the simple recognition that the earth revolved around the sun, and subsequently Johannes Kepler, who taking over the data from his mentor Tycho Brahe, discovered that the orbits of the planets were elliptical, not circular. With one insight Kepler eliminated thousands of unnecessary calculations used to justify previously incongruous planetary motions. Each scientist radically simplified and revolutionized their field by building on the knowledge of their predecessors. Of course, this kind of paradigm shifting requires the introduction of fresh perspectives.

By seeking ways to enlist this largely untapped and rapidly growing resource of motivated citizens, we can give, in a truly liberal spirit, every person a chance to define their own causes. The big political idea, the next "Just Society" will emerge from this movement. Instead of polling the public and writing slogans to sell back to them we can build a society that is passionate and involved.

Simply put, I suggest that in the hurry to address our current problems we remember the great problem solving power of people. I ask each of you to consider the access and opportunity that exists for citizens to have substantial political engagement in your organizations. Wherever possible introduce mechanisms that will perpetuate an influx of ideas and talent. Everyone at this conference can at least individually seek out and reach out to active and interested people, mentoring them, connecting with them, discussing with them, involving them and seeking ways to partner with them.

As we create a more porous, accessible infrastructure and reduce the gap between the people and the politicians we also take a step closer to realizing the fundamental philosophy of liberalism.

Commentary:
Canada and the World

Dunniela Kaufman

ALISON LOAT SPOKE about defining Canada's place in the world from the perspective of the "younger generation." She initiated her comments by outlining a modern concept of an international policy for Canada rather than the more traditional concept of a foreign policy. Foreign policy implies that the only direct role on the global stage can be played by the State rather than focusing on the role that individual Canadians outside of Canada can play in developing and enhancing Canada's role in the world. Canadians are well respected in the world, we are looked upon as a kind, educated and intelligent society. Canadians play significant roles in almost each and every international organization and we, as a country, should engage these people to help us extend our influence on the international stage.

The concept of the sovereign state as the sole participant in the global forum, although still relevant, has expanded, and in so doing, has recreated a role for individuals. If we look to the evolution of international law, it too follows a similar path. Jeremy Bentham's international law, which replaced Hugo Grotius' "Law of Nations," discounted a role for any juridical being save and except the sovereign state. As we moved into a more globalized and integrated world, international organizations officially became juridical beings on the international stage and, with the advent of certain tribunals, individuals have been given certain rights that can be "enforced" in their own right, without the assistance of their governments. These more expansive concepts align themselves more clearly with the younger generation who do not need borders and therefore, the state, to define and identify themselves.

Defining an international policy rather than relying on the more limited concept of a foreign policy for Canada is forward looking in the context of international affairs. Further, it feeds the idea of brain circulation rather than the negative connotations surrounding the over-used term "brain drain." Younger Canadians do not feel the need to live in Canada to be Canadian, they can participate in a global world as Canadians from wherever they are physically located. This is a positive asset for Canada in a global forum. What then becomes key is strengthening the younger generation's identification with Canada. The younger generation is passionate yet not directly engaged. As a corollary to this notion of an international policy, we as a country have to capitalize on this passion and not alienate this generation for leaving Canada; we should embrace their sense of adventure and global mobility and define our role in the world within this context.

This generation is defined by their values and beliefs. Where they are physically located does not confine them, but it can help define them. Government inherently plays a role in defining its citizen's values and beliefs, and it is through this moral centrepiece that Canadians remain connected. It has historically been the glue to bind them, and to eventually bring them home but, to this inter connected generation, who did not live through a world war but saw the fall of communism and the corresponding disrepute of socialist concepts, amidst the hay day of the international prominence of economic and capitalist means and government being driven by economic concerns to the exclusion of their role in providing societal goods, we must question: what kind of relationship did this generation form with its government? Up until the events of September 11 and the corporate scandals that followed, both of which cried out for government intervention, this generation did not objectively ever need to rely on their government. This generation came to political realization during a time when the role of government was being questioned and the government itself was going through a period of budget cuts, government firing, and a general retreat from its societal obligations. It is during this time period where government refrained from providing an atmosphere where all citizens could access a better tomorrow, leaving that to private interests and privatization. Ironically enough, this Charter generation's roots of positive interaction with their government do not run very deep.

The Canadian government has historically had a very positive relationship with its citizenry. Canadians have trusted their government, contrasted by American notions that all government regulation and intervention is a negative, which corresponds with a belief that the free market will properly regulate all of society's ills. Canada has always been about balancing individual rights with societal rights and obligations, and Canadians historically looked to their government to maintain this balance. What this has created is a citizenry that does not define everything in the "I" but has a concept of an "us." There are many young people who appreciate this and long for it when resident outside of Canada. The concept of forsaking individual rights for a greater good was enshrined in Section One of our Charter: the government cannot infringe on your individual rights unless this infringement can be demonstrably justified in a free and democratic society. We must question if this concept of "us," bound together through our relationship with our common government, has been eroded over the last fifteen years. Rights belong to each and every citizen, but Canadians instinctively understand that the concept of individual rights requires some rebalancing of resources and opportunities to truly have meaning, and they believe that their government must play a positive role in providing this balance. The loss of this positive relationship with government, where government reacts to polls rather than embracing the role of leading and inspiring, is what threatens Canadians role in the world and the younger generation's ties to this country, not their sense of adventure. When we cease to offer a different societal model, we cease to have something to offer the world at large and young people will cease to see Canada as something worth returning for.

As a relatively younger Canadian who had the privilege of studying national and international regulation in both Canada and the United States, certain concepts relating to attitudes towards gov-

ernment and regulation become clear. Canada is a "distinct society." As long as Canada continues to nurture this distinctiveness,
young people will continue to return home and upon that return,
they will bring their experience, their knowledge and their connect-
edness with them and share it among their peers and their colleagues feeding Canada's sense of identity not alienating it and this
will help Canada continue to define its role in the world. Further,
and just as important, this distinctly balanced Canadian way is how
Canada exerts its influence in the world. In line with our history as
peacekeepers and strong forces in international organizations, many
developing democracies look to Canada for guidance.

The government of tomorrow has an obligation to re-build the
eroded relationship between the Canadian citizen and their state.
It is a true Canadian belief that there are certain things that government must ensure for each and every one of its member of society. If
it ceases to provide these things, it risks alienating itself from a generation that is defined by its beliefs and values not by borders and
in this context, it risks forever eroding something that is uniquely
Canadian. Government must be more than a tax collector for if it
ceases to provide societal goods with the taxes that it collects, people
will merely become focused on the "I" and cease to believe that they
are a part of an "us." Further, if we cease to offer an alternative kind
of society, or if we believe that there is no alternative, than there
really is no reason to maintain our sovereignty and in that context,
we discourage a sense of pride in our younger generations and we
cease to be a society that produces a kind, educated and intelligent
citizenry that can share their experiences with the world.